Praise for Previous Editions of Home Buying For Dummies

"It is absolutely practical. They cover the basics in straightforward language and go into enough detail to make them the only books you'll need."

— Eric Antonow, President and CEO, Katabat Corporation

"As a first-time home buyer, I found this book to be a quick read and immensely helpful in knowing what to ask my agent, what to look for on walk-throughs, what to expect in terms of offers and counter-offers, as well as the entire time-line and process from open house to moving in. This book really is invaluable to *anyone* purchasing a home, even if you're not a first-time home buyer."

— Travis A. Wise, San Jose, CA

"Because I bought this book, I was able to carry on intelligent conversations with my agent and lender when I recently purchased a home. Even better, I felt prepared for those conversations and much more in control of the situation than I would have had I not read this book. Thanks to the authors for doing such a great job!"

— Jeff C. Benson, Lake Zurich, IL

"I never bought real estate in my life. I never shopped for a mortgage in my life. But after reading this book I am extremely well prepared when I call them and when they walk through the door to meet with me."

— Ben Milano, Lindenhurst, NY

"If you are considering buying a home, don't fail to read this excellent new book. The book is full of profitable 'insider tips' which most real estate writers either don't know or are afraid to reveal. The advice is so good I wish I had written it . . . On my scale of one to 10, this outstanding book rates a 12."

— Robert J. Bruss, Tribune Media Services

" . . . *Home Buying For Dummies* immediately earned a prominent spot on my reference bookshelf . . . takes a holistic approach to home buying."

— Broderick Perkins, *San Jose Mercury News*

" . . . invaluable information, especially for the first time homebuyer . . . "

— Carol Nuckols, *Morning Star-Telegram,* Fort Worth, Texas

Here's what critics have said about Eric Tyson and his previous national best-selling personal finance guides:

"*Personal Finance For Dummies* is the perfect book for people who feel guilty about inadequately managing their money but are intimidated by all of the publications out there. It's a painless way to learn how to take control. My college-aged daughters even enjoyed reading it!"

> — Karen Tofte, producer, National Public Radio's
> *Sound Money*

"Among my favorite financial guides are . . . Eric Tyson's *Personal Finance For Dummies.*"

> — Jonathan Clements, *The Wall Street Journal*

"Smart advice for dummies . . . skip the tomes . . . and buy *Personal Finance For Dummies,* which rewards your candor with advice and comfort."

> — Temma Ehrenfeld, *Newsweek*

"Eric Tyson is doing something important — namely, helping people at all income levels to take control of their financial futures. This book is a natural outgrowth of Tyson's vision that he has nurtured for years. Like Henry Ford, he wants to make something that was previously accessible only to the wealthy accessible to middle-income Americans."

> — James C. Collins, coauthor of the national bestseller
> *Built to Last;* Lecturer in Business, Stanford Graduate
> School of Business

"Eric Tyson . . . seems the perfect writer for a *...For Dummies* book. He doesn't tell you what to do or consider doing without explaining the why's and how's — and the booby traps to avoid — in plain English. . . . It will lead you through the thickets of your own finances as painlessly as I can imagine."

> — Clarence Peterson, *Chicago Tribune*

"*Personal Finance For Dummies* is, by far, the best book I have read on financial planning. It is a simplified volume of information that provides tremendous insight and guidance into the world of investing and other money issues."

> — Althea Thompson, producer, "PBS Nightly Business Report"

Home Buying
FOR
DUMMIES®
3RD EDITION

by Eric Tyson and Ray Brown

WILEY

Wiley Publishing, Inc.

Home Buying For Dummies,® 3rd Edition

Published by
Wiley Publishing, Inc.
111 River St.
Hoboken, NJ 07030-5774
www.wiley.com

Copyright © 2006 Eric Tyson and Ray Brown

Chapter 5 excerpted from *Mortgages For Dummies,* 2nd Edition, Copyright © 2004 by Eric Tyson and
Ray Brown

Published by Wiley Publishing, Inc., Indianapolis, Indiana

Published simultaneously in Canada

For general information on our other products and services, please contact our Customer Care
Department within the U.S. at 800-762-2974, outside the U.S. at 317-572-3993, or fax 317-572-4002.

For technical support, please visit www.wiley.com/techsupport.

Wiley also publishes its books in a variety of electronic formats. Some content that appears in print may
not be available in electronic books.

Library of Congress Control Number: 2005936642

ISBN-13: 978-0-471-76847-0

ISBN-10: 0-471-76847-2

Manufactured in the United States of America

10 9 8 7 6 5 4 3

3O/QZ/QR/QW/IN

WILEY

About the Authors

Eric Tyson is a syndicated personal financial writer, lecturer, and counselor. He is dedicated to teaching people to manage their personal finances better. Eric is a former management consultant to Fortune 500 financial service firms. Over the past two decades, he has successfully invested in securities as well as in real estate, started and managed several growing businesses, and earned a bachelor's degree in economics at Yale and an MBA at the Stanford Graduate School of Business.

An accomplished freelance personal finance writer, Eric is the author of five other national best-sellers in the *For Dummies* series: *Personal Finance For Dummies, Investing For Dummies, Mutual Funds For Dummies, Real Estate Investing For Dummies* (which he coauthored), and *Taxes For Dummies* (which he also coauthored). Eric was an award-winning journalist for *The San Francisco Examiner.* His work has been featured and praised in hundreds of national and local publications, including *Newsweek, Kiplinger's, The Wall Street Journal, Money, Los Angeles Times, Chicago Tribune,* and on NBC's *Today Show,* PBS's *Nightly Business Report,* CNN, *The Oprah Winfrey Show,* ABC, CNBC, Bloomberg Business Radio, CBS National Radio, and National Public Radio.

Eric has counseled thousands of clients on a variety of personal finance, investment, and real estate quandaries and questions. In addition to maintaining a financial counseling practice, he is a much sought after speaker.

Ray Brown is a veteran of the real estate profession with more than three decades of hands-on experience. A former manager for Coldwell Banker Residential Brokerage Company and McGuire Real Estate and founder of his own real estate firm, the Raymond Brown Company, Ray is currently a branch manager and vice president of Pacific Union GMAC Real Estate as well as a writer, consultant, and public speaker on residential real estate topics.

Ray knows that most people are pretty darn smart. When they have problems, it's usually because they don't know the right questions to ask to get the information they need to make good decisions themselves. He always wanted to write a book that focused on what you need to know to make sound home-buying decisions — a book that kept people from manipulating you by exploiting your ignorance. This, at last, is that book!

On his way to becoming a real estate guru, Ray worked as the real estate analyst for KGO-TV (ABC's affiliate in San Francisco), a syndicated real estate columnist for *The San Francisco Examiner,* and he still hosts a weekly radio program, *Ray Brown on Real Estate* for KNBR. In addition to his work for ABC,

Ray has appeared as a real estate expert on CNN, NBC, CBS, and in *The Wall Street Journal* and *Time*.

That's all fine and good. Ray's three proudest achievements, however, are Jeff and Jared, his two extraordinary sons, and more than 40 years of nearly always wedded bliss to the always wonderful Annie B. He's delighted to welcome Jeff's wife, Genevieve, to the family.

Dedications

This book is hereby and irrevocably dedicated to my family and friends, as well as to my counseling clients and customers, who ultimately have taught me everything I know about how to explain financial terms and strategies so that all of us may benefit. — Eric Tyson

This book is lovingly dedicated to my real estate pals who taught me how the game is played, to my clients and friends who honor me with their trust and loyalty, to my brother Steve and best buddy Ben Colwell who made RBCo a reality, to Bruce Koon and Corrie Anders who taught me the dubious joy of writing, to Warren Doane and Dennis Tarmina who encouraged me to follow this dream, to both brother Daves and Bob Agnew for being there, and, saving the best for last, to Annie B., Jeff, Genevieve, and Jared, who have cheerfully (most of the time, anyhow) put up with the "Ray way" all these years. — Ray Brown

Authors' Acknowledgments

Many, many people at Wiley helped to make this book possible and (we hope in your opinion) good. They include Acquisitions Editor Kathy Cox, Project Editors Alissa Schwipps and Kristin DeMint, Copy Editor Jennifer Bingham, and the fine folks in Composition for making this book look great! Thanks also to everyone else at Wiley who contributed to getting this book done and done right.

Extraordinary acclamation, copious praise, and profound gratitude are due our brilliant technical reviewer, Kip Oxman, who toiled long hours to ensure that we did not write something that wasn't quite right.

We also owe a huge debt of gratitude to Craig Watts for his invaluable assistance with the credit scoring chapter; Paul Bragstad for his incredible Internet insights; Robert Bailey, Laura Williamson, and Michelle Budak for helping us obtain the California Association of Realtors' real estate purchase agreement included in Appendix A and the counter offer used in Chapter 12; Warren Camp, Camp Brothers Inspection Services, Inc., for providing the exemplary inspection report included in Appendix B; Robert Jackson, BayCal Financial, for supplying additional forms; and Brian Felix, Old Republic Title Company, who generously allowed us to pick his Einstein-like brain about the complexities of title insurance and escrows.

Publisher's Acknowledgments

We're proud of this book; please send us your comments through our Dummies online registration form located at www.dummies.com/register/.

Some of the people who helped bring this book to market include the following:

Acquisitions, Editorial, and Media Development

Senior Project Editor: Alissa Schwipps

Project Editor: Kristin DeMint

(Previous Editions: Suzanne Snyder and Shannon Ross)

Acquisitions Editor: Kathleen M. Cox

(Previous Editions: Jonathan Malysiak)

Copy Editor: Jennifer Bingham

(Previous Editions: Tina Sims and Diana R. Conover)

Editorial Program Assistant: Courtney Allen

Technical Editor: Kip Oxman

Senior Editorial Manager: Jennifer Ehrlich

Editorial Assistants: Hanna Scott, Nadine Bell

Cover Photos: © White Packert/Getty Images/ The Image Bank

Cartoons: Rich Tennant (www.the5thwave.com)

Composition Services

Project Coordinator: Maridee Ennis

Layout and Graphics: Carl Byers, Andrea Dahl, Denny Hager, Lynsey Osborn, Julie Trippetti

Proofreaders: Leeann Harney, TECHBOOKS Production Services

Indexer: TECHBOOKS Production Services

Special Help: Melissa Wiley

Publishing and Editorial for Consumer Dummies

Diane Graves Steele, Vice President and Publisher, Consumer Dummies

Joyce Pepple, Acquisitions Director, Consumer Dummies

Kristin A. Cocks, Product Development Director, Consumer Dummies

Michael Spring, Vice President and Publisher, Travel

Kelly Regan, Editorial Director, Travel

Publishing for Technology Dummies

Andy Cummings, Vice President and Publisher, Dummies Technology/General User

Composition Services

Gerry Fahey, Vice President of Production Services

Debbie Stailey, Director of Composition Services

Contents at a Glance

Table of Contents

Introduction

Welcome to *Home Buying For Dummies,* 3rd Edition!

For about the cost of a couple of movie tickets, you can quickly and easily discover how to save thousands, perhaps even tens of thousands, of dollars the next time you buy a home.

How can we make such a claim? Easy. Between the two of us, we've spent more than five decades personally advising thousands of people like you about home purchases and other important financial decisions. We've seen how ignorance of basic concepts and practices translates into money-draining mistakes. We know that many of these mistakes are both needless and avoidable.

No one is born knowing how to buy a home. Everyone who'd like to buy a home must learn how to do it. Unfortunately, too many people get a crash course in the school of hard knocks — and learn by making costly mistakes at their own expense.

We know that you're not a dummy. You've already demonstrated an interest in discovering more about home buying by selecting this book, which can help you make smart moves and avoid financial land mines.

In the event that you're still wondering whether to buy this book, allow us a moment, please, to make our case. Buying a home may well be the largest purchase that you ever make. If you're like most people, buying a home can send shock waves through your personal finances and may even cause a sleepless night or two. Buying a home is a major financial step and a life event for most people. It certainly was for us when we bought our first homes. You owe it to yourself to do things right.

About This Book: The Eric Tyson/Ray Brown Difference

We know that many home-buying books are competing for your attention. If the fact that our families are counting on you to purchase this book doesn't sway you, here are several other compelling reasons why this is the best book for you:

✔ **It's in plain English.** Because we work with real people and answer real questions (Eric, through his financial counseling, teaching, and writing; and Ray through his radio show, real estate consulting, and writing), our information is current, and we have a great deal of experience in explaining things. This experience can put you firmly in control of the home-buying process (rather than having it control you).

✔ **It's objective.** We're not trying to sell you an expensive newsletter or some real estate product that you don't need. Our goal is to make you as knowledgeable as possible before you purchase a home. We even explain why you may *not* want to buy a home. We're not here to be real estate cheerleaders.

✔ **It's holistic.** When you purchase a home, that purchase affects your ability to save money and accomplish other important financial goals. We help you understand how best to fit your home acquisition into the rest of your personal-finance plan.

✔ **It's a reference.** You can read this book from cover to cover if you want. However, we know that you're busy and that you likely don't desire to become a real estate expert, so each portion of the book stands on its own. You can read it piecemeal to address your specific questions and immediate concerns.

Conventions Used in This Book

Every book has its own conventions, and this one is no different. To make the most of the information we provide, keep your eye out for these conventions:

✔ *Italics* highlight new terms that we define.

✔ **Boldfaced** text indicates the keywords in explanatory bulleted lists.

✔ `Monofont` sets Web addresses apart.

In addition, you can safely skip text in gray-shaded sidebars without missing anything you need to know. Sidebars contain plenty of helpful information, but the information they contain isn't crucial to your understanding of the topic at hand.

How This Book Is Organized

So you're ready to buy a home. Or maybe you know that you're not ready, but you see a home purchase somewhere on the not-too-distant horizon. This book starts with the premise that many important things should fall into place *before* you sign a contract to buy a home. And even after the deal is done, you'll have questions. Fear not! Our book covers what you need to know.

Part 1: Home Economics

Perplexed about whether or not to buy a home? Concerned that your financial house isn't as neat and tidy as it should be? Don't know what you can afford or how you'll pay for it? This section is for you! Many prospective home buyers make the mistake of buying before they understand their financial options and the home-buying process. As a bonus in this part, we explain real estate market economics, and tell you how to spot a buyer's market (good values) and avoid the perils of a seller's market (inflated prices).

Part 11: Financing 101

One of the most challenging and important aspects of the home-buying process is choosing a mortgage. Although not quite as jargon-prone as an Internal Revenue Service auditor, most mortgage lenders do have a penchant for using terminology — such as *negative amortization* and *points* — that you probably don't use in your daily life. In this important part, we explain the different types of mortgages and cut through all that jargon to help you select the type of mortgage that matches your needs. We discuss the importance of your credit score, how to understand it, and even how to improve it. In addition to explaining how to get the best deal that you can on a mortgage, we guide you through the morass of paperwork required to apply for and obtain your loan.

Part 111: Property, Players, and Prices

After you've decided that you're ready to buy, and you know how much you can really afford (given your budget and other financial objectives), you're ready to explore how the home-buying game is played. In this part, we introduce you to the various types of property you may consider buying and the people you may hire to help you buy a home. In addition to steering you toward winning strategies and players, we help you avoid loser properties and people. We give you a crash course on how to distinguish good buys from overpriced duds so that you won't overpay (and may even get a very good deal) when you purchase your dream home. We also explain how to harness the power on the Internet and tell you which realty Web sites are worth your time.

Part IV: Making the Deal

In this part, we get down to brass tacks — how to negotiate a super deal and how to get your home inspected from roof to foundation so that you know whether it's in perfect shape or riddled with expensive defects. Because you can't close the purchase until you get homeowners insurance, we explain what to buy, where to buy, and how to buy it right. Finally, we describe some of the legal and tax ramifications of your purchase, along with ways to make sure that your deal closes smoothly and without unnecessary costs.

Part V: The Part of Tens

In this part, we tackle shorter topics that didn't seem to fit elsewhere in this book. Here, we list the ten financial musts after you buy, the ten things to know when investing in real estate, and the ten things to consider when selling your house.

Part VI: Appendixes

Besides showing you a good home-inspection report, we also provide a sample home-buying contract so you will be familiar with these documents. Finally, we provide you a comprehensive glossary in case you can't quite remember what a certain real estate word or phrase means.

Icons Used in This Book

Sprinkled throughout this book are cute little icons to help reinforce and draw attention to key points or to flag stuff that you can skip.

This bull's-eye notes key strategies that can improve your real estate deal and, in some cases, save you lots of moola. Think of these as helpful little paternalistic hints we would whisper in your ear if we were close enough to do so!

Numerous land mines await novice as well as experienced home buyers. This explosive symbol marks those mines, and then we tell you how to sidestep them.

Occasionally, we suggest that you do more research or homework. Don't worry: We tell you exactly what you need to do.

Unfortunately, as is the case in all parts of the business world, some people and companies are more interested in short-term profits than in meeting your needs and concerns. We warn you how, when, and where you may be fleeced and, where appropriate, show you how to de-fleece yourself!

"If I've told you once, I've told you a thousand times. . . ." Remember good old Mom and Dad? From time to time, we tell you something quite important and perhaps repeat ourselves. Just so you don't forget the point, this icon serves as a little nag to bring back those childhood memories.

Some of you are curious and have time to spare. Others of you are busy and just want to know the essentials. This geeky icon points out tidbits and information that you don't really have to know, but understanding this stuff can make you more self-confident and proud!

Where to Go from Here

Odds are you're not quite ready to bolt over to the nearest bank and take out a mortgage — and we don't suggest that you blindly call the first Realtor in the Yellow Pages. It's up to you where you go from here, but if you're just beginning to think about buying your first home, we recommend that you read straight through, cover to cover, to maximize your home-buying savvy. But the A-to-Z approach isn't necessary — if you feel pretty confident in your knowledge of certain areas, pick the ones that you're most interested in by either skimming this book's table of contents or by relying on the well-crafted index at the back of the book.

Part I
Home Economics

The 5th Wave — By Rich Tennant

"I bought a software program that should help us save up for a new home, and while I was there, I picked up a few new games, a couple of screen savers, 4 new mousepads, this nifty pull out keyboard cradle..."

In this part . . .

Is home buying for you? Is now the right time? How much can you afford to spend on a home? These questions aren't meant to throw you into a panic. If you don't know how to answer them (and perhaps even if you think that you do), this part is for you! Many people assume that they need to buy a home (or that they don't) without taking a good look at their overall personal financial situation. Don't make that mistake! Read this part to see how a home purchase should fit into your financial puzzle and to understand how and why home prices do what they do.

Chapter 1

Deciding Whether to Buy

* *

In This Chapter

▶ The beauty (and the beast) of buying

▶ Common blunders in making the decision to buy

▶ The rewards and drawbacks of renting

* *

*E*very month, week, and day, we buy things large and small: lunch; a new pair of shoes; and every now and then, a car.

Most people buy things without doing much comparison shopping, but instead draw upon their past experiences. When the counter help at the nearby coffeehouse was friendly and you liked the espresso, you go back for more the next time you need your caffeine fix.

Sometimes purchases lead you by association to related purchases. You get coffee, for instance, and buying a newspaper may naturally follow. By the same token, you buy a home, and before long you have a new television and gardening gloves.

You end up being really happy with some items you purchase. Others fall short of your expectations . . . or worse. When the items in question don't cost you much, it's no big deal. Perhaps you return them or simply don't buy more in the future. But when it comes to buying a home, that kind of sloppy shopping can lead to financial and emotional disaster.

If you're not willing to invest time, and if you don't work with and heed the advice of the best people, you could end up overpaying for a home you hate. Our goals in this book are simple: to ensure that you're happy with the home you buy, that you get the best deal you can, and that owning the home helps you accomplish your financial goals.

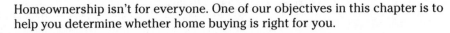

Weighing the Advantages of Owning versus Renting

Nearly everyone seems to have an opinion about buying a home. People in the real estate business — including agents, lenders, property inspectors, and other related people — endorse homeownership. Of course, why wouldn't they? Their livelihoods depend upon it! Therein lies one fundamental problem of nearly all home-buying books written by people who have a vested interest in convincing their readers to buy a home.

Homeownership isn't for everyone. One of our objectives in this chapter is to help you determine whether home buying is right for you.

Consider the case of Peter, who thought that owning a home was the best financial move he could make. What with tax write-offs and living in a place while it made money for him, how could he lose? Peter envied his colleagues at work who'd seemingly made piles of money with property they bought years ago. Peter was a busy man and didn't have time to research other ways to invest his money.

Unfortunately, Peter bought a place that stretched his budget and required lots of attention and maintenance. Adding insult to injury, Peter went to graduate school clear across the country (something he knew he was likely to do at the time he bought) three years after he purchased. During these three years of his ownership, home prices dropped 10 percent in Peter's neighborhood. So after paying the expenses of sale and closing costs, Peter ended up losing his entire down payment when he sold.

Conversely, some people who continue to rent should buy. In her 20s, Melody didn't want to buy a home because she didn't like the idea of settling down. Her monthly rent seemed so cheap compared with the sticker prices on homes for sale.

As it always does, time passed. Melody's 20s turned into 30s, which melted into 40s and then 50s, and she was still renting. Her rent skyrocketed to eight times what it was when she first started renting — that insignificant $150 monthly rent was now over $1,200 per month. But now, home prices really seemed out of sight. She fearfully looked ahead to escalating rental rates in the decades when she hoped to be retired.

Ownership advantages

Most people should eventually buy homes, but not everyone and not at every point in their lives. To decide whether now's the time for you to buy, consider the advantages of buying and whether they apply to you.

Owning should be less expensive than renting

You probably didn't appreciate it growing up, but in addition to the diaper changes, patience during potty training, help with homework, bandaging bruised knees, and countless meals, your folks made sure that you had a roof over your head. Most of us take shelter for granted, unless we don't have it or are confronted for the first time with paying for it ourselves.

Remember your first apartment when you graduated from college or when your folks finally booted you out? That place probably made you appreciate the good deal you had before — even those cramped college dormitories may not have seemed so bad anymore!

But even if you pay several hundred to a thousand dollars or more per month in rent, that expense may not seem so steep if you happen to peek at a home for sale. In most parts of the United States, we're talking about a big number — $150,000, $225,000, $350,000, or more for the sticker price. (Of course, if you're a medical doctor, lawyer, management consultant, or investment banker, you probably think that you can't find a habitable place to live for less than a half-million dollars. Double or triple those figures should you live in costly places such as New York City, Boston, Los Angeles, and San Francisco!)

Here's a guideline that may change the way you view your seemingly cheap monthly rent. To figure out the price of a home you could buy for approximately the same monthly cost as your current rent, simply do the following calculation:

Take your monthly rent and multiply by 200, and you come up with the purchase price of a home.

$ _____ per month   x   200 = $ _____

Example: $ 1,000   x   200 = $200,000

So in the preceding example, if you were paying rent of $1,000 per month, you would pay approximately the same amount per month to own a $200,000 home (factoring in tax savings). Now your monthly rent doesn't sound quite so cheap compared with the cost of buying a home, does it? (Note that in Chapter 3 we show you how to accurately calculate the total costs of owning a home.)

Even more important than the cost *today* of buying versus renting, what about the cost in the *future?* As a renter, your rent is fully exposed to increases in the cost of living, also known as *inflation.* A reasonable expectation for annual increases in your rent is 4 percent per year. Figure 1-1 shows what happens to a $1,000 monthly rent at just 4 percent annual inflation.

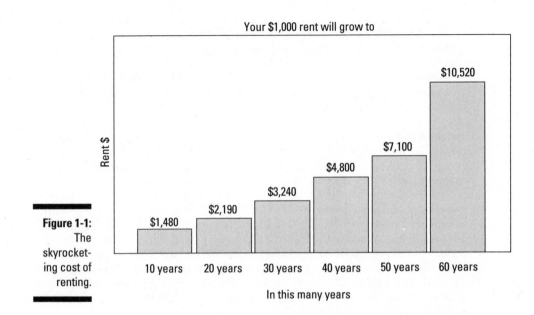

Figure 1-1:
The skyrocketing cost of renting.

When you're in your 20s or 30s, you may not be thinking or caring about your golden years, but look what will happen to your rent over the decades ahead with just modest inflation! Then remember that paying $1,000 rent per month now is the equivalent of buying a home for $200,000. Well, in 40 years, with 4 percent inflation per year, your $1,000-per-month rent will balloon to $4,800 per month. That's like buying a house for $960,000!

In our example, we picked $1,000 for rent to show you what will happen to that rent with a modest 4 percent annual rate of inflation. To see what might happen to your current rent at that rate of inflation (as well as a slightly higher one), simply complete Table 1-1.

Table 1-1	Figuring Future Rent	
Your Current Monthly Rent	**Multiplication Factor to Determine Rent in Future Years at 4 Percent Annual Inflation Rate**	**Projected Future Rent**
$_____	× 1.48	= $_____ in 10 years
$_____	× 2.19	= $_____ in 20 years
$_____	× 3.24	= $_____ in 30 years
$_____	× 4.80	= $_____ in 40 years
$_____	× 7.11	= $_____ in 50 years
$_____	× 10.52	= $_____ in 60 years

Your Current Monthly Rent	Multiplication Factor to Determine Rent in Future Years at 6 Percent Annual Inflation Rate	Projected Future Rent
$ _____	× 1.79	= $_____ in 10 years
$ _____	× 3.21	= $_____ in 20 years
$ _____	× 5.74	= $_____ in 30 years
$ _____	× 10.29	= $_____ in 40 years
$ _____	× 18.42	= $_____ in 50 years
$ _____	× 32.99	= $_____ in 60 years

If you're middle-aged or retired, you may not be planning on having 40 to 60 years ahead of you. On the other hand, don't underestimate how many more years of housing you'll need. U.S. health statistics indicate at age 50, you have a life expectancy of nearly 30 more years, and at age 65, nearly 20 more years.

Although the cost of purchasing a home generally increases over the years, after you purchase a particular home, the bulk of your housing costs aren't exposed to inflation — if you use a fixed-rate mortgage to finance the purchase. As we explain in Chapter 6, a *fixed-rate mortgage* locks your mortgage payment in at a fixed amount (as opposed to an adjustable-rate mortgage payment that fluctuates in value with changes in interest rates). Therefore, only the comparatively smaller property taxes, insurance, and maintenance expenses will increase over time with inflation. (In Chapter 3, we cover in excruciating detail what buying and owning a home costs.)

You're always going to need a place to live. And over the long-term, inflation has almost always been around. Even if you must stretch a little to buy a home today, in the decades ahead, you'll be glad that you did. The financial danger with renting long-term is that *all* of your housing costs (rent) increase over time. We're not saying that everyone should buy because of inflation, but we do think that if you're not going to buy, you should be careful to plan your finances accordingly. We discuss the pros and cons of renting later in the chapter.

You can make your house your own

Think back to all the places you ever rented, including the rental in which you may currently be living. For each unit, make a list of the things you really didn't like that you could have changed if the property were yours: ugly carpeting, yucky exterior paint job, outdated appliances that don't work well, and so on.

Uses for the wealth you build up in your home

Over the many years that you're likely to own it, your home should become an important part of your financial *net worth* — that is, the difference between your *assets* (financial things of value that you own, such as bank accounts, retirement accounts, stocks, bonds, mutual funds, and so on) and your *liabilities* (debts). Why? Because homes generally increase in value over the decades while you're paying down the loan used to buy the home.

Even if you're one of those rare people who owns a home but doesn't see much *appreciation* (increase in the home's value) over the decades of your adult ownership, you will benefit from the monthly forced savings that results from paying down the remaining balance due on your mortgage. Older folks can tell you that owning a home free and clear of a mortgage is a joy.

All that home *equity* (the difference between the market value of a home and the outstanding loan on the home) can help your personal and financial situation in a number of ways. If, like most people, you hope to someday retire, but (also like most people) saving doesn't come easily, your home's equity can help supplement your other sources of retirement income.

How can you tap into your home's equity? There are three main ways:

✔ Some people choose to *trade down* — that is, to move to a less-costly home in retirement. Sell your home for $500,000, replace it with one costing $300,000, and you've freed up $200,000. Subject to certain requirements, you can sell your home and realize up to $250,000 in tax-free profits if you're single, $500,000 if married. (See Chapter 17 to find out more about this homeownership tax break.)

✔ Another way to tap your home's equity is through borrowing. Your home's equity may be an easily tapped and low-cost source of cash (the interest you pay is generally tax deductible — see Chapter 3).

✔ Some retirees also consider what's called a *reverse mortgage.* Under this arrangement, the lender sends you a monthly check you can spend however you want. Meanwhile, a debt balance (that will be paid off when the property is finally sold) is built up against the property.

What can you do with all this home equity? Help pay for your children's college education, start your own business, remodel your home, or whatever!

Although we know some tenants who actually do some work on their own apartments, we don't generally endorse this approach because it takes your money and time, but financially benefits the owner of the building. If, through persistence and nagging, you can get your landlord to make the improvements and repairs at her expense, great! Otherwise, you're out of luck or cash!

When you own your own place, however, you can do whatever you want to it. Want hardwood floors instead of ugly, green shag carpeting? Tear it out. Love neon-orange carpeting and pink exterior paint? You can add it!

In your zest and enthusiasm to buy a place and make it your own, be careful of two things:

- ✔ **Don't make the place too weird.** You'll probably want or need to sell your home someday, and the more outrageous you've made it, the fewer buyers it will appeal to — and the lower the price it will likely fetch. If you don't mind throwing money away or are convinced that you can find a future buyer with similarly (ahem) sophisticated tastes, be as weird as you want. If you do make improvements, focus on those that add value: skylights, a deck addition for an outdoor living area, updated kitchens and bathrooms, and so on.

- ✔ **Beware of running yourself into financial ruin.** Changing, improving, remodeling, or whatever you want to call it costs money. We know many home buyers who have neglected other important financial goals (such as saving for retirement and their kid's college costs) in order to endlessly renovate their homes. Others have racked up significant debts that hang like financial weights over their heads. In the worst cases, homes become money pits that cause owners to build up high-interest consumer debt as a prelude to bankruptcy.

You avoid unpleasant landlords

A final (and not inconsequential) benefit of owning your own home is that you don't have to subject yourself to the whims of an evil landlord. Much is made among real estate investors of the challenges of finding good tenants. As a tenant, perhaps you've already discovered that finding a good landlord isn't easy, either.

The fundamental problem with some landlords is that they're slow to fix problems and make improvements. The best (and smartest) landlords realize that keeping the building ship-shape helps attract and keep good tenants, and maximizes rents and profits. But to some landlords, like Leona Helmsley, maximizing profits means being stingy with repairs and improvements (although some of Leona's tenants took her to court for her "excessive thriftiness").

When you own your home, the good news is that you're generally in control — you can get your stopped-up toilet fixed or your ugly walls painted whenever and however you like. No more hassling with unresponsive, obnoxious landlords. The bad news is that you're responsible for paying for and ensuring completion of the work. Even if you hire someone else to do it, you still must find competent contractors and oversee their work, neither of which is an easy responsibility.

Another risk of renting is that landlords may decide to sell the building and put you out on the street. You should ask your prospective landlords whether they have plans to sell. Some landlords won't give you a truthful answer, but the question is worth asking if this issue is a concern to you.

One way to avoid being jilted by a wayward landlord is to request that the lease contract guarantee you the right to renew your annual lease for a certain number of years, even with a change in building ownership. Unless landlords are planning on selling, and perhaps want to be able to boot you out, they should be delighted with a request that shows you're interested in staying a while. Also, by knowing if and when a landlord desires to sell, you may be able to be the buyer!

Renting advantages

Buying and owning a home throughout most of your adult life makes good financial and personal sense for most people — but not all people and not at all times. Renting works better for some people. The benefits of renting are many:

- **Simplicity:** Yes, searching for a rental unit that meets your needs can take more than a few days (especially if you're in a tight rental market), but it should be a heck of lot easier than finding a place to buy. When you buy, you must line up financing, conduct inspections, and deal with myriad other issues that renters never have to face. When you do it right, finding and buying a good home can be a time-consuming pain in the posterior.

- **Convenience:** After you find and move into your rental, your landlord is responsible for the never-ending task of property maintenance and upkeep. Buildings and appliances age, and bad stuff happens: Fuses blow, plumbing backs up, heaters break in the middle of winter, roofs spring leaks during record-breaking rainfalls, trees come crashing down during windstorms. The list goes on and on and on. As a renter, you can kick back in the old recliner with your feet up, a glass of wine in one hand and the remote control in the other, and say, "Ahhhhh, the joys of *not* being part of the landed gentry!"

- **Flexibility:** If you're the footloose and fancy-free type, you dislike feeling tied down. With a rental, so long as your lease allows (and most leases don't run longer than a year), you can move on. As a homeowner, if you want to move, you must deal with the significant chores of selling your home or finding a tenant to rent it.

- **Increased liquidity:** Unless you're the beneficiary of a large inheritance or work at a high-paying job, you'll probably be financially stretched when you buy your first home. Coming up with the down payment and closing costs usually cleans out most people's financial reserves. In addition, when you buy a home, you must meet your monthly mortgage payments, property taxes, insurance, and maintenance and repair expenses. As a renter, you can keep your extra cash to yourself, and budgeting is also easier without the upkeep-expense surprises that homeowners enjoy, such as the sudden urge to replace a leaking roof or old furnace.

You don't need to buy a home to cut your taxes. Should you have access to a retirement account such as a 401(k), 403(b), SEP-IRA, or Keogh plan (see Chapter 2), you can slash your taxes while you save and invest your extra cash *as a renter.* So saving on taxes should not be the sole motivation for you to buy a home.

✔ **Better diversification:** Many homeowners who are financially stretched have the bulk of their wealth tied up in their homes. As a renter, you can invest your money in a variety of sound investments, such as stocks, bonds, and perhaps your own small business. You can even invest a small amount of money in real estate through stocks or mutual funds if you wish (see Chapter 16). Over the long term, the stock market has produced comparable rates of return to investing in the real estate market. So don't feel that you'll be missing out on good investments if you can't or don't want to purchase real estate. However, you must have the discipline to save and invest your money as a renter.

✔ **Maybe lower cost:** If you live in an area where home prices have rocketed ahead much faster than rental rates, real estate may be overpriced and not a good buy. In Chapter 4, we explain how to compare the cost of owning to the cost of renting in your area and how to spot a potentially overpriced real estate market.

Renting should also be cheaper than buying if you expect to move soon. Buying and selling property costs big bucks. With real estate agent commissions, loan fees, title insurance, inspections, and all sorts of other costs, your property must appreciate approximately 15 percent just for you to break even and recoup these costs. Therefore, buying property that you don't expect to hold onto for at least three (and preferably five or more) years doesn't make much economic sense for you. Although you may sometimes experience appreciation in excess of 15 percent over a year or two, most of the time, you won't. If you're counting on such high appreciation, you're setting yourself up for disappointment.

Pitfalls of the Rent-versus-Buy Decision

When you're considering purchasing a home, you can do lots of reflecting, crunch lots of numbers, and conduct lots of research to help you with your decision. We encourage these activities and show you how to do them in later chapters.

In reality, we know that many people are tempted to jump into making a decision about buying or continuing to rent without setting all their ducks in a row. So at a minimum, we want to keep you from making the common, costly mistakes that many before you have fallen prey to. In the following sections, we go over the biggies to avoid.

Renting because it seems cheaper

As we discuss earlier in this chapter, in the long run, owning should save you money compared with renting a comparable abode. But come on, we're Americans, after all, and we live on — nay, thrive on — instant gratification. We're not generally long-term thinkers — we too often live for today. Well, when you go out to look at homes on the market *today,* the sticker prices are typically in the hundreds of thousands of dollars. Your monthly rent seems dirt-cheap by comparison.

You must compare the *monthly* cost of homeownership with the monthly cost of renting. And you must factor in the tax saving you will realize from home-ownership tax deductions. (We show you how to make these calculations in Chapter 3.) But you must also think about the future. Just as your educational training affects your career prospects and income-earning ability for years to come, your rent-versus-buy decision affects your housing costs, not just this year, but also for years and decades to come.

Fretting too much over job security

Being insecure about your job is natural. Most people are — even corporate chief executives, superstar athletes, and movie stars. And buying a home seems like such a permanent thing to do. Job-loss fears can easily make you feel a financial noose tightening around your neck when you sit down to sign a contract to purchase a home.

Although a few people have real reasons to worry about losing their jobs, the reality is that the vast majority of people shouldn't worry about job loss. We don't mean to say that you *can't* lose your job — almost anyone can, in reality. Just remember that within a reasonable time, your skills and abilities will allow you to land back on your feet in a new, comparable position. We're not career experts, but we've witnessed thousands of people bounce back in just this way.

When losing your job is a high likelihood, and especially if you would have to relocate for a new job, consider postponing the purchase of a home until your employment situation stabilizes. (If you've not demonstrated a recent history of stable employment, most mortgage lenders won't want to lend you money anyway — see Chapters 6 and 7.) When you must move to find an acceptable or desirable job, selling your home and then buying another one can cost you thousands, if not tens of thousands, of dollars in transaction fees.

Buying when you expect to move soon

People move for many reasons other than job loss. You may want to move soon to advance your career, to be nearer to (or farther from!) family, to try living somewhere new, or just to get away from someplace old. Unless you're planning to hold onto your home and convert it to a rental when you move, buying a home rarely makes sound financial sense when you expect to move within three years. (Ideally, stay put for at least five years.)

Succumbing to pushy salespeople

When you buy a house, you're the one who will be coming home to it day after day — and you're the one who will be on the hook for all the expenses. Don't ever forget these facts when you plunge into the thick of purchasing a home. If you have lingering doubts about buying a home, apply the brakes.

Many people involved in home-buying transactions have a vested interest in getting you to buy. They may push you to buy sooner (and buy more) than you intended to or can afford, given your other financial goals and obligations. The reasons: Many people who make their living in the real estate trade get paid only if and when you buy, and the size of their earnings depends upon how much you spend. In Chapter 9, we show you how to put together the best team to assist you in making a decision, rather than push you into making a deal.

Ignoring logistics

Sometimes, when looking at homes, you can lose your perspective on big-picture issues. After months of searching, Frederick finally found a home that met his needs for both space and cost. He bought the home and moved in on a Saturday. Come Monday morning, Frederick hopped in his car and spent the next hour commuting. At the end of his workday, it was the same thing coming home. He was tired and grumpy when he arrived home Monday evening, and after making dinner for himself, he soon had to hit the hay to rise early enough to do it all over again on Tuesday.

Initially, Frederick hoped that the trying traffic was an aberration that would go away — but no such luck. In fact, on many days, his commute was worse than an hour each way. Frederick grew to hate his car, his commute, his job, and his new home.

 When you buy a home, you're also buying the commute, the neighborhood, its amenities, and all the other stuff that comes along for the literal and figurative ride. Understand these issues *before* you buy. In the end, after 18 months of commuter purgatory, Frederick sold his home and went back to renting much closer to his job. Forgetting to consider what the commute from a home to his job would entail was an expensive lesson for Frederick. Don't make the same mistake Frederick made; take your time, and consider all the important factors about the home you're thinking about purchasing.

Overbuying

Many first-time home buyers discover that their desires outstrip their budgets. Nelson and his wife, Laura, had good jobs in the computer industry and together made in excess of $100,000 per year. They got used to buying what they desired — they ate at fancy restaurants, took luxury vacations, and otherwise indulged themselves.

When it came time to purchase a home, they spent the maximum amount and borrowed the maximum amount that the mortgage person told them they could. After the home purchase, Laura got pregnant and eventually left her job to spend more time at home. With the high home-ownership expenses, kid costs, and reduced household income, Nelson and Laura soon found themselves struggling to pay their monthly bills and started accumulating significant credit card debts. Ultimately, they ended up filing bankruptcy.

 Either you own the home, or it owns you. Get your finances in order, and understand how much you can truly afford to spend on a home before you buy (see Chapters 2 and 3).

Underbuying

Remember in the story "Goldilocks and the Three Bears" how Goldilocks had difficulty finding porridge to her liking? In one case, it was too cold, and in another, too hot. Well, just as you can overbuy when selecting a home, you can underbuy. That's what Nathan and Rebecca did when they bought their first home. They believed in living within their means — a good thing — but they took it to an extreme.

Nathan and Rebecca bought a home whose cost was far below the maximum amount they could have afforded. They borrowed $70,000 when they could have afforded to borrow three times that amount. They knew when they bought the home that they would want to move to a bigger home within just a few years. Although this made the real estate agents and lenders happy, all the costs of buying and then selling soon after gobbled a huge chunk of Nathan and Rebecca's original down payment.

Buying because it's a grown-up thing to do

Peer pressure can be subtle or explicit. Some people even impose pressure on themselves. Buying a home is a major milestone and a tangible display of financial maturity and success. If your friends, siblings, and coworkers all seem to be homeowners, you may sometimes feel as though you're being a tad juvenile by not jumping on the same train.

Everyone has different needs; not everyone should own a home and certainly not at every point in their adult lives. Besides, although they may never admit it, some homeowning friends and colleagues are jealous of you and other financially footloose and fancy-free renters.

A study even supports the notion that the life of a typical renter is, in some respects, better than that of the average homeowner. Peter Rossi and Eleanor Weber of the University of Massachusetts Social and Demographic Research Institute conducted a survey of thousands of people. Here are some of their survey findings:

- ✔ Homeowners are less social, on average, than renters — spending less time with friends, neighbors, and co-workers.
- ✔ Homeowners spend more time on household chores.
- ✔ Perhaps for the preceding reasons, renters have more sex and less marital discord, and cope better with parenting than homeowners do!

Buying because you're afraid that escalating prices will lock you out

From time to time, particular local real estate markets experience rapidly escalating prices. During such times, some prospective buyers panic, often with encouragement from those with vested interests in converting prospective renters to buyers. Escalating housing prices make some renters feel left out of the party. Booming housing prices make the front page of the newspaper and the local television news. And gloating homeowners cluck over their equity.

Never in the history of the real estate business have prices risen so high as to price vast numbers of people out of the market. In fact, patient buyers who can wait out a market that has increased sharply in value are often rewarded with steadying and, in some cases, declining prices. Although you won't be locked out of the market forever, you should keep in mind that if you postpone buying for many years, you would likely be able to buy less home for your money thanks to home prices increasing faster than the rate of inflation.

Misunderstanding what you can afford

When you make a major decision, be it personal or financial, it's perfectly natural and human to feel uncomfortable if you're flying by the seat of your pants and don't have enough background. With a home purchase, if you haven't considered and examined your overall financial situation and goals, you're just guessing how much you should be spending on a home.

Again, the vested-interest folks won't generally bring this issue to your attention — partly because of their agendas and motivations, but also because it's not what they're trained and expert at doing. Look in the mirror to see the person who can help you with these important issues. (Chapter 2 walks you through all the important personal financial considerations you should explore before you set out on your buying expedition.)

Chapter 2

Getting Your Financial House in Order

· ·

In This Chapter

▶ Assessing your budget and spending

▶ Determining your savings requirements to achieve your goals

▶ Protecting yourself and your assets with insurance

▶ Remembering what's most important in life

· ·

*W*hen you're shopping for a home, no one else can look out for your overall interests the way that you can . . . with our help. The people involved in typical real estate deals (such as real estate agents, bankers, loan brokers, and the like) are there to get their jobs done. It's *not* within their realm of responsibility to worry about how the real estate purchase fits with the rest of your personal finances and how best to arrange your finances before and after purchasing a home. This chapter explains how you can address these important issues.

Now, time for a parental warning: Skip this chapter at your own peril. In the great history of home buying, many people have bought real estate without first getting their finances in order, setting some goals, and dealing with problems — and they have often paid dearly for this oversight. What are the consequences of plunging headlong into a home purchase before you're financially ready? For starters, you could end up paying tens of thousands of dollars more in taxes and interest over the years ahead. In the worst cases, we've witnessed the financial ruin of intelligent, hardworking people who end up over their heads in debt (and in some situations, even in bankruptcy). We want you to be happy and financially successful in your home — *so please read this chapter!*

Surveying Your Spending

Even if your income and spending fluctuates, you may have unknowingly developed a basic spending routine. Every month, you earn a particular income and then spend most of, all of, or perhaps even more than you earn on the necessities (and the not-so-necessary things) of life. The average American saves less than 5 percent of his take-home (after-tax) income. (Note that this is far less than the average amount saved by people in most similarly industrialized countries.)

When you want to buy a home, saving is one area where it pays to be "above average." Consistently saving more than 5 percent of your income can help turn you from a renter into a financially able and successful homeowner. Why? For two important reasons:

✔ First, in order to purchase a home, you need to accumulate a decent chunk of money for the down payment and closing costs. True, wealthy relatives may help you out, but counting on their generosity is foolhardy. The attached strings may make such a gift or loan undesirable. If you're like most people, you probably don't have any wealthy relatives anyhow.

✔ Second, after you buy a home, your total monthly expenses will probably increase. So if you had trouble saving before the purchase, your finances are really going to be squeezed postpurchase. This will further handicap your ability to accomplish other important financial goals, such as accumulating money for retirement. If you don't take advantage of tax-sheltered retirement accounts, you'll miss out on thousands (if not tens of thousands) of dollars in valuable tax benefits. We discuss the importance and value of funding retirement accounts later in this chapter.

Gathering the data

One of the single most important things that you can and should do before you head out to purchase a home is to examine where (and on what) you're currently spending your money. Completing these financial calisthenics enables you to see what portion of your current income you're saving. Having a handle on your current budget also enables you to see how a given home purchase will fit within or destroy it!

Review your spending data from at least a three-month span to determine how much you spend in a typical month on various things — such as for rent, clothing, income taxes, haircuts, and everything else (see Table 2-1). If your spending fluctuates greatly throughout the year, you may need to analyze and average for 6 (or even 12) months to get an accurate sense of your spending behavior and shenanigans.

Table 2-1	Your Spending, Now and after Purchasing a Home	
Item	*Current Monthly Average ($)*	*Expected Monthly Average with Home Purchase ($)*
Income	_____	_____
Taxes		
Social Security	_____	_____
Federal	_____	_____
State and local	_____	_____
Housing Expenses		
Rent	_____	n/a
Mortgage	n/a	_____
Property taxes	n/a	_____
Homeowners/renters insurance	_____	_____
Gas/electric/oil	_____	_____
Water/garbage	_____	_____
Phone	_____	_____
Cable TV	_____	_____
Furniture/appliances	_____	_____
Maintenance/repairs	_____	_____
Food and Eating		
Supermarket	_____	_____
Restaurants and takeout	_____	_____
Transportation		
Gasoline	_____	_____
Maintenance/repairs	_____	_____
State registration fees	_____	_____
Tolls and parking	_____	_____
Bus or subway fares	_____	_____
Appearance		
Clothing	_____	_____
Shoes	_____	_____
Jewelry (watches, earrings)	_____	_____
Dry cleaning	_____	_____
Haircuts	_____	_____
Makeup	_____	_____
Other	_____	_____

(continued)

Table 2-1 *(continued)*

Item	Current Monthly Average ($)	Expected Monthly Average with Home Purchase ($)
Debt Repayments		
Credit/charge cards	_____	_____
Auto loans	_____	_____
Student loans	_____	_____
Other	_____	_____
Fun Stuff		
Entertainment (movies, concerts)	_____	_____
Vacation and travel	_____	_____
Gifts	_____	_____
Hobbies	_____	_____
Pets	_____	_____
Health club or gym	_____	_____
Other	_____	_____
Advisors		
Accountant	_____	_____
Attorney	_____	_____
Financial advisor	_____	_____
Health Care		
Physicians and hospitals	_____	_____
Drugs	_____	_____
Dental and vision	_____	_____
Therapy	_____	_____
Insurance		
Auto	_____	_____
Health	_____	_____
Life	_____	_____
Disability	_____	_____
Educational Expenses		
Courses	_____	_____
Books	_____	_____
Supplies	_____	_____
Kids		
Day care	_____	_____
Toys	_____	_____
Child support	_____	_____
Charitable Donations/Offerings	_____	_____

Item	Current Monthly Average ($)	Expected Monthly Average with Home Purchase ($)
Other		
_____	_____	_____
_____	_____	_____
_____	_____	_____
_____	_____	_____
_____	_____	_____
Total Spending	_____	_____
Amount Saved	_____	_____
(subtract from income at the beginning of this table)		

Financial software packages, such as Quicken and Microsoft Money, can help with the task of tracking and analyzing your spending, but old-fashioned paper and pencil work fine, too. What you need to do is assemble information that shows what you typically spend your money on. Get out your checkbook register, credit- and charge-card bills, your pay stub, and your most recent tax return.

Whether you use our handy-dandy table or your own software isn't important. What does matter is that you capture the bulk of your spending. But you don't need to account for 100 percent of your spending and track every last penny (or even every last dollar). You're not designing an airplane or performing a financial audit for a major accounting firm here!

As you collect your spending data and consider your home purchase, think about how that purchase will affect and change your spending and ability to save. For example, as a homeowner, if you live farther away from your job than you did when you rented, how much will your transportation expenses increase? Also note that in Chapter 3, we walk you through estimating home-ownership expenses, such as property taxes, insurance, maintenance, and the like.

Analyzing your spending numbers

Tabulating your spending is only half the battle on the path to fiscal fitness and a financially successful home purchase. You must *do* something with and about the personal spending information that you collect.

Trimming the fat from your budget

Most people planning to buy a home need to reduce their spending in order to accumulate enough money for the down payment and closing costs and to create enough slack in their budget to afford the extra costs of homeownership. (Increasing your income is another strategy, but that is usually more difficult to do.) Where you decide to make cuts in your budget is a matter of personal preference — but unless you're independently wealthy or a spendthrift, cut you must.

First, get rid of any and all consumer debt — such as that on credit cards and auto loans. Ridding yourself of such debt as soon as possible is vital to your long-term financial health. Consumer debt is as harmful to your financial health as smoking is to your personal health. Borrowing through consumer loans encourages you to live beyond your means and do the opposite of saving — call it "dis-saving" (or *deficit financing,* as those in Washington, D.C., say). The interest rates on consumer debt are high, and unlike the interest on a mortgage, the interest on consumer debt isn't tax-deductible, so you bear the full brunt of its cost.

Should you have accessible savings to pay down your consumer debts, by all means use those savings. You're surely paying a higher interest rate on such debt than you're earning from interest on your savings. Plus interest on your savings is taxable. Just be sure that you have access to sufficient emergency money through family or other means.

If you lack the savings to make your high-cost debts disappear, start by refinancing your high-cost credit card debt onto cards with lower-interest-rates. Then work at reducing your spending in order to free up cash to pay down these debts as quickly as possible. And if you've had a tendency to run up credit card balances, consider getting rid of your credit cards and obtaining a Visa or MasterCard debit card. These debit cards look like credit cards and are accepted the same as credit cards by merchants, but they function like checks. When you make a purchase with a debit card, the money is deducted from your checking account within a day or two.

Trim unnecessary items from your budget. Even if you're not a high-income earner, some of the things you spend your money on are unnecessary. Although everyone needs food, shelter, clothing, and health care, people spend a great deal of additional money on luxuries and nonessentials. Even some of what we spend on the "necessity" categories is partly for luxury.

Purchase products and services that offer value. High quality doesn't have to cost more. In fact, higher-priced products and services are sometimes inferior to lower-cost alternatives.

Finally, buy in bulk. Most items are cheaper per unit when you buy them in larger sizes or volumes. Wholesale superstores such as Costco and Sam's Club offer family sizes and competitive pricing.

Here, in order of likelihood, are the possible outcomes of your spending analysis:

> ✔ **You spend too much.** When most people examine their spending for the first time, they are somewhat horrified at *how much* they spend overall and *for what* specific things. Perhaps you had no idea that your café latte

addiction is setting you back $100 per month or that you spend $400 per month on eating out.

Your challenge is to decide where to make reductions or cutbacks. (Check out the nearby sidebar, "Trimming the fat from your budget.") Everybody who has enough discretionary income to buy this book has fat in her budget (some have much more than others). In order for most people to reach their financial goals, they must save at least 10 percent of their pretax income. But how much you should be saving depends upon what your goals are and how aggressive and successful an investor you are. If, for example, you want to retire early and don't have much put away yet, you may need to save much more than 10 percent per year to reach your goal.

✔ **You save just right.** You may be one of those people who has mapped out a financial path and is right on track. Great! However, just as a cue ball sends a neatly racked set of billiard balls into disarray, buying a home can disrupt even the most organized and on-track budgets.

Reviewing what your budget may look like with a home in the picture is important. So if you haven't already done so, complete Table 2-1 to analyze your current spending and project how it may look after a home purchase.

✔ **You save a lot.** Perhaps you're one of those rare sorts who saves more than necessary. If so, you may not only be able to skip doing a budget, but you may also be able to stretch the amount you spend and borrow when buying a home. But even if you've made your financial plans and are saving more than enough, you still may want to complete Table 2-1 to ensure that your financial train doesn't get derailed.

Reckoning Your Savings Requirements

Not only do most people not know how much they're currently saving, even more people don't know how much they should be saving. You should know these amounts *before* you buy a home.

How much you should be saving likely differs from how much your neighbors and co-workers should be saving, because each person has a different situation, different resources, and different goals. Focus on your situation.

Setting some goals

Most people find it enlightening to see how much they need to save in order to accomplish particular goals. Wanting to retire someday is a common goal. The challenge is that in your 20s and 30s, it's difficult to have more clearly defined goals — such as knowing that you want to retire at age 58 and move to New Mexico, where you'll join a shared-housing community and buy a home that currently costs $200,000. Not to worry — you don't need to know exactly when, where, and how you want to retire.

But you do want to avoid nasty surprises. When Peter and Nancy hit their 40s, they came to the painful realization that retirement was a long way off because they were still working off consumer debts and trying to initiate a regular savings program. Now they're confronted with a choice: having to work into their 70s to achieve their retirement goals or settling for a much less comfortable lifestyle in retirement.

If retirement isn't one of your goals, terrific! Should you want (and be able) to continue working throughout your 60s, 70s, and 80s, you won't need to accumulate the vast savings that others must in order to be loafing during those golden years. But counting on being able to keep working throughout your lifetime is risky — you don't know what the job market or your personal health may be like later in life.

Retirement savings accounts and a dilemma

Prior years' tax reforms took away many of the previously available tax write-offs, except for one of the best and most available write-offs: funding a retirement-savings plan. Money that you contribute to an employer-based retirement plan — such as a 401(k) or a 403(b) — or to a self-employed plan — such as an SEP-IRA or a Keogh — is generally tax deductible. This saves you both federal and state income taxes in the year for which the contribution is made. Additionally, all of your money in these accounts compounds over time without taxation. (*Note:* The relatively new Roth IRA retirement accounts are unique in offering no up-front tax break but allowing the tax-free withdrawal of investment earnings subject to eligibility requirements.) These tax-reduction accounts are one of the best ways to save your money and make it grow.

The challenge for most people is keeping their spending down to a level that allows them to save enough to contribute to these terrific tax-reduction accounts. Suppose that you're currently spending all of your income (a very American thing to do) and that you want to be able to save 10 percent of your income. Thanks to the tax savings that you'll net from funding your retirement account, if you're able to cut your spending by just 7.5 percent and put those savings into a tax-deductible retirement account, you'll actually be able to reach your 10 percent target.

The wise use of credit

Just because borrowing on credit cards bears a high cost doesn't mean that all credit is bad for you. Borrowing money for long-term purposes can make sense if you borrow for sound, wealth-building investments. Borrowing money for a real estate purchase, for a small business, or for education can pay dividends down the road.

When you borrow for investment purposes, you may earn tax benefits as well. With a home purchase, for example, home mortgage interest and property taxes are generally tax deductible (as we discuss in Chapter 3). When fixed-rate mortgages go for around 7 percent, for example, the effective after-tax cost of borrowing money is just 4.6 percent for a moderate-income earner who is paying approximately 35 percent in federal and state income taxes.

If you own a business, you may deduct the interest expenses on loans that you take out for business purposes. Interest incurred through borrowing against your securities' (stock and bond) investments (through so-called *margin loans*) is deductible against your investment income for the year.

In fact, you can even make wise use of short-term credit on your credit cards to make your money work harder for you. For example, you can use your credit cards for the convenience that they offer, not for their credit feature. When you pay your bill in full and on time during each monthly billing cycle, you've had free use of the money that you owed from the credit card charges that you made during the previous month. (Please see Chapter 5 for details on how to use your positive credit experiences to obtain the best possible mortgage).

Generally speaking, when you contribute money to a retirement account, the money isn't accessible to you unless you pay a penalty. So if you're accumulating down-payment money for the purchase of a home, putting that money into a retirement account is generally a bad idea. Why? Because when you withdraw money from a retirement account, you not only owe current income taxes, but you also owe hefty penalties (10 percent of the amount withdrawn must go to the IRS, plus you must pay whatever penalty your state assesses).

So the dilemma is that you can save outside of retirement accounts and have access to your down-payment money but pay much more in taxes. Or you can fund your retirement accounts and gain tax benefits, but lack access to the money for your home purchase.

There are two ways to skirt this dilemma. See whether your employer allows borrowing against retirement-savings-plan balances. And if you have an Individual Retirement Account (either a standard IRA or a newer Roth IRA), you're allowed to withdraw up to $10,000 (lifetime maximum) toward a home purchase so long as you haven't owned a home for the past two years. Tapping into a Roth IRA is a better deal, because the withdrawal is free from income tax as long as the Roth account is at least five years old. Although a standard IRA has no such time restriction, withdrawals are taxed as income, so you'll net only the after-tax amount of the withdrawal toward your down payment.

Because most of us have limited discretionary dollars, we must decide what our priorities are. Saving for retirement and reducing your taxes are important, but when you're trying to save to purchase a home, some or most of your savings need to be outside a tax-sheltered retirement account. Putting your retirement savings on the back burner for a short time in order to build up your down-payment cushion is okay. Be careful, though, to purchase a home that offers enough slack in your budget to fund your retirement accounts after the purchase. Do the budget exercise in Table 2-1, earlier in this chapter!

Other reasons to save

Wanting to have the financial resources to retire someday is hardly the only reason to save. Most people have several competing reasons to squirrel away money. Here are some other typical financial objectives or goals that motivate people (or should be motivating them) to save money. We tell you how to fit each goal into your home-purchasing desires and your overall personal financial situation:

 ✔ **Emergency reserve:** Whether random bad things happen isn't so much the issue as *when* they happen. You simply can't predict what impact a job loss, death in the family, accident, or unexpectedly large expense may have on you and your family. That's why it's a good idea to have an easily accessible and safe reservoir of money that you can tap should the need arise.

 Make sure that you have access to at least three months' worth of expenses (if you have a highly unstable job and volatile income, perhaps even six months' worth). Ideally, you should keep this money in a money market fund because such funds offer you both high yields and liquidity. The major mutual fund companies (such as Vanguard, Fidelity, and T. Rowe Price) offer money funds with competitive yields, check-writing privileges, and access to other good investments. (See Chapter 3 to find out more about these funds and how you can use them for investing your down-payment money.) Alternatively, a bank savings account can work, but it will likely offer a lower yield. Should you have benevolent relatives who are willing to fork over some dough in a flash, they may serve as your emergency reserve as well.

✔ **Educational expenses:** If you have little cherubs at home, you want the best for them, and that typically includes a good college education. So when the first cash gifts start rolling in from Grandma and Grandpa, many a new parent establishes an investment account in the child's name.

Your best intentions could come back to haunt you, however, when Junior applies to enter college. All things being equal, the more you have available in your no-retirement accounts and in your child's name, the less financial aid your child will qualify for. (By financial aid, we mean all types of assistance, including grants and loans that aren't based on need.) Unless you're wealthy or are sure that you can afford to pay for the full cost of a college education for your kids, think long and hard before putting money in your child's name. Although it may sound selfish, you actually do yourself and your child a financial favor by taking full advantage of opportunities to fund your retirement accounts. Remember, too, that one of the advantages of being a homeowner is that you can borrow against your home's equity to help pay for your child's college expenses.

✔ **Startup business expenses:** Another reason to save money is if you hope to start or purchase a business someday. When you have sufficient equity in your home, you can borrow against that equity to fund the business. But you may desire to accumulate a separate investment pool to fund your business.

No matter what your personal and financial goals are, you're likely going to need to save a decent amount of money to achieve them. Consider what your goals are and how much you need to save to accomplish those goals, especially for retirement. Get your finances in order before you decide how much you can really afford to spend on a home. Otherwise, you may end up being a financial prisoner to your home.

Protecting Yourself, Your Dependents, and Your Assets

Not carrying proper insurance is potentially disastrous — both to yourself and your dependents. We're not talking about homeowners insurance here. (Heck, we haven't even explained how to find a home or get a loan yet! We get to homeowners insurance in Chapter 13.)

You need proper insurance protection for yourself personally, as well as for your assets. Sure, you can take your chances and hope that you never contract a dreaded disease, get into a horrible auto accident, or suffer some other misfortune or bad luck. But misfortune and bad luck usually come knocking without a warning.

Trust us when we say that we're optimistic, positive thinkers. However —
and this is a big *however* — we know more than a few folks who got themselves (or their families or both) into major financial trouble after purchasing
a home because they neglected to obtain proper insurance.

Here are a few cautionary tales:

- ✔ Steve bought a home and then learned from his doctor that he had multiple sclerosis. Steve had to cut back dramatically on work, and because
  he lacked proper long-term-disability insurance and now earned much
  lower work income, he was forced to sell his home at a large loss due to
  a soft real estate market in his area.

- ✔ Mary owned a home in California and, despite the known risk of earthquakes, didn't purchase earthquake coverage. "It's so expensive, and
  besides, the insurance companies won't be able to meet the claims in a
  major quake. Government assistance will help," she said. Mary's home
  was a total loss in an earthquake, and although the government made a
  loan, it did not *pay for* the loss — ultimately, the money came out of
  Mary's pocket.

- ✔ Maggie and Donald were living a charmed life in the New England coun-
  tryside with their two children, a white farmhouse, and a dog and a cat —
  until Maggie came down with cancer. She left her job, which placed some
  strain on the family finances. After much treatment, Maggie died. Donald
  and the kids were forced to move because Maggie lacked proper life
  insurance.

- ✔ Michelle had a walkway in disrepair. Unfortunately, one day an older
  man tripped and severely injured himself. To make a long story short,
  after lengthy legal proceedings, the settlement in favor of the man was
  significant enough to force Michelle to sell her home. A good chunk of
  the settlement money came out of Michelle's pocket because she lacked
  sufficient liability insurance.

Now, we're not about to try to tell you that insurance would have made these
situations come out fine. Insurance generally can't prevent most major medical problems, keep a person from dying, or stop someone from suing you.
However, proper insurance can protect you and your family from the adverse
and severe financial consequences of major problems. The right kind of
insurance can make the difference between keeping versus losing your home,
and it can help you and your family maintain your standard of living.

Wanting to skip insurance is tempting and a natural human tendency. After
all, insurance costs you your hard-earned, after-tax dollars, and (unlike a
meal out, a vacation, or a new stereo) insurance has no up-front, tangible
benefit.

You hope that you won't need to use insurance, but if you need it, you're glad it's there to protect you and, in some cases, your dependents. Buy too little insurance, and it won't protect you and yours against a real catastrophe. So you need the right amount of coverage that balances good protection against cost.

Insuring yourself

Before you buy a home, get your insurance protection (for yourself and for your valuable assets) in order. Not doing so is the financial equivalent of driving down the highway in an old subcompact car at 90 miles per hour without a seat belt. You should purchase sufficient protection to prevent a financial catastrophe.

Disability insurance

Your ability to produce income should be insured. During your working years, your future income-earning ability is likely your most valuable asset — far more valuable than a car or even your home.

Long-term-disability insurance replaces most of your lost income in the event that a disability prevents you from working. Major disabilities are usually the result of accidents or medical problems — occurrences that of course can't be predicted. Even when you don't have financial dependents, you probably need disability coverage. Unless you're quite wealthy and no longer need to work for income, aren't *you* financially dependent upon your paycheck? Although many larger companies offer long-term-disability insurance, many small-company employees and self-employed people have no coverage — a risky situation.

Life insurance

When you have dependents, you may also need life insurance protection. The question to ask yourself and your family is how they would fare financially if you died and they no longer had your income coming in. If your family is dependent upon your income, and you want them to be able to maintain their current standard of living in your absence, you need life insurance.

Term life insurance, like most other forms of insurance, is pure insurance protection and is the best type of insurance for the vast majority of people. The amount of coverage you buy should be based upon how many years' *worth* of your income you desire to provide your family in the event of your passing.

Wills, living trusts, and estate planning

Although some of us don't like to admit or even think about it, we're all mortal. Because of the way our legal and tax systems work, it's often beneficial to have legal documents in place specifying important details such as what should be done with your assets (including your home) when you die.

A *will* is the most basic of such documents and for most people, particularly those who are younger or don't have great assets, the only critical one. Through a will, you can direct to whom your assets will go upon your death, as well as who will serve as guardian for your minor children. In the absence of a will, state law dictates these important issues.

Along with your will, also consider signing a *living will* and a *medical power of attorney*. These documents help your doctor and family members make important decisions regarding your health care, should you be unable to make those decisions for yourself.

Even a will and supporting medical and legal documents may not be enough to get your assets to your desired heirs, as well as minimize taxes and legal fees. When you hold significant assets (such as a home and business) outside tax-sheltered retirement accounts, in most states, those assets must be *probated* — which is the court-administered process for implementing your will.

Attorneys' probate fees can run quite high — up to 5 percent of the value of the probated assets. Establishing and placing your home and other assets in a *living trust* can eliminate much of the hassle and cost of probate.

Finally, if your *net worth* (assets minus liabilities) exceeds $2 million upon your death, the federal (and perhaps your state's) government will levy significant estate taxes. (By 2009, the amount you can pass on free of estate tax will rise to $3.5 million.) Estate planning can help minimize the portion of your estate subject to such taxation. One simple but powerful estate-planning strategy is to give money to your desired heirs in order to reduce your taxable estate. (If your relatives are in the fortunate position of having great wealth, they may give, free of tax, up to $11,000 yearly to as many recipients as they want. If they give you $11,000, you can use this money toward your home's down payment.)

Wills, living trusts, and estate planning are nothing more than forms of insurance. Remember that it takes both time and money to generate these documents, and the benefits may be a long time off, so don't get carried away with doing too many of these things before you're older and have significant assets. Read the latest edition of *Taxes For Dummies* (Wiley), which Eric co-authored, to find out more about estate planning.

Insurance brokers love to sell *cash-value life insurance* (also known as *whole* or *universal* life insurance) because of the hefty commissions that they can earn by selling this type of insurance. (These commissions, of course, come out of your pocket.) Some mortgage lenders lobby you to buy the mortgage life insurance that they sell. Skip both these options. Mortgage life insurance is simply overpriced term insurance, and cash-value life insurance generally combines overpriced life insurance with a relatively low-return investment account.

Health insurance

In addition to disability and life insurance, everyone should have a comprehensive health insurance policy. Even if you're in good health, you never know when an accident or illness can happen. Medical bills can mushroom into tens or hundreds of thousands of dollars in no time. Don't be without comprehensive health insurance.

Insuring your assets

As your wealth builds over the years (ideally, at least in part, due to the increasing value of the home that we help you buy), so does the risk of losing — or facing a lawsuit arising from — your valuable assets. For example, you should have comprehensive insurance on your home and car(s). Should your home burn to the ground, a comprehensive homeowners insurance policy would pay for the cost of rebuilding the home. Likewise, if your car is totaled in an accident, auto insurance should pay to replace the car.

With all types of insurance that you purchase, take the highest deductible that you can comfortably afford. The *deductible* represents the amount of money that you must pay out of your own pocket when you have a loss for which you file a claim. High deductibles help keep the cost of your coverage low and also eliminate the hassle associated with filing small claims.

Along with buying insurance to cover the replacement costs for loss of or damage to your valuable assets, you can (and should) purchase adequate liability insurance for those assets. Both homeowners insurance and auto insurance come with liability protection. Make sure that you carry liability coverage for at least twice the value of your *net worth* (assets minus liabilities).

In addition to the liability protection that comes with auto and homeowners insurance, you may purchase a supplemental liability insurance policy known as an *umbrella* or *excess liability policy*. Purchased in increments of $1,000,000, this coverage can protect people with larger net worth. Note that this coverage doesn't protect against lawsuits arising from your work.

Invest in Yourself

Last but not least, in your zest to build your financial empire and buy ever bigger and more expensive homes, don't forget your best investment: you. Don't run your life and body into the ground by working horrendous hours just to afford what you consider your dream home.

In addition to investing in your health, your family, and your friends, invest in educating yourself and taking charge of your finances. If you need more help with assessing your current financial health; reducing your spending, your taxes, and your debts; and mapping out an overall financial plan (including dealing with your investments and insurance), be smart and pick up a copy of the latest edition of Eric's *Personal Finance For Dummies* (Wiley).

Chapter 3

What Can You Afford to Buy?

*W*hen you walk into an auto showroom, one of the first questions the salespeople ask (after you pry them off you) is "What is your budget?" or "How much can you afford to spend on a car?" Of course, they hope that a large number rolls off your tongue. If you're like many car buyers, you may be likely to say something along the lines of "I'm not really sure."

Many car buyers today finance the purchase — so they allow a banker or other lender to determine how much car they can afford. Such determinations are based upon a buyer's income and other debt obligations.

But here's where most people get confused. When a lender says that you qualify to borrow, say, $30,000 for a car purchase, this doesn't mean that you can *afford* to spend that much on a car. What the lender is effectively saying to you is "Based on what little I know about your situation and the fact that I can't control your future behavior, this is the maximum amount that I think is a prudent risk for my organization to lend to you."

The lending organization normally requires a certain down payment to protect itself against the possibility that you may default on the loan. Should you default on an auto loan, for example, the lender has to send the repo man out to take away and sell your car. This process takes time and money, and the lender will surely get less for the car than the amount that you paid for it.

Lenders Can't Tell You What You Can Afford

Ultimately, a lender doesn't care about you, your financial situation, or your other needs so long as it has protected its financial interests. This is true whether you're borrowing to buy a car or a home. The lender doesn't know or care whether, for example, you're

- Falling behind in saving for retirement
- Wanting to save money for other important financial goals, such as starting or buying your own small business
- Parenting a small army of kids (or facing steep private-schooling costs)
- Lacking proper personal insurance protection

And therein lies the problem of making your decision about how much home (or car) you can afford to buy on the basis of how much money a lender is willing to lend you. That's what Walter and Susan did. They set out to purchase a home when Walter's business was booming. They were making in excess of $200,000 per year.

Walter and Susan really wanted to buy the biggest and best house that they could afford. When they met with their friendly neighborhood banker, he was more than willing to show them how they could borrow $900,000 by getting an adjustable-rate mortgage. (You can read all about these mortgages in Chapter 6. We'll simply tell you here that because some adjustable mortgages start out at an artificially low "teaser" interest rate, they enable you to qualify to borrow a good deal more than would be the case with a traditional, fixed-rate mortgage.)

Walter and Susan bought their dream home with an adjustable-rate $900,000 mortgage. Within a few years, Walter and Susan's dream home turned into the Nightmare on Oak Street. Their mortgage became a financial noose around their necks.

Now blessed with young children, Walter and Susan didn't want to work crazy hours anymore; yet they were forced to do so in order to meet their gargantuan mortgage payments. The initial payments on their adjustable-rate mortgage were high, but they ballooned gigantically as the loan's interest rate increased.

The financial strain led to personal strain as Walter and Susan had frequent arguments about money and child care. We know of others who stretched themselves the same way that Walter and Susan did. Many of them continue slaving away long hours in jobs that they don't like and making other unnecessary sacrifices, such as limiting the time they spend with family, in order to make their housing payments. Some end up divorcing, due in part to the financial strains. Others default on their loans, and lose their homes and their good credit.

People at all income levels, even the affluent, can get into trouble and overextend themselves by purchasing more house than they can afford and by taking on more debt than they can comfortably handle. Just because a lender or real estate agent says that you're eligible for, or can qualify for, a certain-size loan doesn't mean that's what you can afford given your personal financial situation. Lenders *can't* tell you what you can afford — they can tell you *only* the maximum that they will allow you to borrow.

The Cost of Buying and Owning a Home

Before you set out in search of your dream home, one of the single most important questions you should answer is "What can I afford to spend on a home?" In order to answer that question intelligently, you first need to understand what your financial goals are, what it will take to achieve them, and where you are today. If you haven't yet read Chapter 2, now's the time (unless you're 100 percent sure that your personal finances are in tip-top shape).

In the following sections, we dig into the costs of buying and owning a home.

Mortgage payments

In Chapter 6, we discuss selecting the best type of mortgage that fits with your particular circumstances. In the meantime, you must still confront mortgages (with our assistance), because mortgages undoubtedly constitute the biggest component of the total cost of owning a home.

Start with the basics: A *mortgage* is a loan you take out to buy a home. A mortgage allows you to purchase a $150,000 home even though you yourself have far less money than that to put toward the purchase.

With few exceptions, mortgage loans in the United States are typically repaid over a 15- or 30-year time span. Almost all mortgages require monthly payments. Here's how a mortgage works. Suppose that you are purchasing a $150,000 home and that (following our sage advice, appearing later in this chapter) you have diligently saved a 20 percent ($30,000, in this example) down payment. Thus, you are in the market for a $120,000 mortgage loan.

You sit down with a mortgage lender who asks you to complete a volume of paperwork (we navigate you through that morass in Chapter 7) that dwarfs the stack required for your annual income tax return. Just when you think the worst is over (after the paperwork blizzard subsides), the lender proceeds to give you an even bigger headache by talking about the literally hundreds of mortgage permutations and options.

Don't worry — we can help you cut through the clutter! Imagine, for a moment, a simple world where the mortgage lender offers you only two mortgage options: a 15-year fixed-rate mortgage and a 30-year fixed-rate mortgage (*fixed-rate* simply means that the interest rate on the loan stays fixed and level over the life of the loan). Here's what your monthly payment would be under each mortgage option:

$120,000, 15-year mortgage @ 7.00 percent = $1,079 per month

$120,000, 30-year mortgage @ 7.25 percent = $819 per month

As we discuss in Chapter 6, the interest rate is typically a little bit lower on a 15-year mortgage versus a 30-year mortgage because shorter-term loans are a little less risky for lenders. Note how much higher the monthly payment is on the 15-year mortgage than it is on the 30-year mortgage. Your payments must be higher for the 15-year mortgage because you're paying off the same-size loan 15 years faster.

But don't let the higher monthly payments on the 15-year loan cause you to forget that at the end of 15 years, your mortgage payments disappear, whereas with the 30-year mortgage, you still have 15 more years' worth of monthly payments to go. So although you do have a higher required monthly payment with the 15-year mortgage, check out the difference in the total payments and interest on the two mortgage options:

Mortgage Option	Total Payments	Total Interest
15-year mortgage	$194,147	$74,147
30-year mortgage	$294,700	$174,700

Note: In case you're curious about how we got the total interest amount, we simply subtracted the amount of the loan repaid ($120,000) from the "Total Payments." Also, the monthly payment numbers previously cited, as well as these total payments and interest numbers, are rounded off, so if you try multiplying 180 or 360 by the monthly payment numbers, you won't get answers identical to the above.

With the 30-year mortgage (compared with the 15-year mortgage), because you're borrowing the money over 15 additional years, it shouldn't come as a great surprise that (with a decent-size mortgage loan like this one) you end up paying more than $100,000 additional interest. The 30-year loan isn't necessarily inferior; for example, its lower payments may better allow you to accomplish other important financial goals, such as saving in a tax-deductible retirement account. (See Chapter 6 for more information about 15-year versus 30-year mortgages.)

In the early years of repaying your mortgage, nearly all of your mortgage payment goes toward paying interest on the money that you borrowed. Not until the later years of your mortgage do you begin to rapidly pay down your loan balance, as shown in Figure 3-1.

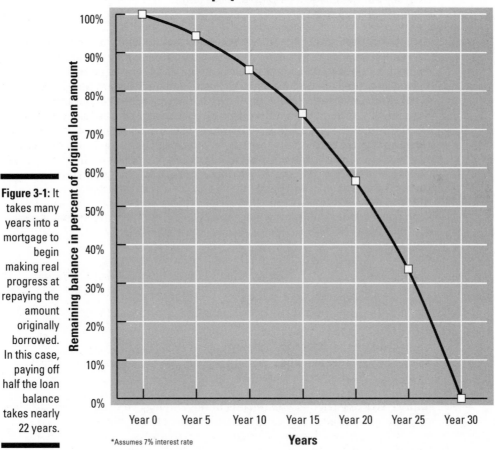

Figure 3-1: It takes many years into a mortgage to begin making real progress at repaying the amount originally borrowed. In this case, paying off half the loan balance takes nearly 22 years.

As interest rates increase, so does the time required to pay off half the loan. For example, at a 10 percent interest rate, paying off half the loan takes almost 24 years of the loan's 30-year term, and at a 14 percent interest rate, paying off half the loan takes over 25 years of the loan's 30-year life.

Lender's limits

Because we have personally seen the financial consequences of people borrowing too much (yet still staying within the boundaries of what mortgage lenders allow), you won't hear us saying in this section that lenders can tell you the amount that you can afford to spend on a home. They can't. All that mortgage lenders can do is tell you their criteria for approving and denying mortgage applications, and calculating the maximum that you're eligible to borrow. (For the inside scoop on lenders and their limits, please see the first section of this chapter.)

Most, but by no means all, mortgage lenders follow similar loan-evaluation criteria because they actually sell the mortgage loans they originate in the financial markets to picky investors. Government agencies — such as *Fannie Mae* (FNMA: the Federal National Mortgage Association) and *Ginnie Mae* (GNMA: the Government National Mortgage Association) — guarantee the repayment of principal and interest on such loans so long as the bank that originates the mortgage adheres to certain specific criteria for accepting or rejecting the mortgage loan. Perhaps, in the often-confusing world of investments, you've heard of *Ginnie Maes.* Well, when you invest in these mortgage-backed securities, what you're basically buying are bonds that are mortgages, perhaps even yours!

A mortgage lender tallies up your monthly *housing expense,* the components of which they consider to be

	Mortgage payment	(*PI* for principal and interest)
+	Property taxes	(*T* for taxes)
+	Insurance	(*I* for insurance)
=	Lender's definition of *housing expense*	(PITI is the common acronym)

For a given property that you're considering buying, a mortgage lender calculates the housing expense and normally requires that it not exceed a certain percentage (typically around 35 percent or so) of your monthly before-tax *(gross)* income. (Some lenders allow the percentage to go a bit higher.) So, for example, if your monthly gross income is $6,000, your lender will not allow your expected monthly housing expense to exceed $2,100 (if the lender is using 35 percent). When you're self-employed and complete IRS *Form 1040, Schedule C,* mortgage lenders use your after-expenses *(net)* income, from the bottom line of *Schedule C.*

Stretching more than lenders allow

Sometimes, prospective home buyers feel that they can handle more debt than lenders will allow. Such home buyers may seek to borrow more money from family or fib on their mortgage application about their income. (Self-employed people have the greatest opportunity to do this.) Such behavior isn't unlike the shenanigans of some teenagers who drive above the speed limit, drink and smoke forbidden things, or stay out past curfew and sneak in the back door.

Although a few of these teenagers get away with such risky behavior, others end up in trouble academically or psychologically (or worse). The same is true of homeowners who stretch themselves financially thin to buy a more costly property. Some survive just fine, but others end up in financial and emotional trouble.

And, increasingly, home buyers who lie on their mortgage applications are getting caught. How? When you're ready to close on your loan, lenders can (and often do) ask you to sign a form authorizing them to request a copy of your income tax return from the IRS. This allows the lender to validate your income. (See Chapter 7 for more details.)

So although we've said that the lender's word isn't the gospel as to how much home you can truly afford, we will go on record as saying that telling the truth on your mortgage application is the only way to go (and prevents you from committing perjury and fraud). Telling the truth isn't only honest, but also helps keep you from getting in over your head. Bankers don't want you to default on your loan, and you shouldn't want to take the risk of doing so either.

Now, if you've been paying attention thus far in this chapter, you should smell something terribly wrong with such a simplistic, one-number-fits-all approach. This housing-expense ratio completely ignores almost all your other financial goals, needs, and obligations. It also ignores maintenance and remodeling expenses, which can gobble up a lot of a homeowner's dough.

About the only other financial considerations a lender takes into account (besides your income) are your other debts. Specifically, mortgage lenders examine the required monthly payments for student loans, an auto loan, credit card bills, and other debts. In addition to the percentage of your income lenders allow for housing expenses, lenders typically allow an additional 5 percent of your monthly income to go toward other debt repayments. Thus, your monthly housing expense and monthly repayment of nonhousing debts can total up to, but generally be no more than, 40 percent.

Should you have consumer debt, be sure to read Chapter 2. Suffice it to say here that you should get out (and stay out) of consumer debt. Consumer debt has a high cost, and unlike the interest on a mortgage loan, the interest on consumer debt isn't tax deductible. And consumer debt handicaps your ability to qualify for and pay back your mortgage. *Consumer debt is the financial equivalent of cancer.*

Figuring the size of your mortgage payments

Calculating the size of your mortgage payment, after you know the amount you want to borrow, is simple. The hard part for most people is determining how much they can afford to borrow. If you already know how large a monthly mortgage payment you can afford, terrific! Go to the head of the class. Suppose that you worked through your budget in Chapter 2 and calculated that you can afford to spend $1,500 per month on housing. Determining the exact amount of mortgage that allows you to stay within this boundary is a little challenging, because the housing cost you figure that you can afford ($1,500, in our example) is made up of several components. Lucky for you, we cover each of these components in this chapter, including mortgage payments, property taxes, insurance, and maintenance. (Note that although lenders don't care about maintenance expenses in figuring what you can afford to buy, you shouldn't overlook this very real and significant expense.)

As you change the amount that you're willing to spend on a home, the size of the mortgage you choose to take out also usually changes, but so do the other property cost components. So you may have to play with the numbers a bit to get them to work out just right. You may pick a certain-price home and then figure the property taxes, insurance, maintenance, and the like. When you tally everything up, you may find that the total comes in above or below your desired target ($1,500, in our example). Obviously, if you come out a little high, you need to cut back a bit and choose a slightly less-costly property and/or get a smaller mortgage.

Using Table 3-1, you can calculate the size of your mortgage payments based on the amount you want to borrow, the loan's interest rate, and the length (in years) the mortgage payments last. To determine the monthly payment on a mortgage, simply multiply the relevant number from Table 3-1 by the size of your mortgage expressed in (divided by) thousands of dollars. For example, if you will be taking out a $150,000, 30-year mortgage at 7.50 percent, multiply 150 by 6.99 (from Table 3-1) to arrive at a $1,048.50 monthly payment.

Table 3-1	Monthly Mortgage Payment Calculator	
Interest Rate	*15-Year Mortgage*	*30-Year Mortgage*
4	7.40	4.77
4⅛	7.46	4.85
4¼	7.52	4.92
4⅜	7.59	4.99
4½	7.65	5.07
4⅝	7.71	5.14
4¾	7.78	5.22

Interest Rate	15-Year Mortgage	30-Year Mortgage
4⅞	7.84	5.29
5	7.91	5.37
5⅛	7.98	5.45
5¼	8.04	5.53
5⅜	8.11	5.60
5½	8.18	5.68
5⅝	8.24	5.76
5¾	8.31	5.84
5⅞	8.38	5.92
6	8.44	6.00
6⅛	8.51	6.08
6¼	8.58	6.16
6⅜	8.65	6.24
6½	8.72	6.33
6⅝	8.78	6.41
6¾	8.85	6.49
6⅞	8.92	6.57
7	8.99	6.66
7⅛	9.06	6.74
7¼	9.13	6.83
7⅜	9.20	6.91
7½	9.28	7.00
7⅝	9.35	7.08
7¾	9.42	7.17
7⅞	9.49	7.26
8	9.56	7.34
8⅛	9.63	7.43
8¼	9.71	7.52

(continued)

Table 3-1 *(continued)*

Interest Rate	15-Year Mortgage	30-Year Mortgage
8⅜	9.78	7.61
8½	9.85	7.69
8⅝	9.93	7.78
8¾	10.00	7.87
8⅞	10.07	7.96
9	10.15	8.05
9⅛	10.22	8.14
9¼	10.30	8.23
9⅜	10.37	8.32
9½	10.45	8.41
9⅝	10.52	8.50
9¾	10.60	8.60
9⅞	10.67	8.69
10	10.75	8.78
10⅛	10.83	8.87
10¼	10.90	8.97
10⅜	10.98	9.06
10½	11.06	9.15
10⅝	11.14	9.25
10¾	11.21	9.34
10⅞	11.29	9.43
11	11.37	9.53
11¼	11.53	9.72
11½	11.69	9.91
11¾	11.85	10.10
12	12.01	10.29
12¼	12.17	10.48
12½	12.17	10.48

Use this handy-dandy workspace (reproduced throughout the chapter) to track your estimated homeownership expenses, starting with the mortgage payment:

Item		*Estimated Monthly Expense*
Mortgage payment		$ _____
Property taxes	+	$ _____
Insurance	+	$ _____
Improvements, maintenance, and other	+	$ _____
Homeownership expenses (pretax)	=	$ _____
Tax savings	−	$ _____
Homeownership expenses (after-tax benefits)	=	$ _____

Property taxes

If you live and breathe, escaping taxes is darn near impossible. When you buy and own a home, your local government (typically through what is called a County Tax Collector's office) sends you an annual, lump-sum bill for property taxes. Receiving this bill and paying it are never much fun, because most communities bill you just once or twice per year. And some homeowners find it aggravating to be paying so much in property taxes on top of all the federal and state income and sales taxes they pay. In case you're wondering, property taxes go toward expenses of the local community, such as the public schools and snow plowing (for those of us foolish enough to locate where the winters are cold). Especially in higher-cost areas with few retail and commercial properties paying taxes, residential property taxes can be quite significant.

Should you make a small down payment (typically defined as less than 20 percent of the purchase price), many lenders insist upon property tax and insurance *impound accounts.* These accounts require you to pay your property taxes and insurance to the lender each month along with your mortgage payment.

Property taxes are typically based on the value of a property. Although an average property tax rate is about 1.5 percent of the purchase price of the property per year, you should understand what the exact rate is in your area. Call the Tax Collector's office (you can find the phone number in the government pages section of your local phone directory under such headings as "Tax Collector," "Treasurer," or "Assessor") in the town where you're contemplating buying a home, and ask what the property tax rate is and what additional fees and assessments may apply.

Be careful to make sure that you're comparing apples with apples when comparing communities and their property taxes. For example, some communities may nickel-and-dime you for extra assessments for services that are included in the standard property tax bills of other communities.

Real estate listings, which are typically prepared by real estate agents, may list what the current property owner is paying in taxes. But relying on such data to understand what your real estate taxes will be if you buy the property can be financially dangerous. The current owner's taxes may be based upon an outdated and much lower property valuation. Just as it's dangerous to drive forward by looking in the rearview mirror of your car, you shouldn't buy a property and budget for property taxes based upon the current owner's taxes. Your property taxes (if you buy the home) will probably be recalculated based upon the price you paid for the property.

Item	*Estimated Monthly Expense*
Mortgage payment	$ _____
Property taxes	+ $ _____
Insurance	+ $ _____
Improvements, maintenance, and other	+ $ _____
Homeownership expenses (pretax)	= $ _____
Tax savings	− $ _____
Homeownership expenses (after-tax benefits)	= $ _____

Insurance

When you purchase a home, your mortgage lender almost surely won't allow you to close the purchase until you've demonstrated that you have proper homeowners insurance. Lenders aren't being paternalistic, but self-interested. You see, if you buy the home and make a down payment of, say, 20 percent of the purchase price, the lender is putting up the other 80 percent of the purchase price. So if the home burns to the ground and is a total loss, the lender may care more, at least financially, than you do. In most states, your home is the lender's security for the loan.

Some lenders, in years past, learned the hard way that some homeowners may not care about losing their homes. In some cases, where homes were total losses, homeowners with little financial stake in the property and insufficient insurance coverage simply walked away from the problem and left the lender with the financial mess. Because of cases like this, almost all lenders today require you to purchase *private mortgage insurance* (PMI) if you put down less than 20 percent of the purchase price when you buy. (We discuss PMI further later in this chapter, in the section titled "The 20 percent solution.")

When you buy a home, you should want to protect your investment in the property (as well as cover the not-so-inconsequential cost of replacing your personal property, if it is ever damaged or stolen). In short order, your clothing, furniture, kitchen appliances, and beer-can collection can tally up to a lot of dollars to replace.

When you purchase homeowners insurance, you should buy the most comprehensive coverage that you can and take the highest deductible that you can afford to help minimize the cost. In Chapter 13, we explain how to do all that. In order to estimate what homeowners insurance may cost you, we suggest that you contact some of the insurers we recommend in Chapter 13. Explain to them what type and price range of properties you're considering buying in which communities (zip codes), and they should be able to give you a ballpark monthly cost estimate for insurance. Calling insurance agents now will also enable you to begin to evaluate which insurers offer the service and coverage you desire when the time comes to actually buy your dream home.

Just as you should do when you shop for a car, get quotes on insuring properties as you evaluate them, or ask current owners what they pay for their coverage. (Just remember that some homeowners overpay or don't buy the right kind of protection, so don't take what they pay as gospel.) If you overlook insurance costs until after you've agreed to buy a property, you could be in for a rude awakening.

Item	Estimated Monthly Expense
Mortgage payment	$ _____
Property taxes	+ $ _____
Insurance	+ $ _____
Improvements, maintenance, and other	+ $ _____
Homeownership expenses (pretax)	= $ _____
Tax savings	− $ _____
Homeownership expenses (after-tax benefits)	= $ _____

Maintenance and other costs

As a homeowner, you *must* make your mortgage and property-tax payments. If you don't, you'll eventually lose your home. Homes also require maintenance

Tax difference between maintenance and improvements

While you own your home, it is in your interest to track the amount that you spend on improvements. Why? Well, when you go to sell your home someday, the IRS allows you to exclude from taxation that portion of your profit that was due to capital improvements. (As we discuss in Chapter 15, IRS home-sale tax rules also enable qualifying taxpayers to exclude from federal taxation a large chunk of profit — up to $250,000 for single taxpayers, $500,000 for married couples filing jointly.)

For tax purposes, the IRS enables you to add the cost of *improvements* (but not money spent on *maintenance*) to your original purchase price. What's the difference? Well, there *is* a difference, but as with all matters on which the IRS has an opinion, that difference isn't always crystal clear.

✔ *Capital improvements* are things that you do to your home that permanently increase its value and lengthen its life. Capital improvements include such things as landscaping your yard, adding a deck, purchasing new appliances (as long as you leave them when you sell), installing a new heating system or roof, remodeling and adding rooms, and so on.

✔ *Maintenance and repair expenses,* in contrast, include those types of fix-up items that need to be done throughout your home from time to time. Maintenance and repairs include such things as fixing a leaky pipe or toilet, painting, paying someone to cut your lawn and pull weeds, and the like.

So when you buy a home, keep handy a file folder into which you can dump receipts for your home-improvement expenditures. If you're in doubt as to whether an expense is an improvement or a maintenance item, keep the receipt, and figure it out when the time comes to sell your home.

over the years. You must do some kinds of maintenance (repairs, for example) at a certain time. You never know precisely when you may need to fix an electrical problem, patch a leaking roof, or replace the washer and dryer — until the problem rears its ugly head, which is why maintenance is difficult to budget for. (Painting and other elective improvements can take place at your discretion.)

As a rule of thumb, expect to spend about 1 percent of the purchase price of your home each year on maintenance. So, for example, if you spend $150,000 on a home, you should budget about $1,500 per year (or about $125 per month) for maintenance. Although some years you may spend less, other years you may spend more. When your home's roof goes, for example, replacing it may cost you several years' worth of your budgeted maintenance expenses. With some types of housing, such as condominiums, you actually pay monthly dues into a homeowners association, which takes care of the maintenance for the complex. In that case, you're responsible for maintaining only the interior of your unit. Before you buy such a unit, check with the association to see what the dues are running and whether any new assessments are planned for future repairs. (See Chapter 8 for more information.)

In addition to necessary maintenance, you should be aware (and beware) of what you may spend on nonessential home improvements. This *Other* category can really get you into trouble. Advertisements, your neighbors, and your co-workers can all entice you into blowing big bucks on new furniture, endless remodeling projects, landscaping, and you-name-it.

Should you budget for these nonessentials? In general, yes. The potential problem is that your home can become a money pit by causing you to spend too much, not save enough, and (possibly) go into debt via credit cards and the like. (We cover the other dangers of overimprovement in Chapter 8.) Unless you're a terrific saver, can easily accomplish your savings goal, and have lots of slack in your budget, be sure not to overlook this part of your home-expense budget.

The amount you expect to spend on improvements is just a guess. It depends upon how *finished* a home you buy and on your personal tastes and desires. Consider your previous spending behavior and the types of projects you expect to do as you examine potential homes for purchase.

Item	*Estimated Monthly Expense*
Mortgage payment	$ _____
Property taxes	+ $ _____
Insurance	+ $ _____
Improvements, maintenance, and other	+ $ _____
Homeownership expenses (pretax)	= $ _____
Tax savings	− $ _____
Homeownership expenses (after-tax benefits)	= $ _____

The tax benefits of homeownership

One of the benefits of homeownership is that the IRS and most state governments allow you to deduct, within certain limits, mortgage interest and property taxes when you file your annual income tax return. When you file your Federal IRS *Form 1040,* the mortgage interest and property taxes on your home are itemized deductions on *Schedule A* (see Figure 3-2). On mortgage loans now taken out, you may deduct the interest on the first $1 million of debt, as well as all of the property taxes. The good folks at the IRS also allow you to deduct the interest costs on a *home equity* loan (second mortgage) to a maximum of $100,000 borrowed.

But just because mortgage interest and property taxes are allowable deductions on your income tax return, don't think that the government is literally paying for these items for you. Consider that when you earn a dollar of income and must pay income tax on that dollar, you don't pay the entire dollar back to the government in taxes. Your tax bracket (see Table 3-2) determines the amount of taxes you pay on that dollar.

SCHEDULES A&B (Form 1040)
Department of the Treasury Internal Revenue Service (99)

Schedule A—Itemized Deductions
(Schedule B is on back)
► Attach to Form 1040. ► See Instructions for Schedules A&B (Form 1040).

OMB No. 1545-0074
2005
Attachment Sequence No. **07**

Name(s) shown on Form 1040 | **Your social security number**

Section	Line	Description	Box
Medical and Dental Expenses		**Caution.** Do not include expenses reimbursed or paid by others.	
	1	Medical and dental expenses (see page A-2)	1
	2	Enter amount from Form 1040, line 38 [2]	
	3	Multiply line 2 by 7.5% (.075)	3
	4	Subtract line 3 from line 1. If line 3 is more than line 1, enter -0-	4
Taxes You Paid (See page A-2.)	5	State and local **(check only one box)**: a ☐ Income taxes, **or** b ☐ General sales taxes (see page A-3)	5
	6	Real estate taxes (see page A-5)	6
	7	Personal property taxes	7
	8	Other taxes. List type and amount ►	8
	9	Add lines 5 through 8	9
Interest You Paid (See page A-5.)	10	Home mortgage interest and points reported to you on Form 1098	10
	11	Home mortgage interest not reported to you on Form 1098. If paid to the person from whom you bought the home, see page A-6 and show that person's name, identifying no., and address ►	11
Note. Personal interest is not deductible.	12	Points not reported to you on Form 1098. See page A-6 for special rules	12
	13	Investment interest. Attach Form 4952 if required. (See page A-6.)	13
	14	Add lines 10 through 13	14
Gifts to Charity If you made a gift and got a benefit for it, see page A-7.	15a	Total gifts by cash or check. If you made any gift of $250 or more, see page A-7	15a
	b	Gifts by cash or check after August 27, 2005, that you elect to treat as qualified contributions (see page A-7) [15b]	
	16	Other than by cash or check. If any gift of $250 or more, see page A-7. You **must** attach Form 8283 if over $500	16
	17	Carryover from prior year	17
	18	Add lines 15a, 16, and 17	18
Casualty and Theft Losses	19	Casualty or theft loss(es). Attach Form 4684. (See page A-8.)	19
Job Expenses and Certain Miscellaneous Deductions (See page A-8.)	20	Unreimbursed employee expenses—job travel, union dues, job education, etc. Attach Form 2106 or 2106-EZ if required. (See page A-8.) ►	20
	21	Tax preparation fees	21
	22	Other expenses—investment, safe deposit box, etc. List type and amount ►	22
	23	Add lines 20 through 22	23
	24	Enter amount from Form 1040, line 38 [24]	
	25	Multiply line 24 by 2% (.02)	25
	26	Subtract line 25 from line 23. If line 25 is more than line 23, enter -0-	26
Other Miscellaneous Deductions	27	Other—from list on page A-9. List type and amount ►	27
Total Itemized Deductions	28	Is Form 1040, line 38, over $145,950 (over $72,975 if married filing separately)? ☐ **No.** Your deduction is not limited. Add the amounts in the far right column for lines 4 through 27. Also, enter this amount on Form 1040, line 40. ☐ **Yes.** Your deduction may be limited. See page A-9 for the amount to enter. ►	28
	29	If you elect to itemize deductions even though they are less than your standard deduction, check here ► ☐	

For Paperwork Reduction Act Notice, see Form 1040 instructions. Cat. No. 11330X **Schedule A (Form 1040) 2005**

Figure 3-2: Itemize mortgage interest and property tax deductions on Schedule A of your 1040.

Table 3-2	2001 Federal Income Tax Brackets and Rates	
Singles	*Married-Filing-Jointly Taxable Income*	*Federal Tax Rate Taxable Income*
Less than $7,550	Less than $15,100	10%
$7,550 to $30,650	$15,100 to $61,300	15%
$30,650 to $74,200	$61,300 to $123,700	25%
$74,200 to $154,800	$123,700 to $188,450	28%
$154,800 to $336,550	$188,450 to $336,550	33%
More than $336,550	More than $336,550	35%

Technically, you pay federal and state taxes, so you should consider your state tax savings as well when calculating your homeownership tax savings. However, to keep things simple and still get a reliable estimate, simply multiply your mortgage payment and property taxes by your *federal* income tax rate. This shortcut works well because the small portion of your mortgage payment that isn't deductible (because it is for the loan repayment) approximately offsets the overlooked state tax savings.

Item	*Estimated Monthly Expense*
Mortgage payment	$ _____
Property taxes	+ $ _____
Insurance	+ $ _____
Improvements, maintenance, and other	+ $ _____
Homeownership expenses (pretax)	= $ _____
Tax savings	− $ _____
Homeownership expenses (after-tax benefits)	= $ _____

You may also be interested in knowing — but more likely don't care — that the deductibility of the mortgage interest on up to $1 million borrowed covers debt on both your primary residence and a second residence. (Buying and maintaining two homes is an expensive proposition and something few people can afford, so don't get any silly ideas from our mentioning this tax tidbit!)

Congratulations! You've totaled what your dream home should cost you on a monthly basis after factoring in the tax benefits of homeownership. Don't forget to plug these expected homeownership costs into your current monthly spending plans (see Chapter 2) to make sure that you can afford to spend this much on a home and still accomplish your financial goals.

Closing Costs

On the day when a home becomes yours officially (known as *closing day*), many people (in addition to the seller) will have their hands in your wallet. Myriad one-time closing costs can leave you poor and destitute, or send you running to your parents or your in-laws for financial assistance.

We don't want you to be unable to close your home purchase or be forced to get down on your hands and knees and beg for money from your mother-in-law. (Not only is such groveling hard on your ego, but also, she will likely charge you 25 percent interest on the borrowed money and expect three grandchildren in the next five years to boot.) Advance preparation for the closing costs saves your sanity and your finances.

Here are some typical closing costs (listed from those that are usually largest to those that are typically tiniest) and how much to budget for each (exact fees vary by property cost and location):

✔ **Loan-origination fees (points) and other loan charges:** These fees and charges range from nothing to 3 percent of the amount borrowed. Lenders generally charge all sorts of fees for things such as appraising the property, pulling your credit report, preparing loan documents, and processing your application, as well as charging a loan-origination fee, which may be 1 or 2 percent of the loan amount. If you're strapped for cash, you can get a loan that has few or no fees; however, such loans have substantially higher interest rates over their lifetimes. As Chapter 12 explains, you may be able to cut a deal with the seller to pay these loan-closing costs.

✔ **Escrow fees:** Escrow fees range from several hundred to over a thousand dollars, based on the purchase price of your home. These fees cover the cost of handling all the purchase-related documents and funds. We explain escrows in much more detail in Chapters 9 and 14.

✔ **Homeowners insurance:** This insurance typically costs several hundred to a thousand dollars plus per year, depending on the value of your home and how much coverage you want. As we discuss earlier in this chapter, you can't get a mortgage unless you prove to the lender that you have adequate homeowners insurance coverage. Promising to get this coverage isn't enough; lenders usually insist that you pay the first year's premium on said insurance policy at the time of the closing.

✔ **Title insurance:** This insurance typically costs several hundred to a thousand dollars, depending on the home's purchase price. Lenders require that you purchase title insurance when you buy your home to make sure that you have clear, marketable title to the property. Among other things, *title insurance* protects you and the lender against the remote possibility that the person selling you the home doesn't legally own it. We discuss title insurance in detail in Chapter 13.

✔ **Property taxes:** These taxes typically cost several hundred to a couple thousand dollars and are based upon the home's purchase price and the date that escrow closes. At the close of escrow, you may have to reimburse the sellers for any property taxes that they paid in advance. For example, suppose that (before they sold their home to you) the sellers had already paid their property taxes through June 30. If the sale closes on April 30, you owe the sellers two months' property taxes — the tax collector won't refund the property taxes they have already paid for May and June.

✔ **Legal fees:** These fees range anywhere from nothing to hundreds of dollars. In some Eastern states, lawyers are routinely involved in real estate purchases. In most states, however, lawyers aren't needed for home purchases as long as the real estate agents use standard, fill-in-the-blank contracts. Such contracts have the advance input and blessing of the legal eagles.

✔ **Inspections:** Inspection fees can run from $200 to $1,000 (depending upon the size of the property and the scope of the inspection). As we explain in Chapter 13, you should never, ever consider buying a home without inspecting it. Because you're likely not a home-inspection expert, you'll benefit from hiring someone who inspects property as a full-time job. Sometimes, you simply pay these costs directly; at other times, you pay these costs at the closing.

✔ **Private mortgage insurance (PMI):** Should you need it, this insurance can cost you several hundred dollars — or more — annually. As we explain in the next section of this chapter, if you put less than 20 percent down on a home, many mortgage lenders require that you take out private mortgage insurance. This type of insurance protects the lender in the event that you default on the loan. At closing, you need to pay anywhere from a couple months' premiums to more than a year's premium in advance. If you can, avoid this cost by making a 20 percent down payment or by obtaining 80-10-10 financing, which we explain in the section "Ways to buy with less money down," later in this chapter.

✔ **Prepaid loan interest:** Lenders charge up to 30 days' interest on your loan to cover the interest that accrues from the date your loan is funded (usually, one business day before the escrow closes) up to 30 days prior to your first regularly scheduled loan payment. How much interest you actually have to pay depends on the timing of your first loan payment. If you're smart, and we know that you are, you can work this timing out with the lender so you don't have to pay any advance loan interest.

To avoid paying three useless days of interest charges, *never schedule your escrow to close on a Monday.* Should you close on a Monday, the lender has to put your mortgage funds into escrow the preceding Friday. As a result, you're charged interest on your loan for Friday, Saturday, and Sunday even though you won't own the home until escrow closes on Monday. (This little tip more than pays for this book all by itself. Don't you feel smart now?)

✔ **Recording:** The fee to record the deed and mortgage usually runs about $50.

✔ **Overnight/courier fees:** These fees usually cost $50 or less. Remember the times when you sent something via the U.S. Postal Service to a destination that you could have driven to in less than a few hours, and it took them the better part of a week to get it there (or perhaps they lost it)? Well, lenders and other players in real estate deals know that these snags can occur without warning, and because they don't want to derail your transaction or cost themselves money, they often send stuff the fastest way they can. And why not — it's your money!

✔ **Notary:** Notary fees run from $10 to $20 *per signature per buyer.* At the close of escrow, you sign all sorts of important documents pledging your worldly possessions and firstborn child, should you renege on your mortgage. Therefore, you need to have your signature verified by a notary so everybody in the transaction knows that you really are who you say you are.

As you can see, closing costs can mount up in a hurry. In a typical real estate deal, closing costs total 2 to 5 percent of the purchase price of the property. Thus, you shouldn't ignore them in figuring the amount of money you need to close the deal. Having enough to pay the down payment on your loan just isn't sufficient.

When you're short of cash and hot to buy a home sooner rather than later, you can take out a mortgage with no out-of-pocket fees and points (see Chapter 6) and try to negotiate with the property seller to pay other closing costs (see Chapter 12). Expect to pay a higher mortgage interest rate for a low-up-front-fee loan. And all other things being equal, expect to pay a higher purchase price (with a correspondingly bigger mortgage) to entice the seller to pay your other closing costs. Also, don't blindly accept all the closing costs come closing time. In Chapter 14, we explain the importance of auditing your closing statement.

Accumulating the Down Payment

Jeremy went house hunting and soon fell in love with a home. Unfortunately, after he found his dream home, he soon discovered all the loan-documentation requirements and the extra fees and penalties he would have to pay for having such a small down payment. Ultimately, he couldn't afford to buy the home that he desired because he hadn't saved enough. "If I had known, I would have started saving much sooner — I thought that saving for the future was something you did when you turned middle-aged," he told Eric.

We don't want you to be surprised when you finally set out to purchase a home. That's why now, in the comfort of your rental, commuter train, or bus (or anywhere else you may be reading this book), we'd like you to consider the following:

- How much money you should save for the down payment and closing costs for the purchase of your home
- Where your down-payment money is going to come from
- How you should invest this money while you're awaiting the purchase and closing

The 20 percent solution

Ideally, you should purchase a home and have enough accumulated for a down payment so that your down payment represents 20 percent of the purchase price of the property. Why 20 percent and not 10 or 15 or 25 or 30 percent? Twenty percent down is the magic number because it's a big enough cushion to protect lenders from default. Suppose, for example, that a buyer puts only 10 percent down; property values drop 5 percent; and the buyer defaults on the loan. When the lender forecloses — *after* paying a real estate commission, transfer tax, and other expenses of sale — the lender will be in the hole. Lenders don't like losing money. They found that they are far less likely to lose money on mortgages where the borrower has put up a down payment of at least 20 percent of the value of the property.

If, like most people, you plan to borrow money from a bank or other mortgage lender, be aware that almost all require you to obtain (and pay for) private mortgage insurance (PMI) if your down payment is less than 20 percent of the purchase price of the property. Although PMI typically adds several hundred dollars annually to the cost of your loan, it protects the lender financially if you default. Should you buy an expensive home — into the hundreds-of-thousands-of-dollars price range — PMI can add $1,000 or more, annually, to your mortgage bill. (You can also expect worse loan terms, such as higher up-front fees and/or a higher ongoing interest rate on a mortgage, when you make a down payment of less than 20 percent.)

PMI isn't a permanent cost. Your need for PMI vanishes when you can prove that you have at least 20 percent *equity* (home value minus loan balance outstanding) in the property. The 20 percent can come from loan paydown, appreciation, improvements that enhance the value of the property, or any combination thereof. Note also that to remove PMI, most mortgage lenders require that an appraisal be done — at your expense.

Note: If you have (or expect to have) the 20 percent down payment and enough money for the closing costs, skip the next section, and go to the section on how to invest your down-payment money.

Ways to buy with less money down

Especially if you're just starting to save or are still paying off student loans or worse — digging out from consumer debt — saving 20 percent of a property's purchase price as a down payment plus closing costs can seem like a financial mountain.

Don't panic, and don't give up. Here's a grab bag filled with time-tested ways to overcome this seemingly gargantuan obstacle:

- ✔ **Boost your savings rate.** Say that you want to accumulate $30,000 for your home purchase, and you're saving just $100 per month. At this rate, it will take you nearly two decades to reach your savings goal! However, if you can boost your savings rate by $300 per month, you should reach your goal in about five years.

  Being efficient with your spending is always a good financial habit, but saving faster is a *necessity* for nearly all prospective home buyers. Without benevolent, loaded relatives or other sources for a financial windfall, you're going to need to accumulate money the old-fashioned way that millions of other home buyers have done in the past: by gradually saving it. Most people have fat in their budgets. Start by reading Chapter 2 for ways to assess your current spending and boost your savings rate.

- ✔ **Set your sights lower.** Twenty percent of a big number is a big number, so it stands to reason that 20 percent of a smaller number is a smaller number. If the down payment and closing costs needed to purchase a $300,000 home are stretching you, scale back to a $240,000 or $200,000 home, which should slash your required cash for the home purchase by about 20 to 33 percent.

- ✔ **Check out low-down-payment loan programs.** Some lenders offer low-down-payment mortgage programs where you can put down as little as 3 to 10 percent of the purchase price. To qualify for such programs, you generally must have excellent credit and purchase private mortgage insurance (PMI). In addition to the extra expense of PMI, expect to get worse loan terms — higher interest rates and more up-front fees — with such low-money-down loans. Check with local lenders and real estate agents in your area.

Unless you're champing at the bit to purchase a home, take more time, and try to accumulate a larger down payment. However, if you're the type of person who has trouble saving and may never save a 20 percent down payment, buying with less money down may be your best option. In this situation, be sure to shop around for the best loan terms.

✔ **Access retirement accounts.** Some employers allow you to borrow against your retirement-savings plan. Just be sure that you understand the repayment rules so that you don't get tripped up and forced to treat the withdrawal as a taxable distribution. You're allowed to make penalty-free withdrawals from Individual Retirement Accounts for a first-time home purchase (see Chapter 2).

✔ **Get family help.** Your folks or grandparents may like, perhaps even love, to help you with the down payment and closing costs for your dream home. Why would they do that? Well, perhaps they had financial assistance from family when they bought a home, way back when. Another possibility is that they have more money accumulated for their future and retirement than they may need. If they have substantial assets, holding onto all these assets until their death could trigger unnecessary estate taxes. A final reason that they may be willing to lend you money is that they're bank-and-bond-type investors and are earning paltry returns.

If your parents or grandparents (or other family members, for that matter) broach the topic of giving or lending you money for a home purchase, go ahead and discuss the matter. But in many situations, you (as the prospective home buyer) may need to raise the issue first. Some parents just aren't comfortable bringing up the topic of money or may be worried that you'll take their offer in the wrong way.

✔ **Look into seller financing.** Some sellers don't need all the cash from the sale of their property when the transaction closes escrow. These sellers may be willing to offer you a second mortgage to help you buy their property. In fact, they often advertise that they're willing to assist with financing. Seller financing is usually due and payable in five to ten years. This gives you time to build up equity or save enough to refinance into a new, larger 80 percent conventional mortgage before the seller's loan comes due.

Be cautious about seller financing. Some sellers who offer property with built-in financing are trying to dump a house that has major defects. It's also possible that the house may be priced far above its fair market value. Before accepting seller financing, make sure that the property doesn't have fatal flaws (have a thorough inspection conducted, as we discuss in Chapter 13) and is priced competitively. Also be sure that the seller financing interest rate is as low as or lower than the rate you can obtain through a traditional mortgage lender.

✔ **Check out 80-10-10 financing.** It's called 80-10-10 because a bank, savings and loan association, or other institutional lender makes a traditional 80 percent first mortgage, and you get a 10 percent second mortgage and make a cash down payment equal to 10 percent of the home's purchase price. You can get the second mortgage either from the institutional lender that provided the 80 percent first mortgage or the previously mentioned seller. From a lender's perspective, 80-10-10 financing is as good as 20 percent down.

Don't get hung up on the name. Just because this is known as 80-10-10 financing doesn't mean you must put down 10 percent cash. The exact same principle applies if, for example, you can afford to put only 5 percent cash down — 80-15-5 financing is also available. Because a smaller cash down payment increases the lender's risk of default, however, you'll no doubt have to pay higher loan fees and a higher mortgage interest rate for 80-15-5 financing than you'd pay for 80-10-10. *Mortgages For Dummies* (Wiley), which we co-wrote, delves into the intricacies of special situation loans like this.

✔ **Get partners.** With many things in life, there is strength in numbers. You may be able to get more home for your money and may need to come up with less up-front cash if you find partners for a multiunit real estate purchase. For example, you could find one or two other partners and go in together to purchase a duplex or triplex.

Getting involved in the real estate version of Siamese twins or triplets isn't without risk, however. Before you go into a partnership to buy a building, be sure to consider all the "what ifs." (What if one of you wants out after a year? What if one of you fails to pay the pro-rata share of expenses? What if one of you wants to remodel and the other doesn't? And so forth.) Have a lawyer prepare a partnership agreement that explicitly delineates how issues like these will be dealt with. Otherwise, you could face some major disagreements down the road, even if you go in together with friends or people you think you know well. We cover the pros and cons of partnerships in Chapter 8.

Where to invest the down payment

As with all informed investing decisions, which investment(s) you consider for money earmarked for your down payment should be determined by how soon you need the money back. The longer the time frame during which you can invest, the more growth-oriented and riskier (that is, more *volatile*) an investment you may consider. Conversely, when you have a short time frame — five years or less — during which you can invest, choosing volatile investments is dangerous.

Buying a home with "no money down"

More than a few books written by (and high-priced seminars led by) real estate "gurus" claim that not only can you buy property with no money down, but you can also make piles of money doing so. A generation ago, this way of thinking was popularized by Robert Allen in his book *Nothing Down*.

Allen says that the key to buying property with no money down is to find a seller who is a don't-wanter — that is, someone who "will do anything to get rid of his property." Why would someone be that desperate? Well, perhaps the person is in financial trouble because of a job loss, an overextension of credit, or a major illness.

Perhaps, back when more people used to live in smaller, tight-knit communities where everyone supported one another, this type of vulture capitalism may not have flourished. But in these times, Allen says, a don't-wanter can offer you the most favorable mortgage terms, such as a low down payment and interest rate.

How do you find such downtrodden souls who are just waiting for you to take advantage of them? According to Allen's estimates, 10 percent of the sellers in the real estate market are don't-wanters. Simply call people who have property listed for sale in the newspaper, or place ads yourself saying that you'll buy in a hurry.

In our experience, finding homes that can be bought with no money down isn't easy to do. If you can find such a desperate seller, be aware that the property may have major flaws. If the property were a good one, logic dictates that the seller wouldn't have to sell under such lousy terms. Should you have the patience to hunt around and sift through perhaps hundreds of properties to find a good one available with seller financing at no money down, be our guest. Just don't expect the task to be easy or all that lucrative. Better to look for good properties and low down payment lender financing and to start saving a healthy down payment so that you can qualify for a better loan.

When the stock market is rising, as it did so often in the 1990s, you may be tempted to keep your down payment money in stocks. After all, when you're getting returns of 20 percent or more annually, you'll reach your down payment savings goal far more quickly. Greedier investors lusting after high-flying technology and Internet stocks that seem to double in value every 90 days hope to quickly parlay their small savings for a shack into a money mountain for a mansion.

Investing down-payment money in stocks is a dangerous strategy. Your expected home purchase may be delayed for years due to a sinking investment portfolio. Stocks are a generally inappropriate investment for down-payment money you expect to tap within the next five years. More aggressive individual stocks should have even a longer time horizon — ideally, seven to ten or more years. Consider what happened to the home-buying dreams of folks who foolishly parked their home-down-payment money in the stock market before and during the severe stock market decline of the early 2000s.

Investments for five years or less

Most prospective home buyers aren't in a position to take many risks with their down-payment money. The sooner you expect to buy, the less risk you should take. Unless you expect to buy in more than five years, you shouldn't even consider investing in more growth-oriented investments, such as stocks.

Although it may appear boring, the first (and likely best) place for accumulating your down-payment money is in a money-market mutual fund. As with bank savings accounts, money-market mutual funds don't put your principal at risk — the value of your original investment (principal) doesn't fluctuate. Rather, you simply earn interest on the money that you've invested. Money-market funds invest in supersafe investments, such as in Treasury bills, bank certificates of deposit, and *commercial paper* (short-term IOUs issued by the most creditworthy corporations).

Money-market funds are one of the three major types of mutual funds — the other two being those that focus on bonds (bond funds) and those that focus on stocks (stock or equity funds). Many people think of mutual funds as being risky investments, partly because they equate funds with stock market investing. However, the reality is that under Securities and Exchange Commission regulations, money-market funds can invest only in safe securities, and money funds' investments must have an average maturity of less than 90 days. The short-term nature of these funds eliminates the risk of money-market funds' being sensitive to changes in interest rates in the way that bonds and bond funds are.

Although some bank savings accounts pay reasonable interest rates, nearly all pay less in interest than the best money-market funds. Why? Because banks aren't as efficient and low-cost as money markets. Who do you think is paying for the rent in all those bank branches, anyway?

If you really want to save through a bank, shop, shop, shop around. Smaller savings-and-loans and credit unions tend to offer more competitive yields than do the larger banks that spend gobs on advertising and have branches on nearly every corner. Remember, more overhead means lower yields for your money.

In addition to higher yields, the best money-market funds offer check writing (so that you can easily access your money) and come in tax-free versions. If you're in a higher income tax bracket, a tax-free money-market fund may allow you to earn a higher effective yield than a money fund that pays taxable interest. (***Note:*** You pay tax only on money invested outside tax-sheltered retirement accounts.) When you're in a high tax bracket (refer to Table 3-2 earlier in this chapter), you should come out ahead by investing in tax-free money market funds. If you reside in a state with high income taxes, consider a state money-market fund, which pays interest that's free of both federal and state tax.

The better money-market funds also offer telephone exchange and redemption and automated, electronic exchange services with your bank account. Automatic investment comes in handy for accumulating your down payment for a home purchase. Once per month, for example, you can have money zapped from your bank account into your money-market fund.

Because a particular type of money-market fund (general, Treasury, or tax-free municipal) is basically investing in the same securities as its competitors, opt for a money-market fund that keeps lean-and-mean expenses. A money fund's operating expenses, which are deducted before payment of dividends, are the major factor in determining a money fund's yield. As with the high overhead of bank branches, the higher a money fund's operating expenses, the lower its yield. Excellent money funds from the best mutual fund companies are yours for the asking for annual operating expenses of 0.5 percent or less. We recommend good ones in this section.

When you're not in a high federal-tax bracket, and you're not in a high state-tax bracket (that is, you pay less than 5 percent in state taxes), consider the following taxable money-market funds for your home down-payment money:

- Fidelity Cash Reserves ($2.5K to open)

- Fidelity's Spartan Money Market (higher yields if you have $20K to invest)

- T. Rowe Price Summit Cash Reserves ($25K to open)

- Vanguard's Prime Money Market ($3K to open)

If you sleep better at night after lending your money to an organization with more than $7 trillion in debt outstanding, you can invest in a money-market fund that invests in U.S. Treasury money market funds, which have the backing of the U.S. federal government — for what that's worth! From a tax standpoint, because U.S. Treasuries are state-tax-free but federally taxable, U.S. Treasury money-market funds are appropriate when you're not in a high federal-tax bracket but you are in a high state-tax bracket (5 percent or higher). Should you choose to invest in a money-market fund that invests in the U.S. Treasury, consider these:

- Fidelity's Spartan U.S. Treasury Money Market ($20K to open)

- USAA's Treasury Money Market ($3K to open)

- Vanguard Treasury Money Market ($3K to open)

- Vanguard's Admiral Treasury Money Market (higher yields if you have $50K to invest)

Getting in touch with mutual fund companies

Most mutual fund companies don't have many (or any) local branch offices. Generally, this fact helps mutual fund companies keep their expenses low so they can pay you greater yields on their money-market funds.

So how do you deal with an investment company without a location near you? Simple: You open and maintain your mutual fund account via the fund's toll-free phone line, the mail, and the Web. Some fund providers also have branch offices.

Here's how to reach, by phone or through online access, the major fund companies recommended in this section:

- Fidelity: 800-544-8888; www.fidelity.com

- T. Rowe Price: 800-638-5660; www.troweprice.com

- USAA: 800-382-8722; www.usaa.com

- Vanguard: 800-662-7447; www.vanguard.com

Municipal (also known as *muni*) money-market funds invest in short-term debt issued by state and local governments. A municipal money-market fund, which pays you federally tax-free dividends, invests in munis issued by state and local governments throughout the country. A state-specific municipal fund invests in state and local government-issued munis for one state, such as New York. So if you live in New York and buy a New York municipal fund, the dividends on that fund are generally free of both federal and New York state taxes.

So how do you decide whether to buy a nationwide or state-specific municipal money-market fund? Federal-tax-free-only money-market funds are appropriate when you're in a high federal-tax bracket but not a high state-tax bracket (less than 5 percent). Your state may not have good (or any) state-tax-free money-market funds available. If you live in any of those states, you're likely best off with one of the following national money market funds:

- T. Rowe Price Summit Municipal Money Market ($25K to open)

- USAA Tax-Exempt Money Market ($3K to open)

- Vanguard Tax-Exempt Money Market ($3K to open)

State-tax-free money market funds are appropriate when you're in a high federal-tax bracket and a high state-tax bracket (5 percent or higher). Contact fund companies listed in the sidebar "Getting in touch with mutual fund companies" to see if they offer a money fund for your state.

Short-term bonds and bond funds

You may be thinking, "Three to five years is an awfully long time to keep my money dozing away in a money-market fund."

Well, yes and no. During some time periods, investors who bought bonds maturing in five years got very little in the way of extra yield versus what they could get in a good money-market fund. During other periods, three-year to five-year bonds yielded a good deal more interest than money-market funds yielded.

Whenever you invest in bonds that won't mature soon, you take on risk. First is the risk that the bond issuer may fall into financial trouble between the time that you buy the bond and the time that it is due to mature. Second is the risk that interest rates in general could greatly increase. If the latter happens, typically caused by unexpected inflation, you may end up holding a bond that pays you less interest than the rate of inflation.

Most of the time, bonds that mature in a few years should produce a slightly higher rate of return for you than a money-market or savings account. However, if you invest in such bonds, recognize that you may end up earning the same (or perhaps even less) than you would have earned had you stuck with a money-market fund. Rising interest rates can deflate the value of an investment in bonds.

Invest in bonds only if you expect to hold them for at least three to five years. If you want to invest in individual bonds, and you're not in a high tax bracket, consider Treasury bonds, which don't require monitoring of credit risk — that is, unless the U.S. government slips into default! Also look at the yield on bank certificates of deposit. You may also consider some high-quality, short-term bond mutual funds that invest in — you guessed it — short-term bonds. A solid one is Vanguard's Short-Term Investment Grade Portfolio.

If you're in a high tax bracket, a tax-free money-market fund is hard to beat. Some federal-tax-free bond funds to peruse include Vanguard's Short-Term Tax-Exempt and Vanguard's Limited-Term Tax-Exempt funds. Good, double-tax-free, short-term bond funds just don't exist.

Investments for more than five years

Should you expect to hold onto your home down-payment money for more than five years, you can comfortably consider riskier investments, such as longer-term bonds, as well as more conservative stocks. Eric covers these investments and many others in the latest editions of his books *Investing For Dummies* and *Mutual Funds For Dummies* (both published by Wiley).

Chapter 4

Why Home Prices Rise and Fall

In This Chapter

▶ Determining present and future home values

▶ Figuring where home prices may be headed in your community

▶ Buying strategies to get more for your money in any type of market

*I*f you're contemplating the purchase of a home, you may be concerned about the future direction of home prices. After all, who wants to buy a home just before prices plunge? Conversely, who in their right mind wouldn't love to jump into the real estate market before prices head skyward? To understand what drives home prices, you must examine what drives the supply of, and demand for, homes.

As we discuss what causes home prices to rise and fall in this chapter, please keep the following in mind: When it comes to buying and owning a home, don't get too hung up on the current state of your local market. If you take the perspective that after you buy a home, you're likely to own a home for many decades, worrying about timing your purchase is generally not worth the trouble. *Timing* — that is, buying when prices are at rock bottom and getting out when you think that home values are cresting — is extraordinarily difficult to do. We know people who started waiting for lower home prices a generation ago — they're still waiting!

Predicting what's going to happen with real estate prices in a particular neighborhood, town, region, or state over the next one, two, three, or more years isn't easy. Ultimately, the demand for and prices of homes in an area are driven largely by the economic health and vitality of that area. With an increase in jobs, particularly ones that pay well, comes a greater demand for housing.

If you first buy a home when you're in your 20s, 30s, or even your 40s, you'll likely end up being a homeowner for several decades or more. Over such a lengthy time, the real estate markets in which you have your money invested will surely experience more than a few ups and downs. History shows that real estate prices experience more and bigger ups than downs over the long-term, so don't fret about the cloudiness of your real estate crystal ball.

That said, you may be ambivalent about buying a home at particular times in your life. Perhaps you're not sure that you will stay put for more than three to five years. The shorter the time period you expect to hold onto your home, the more important it is to be careful about when you buy. Thus, part of your home-buying decision may hinge on whether current home prices in your area offer you a good value. Even if you expect to stay put for a while, understanding what causes home prices to rise and fall, and knowing ways to maximize your chances of getting a good buy, can also be worth your while. This chapter helps you grasp these points.

What Drives Real Estate Markets and Prices?

If you're going to buy a home, you're making a significant investment — perhaps the single biggest investment you've ever made. You can do a mountain of research to decide what, where, and when to buy.

In the rest of this chapter, we explain what to look for, from an investment standpoint, both in a community and in the property that you buy. Some of the information that we provide requires you to think like an investor. Of course, for many people, buying a home in which you will live is different from buying a piece of investment real estate to rent out.

Note: We discuss different types of properties (single-family homes, condominiums, and the like) and their investment desirability in Chapter 8.

Jobs, glorious jobs

A home provides shelter from the elements and a place to store and warehouse your consumer possessions. Because houses cost money to buy and maintain — and you're likely not a descendant of the Rockefellers, the Gettys, or Bill Gates — you need an ongoing source of money in order to afford your home. Where does this money come from? A job.

Okay, you may call it your *career* or (even better) one of your *passions*. But if you're like most folks, you work to pay your bills. And a home and its accompanying expenses are one of the biggest sources of expenses that people have (hence, one of the reasons we end up working so many decades as adults)!

So it stands to reason that the demand for housing and the ability to pay for housing are deeply affected by the abundance and quality of jobs in a community or area. From an investment perspective, an ideal area where homes appreciate in value at a relatively high rate has the following characteristics:

✔ **Job growth:** So what if an area has hundreds of thousands or millions of jobs if the number of jobs is shrinking? The New York City metropolitan area had millions of jobs yet experienced declining real estate prices in the early 1990s due to a deteriorating job base. Job *creation* is the lifeblood of a healthy local real estate market. Check out the unemployment situation, and examine how the jobless rate has changed in recent years. Good signs are a declining unemployment rate and increasing job growth.

✔ **Job diversity:** No, we're not talking about political correctness here. If a community is reliant on a paper manufacturer and an underwear maker for half of all its jobs, you ought to be wary of buying a home there. Should both of these companies go in the tank, the real estate market will follow. This type of scenario has played out in smaller communities that were badly hurt when large defense manufacturers and military bases lost many employees due to defense cutbacks.

✔ **Job quality:** All jobs aren't created equal. Which area do you think has faster-appreciating real estate prices: an area with more high-paying jobs in growth industries (such as technology) or an area that's producing mostly low-pay, low-skill jobs (such as those jobs found at fast-food joints)? As with food, entertainment, and sex, quality is just as important as (if not more important than) quantity. When most of the jobs in a community come from slow-growing or shrinking employment sectors (such as farms, small retailers, shoe and apparel manufacturers, and government), real estate prices are unlikely to rise quickly in the years ahead. On the other hand, areas with a preponderance of high-growth industries (such as technology) should have a greater chance of experiencing faster price appreciation.

So how can you get your hands on data that gives you this type of perspective? The U.S. Bureau of Labor Statistics compiles employment and unemployment data for metropolitan areas and counties. You can find this department's treasure trove of data via your computer at www.bls.gov, or try visiting a good local library or chamber of commerce. A real estate agent also may be able to help you track it down.

Available housing

Although jobs create the demand for housing, the amount of housing available — both existing and new — is the supply side of the supply-and-demand equation. Even though jobs are being created, housing values may be stagnant if an overabundance of available housing exists. Conversely, a relatively low employment growth rate in an area with a housing shortage could trigger significant real estate price increases.

Start by examining how well the existing supply of housing is being utilized. Vacancy rates, which measure how much or little demand there is for existing rental units, are a useful indicator to investigate. The *vacancy rate* is calculated simply by dividing the number of empty (unrented) rental units by the total number of rental units available. So, for example, if 50 rental units are vacant in Happy Valley, Tennessee, and 1,000 total units are available, the vacancy rate is 5 percent (50 divided by 1,000).

A low vacancy rate (under 5 percent) is generally a good indicator of future real estate price appreciation. When the vacancy rate is low and declining, more competition for few available rental units exists (or will soon exist). This competition tends to drive up rental rates, making renting more expensive and less attractive.

On the other hand, high vacancy rates indicate an excess supply of rentals, which tends to depress rents as landlords scramble to find tenants. All things being equal, high (more than 7 to 10 percent) and increasing vacancy rates are generally a sign — bad for real estate sellers and prices but good for prospective home buyers.

In addition to checking out vacancy rates, which tell you how well the existing housing supply is being used, smart real estate investors look at what's happening with building permits. In order to build new housing, a permit is required. The trend in the number of building permits can tell you how fast or how slowly the supply of real estate properties may be changing in the future.

A significant increase in the number of permits being issued can be a red flag because it may signal a future glut of housing. Such increases often happen after a sustained rise in housing prices in an area. As prices reach a premium level, builders race to bring new housing to market to capitalize on the high prices.

Conversely, depressed prices or a high cost of building can lead to little new housing being developed. Eventually, this trend should bode well for local real estate prices.

The supply of housing is also determined in part by the amount of land available to develop. Unless you think that houseboats or landfill sites are the waves of the future, you'll agree that land is needed to build housing. A limited supply of land generally bodes well for long-term real estate price appreciation in an area. Thus, real estate has appreciated very well over the decades (and is expensive today) in areas such as Manhattan, San Francisco, Hawaii, Hong Kong, and Tokyo, which are surrounded by water. Conversely, home prices tend to rise slowly in areas with vast tracts of developable land.

Inventory of homes for sale and actual sales

Just as scads of developable land and a barrage of new buildings place a lid on potential real estate price increases in the future, so do escalating numbers of properties listed for sale. Local associations of real estate agents, through their Multiple Listing Service (MLS), typically track the total number of *listings* (employment agreements between a property owner and a real estate agent). Properties that are "for sale by owner" (that is, without an agent) aren't included in this total, but such unlisted sales tend to follow the same trends as property listed with agents. (We aren't aware of anyone tracking the total number of properties for sale by owner.)

In a normal real estate market, the number of homes listed for sale stays at a relatively constant level as new homes come on the market and other homes sell. But as property prices start to reach high levels, and some real estate owners/investors seek to cash in and invest elsewhere, the *listing inventory* (number of listings) can increase significantly. When home prices reach a high level relative to the cost of renting (see the next section), increasing numbers of potential buyers choose to rent. Buyer interest also may dry up because of an economic slowdown.

An increase in the number of newly listed houses for sale and a high inventory of unsold homes are two signs that soft home prices likely lie ahead. With many options to choose among, prospective buyers can be picky about what they buy. This competition among many sellers for a few buyers is what begins to exert downward pressure on prices and can create a *buyer's market* — a market that buyers prefer because prices are soft due to supply far exceeding demand.

A decreasing number of new listings and a low inventory of properties listed for sale bode well for home price increases. Few listings, multiple purchase offers, and rapid sales indicate that the demand from buyers exceeds the supply of property listed for sale — a *seller's market.*

When the local economy is strong, and housing isn't expensive compared with rental rates, more renters elect to (and can afford to) purchase, thus increasing sales activity. If you're a seller, you're in heaven. As a buyer, you may be frustrated by dealing with constant price increases, losing homes in multiple-offer situations, or being beaten by other bidders in the race to a new listing.

The rental market

Rental rates provide a useful indicator as to the demand for housing. When the demand for rental housing exceeds the supply of rental housing, and the local economy continues to grow, rents generally increase. This situation is a plus for future home price increases. As the cost of renting increases, purchasing a home looks all the more attractive to renters who are on the fence and are considering buying.

The trend in rents and the absolute level of rents don't tell you all that you need to know. Suppose that a two-bedroom, one-bath, 1,100-square-foot home in a decent neighborhood in your town is renting for $1,200 per month. So what? What you also need to know is how this rental cost compares with the cost of purchasing and owning the same home.

Compare the cost of renting a given home with the cost of owning it. Such a comparison is effectively what current renters do when they weigh the costs of buying a home and leaving their landlord behind. Comparing the cost of owning a home with the cost of renting that same property serves as a reality check on home prices.

In order to make a fair comparison between renting and owning, you must compare the monthly cost of renting with the monthly cost of owning. If you compare the cost of renting a home for $1,200 per month with the sticker price of buying that same home for $250,000, you're comparing apples with oranges. That $250,000 is the total purchase price of the home, not your monthly cost of owning it.

Interest rates and home prices

Because the biggest expense of owning a home generally is the monthly mortgage payment, the level of interest rates on mortgages should have a big impact on home prices. As interest rates drop, so can payments on mortgages of a given size.

Consider a $100,000, 30-year, fixed-rate mortgage. If the interest rate is 6 percent, the monthly mortgage payment is $600. At an interest rate of 10 percent, the mortgage payment balloons to $878.

It certainly is true that low interest rates enable more renters to become homeowners. So you may think that declining interest rates would cause home prices to rise and, conversely, that increasing interest rates would lead to falling home prices. That this isn't the way that the world operates is proved by the fact that many parts of the United States, in the late 1980s and early 1990s, experienced falling home prices at the same time that interest rates were declining. Even though interest rates trended higher in the late 1990s, home prices were rising briskly in many communities nationwide.

Clearly, other factors do influence home prices, especially the health of the local and national economies and consumer confidence. And although low interest rates make housing more affordable, low rates also make building more housing at lower costs possible. A larger supply of housing tends to dampen housing price increases.

What's the lesson of this story? Don't try to time your housing purchase based upon what is happening, or what you expect to happen, with interest rates. The future change in your home's value could very well surprise you.

And when you calculate homeownership costs, you must also factor in tax benefits. Your biggest homeownership expenses — mortgage interest and property taxes — are generally tax deductible (see Chapter 3).

The following real-life example illustrates how to compare monthly rental and ownership costs. In the mid-1980s, three-bedroom homes on modest lots in popular communities on the San Francisco peninsula were selling for about $250,000. You could rent these same homes for about $1,200 per month. The cost of owning such a home (assuming a 20 percent down payment) amounted to approximately $1,300 per month, factoring in the mortgage interest and property tax write-offs.

Thus, at that time, you could have bought a home in this beautiful, economically robust, and diverse area and have had monthly ownership costs about equal to the cost of renting the very same home. And don't forget that over time, the costs of renting would be fully exposed to inflation, whereas, if you had bought your home with a fixed-rate mortgage, the costs of owning would largely be constant (see Chapter 3). Buying a home at this time was a good deal, given these facts.

Now fast-forward to 1990. In the short span of just a few years, home prices in that area skyrocketed. Those $250,000 homes were selling for $400,000. Rents had risen slowly. Thus, the cost of owning such a home amounted to more than $2,400 per month, although the cost of renting remained at $1,300. Thus, in 1990, home buyers in this area were paying a substantial premium to own (versus renting) a comparable home.

Signs abounded that the home-buying market was overheated, but the biggest factor to focus on was that the monthly ownership costs greatly exceeded the monthly rental costs for property. *Guess what happened next?* Well, fewer renters could afford to buy because buying had gotten so expensive. And fewer renters wanted to buy because, by comparison, renting was such a good deal. So the demand for home purchases dropped, which had a depressing effect on home prices. The demand for rentals increased, which ultimately had a buoyant effect on rents. The laws of supply and demand correct a system out of balance. When the economy started to slow, as it eventually does, prospective buyers got very cold feet about spending so much on a home and carrying such a large mortgage.

Now fast-forward five more years. Lo and behold, the market did correct the imbalance. Those $400,000 homes dropped in value to about $350,000 by 1995. Meanwhile, rents increased as the rental market tightened up. The cost of buying this home in 1995 was about $1,790 per month (versus $1,600 per month in rent). In other words, you could own for just a slightly higher cost than the cost of renting — just like things were back in the mid-1980s! (Over this same time period, interest rates dropped, also helping reduce ownership costs.)

Are real estate prices a bubble about to burst?

Even during the major stock market decline in the early 2000s, housing prices in most communities continued their upward march, which began in the mid-1990s. Commentators and pundits increasingly wondered and predicted that prices were being set up for a major fall.

In one such article titled "That Sinking Feeling," the writer argues that real estate prices are the next investment bubble. Unfortunately, the author completely overlooked the most useful indicator of all for potential home buyers when trying to figure out whether housing is a good value or not. That can be done by comparing the monthly after-tax cost of buying a given home with the cost of renting that same home. If the cost of owning is substantially more, that's a potential red flag of inflated housing prices. As we discuss elsewhere in this chapter, anyone who is concerned about housing prices in a given area being too high should do this simple analysis before committing to buy.

We found the writer's analysis to be highly simplistic. He basically argued that home values are too high because rates of appreciation have outstripped income growth. That is almost always true over the long term, especially during periods of declining interest rates.

Prospective home buyers have the option of renting, which is why the rent-versus-buy analysis is an amazingly simple yet powerful tool for dissecting whether home prices are too high, too low, or just about right.

Homes have never suddenly lost favor with homeowners the way stocks have with stockholders. Remember when Enron's stock plunged from $49 a share in September 2001 to 25 cents a share by the end of November 2001, after word got out about corporate malfeasance? How about the double whammy of Black Friday and Meltdown Monday in October 1987, when the Dow Jones average lost about 25 percent of its value in two days?

Even in the worst of times, home prices have never burst. Sure, prices sagged now and then, but they never burst. Don't confuse the way the stock market operates with how the residential real estate market behaves.

Homeowners don't have the herd mentality of stockholders. Suppose that mortgage rates suddenly zoomed to double digits, as they did in the early 1980s. Would all homeowners simultaneously put their houses on the market? Of course not. Higher rates on new loans wouldn't affect tens of millions of existing mortgages. Life would go on.

Sure, home prices would head south for a while. And sooner or later, as they always do, interest rates would return to normal. Ditto property values.

If you don't sell when prices are down, you don't lose money. If you must sell in a depressed market due to divorce, retirement, or another major life change, you'll find the real estate gods are scrupulously fair. Whatever you lose when you sell, you'll usually recapture when you purchase your next home. Home prices are like corks floating on a pond: They all tend to go up and down together.

Homeownership isn't just an investment. It offers a rainbow of benefits: physical shelter, an inflation hedge, and tax write-offs for mortgage interest and property taxes. Under the current tax laws, house sellers can exclude a hefty portion of their capital gains from tax (more about this delightful tax break in Chapter 17). Homes are an excellent *long-term* investment.

Since 1995, housing prices in the San Francisco Bay Area have again skyrocketed — more than doubling in value in most communities. Rents likewise have soared.

The overall economic health of the region in which you live also clearly has a direct impact on housing prices. If companies in your area have to make cutbacks, and employees' compensation stagnates or even falls, consumers would have less disposable income to spend on housing, and housing prices would suffer.

A correction (reduction) in housing prices of 20 percent is entirely possible under these circumstances. Those who think that a slowdown in price increases or a period of stable prices is the worst that could happen would be in for a rude awakening.

 Comparing the cost of owning a home with the cost of renting that same home is a simple yet powerful indicator of whether real estate in an area is overpriced, underpriced, or priced just right. Buying is generally safer (and a good value) when it costs about the same as renting. However, in some particularly desirable and in-demand communities, homeownership almost always costs more than renting. What's a reasonable premium? There's no simple answer, but if the monthly cost of owning is pushing past 20 to 30 percent more than the monthly cost of renting, be cautious.

After you purchase a home, you'll probably own it for decades to come. So don't worry about timing your first home purchase. Trying to time your purchase has more importance if you may be moving in fewer than five years. In that case, be careful to avoid buying in an overheated market. The level of real estate prices compared with rents, the state of the job market, and the number of home listings for sale are useful indicators of the health of the housing market.

How to Get a Good Buy in Any Market

Well, what if you have to (or want to) buy in a seller's market? Or you're simply frightened that you're going to overpay in any market because you're a home-buying novice? No one likes to be taken. And most folks like to feel or believe that they're getting a bargain.

Many times, when you purchase products and services through businesses (especially through retailers), the sellers like to tell you how much of a discount or markdown they're offering you:

> 60 PERCENT OFF!
>
> GOING-OUT-OF-BUSINESS SALE — EVERYTHING MUST GO!
>
> SAVE UP TO $3 PER POUND!
>
> SPRING CLEARANCE SALE!

Real estate get-rich-quick schemes

Scores of books have been written and high-priced seminars conducted claiming to have the real estate investing approach that can "beat the system." Often, these promoters claim that you can become a multimillionaire through buying *distressed* property — property with financial, legal, or physical problems. One suggested strategy is to buy property on which a seller has defaulted or is about to default. Or how about buying a property in someone's estate through probate court? Maybe you'd like to try your hand at investing in a property that has been condemned or has toxic-waste contamination!

Getting a "good buy" and purchasing a problem property at a discount larger than the cost of fixing the property are possible. But these opportunities are hard to find, and sellers of such properties are often unwilling to sell at a large enough discount to leave you sufficient profit. If you don't know how to thoroughly and correctly evaluate the problems of a property, you could end up overpaying. You may even get stuck with a property that has incurable defects such as poor location, excessive noise, or no backyard. (We tell you how to separate dumps from diamonds-in-the-rough fixer-upper properties in Chapter 8.)

In some cases, the strategies that these real estate gurus advocate involve taking advantage of people's lack of knowledge. For example, some people don't know that they can protect the equity in their home through filing personal bankruptcy. When you can find sellers in such dire financial straits, you may be able to get bargain buys on their homes.

Other methods of getting a good buy take a great deal of time and digging. Some involve cold-calling property owners to see whether they're interested in selling. If you phone thousands of people, you may eventually find a good candidate this way. However, when you factor in the value of your time, these deals rarely appear attractive.

Some home sellers and (more often) their agents like to use the same type of advertising. The following examples are from actual home-for-sale ads:

HUGE PRICE REDUCTION!

PRICE SLASHED $20,000!

REDUCED! BACK ON THE MARKET — OWNER MUST SELL!

Whenever you see these types of ads, rather than thinking, "Gee, that sounds like a good deal," you should be thinking, "That home must have been over-priced before, and/or it probably has a significant defect."

Now, we're not trying to tell you that you can't get a *deal* (in other words, buy a home at less than its *fair market value*). But doing so isn't easy, and finding just the right situation takes a great deal of work. For most people, not over-paying — in other words, paying fair market value (which isn't necessarily the asking price) — is a good objective. See Chapter 10 to find out more about determining home values.

Read our suggestions for finding a good buy even if you're willing to pay fair market value. These ideas can help prevent you from overpaying.

Seek hidden opportunities to add value

The easiest problems to correct are cosmetic. Some sellers and their agents are lazy and don't even bother to clean a property. Painting, tearing up dingy carpeting, refinishing hardwood floors, replacing outdated cabinets and appliances, and installing new landscaping need not be difficult projects. And such changes can make some properties look much better.

A somewhat more complicated way to add value is to identify properties not being fully used or developed according to the zoning of the property. Sometimes, you can make more productive use of a property. For example, you may be able to convert a duplex to two separate condominiums. Some single-family residences may incorporate a rental unit if local zoning allows. Perhaps you can add another level to create a panoramic view. A good real estate agent, a contractor, and the local planning office in the town or city in which you're looking at property should be able to help you identify properties for which the use can be changed.

Identifying, evaluating, buying, and fixing up a property take valuable time and energy. If you have a talent for finding hidden opportunities and are willing to invest the time required to coordinate the fix-up work, by all means try your hand and money at it! Just be sure to be realistic when you assess whether the major defects can be corrected, how much money you may need to spend to improve the property, and how much value your improvements can really add. Also, be sure to hire a competent property inspector (see Chapter 13).

Buy when others are scared to buy

When the economy hits the skids, unemployment rises, and the mood is somber and gloomy, the number of home purchases usually drops. Prices tend to fall as well. This situation can signal a great time to step up and buy. Buy when homes are "on sale" and when you don't have to compete with many other buyers. Buy when you can have your pick of a larger inventory of homes for sale.

Few people feel comfortable buying an investment that has gone down in value, especially when things look bleak. (For some perverse psychological reason, though, many of us love shopping for bargains in retail stores.) Here are several signs that a soft real estate market is beginning to firm up:

✔ The monthly cost of owning a home approximates the monthly cost of renting a similar property. One of the beauties of a major real estate price decline is that it can bring homeownership costs back in line with rent costs.

✔ The inventory of homes listed for sale starts to fall from its peak as home sales pick up.

✔ The rental market tightens (as evidenced by increasing rents and a low vacancy rate). Another good sign is that little new housing is being built.

✔ The job market improves. Remember that jobs fuel the demand for housing. Home prices tend to rebound when employment increases. Watch for a decrease in the unemployment rate in your region.

Despite lower home prices, an improving economy, and tightening rental and homes-for-sale inventories, prospective home buyers generally show far less interest in buying a home when things still look bleak. It takes courage to buy during those times when newspaper headlines and the television news reports trumpet the latest round of layoffs. Keep a level head, and take advantage of buying opportunities when they occur. Years down the road, you may be glad that you did.

Find a motivated seller

When you take your time and peruse enough properties, you eventually cross paths with a property owner who really needs or wants to sell. The owner may need to relocate to another part of the country for a job, or perhaps the owner is trading up to a larger home and needs the cash from the sale of the current one in order to buy the new home. Sometimes, a property owner simply can't afford to own and maintain a home any longer due to personal financial troubles.

Whatever the reason, buying a home at or below its fair market value is far easier if the seller is what we call *motivated*. How do you find a motivated seller? Simple: You ask questions! The number of prospective buyers who are too shy to (or don't think to) ask why a seller is selling is amazing. Many sellers will be honest, and more than a few real estate agents (especially those who love to talk) have loose lips and share plenty of details. But you gotta ask!

Buy during slow periods

Most local real estate markets go through predictable busy and slow periods like clockwork. Just as it makes good sense to buy when the overall real estate market in an area is depressed, it can be beneficial to buy during those typical slow periods.

For example, far fewer prospective buyers tend to be looking for homes during the holiday season in the dead of winter. In most markets, the period from Thanksgiving through January or February tends to be quite slow. The colder the region in which you live, the later into the new year this slow period lasts. In the blustery and snowy northernmost regions of the United States, the real estate market doesn't really start to pick up until April. In locales that are sunny and warm year 'round, such as Florida and Southern California, home sales start to pick up as early as February.

Another typically slow period is during the summer months of July and August. Many people take vacations then, and those families who wanted to buy in time for the next school year have likely already bought. The oppressive heat in the southern regions also keeps people indoors and near their air conditioners and iced tea.

The advantage of looking during the slow periods is that you have far less competition from other potential buyers. If you can find a motivated seller, you may really be able to negotiate a great deal without the intrusion of other potential buyers.

We're not saying, however, to look only during slow periods of the year or that you can definitely get a good buy during these times. You must be realistic. In most markets, most of the time, fewer properties are for sale during the slow periods. Smart sellers get their properties sold during the more active periods in the spring and fall. Also, be aware that a good portion of those properties on the market during slow periods may be the unwanted leftovers.

Become a great negotiator

Getting a good buy can be as simple as being a good negotiator. Good negotiation skills may enable you to buy a property at less than fair market value, especially if you find a seller who needs to sell soon.

Your negotiating position is also better if you're in a situation where you don't *have* to buy. The more patient you are and the more willing you are to walk away if you don't get a good deal, the better able you will to negotiate a good buy. Having a backup property in mind (or remembering that many other properties are out there for you to buy) also helps. See Chapter 12 to discover how to be a world-class negotiator.

Buy in a good neighborhood

If you buy a home in a desirable area, you should have a better chance at making a good investment. We explain how to find out whether a neighborhood is good in Chapter 8.

When you buy good real estate and hold it for the long-term, you should earn a decent return on your investment. Over the long haul, having bought a property at a small discount becomes an insignificant issue. You'll make money from owning a home (and perhaps other real estate investments) as the overall real estate market appreciates.

Part II
Financing 101

The 5th Wave — By Rich Tennant

"Can you explain your mortgage program again, this time without using the phrase 'yada, yada, yada'?"

In this part . . .

For some people, just the word *mortgage* can bring on a stomachache. Don't be intimidated. Read these chapters to understand the different types of mortgages, to see how to cut through all the mortgage-related jargon, and to find out how to select the type of mortgage that best meets your needs. In addition to explaining how to get the best deal that you can on a mortgage, we also guide you through the maze of paperwork you face when applying for your mortgage loan as well as how to understand and even improve your credit score.

Chapter 5

Understanding and Improving Your Credit Score

*Y*ou can't play the home-buying game if you can't pay. And most people can't pay without a mortgage.

When you apply for a loan, lenders try to determine your credit risk level. If they decide to loan you money, what are the odds that you'll pay them back on time? To understand your credit risk, most lenders look at your credit score. Your score influences the credit that's available to you and the terms of any mortgage that lenders offer you.

Most lenders also use a number of other facts to make credit decisions. They usually look at the amount of debt you can reasonably handle given your income, your employment history, and your credit history. Based on their perception of this information, as well as their specific underwriting policies, lenders may extend credit to you although your score is low or decline your request for credit although your score is high. But your chances for getting approved at the best possible loan terms improve when you have a good score.

 Understanding your credit score can help you manage your credit health. By knowing how lenders evaluate your credit risk, you can take action to lower your credit risk — and thus raise your score — over time. A better score may mean better loan options for you.

Follow the tips in this chapter to manage your credit score efficiently. Improving your score can help you:

✔ Get better credit offers

✔ Lower your interest rates

✔ Speed credit approvals

The Record You Can't Ignore: Your Credit Report

You've probably heard about credit reports and realize that they can make or break your application for a loan. However, these reports are mysterious to most of us because we don't know what goes into a credit report, nor do we understand what we can do to improve our credit score. Wonder no more. . . .

What your credit history comprises

Credit reports tell a lender how well you manage your finances. Your report details your credit history as it has been reported to the credit reporting agency by lenders who have extended credit to you. Your credit report lists

✔ What types of credit you use

✔ The length of time your accounts have been open

✔ Whether you've paid your bills on time

It tells lenders how much credit you've used and whether you're seeking new sources of credit. It gives lenders a broader view of your credit history than one bank's own customer records (unless all of your previous credit has been drawn from that one bank).

What goes into your credit report

Although each credit reporting agency formats and reports information differently, all credit reports contain basically the same kinds of information:

✔ **Identifying information:** Your name, address, Social Security number, date of birth, and employment information are used to identify you. These factors aren't used to calculate your score, however. Updates to this information come from information you supply to lenders.

✔ **Trade lines:** These are your credit accounts. Lenders report each account you've established with them. They report the type of account (credit card, auto loan, mortgage, and so on), the date you opened the account, your credit limit or loan amount, the account balance, your payment history, and when you closed the account.

✔ **Inquiries:** When you apply for a loan, you authorize your lender to ask for a copy of your credit report. This is how inquiries appear on your credit report. The inquiries section contains a list of everyone who accessed your credit report within the past two years. The report you see lists both *voluntary* inquiries, spurred by your own requests for credit, and *involuntary* inquires, such as when lenders order your report so as to make you a preapproved credit offer in the mail.

✔ **Public record and collection items:** Credit reporting agencies also collect public record information from state and county courts, and information on overdue debt from collection agencies. Public record information includes bankruptcies, foreclosures, suits, wage attachments, liens, and judgments.

Along with the credit report, lenders can buy a credit score based on the information in the report.

Why you should check your credit report

If your credit report contains errors, the report may be incomplete or contain information about someone else. This typically happens because:

✔ You applied for credit under slightly different names (Robert Jones, Bob Jones, and so on).

✔ Someone made a clerical error in reading or entering name or address information from a handwritten application.

✔ Someone gave an inaccurate Social Security number, or the lender misread the number.

✔ Loan or credit card payments were inadvertently applied to the wrong account.

Derogatory information on your credit report may force you into a mortgage with a higher interest rate and fees or cause your mortgage application to be denied. If you find an error, the credit reporting agency must investigate and respond to you within 30 days. If you're in the process of applying for a loan, immediately notify your lender of any incorrect information in your report. Please see the last section in this chapter for info on how to contact the credit reporting agencies to obtain your credit report.

The Most Popular Kid on the Block: FICO Scores

The credit score most lenders use today was developed by Fair Isaac Corporation and is called a *FICO score*. FICO scores range from a low of 300 to a maximum of 850. The higher your FICO score, the lower the potential risk you pose for lenders. They're provided to lenders by the three major credit reporting agencies: Equifax, Experian, and TransUnion.

Although FICO scores are the most commonly used credit risk scores in the United States, lenders may use other scores to evaluate your credit risk. These include

- ✔ **Application risk scores:** Many lenders use scoring systems that include the FICO score but also consider information from your loan application.

- ✔ **Customer risk scores:** A lender may use these scores to make credit decisions about its current customers. Also called *behavior scores,* these scores generally consider the FICO score along with information on how you've paid that lender in the past.

- ✔ **Other credit bureau scores:** These scores may evaluate your credit report differently than FICO scores, and in some cases a higher score may mean more risk, not less risk, as with FICO scores.

If you've been turned down for credit, the federal Equal Credit Opportunity Act (ECOA) gives you the right to find out why within 30 days. You're also entitled to a free copy of your credit agency report within 60 days, which you can request from the credit reporting agencies. If your credit score was a primary part of the lender's decision, the lender will use the score reasons to explain why you didn't qualify for the credit.

How scores work — the short version

Each credit score is calculated by a mathematical equation that evaluates many types of information from your credit report at that agency. By comparing this information with the patterns in hundreds of thousands of past credit reports, the score identifies your level of estimated future credit risk.

In order for a FICO score to be calculated from your credit report, the report must contain at least one account that has been open for six months or longer. In addition, the report must contain at least one account that has been updated in the past six months. This ensures that enough recent information is in your report to calculate a score.

FICO scores can differ among bureaus

Fair Isaac makes the FICO scores as consistent as possible among the three credit reporting agencies. If your information were exactly identical at all three credit reporting agencies, your scores from all three should be within a few points of each other.

But sometimes your FICO score may be quite different at each of the three credit reporting agencies. The way lenders and other businesses report information to the credit reporting agencies sometimes results in different information being in your credit report at the different agencies. The agencies may also report the same information in different ways. Even small differences in the information at the three credit reporting agencies can affect your scores.

Because lenders may review your score and credit report from any one of the three credit reporting agencies, go ahead and check your credit report at all three to make sure each is correct (see the last section in this chapter to find out how to do that).

Your score can change whenever your credit report changes. But your score probably won't change a lot from one month to the next.

Although a bankruptcy or late payment can quickly lower your score, improving your score takes time. That's why it's a good idea to check your score (especially if you have reason to be concerned about your credit history) at least six months before applying for a mortgage. That gives you time to take corrective action if needed. If you're actively working to improve your score, you should check it quarterly or even monthly to review changes.

But no score, no matter how high or low, says whether you will be a "good" or "bad" customer. Although many lenders use FICO scores to help them make lending decisions, each lender also has its own strategy, including the level of risk it finds acceptable for a given type of loan. There is no single minimum score used by all lenders.

How a FICO score assesses your credit history — the long version

The FICO score evaluates several categories of information: your payment history, the amount you owe, the length of your credit history, new credit you've acquired, types of credit you have in use, and the number of credit queries. Some, as you'd expect, are more important than others. It is important to note that:

✔ **A score considers all these categories of information, not just one or two**. No one piece of information or factor alone determines your score.

✔ **The importance of any factor depends on the overall information in your credit report.** A given factor may be more important for some people than for others who have a different credit history. In addition, as the information in your credit report changes, so does the importance of any factor in determining your score. That is why it's impossible to say exactly how important any single factor is in determining your score — even the levels of importance shown in the following subsections are for the general population and differ for different credit profiles.

✔ **Your FICO score looks only at information in your credit report.** Lenders often also look at other things when making a credit decision, including your income, how long you've worked at your present job, and the kind of credit you're requesting.

✔ **Your score considers both positive and negative information in your credit report.** Late payments lower your score, but establishing or reestablishing a good track record of making payments on time raises your score.

✔ **Raising your score is a bit like getting in shape.** It takes time, and there is no quick fix. In fact, quick-fix efforts can backfire. The best advice is to manage credit responsibly over time.

These percentages are based on the importance of the five categories for the general population. For particular groups — for example, people who have not been using credit long — the importance of these categories may be different.

The following sections offer a complete look at the information that goes into a FICO score. For a visual graphic of what contributes to your credit score, please see Figure 5-1.

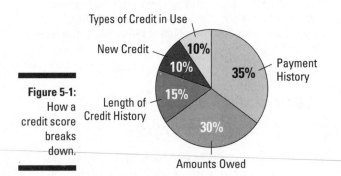

Figure 5-1:
How a credit score breaks down.

Types of Credit in Use — **10%**
New Credit — **10%**
Length of Credit History — **15%**
Amounts Owed — **30%**
Payment History — **35%**

Your payment history

The first thing any lender wants to know is whether you've paid past credit accounts on time. Your track record for repaying creditors affects roughly 35 percent of your score.

Late payments aren't an automatic "score-killer." An overall good credit picture can outweigh one or two instances of, say, late credit card payments. And on the other hand, having no late payments in your credit report doesn't mean you automatically get a great score. Some 60 to 65 percent of credit reports show no late payments at all. Your payment history is just one piece of information used in calculating your score.

In the area of payments, your score takes into account:

- ✔ **Payment information on many types of accounts:** These include credit cards such as Visa, MasterCard, American Express, and Discover; credit cards from stores where you do business; *installment loans* (loans such as a mortgage on which you make regular payments); and finance-company accounts.

- ✔ **Public record and collection items:** These items include reports of events such as bankruptcies, foreclosures, suits, wage attachments, liens, and judgments. They're considered quite serious, although older items and items with small amounts count less than more recent items or those with larger amounts. Bankruptcies stay on your credit report for seven to ten years, depending on the type.

- ✔ **Details on late or missed payments *(delinquencies)* and public record and collection items:** The FICO score considers how late such payments were, how much was owed, how recently they occurred, and how many there are. As a rule, a 60-day late payment isn't as damaging as a 90-day late payment. A 60-day late payment made just a month ago, however, penalizes you more than a 90-day late payment from five years ago.

- ✔ **How many accounts show no late payments:** A good track record on most of your credit accounts increases your credit score.

How to improve your FICO score:

- ✔ **Pay your bills on time.** Delinquent payments and collections can have a major negative impact on your score.

- ✔ **If you've missed payments, get current, and stay current.** The longer you pay your bills on time, the better your score.

- ✔ **Paying off or closing an account doesn't remove it from your credit report.** The score still considers this information because it reflects your past credit pattern.

- ✔ **If you're having trouble making ends meet, get help.** This doesn't improve your score immediately, but if you can begin to manage your credit and pay on time, your score gets better over time. Please see our advice in Chapter 2 for credit-problem-solving strategies.

The amount you owe

About 30 percent of your score is based on your current debt. Having credit accounts and owing money on them doesn't mean you're a high-risk borrower who'll receive a low score. However, owing a great deal of money on many accounts can indicate that a person is overextended and is more likely to make some payments late or not at all. Part of the science of scoring is determining how much is too much for a given credit profile.

In the area of debts, your score takes into account:

- ✔ **The amount owed on all accounts.** Note that even if you pay off your credit cards in full every month, your credit report may show a balance on those cards. The total balance on your last statement is generally the amount that will show in your credit report.

- ✔ **The amount owed on all accounts and on different types of accounts.** In addition to the overall amount you owe, the score considers the amount you owe on specific types of accounts, such as credit cards and installment loans.

- ✔ **Whether you show a balance on certain types of accounts.** In some cases, having a small balance without missing a payment shows that you've managed credit responsibly. On the other hand, closing unused credit accounts that show zero balances and that are in good standing doesn't raise your score.

- ✔ **How many accounts have balances.** A large number can indicate higher risk of overextension.

- ✔ **How much of the total credit line is being used on credit cards and other *revolving credit* (carrying a debt balance month to month) accounts.** Someone closer to "maxing out" on many credit cards may have trouble making payments in the future.

- ✔ **How much of installment loan accounts is still owed** compared with the original loan amounts. For example, if you borrowed $10,000 to buy a car, and you have paid back $2,000, you owe (with interest) more than 80 percent of the original loan. Paying down installment loans is a good sign that you're able and willing to manage and repay debt.

How to improve your FICO score:

- ✔ **Keep balances low on credit cards and other revolving credit.** High outstanding debt can adversely affect a score.

- ✔ **Pay off debt.** The most effective way to improve your score in this area is by paying down your revolving credit.

- ✔ **Don't close unused credit cards as a short-term strategy to raise your score.** Generally, this doesn't work. In fact, it may *lower* your score. Late payments associated with old accounts won't disappear from your credit report if you close the account. Long-established accounts show you have a longer history of managing credit, which is a good thing. And having available credit that you don't use doesn't lower your score. You may have reasons other than your score to shut down old credit card accounts that you don't use. But don't do it in hopes of getting a better score.

✓ **Don't open new credit cards that you don't need, just to increase your available credit.** This approach could backfire and actually lower your score.

The length of your credit history

How established is your credit history? About 15 percent of your score is based on this area. In general, a longer credit history will increase your score. However, even people who haven't been using credit long may get high scores, depending on how the rest of the credit report looks.

In this area, your score takes into account:

✓ **How long your credit accounts have been established, in general.** The score considers both the age of your oldest account and an average age of all your accounts.

✓ **How long specific credit accounts have been established.**

✓ **How long it has been since you used certain accounts.**

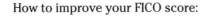

How to improve your FICO score:

✓ **If you have been managing credit for a short time, don't open a lot of new accounts too rapidly.** New accounts lower your average account age, which will have a larger effect on your score if you don't have a lot of other credit information. Also, rapid account buildup can look risky if you're a new credit user.

New credit you've acquired

Taking on a lot of new debt affects your score, too. About 10 percent of your score is based on new credit and credit applications.

People tend to have more credit today and to shop for credit — via the Internet and other channels — more frequently than ever. Credit scores reflect this fact. However, research shows that opening several credit accounts in a short period does represent more risk — especially for people who don't have a long-established credit history.

Applying for several new credit cards or accounts also represents more risk. However, FICO scores do a good job of distinguishing between a search for *many* new credit accounts and rate shopping for *one* new account.

In the area of new credit, your score takes into account:

✔ **How many new accounts you have.** The score looks at how many new accounts you have by type of account (for example, how many newly opened credit cards you have). It also may look at how many of your accounts are new accounts.

✔ **How long it has been since you opened a new account.** Again, the score looks at this by type of account.

✔ **How many recent requests for credit you have made.** This is indicated by inquiries to the credit reporting agencies. Inquiries remain on your credit report for two years, although FICO scores consider only inquiries from the last 12 months. The scores have been carefully designed to count only those inquiries that truly impact credit risk.

✔ **Length of time since lenders made credit report inquiries.** The older the lender inquiries, the better. Inquiries more than a year old are ignored. In this case, being ignored is good.

✔ **Whether you have a good recent credit history following past payment problems.** Reestablishing credit and making payments on time after a period of late payment behavior both help raise a score over time.

How to improve your FICO score:

✔ **Do your rate shopping for a specific loan within a focused period of time.** FICO scores distinguish between a search for a single loan and a search for many new credit lines, in part by the length of time over which inquiries occur. For more on this topic, see the section "The number of credit inquiries," later in the chapter.

✔ **Reestablish your credit history if you've had problems.** Opening new accounts responsibly and paying them off on time will raise your score in the long-term.

✔ **It's okay to request and check your own credit report and FICO score.** This doesn't affect your score, as long as you order your credit report directly from the credit reporting agency or through an organization authorized to provide credit reports to consumers, such as www.myfico.com.

Types of credit you have in use

The credit mix usually isn't a key factor in determining your score — but is given more weight if your credit report doesn't have a lot of other information on which to base a score. About 10 percent of your score is based on this category.

In this area, your score takes into account:

- ✔ **What kinds of credit accounts you have.** Your score considers your mix of credit cards, retail accounts, installment loans, finance company accounts, and mortgage loans. Don't feel obligated to have one of each.

- ✔ **How many of each type of credit account you have.** The score looks at the total number of accounts you have. How many is too many varies depending on the credit type. You don't need to have one of each type. Don't open credit accounts you don't intend to use just to hype up your total.

How to improve your FICO score:

- ✔ **Apply for and open new credit accounts only as needed.** Don't open accounts just to have a better credit mix — it probably won't raise your score.

- ✔ **Have credit cards — but manage them responsibly.** In general, having credit cards and installment loans (and making timely payments) raises your score.

- ✔ **Note that closing an account doesn't make it go away.** A closed account still shows up on your credit report and may be included in the score.

The number of credit inquiries

A search for new credit can mean greater credit risk. This is why the FICO score counts inquiries — those requests a lender makes for your credit report or score when you apply for credit.

FICO scores consider inquiries very carefully because not all inquiries are related to credit risk. You should note three things about credit inquiries:

- ✔ **Inquiries don't affect scores very much.** For most people, one additional credit inquiry will take less than 5 points off their FICO score. However, inquiries can have a greater impact if you have few accounts or a short credit history. Large numbers of inquiries also mean greater risk: People with six inquiries or more on their credit reports are eight times more likely to declare bankruptcy than people with no inquiries on their reports.

- ✔ **Many kinds of inquiries aren't counted at all.** The score doesn't count it when you order your credit report or credit score from a credit reporting agency. Also, the score doesn't count requests a lender has made for your credit report or score in order to make you a preapproved credit offer or to review your account with them, even though you may see these inquiries on your credit report. Requests that are marked as coming from employers aren't counted either.

✔ **The score looks for *rate shopping*.** Looking for a mortgage or an auto loan may cause multiple lenders to request your credit report, even though you're looking for only one loan. To compensate for this, the score counts multiple inquiries in any 14-day period as just one inquiry. In addition, the score ignores *all* inquiries made in the 30 days prior to scoring. So if you find a loan within 30 days, the inquiries won't affect your score while you're rate shopping.

What FICO scores ignore

FICO scores consider a wide range of information on your credit report. However, they don't consider

✔ Your race, color, religion, national origin, sex, and marital status

U.S. law prohibits credit scoring from considering these facts, as well as any receipt of public assistance, or the exercise of any consumer right under the Consumer Credit Protection Act.

✔ Your age

✔ Your salary, occupation, title, employer, date employed, or employment history

Lenders may consider this information, however:

✔ Where you live

✔ Any interest rate being charged on a particular credit card or other account

✔ Any items reported as child/family support obligations or rental agreements

✔ Certain types of inquiries (requests for your credit report or score)

The score does *not* count any requests you make, any requests from employers, and any requests lenders make without your knowledge.

✔ Any information not found in your credit report

✔ Any information not proved to be predictive of future credit performance

Why your score is what it is

When a lender receives your FICO score, up to four *score reasons* are also delivered. These are the top reasons why your score wasn't higher. If the lender rejects your request for credit, and your FICO score was part of the reason, these score reasons can help the lender tell you why.

These score reasons can be more useful to you than the score itself. They help you determine whether your credit report may contain errors and how you may improve your credit score. However, if you already have a high FICO score (for example, in the mid-700s or higher) some of the reasons may not be helpful because they may be marginal factors related to less important categories, such as your length of credit history, new credit, and types of credit in use.

Getting Hold of Your Report and Score

Getting and retaining a copy of your personal credit report is a good idea. Because your personal credit report contains a history of your use (and abuse!) of credit, it's important that you're aware of what it contains and whether the information is accurate.

If you're applying for a mortgage, you can ask at that time for a copy of your credit report — after all, you're paying for it! You should also know that lenders are required to give you a copy of your credit report without charge if they turn you down for a loan.

Congress gave each of us the right to get one free credit report from each of the three big credit bureaus — Experian (888-397-3742; www.experian.com), Equifax (800-685-1111; www.equifax.com), and Trans Union (800-888-4213; www.transunion.com) — every year. Credit bureaus are also generally required to provide you with a free copy of your report if you were denied credit, employment, housing, or insurance over the most recent 60 days due to information in their credit files. You may also purchase a copy of your credit report from any of the three big bureaus (generally for less than $10). At the least, we encourage you to get your free reports annually. Only the report is free, however. You still have to pay to find out what your credit score is.

It's easy to check your FICO score and to find out specific things that you can do to raise it. The Web sites for many banks, financial services sites, and credit reporting agencies offer FICO scores for a fee, as does Fair Isaac's myFICO site at www.myfico.com. Information you receive includes

- ✔ Your current FICO score
- ✔ Your credit report on which your FICO score is based
- ✔ An explanation of your score, the positive and negative factors behind it, and how lenders view your credit risk
- ✔ A FICO score simulator you can use to see how specific actions, such as paying off all your card balances, would affect your score
- ✔ Specific tips on what you can do to improve your FICO score over time

In addition, you can see current information on the average interest rates for home loans for different FICO score ranges.

Chapter 6

Selecting a Mortgage

• •

• •

*M*ost of us need to take out a mortgage to buy a home for the simple reason that doing so is the only way we can afford a home that meets our needs. This chapter helps all nonwealthy folks comprehend mortgages and then choose one. (If you *are* wealthy and have a great deal of money to put into a property, this chapter can also help you decide how much of your loot to put into your home purchase.)

Start with the basics. What is a mortgage? A *mortgage* is nothing more than a loan that you obtain to close the gap between the cash you have for a down payment and the purchase price of the home that you're buying. Homes in your area may cost $70,000, $170,000, or $770,000. No matter — most people don't have that kind of spare cash in their piggy banks.

Mortgages typically require that you make monthly payments to repay your debt. The mortgage payments comprise *interest,* which is what the lender charges for use of the money you borrowed, and *principal,* which is repayment of the original amount borrowed.

Figuring out how to select a mortgage to meet your needs ensures that you'll be a happy homeowner for years to come. You also need to understand how to get a good deal when shopping around for a mortgage because your mortgage is typically the biggest monthly expense of homeownership (and perhaps of your entire household budget). Paying more in total interest charges over the life of your mortgage than you originally paid for your humble abode itself isn't unusual.

Suppose that you borrow $144,000 (and contribute $36,000 from your savings as the down payment) for the purchase of your $180,000 dream palace. If you borrow that $144,000 with a 30-year fixed-rate mortgage at 7 percent, you end up paying a whopping $200,892 in interest charges alone over the life of your loan. That $200,892 is not only a great deal of interest — but also more than the purchase price of the home or the loan amount you originally borrowed!

So that you don't spend any more than you need to on your mortgage, and so that you get the mortgage that best meets your needs, the time has come to get on with the task of understanding the mortgage options out there.

Fixed or Adjustable? That Is the Interest (ing) Question

You may remember the skit from *Saturday Night Live* where Dan Aykroyd and John Belushi worked in a restaurant that served only cheeseburgers, chips, and Pepsi. Customers who tried to order a hamburger, fries, and Coke were out of luck. No hamburgers, just cheeseburgers; no fries, just chips; and no Coke, just Pepsi. At that restaurant, your choices were already made. If only you were so lucky with mortgages.

Like some other financial and investment products, many different mortgage options are available for your choosing. The variations can be significant or trivial, expensive or less costly.

You will note throughout this chapter that two fundamentally different types of mortgages exist. Mortgages differ in terms of how their interest rate is determined. The two types of mortgages are fixed-rate mortgages and adjustable-rate mortgages.

Distinguishing fixed from adjustables

Before adjustable-rate mortgages came into being, only fixed-rate mortgages existed. Usually issued for 15- or 30-year periods, *fixed-rate mortgages* (as the name suggests) have interest rates that are *fixed* (unchanging) during the entire life of the loan.

With a fixed-rate mortgage, the interest rate stays the same, and your monthly mortgage payment amount never changes. No surprises, no uncertainty, and no anxiety for you over interest-rate changes and changes in your monthly payment. If you like the predictability of your favorite television show airing at the same time daily, you'll probably like fixed-rate mortgages.

On the other hand, *adjustable-rate mortgages* (ARMs for short) have an interest rate that varies (or *adjusts*). The interest rate on an ARM typically adjusts every 6 to 12 months, but it may change as frequently as every month.

As we discuss later in this chapter, the interest rate on an ARM is primarily determined by what's happening overall to interest rates. When interest rates are generally on the rise, odds are that your ARM will experience increasing rates, thus increasing the size of your mortgage payment. Conversely, when interest rates fall, ARM interest rates and payments generally fall.

If you like change, you may think that adjustable-rate mortgages sound good. Change is what makes life interesting, you say. Please read on, because even if you believe that variety is the spice of life, you may not like the financial variety and spice of adjustables!

Looking at hybrid loans

If only the world were so simple that only pure fixed-rate and pure adjustable-rate loans were available. But one of the rewards of living in a capitalistic society is that you often have a wide array of choices. Enter *hybrid loans* (or what lenders sometimes call *intermediate ARMs*). Such loans start out like a fixed-rate loan — the initial rate may be fixed for three, five, seven, or even ten years — and then the loan converts to an ARM, usually adjusting every 6 to 12 months thereafter (although some have just one adjustment).

Starting out risky: Interest-only mortgages

As housing prices mushroomed in already-high-cost urban areas and surrounding desired suburbs, lenders responded with yet another twist and began pushing interest-only loans. Unlike a traditional mortgage, *interest-only mortgages* entice borrowers with artificially low payments in their early years. This is possible because the initial payments simply consist of interest (hence the name of the loans) with no repayment of principal.

At some predetermined point down the road (three, five, seven, or ten years), repayment of principal begins, and the monthly loan payment amount takes a significant jump of 20, 30, or 40 percent or more. And therein lies the major problem with these loans; some borrowers may be financially unprepared for the much higher payments. In the worst cases, these loans are actually balloon loans in disguise (see the sidebar later in this chapter) carrying all the additional warts of balloon loans.

As you may have gathered, we're not big fans of interest-only mortgages. We urge you to completely understand all the terms and conditions before agreeing to take one.

Making the fixed/adjustable decision

So how do you choose whether to take a fixed-rate or an adjustable-rate loan? Is it as simple as a personality test?

In this section, we talk you through the pros and cons of your mortgage options, but as we do, please keep one very important fact in mind: In the final analysis, the mortgage that is best for you hinges on your personal and financial situation. *You* are the one who is best positioned to make the call as to whether a fixed or an adjustable loan better matches your situation and desires.

Fixed-rate mortgages

It stands to reason that because the interest rate doesn't vary with a fixed-rate mortgage, the advantage of this type of mortgage is that you always know what your monthly payment is going to be. Thus, budgeting and planning are easier.

You will pay a premium, in the form of a higher interest rate, to get a lender to commit to lending you money over many years at a fixed rate. The longer the mortgage lender agrees to accept a fixed interest rate, the more risk that lender is taking. A lender who agrees to loan you money, for example, over 30 years at 8 percent will be weeping if interest rates skyrocket (as they did in the early 1980s) to the 15-plus percent level. (With the rise of interest rates and inflation at that time, mortgage lenders were paying interest rates to depositors that were almost double the levels of the interest that they were charging for mortgages that had commenced a decade before. Not a profitable way to run a bank!)

In addition to paying a premium interest rate when you take the loan out, another potential drawback to fixed-rate loans is that if interest rates fall significantly after you take out your mortgage, you face the risk of being stranded with your costly mortgage. That could happen if (due to a deterioration in your financial situation or a decline in the value of your property) you don't qualify to *refinance* (get a new loan to replace the old). Even if you do qualify to refinance, doing so takes time and usually costs money for a new appraisal, loan fees, and title insurance.

Here are a couple other possible minor drawbacks to be aware of with some fixed-rate mortgages:

- If you sell your house before paying off your fixed-rate mortgage, your buyers probably won't be able to assume that mortgage. The ability to pass your loan on to the next buyer (in real estate talk, the next buyer assumes your loan) can be useful if you're forced to sell during a rare period of ultra-high interest rates, such as occurred in the early 1980s.

- Fixed-rate mortgages sometimes have prepayment penalties (explained in the sidebar "Avoid loans with prepayment penalties").

Balloon loans

One type of mortgage, known as a *balloon loan,* appears at first blush to be somewhat like a hybrid loan. The interest rate is fixed, for example, for five, seven, or ten years. However, and this is a big *however,* at the end of this time period, the full loan balance becomes due. In other words, you must pay off the *entire* loan.

Borrowers are attracted to balloon loans for the same reason that they're attracted to hybrid or ARM loans — because balloon loans start at a lower interest rate than do fixed-rate mortgages. Buyers are sometimes seduced into such loans during high-interest-rate periods or when they can't qualify for or afford the payments of a traditional mortgage.

We don't like balloon loans because they can blow up in your face. You may become trapped without a mortgage if you're unable to *refinance* (obtain a new mortgage to replace the old loan) when the balloon loan comes due. You may have problems refinancing if, for example, you lose your job, your income drops, the value of your property declines and the appraisal comes in too low to qualify you for a new loan, or interest rates increase and you can't qualify for a new loan at those higher rates.

In the real estate trade, balloon loans are also called *bullet loans.* Why? If the loan comes due during a period of high mortgage rates, industry people say that it's like getting hit by a bullet.

Remember that refinancing a mortgage is *never* a sure thing. Taking a balloon loan may be a financially hazardous short-term solution to your long-term financing needs.

The one circumstance under which we say that it's okay to *consider* a balloon loan is if you absolutely must have a particular property, and the balloon loan is your one and only mortgage option. If that's the case, you should also be as certain as you can be that you'll be able to refinance when the balloon loan comes due. If you have family members who could step in to help with the refinancing, either by cosigning or by loaning you the money themselves, that's a big backup plus. Oh, and if you *must* take out a balloon loan, get as long a term as possible, ideally for no less than seven years (and preferably for ten years).

Adjustable-rate mortgages

Fixed-rate mortgages aren't your only option. Mortgage lenders were intelligent enough to realize that they couldn't foresee how much future interest rates would rise or fall; thus, adjustable-rate mortgages (*adjustables* for short) were born.

Although some adjustables are more volatile than others, all are similar in that they *fluctuate* (or float) with the market level of interest rates. If the interest rate fluctuates, so does your monthly payment. And therein lies the risk: Because a mortgage payment is likely to be a big monthly expense for you, an adjustable-rate mortgage that is adjusting upward may wreak havoc with your budget.

Given all the trials, tribulations, and challenges of life as we know it, you may rightfully ask, "Why would anyone choose to accept an adjustable-rate

---

Avoid loans with prepayment penalties

Some mortgages come with a provision that penalizes you for paying off the loan balance faster. Such penalties can amount to as much as several percentage points of the amount of the mortgage balance that is paid off early.

When you pay off a mortgage early because you sold the property or because you want to refinance the loan to take advantage of lower interest rates, some lenders won't enforce their loan's prepayment penalties as long as they get to make the new mortgage. Even so, your hands are tied financially unless you go through the same lender.

Many states place limits on the duration and amount of prepayment penalty that lenders may charge for mortgages made on owner-occupied residential property. The only way to know whether a loan has a prepayment penalty is to ask and to carefully review the federal truth-in-lending disclosure and the promissory note the mortgage lender provides you. We think that you should avoid such loans. (Many so-called *no-points* loans have prepayment penalties.)

---

mortgage?" Well, people who are stretching themselves — such as some first-time buyers or those *trading up* to a more expensive home — may financially force themselves into accepting adjustable-rate mortgages. Because an ARM starts out at a lower interest rate, such a mortgage enables you to *qualify* to borrow more. As we discuss in Chapter 2, just because you can qualify to borrow more doesn't mean that you can *afford* to borrow that much, given your other financial goals and needs.

Some home buyers who can qualify for either an adjustable-rate or a fixed-rate mortgage of the same size have a choice and choose the fluctuating adjustable-rate mortgage. Why? Because they may very well save themselves money, in the form of smaller total interest charges, with an adjustable-rate loan rather than a fixed-rate loan.

Because you accept the risk of a possible increase in interest rates, mortgage lenders cut you a little slack. The *initial interest rate* (also sometimes referred to as the *teaser rate*) on an adjustable should be less than the initial interest rate on a comparable fixed-rate loan. In fact, an ARM's interest rate for the first year or two of the loan is generally lower than the rate on a fixed-rate mortgage.

Another advantage of an ARM is that if you purchase your home during a time of high interest rates, you can start paying your mortgage with the artificially depressed initial interest rate. Should interest rates subsequently decline, you can enjoy the benefits of lower rates without refinancing.

Another situation when adjustable-rate loans have an advantage over their fixed-rate brethren is when interest rates decline and you don't qualify to refinance your mortgage to reap the advantage of lower rates. The good news for

When to consider hybrid loans

If you want more stability in your monthly payments than you can get with a regular adjustable, and you expect to keep your loan for no more than five to ten years, a *hybrid* (or intermediate ARM) loan, which is explained earlier in this chapter, may be the best loan for you.

The longer the initial interest rate stays locked in, the higher it will be, but the initial rate of a hybrid ARM is almost always lower than the interest rate on a 30-year fixed-rate mortgage. However, because the initial rate of hybrid loans is locked in for a longer period of time than the six-month or one-year term of regular ARMs, hybrid ARMs have higher initial interest rates than regular ARM loans.

During periods when little difference existed between short-term and long-term interest rates, the interest-rate savings with a hybrid or regular adjustable (versus a fixed-rate loan) were minimal (less than 1 percent). In fact, during certain times, the initial interest rate on a 7- or 10-year hybrid was exactly the same as on a 30-year fixed-rate loan. During such periods, fixed-rate loans offer the best overall value.

To evaluate hybrids, weigh the likelihood that you'll move before the initial loan interest rate expires. For example, with a 7-year hybrid, if you're saving, say, 0.5 percent per year versus the 30-year fixed-rate mortgage, but you're quite sure that you will move within seven years, the hybrid will probably save you money. On the other hand, if you think that there's a reasonable chance that you'll stay put for more than seven years, and you don't want to face the risk of rising payments after seven years, you should opt for a 30-year, fixed-rate mortgage instead.

homeowners who are unable to refinance and who have an ARM is that they usually capture many of the benefits of the lower rates. With a fixed-rate loan, you must refinance in order to realize the benefits of a decline in interest rates.

The downside to an adjustable-rate loan is that if interest rates in general rise, your loan's interest and monthly payment will likely rise, too. During most time periods, if rates rise more than 1 or 2 percent and stay elevated, the adjustable-rate loan is likely to cost you more than a fixed-rate loan.

Before you make the final choice between a fixed-rate mortgage versus an adjustable-rate mortgage, read the following two sections.

What would rising interest rates do to your finances?

Far too many home buyers, especially first-timers, take out an adjustable-rate mortgage because doing so allows them to stretch and borrow more and buy a more expensive home. Although some of this overborrowing is caused by the modern-day American spendthrift "I gotta have it today" attitude, over-borrowing is also encouraged by some real estate and mortgage salespeople. After all, these salespeople's income, in the form of a commission, is a function of the cost of the home that you buy and the size of the mortgage that you take on.

If you haven't already done so, let your fingers do the walking back to Chapters 2 and 3. Read and digest these chapters in order to understand how much you can really afford to spend on a home, given your other financial needs, commitments, and goals.

When considering an ARM, you absolutely, positively must understand what rising interest rates (and, therefore, a rising monthly mortgage payment) would do to your personal finances. Consider taking an ARM only if you can answer all of the following questions in the affirmative:

✔ Is your monthly budget such that you can afford higher mortgage payments and still accomplish other financial goals that are important to you, such as saving for retirement?

✔ Do you have an emergency reserve (equal to at least six months of living expenses) that you can tap into to make the potentially higher monthly mortgage payments?

✔ Can you afford the highest payment allowed on the adjustable-rate mortgage?

The mortgage lender can tell you the highest possible monthly payment, which is the payment that you would owe if the interest rate on your ARM went to the lifetime interest-rate cap allowed on the loan.

✔ If you're stretching to borrow near the maximum the lender allows or an amount that will test the limits of your budget, are your job and income stable?

✔ If you expect to be having children in the future, have you considered that your household expenses will rise and your income may fall with the arrival of those little bundles of joy?

✔ Can you handle the psychological stress of changing interest rates and mortgage payments?

If you're fiscally positioned to take on the financial risks inherent to an adjustable-rate mortgage, by all means consider taking one — we're not trying to talk you into a fixed-rate loan. The odds are with you to save money, in the form of lower interest charges and payments, with an ARM. Your interest rate starts lower (and generally stays lower, if the overall level of interest rates doesn't change). Even if rates do go up, as they are sometimes prone to do, they will surely come back down. So if you can stick with your ARM through times of high and low interest rates, you should still come out ahead.

Also recognize that although ARMs do carry the risk of a fluctuating interest rate, almost all adjustable-rate loans limit, or *cap,* the rise in the interest rate allowed on your loan. We certainly wouldn't recommend that you take an ARM without caps. Typical caps are 2 percent per year and 6 percent over the life of the loan. (We cover ARM interest-rate caps in detail later in this chapter.)

Short-term versus long-term interest rates

When choosing between an adjustable-rate mortgage and a fixed-rate mortgage, many people don't realize that they're making a choice between a mortgage on which the interest rate is determined by either short-term or long-term interest rates.

"What's a short-term versus a long-term interest rate?" you ask. Glad you asked. When a mortgage lender quotes an interest rate for a particular type of loan, he should specify (in terms of how many years until the loan is completely paid off) the length of the loan.

Most of the time, borrowers must pay a higher interest rate to borrow money for a longer period of time. Conversely, borrowers generally pay a lower rate of interest for shorter-term loans. So?

Well, the interest rates that are used to determine most adjustable-rate mortgages are *short-term interest rates,* whereas fixed-rate mortgage interest rates are dictated by *long-term interest*

rates. During most time periods, longer-term interest rates are higher than shorter-term rates because of the greater risk the lender accepts in committing to a longer-term rate.

It stands to reason, therefore, that when little difference exists in the market level of short-term and long-term interest rates, the rates of fixed-rate mortgages shouldn't be all that different from the rates of adjustable-rate mortgages. Thus, adjustables appear less attractive, and fixed-rate mortgages appear more alluring.

On the other hand, when short-term interest rates are significantly lower than long-term interest rates, adjustable-rate mortgages should be available at rates a good deal lower than the rates for fixed-rate loans. All things being equal, adjustables appear more attractive during such time periods and save you more money during the early years of your loan.

Consider an adjustable-rate mortgage only if you're financially and emotionally secure enough to handle the maximum possible payments over an extended period of time. ARMs work best for borrowers who take out smaller loans than they're qualified for or who consistently save more than 10 percent of their monthly income. If you do choose an ARM, make sure that you have a significant cash cushion that is accessible in the event that rates go up. Don't take an adjustable just because the initially lower interest rate allows you to afford a more expensive home. Better to buy a home that you can afford with a fixed-rate mortgage. (And don't forget hybrid loans if you want a loan with more payment stability but aren't willing to pay the premium of a long-term, fixed-rate loan.)

How long do you expect to stay in the home/mortgage?

As we explain earlier in this chapter, a mortgage lender takes more risk when lending money at a fixed rate of interest for many (15 to 30) years. Lenders charge you a premium, in the form of a higher interest rate than what the ARM starts at, for the interest-rate risk that they assume with a fixed-rate loan.

If you don't plan or expect to stay in your home for a long time, you should consider an ARM. Saving money on interest charges for most adjustables is usually
guaranteed in the first two to three years, because an ARM starts at a lower
interest rate than a fixed-rate loan does. If you're reasonably certain that you'll
hold onto your home for fewer than five years, you should come out ahead with
an adjustable. However, you should also ask yourself why you're going to all the
trouble and expense of buying a home that you expect to sell so soon.

If you expect to hold onto your home and mortgage for a long time — more
than five to seven years — a fixed-rate loan may make more sense, especially
when you're not in a position to withstand the fluctuating monthly payments
that come with an ARM.

When you're in the intermediate area (expecting to stay seven to ten years,
for example), consider the hybrid loans we discuss earlier in this chapter.

If you're still stuck on the fence, go with the fixed-rate loan. A fixed-rate loan
is financially safer than an ARM — and easier to shop for.

Deciding on your loan's life: 15 years or 30?

After you've decided which type of mortgage — fixed or adjustable — you want,
you may think that your mortgage quandaries are behind you. Unfortunately,
they're not. You also need to make another important choice — typically
between a 15-year and a 30-year mortgage. (Not all mortgages come in just
15- and 30-year varieties. You may run across some 20- and 40-year versions,
but that won't change the issues we're about to tackle.)

When you're stretching to buy the home that you want, you may also be forc-
ing yourself to take the longer-term, 30-year mortgage. Doing so isn't necessarily bad and, in fact, has advantages.

The main advantage that a 30-year mortgage has over its 15-year peer is that
it has lower monthly payments that free up more of your monthly income for
other purposes, including saving for other important financial goals (such as
retirement). You may want to have more money so that you aren't a financial
prisoner to your home and can just have a life! A 30-year mortgage has lower
monthly payments because you have a longer period to repay it (which translates into more payments). A fixed-rate 30-year mortgage with an interest rate
of 7 percent, for example, has payments that are approximately 25 percent
lower than those on a comparable 15-year mortgage.

What if you can afford the higher payments that a 15-year mortgage requires?
You shouldn't necessarily take it. What if, instead of making large payments
on the 15-year mortgage, you make smaller payments on a 30-year mortgage
and put that extra money to productive use?

No one can predict where interest rates are headed

All the logicians out there are probably commenting that the choice between an adjustable-rate mortgage and a fixed-rate mortgage is simple. All you need to know in order to make a decision is the direction of interest rates. It's only logical. When interest rates are about ready to rise, a fixed-rate mortgage would be favorable. Lock in a low rate, and smile smugly when interest rates skyrocket.

Conversely, if you thought that rates were going to stay the same or drop, you would want an ARM. Some real estate books that we've read even go so far as to say that your own personal interest-rate forecast should determine whether to take an ARM or fixed-rate mortgage! "Interest-rate forecasts should be the major factor in deciding whether or not to get an ARM," argues one such book.

Now, we don't think that you're stupid, but you are _not_ going to figure out which way rates are headed. The movement of interest rates isn't logical, and you certainly can't predict it. If you could, you would make a fortune investing in bonds, interest-rate futures, and options.

Even the money-management pros who work with interest rates and bonds as a full-time job can't consistently predict interest rates. Witness the fact that bond-fund managers at mutual fund companies have a tough time beating the buy-and-hold bond-market indexes. If bond-fund managers could foresee where rates were headed, they could easily beat the averages by trading into and out of bonds when they foresaw interest-rate changes on the horizon.

 If you do, indeed, make productive use of that extra money, the 30-year mortgage may be for you. A terrific potential use for that extra dough is to contribute it to a tax-deductible retirement account that you have access to. Contributions that you add to employer-based 401(k) and 403(b) plans (and self-employed SEP-IRAs or Keoghs) not only give you an immediate reduction in taxes, but also enable your investment to compound, tax deferred, over the years ahead. Everyone with employment income may also contribute to an Individual Retirement Account (IRA). However, your IRA contributions may not be immediately tax deductible if your (or your spouse's) employer offers a retirement account or pension plan.

 If you've exhausted your options for contributing to all the retirement accounts that you can, and if you find it challenging to save money anyway, the 15-year mortgage may offer you a good forced-savings program.

When you elect to take a 30-year mortgage, you retain the flexibility to pay it off faster if you so choose. (Just be sure to avoid those mortgages that have a prepayment penalty.) Constraining yourself with the 15-year mortgage's higher monthly payments does carry a risk. Should you fall on tough financial times, you may not be able to meet the required mortgage payments.

Finding a Fixed-Rate Mortgage

If you decide, based upon our advice and selection criteria, to go with a fixed-rate loan, great! You shouldn't be disappointed. You'll have the peace of mind that comes with stable mortgage payments. And because fixed-rate loans have fewer options, they're a good deal easier to compare than adjustable-rate loans.

However, we don't want to give you the false impression that fixed-rate loans are as simple to shop for as carbonated beverages. Unfortunately, because of the hundreds of lenders that offer such loans and the seemingly endless number of extra fees and expenses that lenders tack onto loans, you need to put on your smart-consumer hat and sharpen your No. 2 pencil.

Be sure that you understand the following sections before you attempt to choose the best fixed-rate loan to meet your needs.

The all-important interest rate

If you've ever borrowed money, you know that lenders aren't charities. Lenders make money by charging you, in the form of interest, for the use of their money. Lenders normally quote the *rate of interest* as a percentage per year of the amount borrowed. You may be familiar with rates of interest if you've ever borrowed money through student loans, credit cards, or auto loans. In these cases, lenders may have charged you 8, 10, 12, or perhaps even 18 percent or more for the privilege of using their money. Similarly, mortgage lenders also quote you an annual interest rate.

You've shopped for other products and services by phone, so you may as well get on the horn and call lenders, as well. The first one you call may be offering a fixed-rate loan at an interest rate of 7.5 percent. Then you call another lender to try to beat that rate, and that lender says, "Sure, we can get you into a fixed-rate loan at 7.25 percent."

The finer points of points

If you blindly choose a 7.25 percent loan, you could be making a very expensive mistake. You have an idea of what we mean if you've heard the expression "Don't judge a book by its cover." You shouldn't judge a mortgage solely by its interest rate, either. You must also understand the points and other loan fees that the lender assesses.

Just as Abbott goes with Costello, Laurel goes with Hardy, and Calvin is inseparable from Hobbes, the interest rate on a mortgage should go together, in your mind, with the points on the loan. We aren't talking about the kind of points that a basketball player tallies during a game for each successful shot. Points on a mortgage cost you money.

Points are up-front interest. Lenders charge points as a way of being paid for the work and expense of processing and approving your mortgage. When you buy a home, the points are tax deductible — you get to claim them as an itemized expense on *Schedule A* of your IRS *Form 1040* (see Chapter 3). When you refinance, in contrast, the points must be spread out for tax purposes and deducted over the life of the new loan.

Lenders quote points as a percentage of the mortgage amount and require you to pay them at the time that you close on your home purchase and begin the lengthy process of repaying your loan. One *point* is equal to 1 percent of the amount that you're borrowing. For example, if a lender says that the loan being proposed to you has two points, that simply means that you must pay 2 percent of the loan amount as points. On a $120,000 loan, for example, two points cost you $2,400. That's not chump change!

The interest rate on a fixed-rate loan has an inverse relationship to that loan's points. When you're able to (or desire to) pay more points on a mortgage, the lender should reduce the ongoing interest rate. This reduction may be beneficial to you if you have the cash to pay more points and want to lower the interest rate that you'll pay year after year. If you expect to hold onto the home and mortgage for many years, the lower the interest rate, the better.

Conversely, if you want to (or need to) pay fewer points (perhaps because you're cash-constrained when you make the home purchase), you can pay a higher ongoing interest rate. The shorter the time that you expect to hold onto the mortgage, the more sense this strategy of paying less now makes.

Don't get suckered into believing that "no-point" loans are a good deal. There are no free lunches in the real estate world. Remember the points/interest-rate trade-off: If you pay less in points, the ongoing interest rate is higher. So if a loan has zero points, it must have a higher interest rate. This doesn't necessarily mean that the loan is better or worse than comparable loans from other lenders. However, it has been our experience that lenders who aggressively push no-point loans aren't the most competitive lenders in terms of pricing. No-point loans make sense only when you're really tight on cash for your home purchase and expect not to hold onto the home and mortgage for the long-term.

Take a look at a couple of specific mortgage options to understand the points/interest-rate trade-off. Suppose that you want to borrow $150,000. One lender quotes you 7.25 percent on a 30-year fixed-rate loan and charges one point (1 percent). Another lender quotes 7.75 percent and doesn't charge any points. Which offer is better? The answer depends mostly on how long you plan to keep the loan.

The 7.25-percent loan costs $1,024 per month compared with $1,075 per month for the 7.75-percent mortgage. You can save $51 per month with the 7.25-percent loan, but you'd have to pay $1,500 in points to get it.

To find out which loan is better for you, divide the cost of the points by the monthly savings ($1,500 divided by $51 equals 29.4). This gives you the number of months (in this case, 29.4) it will take you to recover the cost of the points. The 7.25-percent loan costs 0.5 percent less in interest annually than the 7.75-percent loan. Year after year, the 7.25-percent loan saves you 0.5 percent. But because you have to pay one point up front on the 7.25-percent mortgage, it will take you about 30 months to earn back the savings to cover the cost of that point. So if you expect to keep the loan more than 30 months, go with the 7.25-percent, one-point option. If you don't plan to keep the loan for 30 months, choose the no-points loan.

To make a fair comparison of mortgages from different lenders, have the lenders provide interest-rate quotes at the *same* point level. Ask the mortgage contenders, for example, to tell you what their fixed-rate mortgage interest rate would be at one point. Also, make sure that the loans are of the same term — for example, 30 years.

Other lender fees

You may think that because you're paying points with your mortgage, you won't have to pay any other up-front fees. Well, think again. There is no shortage of up-front loan-processing charges for you to investigate when making mortgage comparisons. If you don't understand the fee structure, you may end up with a high-cost loan or come up short of cash when the time comes to close on the purchase of your home.

Ask each lender whose services you're seriously considering for a written itemization of all of these "other" charges. To reduce your chances of throwing money away on a mortgage for which you may not qualify, ask the lender whether your application may be turned down for some reason. For example, disclose any potential problems with the property that were discovered during inspections of the property.

Just as some lenders have no-point mortgages, some lenders also have *no-fee mortgages*. If a lender is pitching a no-fee loan, odds are that the lender will charge you more in other ways, namely in the ongoing interest rate on your loan.

Application and processing fees

Lenders generally charge $200 to $300 up front as an *application* or *processing fee.* This charge is mainly to ensure that you're serious about wanting a loan from them and to compensate them in the event that your loan is rejected.

Lenders want to cover their costs to keep from losing money on loan applications that don't materialize into actual loans. A few lenders don't charge this fee, or if they do, they return it if you take their loan.

Credit report

Your credit report tells a lender how responsibly you've dealt with prior loans. Did you pay all of your previous loans back (and on time)? Credit reports don't cost a great deal, but you can expect to pay about $50 for the lender to obtain a current copy of yours.

If you know that you have blemishes on your credit report, address those problems *before* you apply for your mortgage. Otherwise, you're wasting your time and money. Don't apply for a loan that you know you'll be denied.

Appraisal

Mortgage lenders want an independent assessment to ensure that the property that you're buying is worth approximately what you agreed to pay — that's the job of an appraiser. Why would the lender care? Simple — because the lender is likely loaning you a large portion of the purchase price of the property. If you overpay and home values decline, or you end up in financial trouble, you may be willing to walk away from the property and leave the lender holding the bag.

The cost of an appraisal varies with the size, complexity, and value of property. Expect to pay a few hundred dollars for an appraisal of most modestly priced, average-type properties.

Arriving at the Absolute Best Adjustable

If you're the calm and collected type of person who isn't prone to panicking, can stomach interest-rate volatility, and have decided based on our sage advice to go with an adjustable-rate mortgage (ARM), you'll need to understand a bit more in order to choose a good one. Adjustables are more complicated to evaluate and select than fixed-rate mortgages are.

In addition to understanding points and other loan fees that we cover in the preceding section on fixed-rate loans, you'll be bombarded with such jargon as *margins, caps,* and *indexes.* Numbers geeks can easily spend hundreds of hours comparing different permutations of ARMs and determining how they might behave in different interest-rate environments.

Unlike with a fixed-rate mortgage, precisely determining the amount of money a particular ARM is going to cost you isn't possible. As with choosing a home to buy, selecting an ARM that meets your needs and budget involves compromising and deciding what's important to you. So here's your crash course in understanding ARMs.

Where an ARM's interest rate comes from

Most ARMs start at an artificially low interest rate. Selecting an ARM based on this rate is likely to be a huge mistake, because you won't be paying this low rate for long, perhaps for just 6 to 12 months — or maybe even just 1 month! Lenders and mortgage brokers are like many other salespeople; they like to promote something that will catch your attention and get you thinking you're going to get a great deal. That's why lenders and brokers are most likely to tell you first about the low teaser rate.

The starting rate on an ARM isn't anywhere near as important as what the future interest rate is going to be on the loan. How the future interest rate on an ARM is determined is the single most important feature for you to understand when evaluating an ARM.

All ARMs that we've ever seen are based on an equation that includes an index and margin, the two of which are added together to determine and set the future interest rate on the loan. Before we go further, please be sure that you understand these terms:

- **Index:** The index is a measure of interest rates that the lender uses as a reference. For example, the six-month bank certificate of deposit index is used as a reference for many mortgages. Suppose that the going rate on six-month CDs is approximately 5 percent. The index theoretically indicates how much it costs the bank to take in money that it can then lend.

- **Margin:** The margin is the lenders' profit (or markup) on the money that they intend to lend. Most loans have margins of around 2.5 percent, but the exact margin depends on the lender and the index that lender is using. When you compare loans that are tied to the same index and are otherwise the same, the loan with the lower margin is better (lower cost) for you.

- **Interest rate:** The interest rate is the sum of the index and the margin. It is what you will pay (subject to certain limitations) on your loan.

Putting it all together, in our example of the six-month CD index at 5 percent, plus a margin of 2.5 percent, we get an interest rate sum of 7.5 percent. This figure is known as the *fully indexed rate*. If this loan starts out at 5 percent, for example, the fully indexed rate tells you what interest rate this ARM would increase to if the market level of interest rates, as measured by the CD index, stays constant. Never take an ARM unless you understand this important concept of the fully indexed rate:

Index + margin = interest rate

Many mortgage lenders know that more than a few borrowers focus on an ARM's initial interest rate, and ignore the margin and the index that determine the loan rate. Take our advice, and look at an ARM's starting rate *last*.

Begin to evaluate an ARM by understanding what index it is tied to and what margin it has. The sections that follow explain common ARM indexes.

Treasury bills

The U.S. federal government is the largest borrower in the universe as we know it, so it should come as no surprise that at least one ARM index is based on the interest rate that the government pays on some of this pile of debt. The most commonly used government interest rate indexes for ARMs are for 6-month and 12-month Treasury bills.

The Treasury-bill indexes tend to be among the faster-moving ones around. In other words, they respond quickly to market changes in interest rates.

Certificates of deposit

Certificates of deposit (CDs) are interest-bearing bank investments that lock you in for a specific period of time. Adjustable-rate mortgages are usually tied to the average interest rate that banks are paying on six-month CDs.

As with Treasury bills, CDs tend to move rapidly with overall changes in interest rates. However, CD rates tend to move up a bit more slowly when rates rise, because profit-minded bankers like to drag their feet when paying more interest to depositors. Conversely, CD rates tend to come down quickly when rates decline, so that bankers can maintain their profits.

The 11th District Cost of Funds Index

The 11th District Cost of Funds Index (also known as COFI, pronounced like the caffeinated brew that some people drink in the morning) is published monthly by the Federal Home Loan Bank Board. This index shows the monthly weighted average cost of savings, borrowings, and advances for its member banks located in California, Arizona, and Nevada (the 11th District). Because the COFI is a moving average of the rates that bankers have paid depositors over recent months, it tends to be a relatively stable index.

An ARM tied to a slower-moving index, such as the 11th District Cost of Funds Index, has the advantage of increasing more slowly when interest rates are on the upswing. On the other hand, you have to be patient to benefit from falling interest rates when rates are on the decline. The 11th District is slow to fall when interest rates overall decline.

Because ARMs tied to the 11th District Cost of Funds Index are slower to rise when overall interest rates rise, they generally begin at a higher rate of interest than do ARMs tied to faster-moving indexes.

The London Interbank Offered Rate Index

Okay, now for a more unusual index. The *London Interbank Offered Rate index (LIBOR)* is an average of the interest rates that major international banks charge one another to borrow U.S. dollars in the London money market. Like the U.S. Treasury and CD indexes, LIBOR tends to move and adjust quite rapidly to changes in interest rates.

Why do we need an *international* interest-rate index? Well, foreign investors buy American mortgages as investments, and not surprisingly, these investors like ARMs tied to an index that they understand and are more familiar with.

How often does the interest rate adjust?

Lenders usually adjust the interest rates on their ARMs every 6 or 12 months, using the mortgage-rate formula discussed earlier in this section. Some loans adjust monthly. (Monthly adjustments are usually a red flag for negative amortization loans; we explain why to stay away from these loans in the "Avoid adjustables with negative amortization" sidebar.) In advance of each adjustment, the mortgage lender should send you a notice spelling out how the new rate is calculated according to the agreed-upon terms of your ARM.

The less often your loan adjusts, the less financial risk you're accepting. In exchange for taking less risk, the mortgage lender normally expects you to pay a higher initial interest rate.

Limits on interest-rate adjustments

Despite the fact that an ARM has a system for calculating future interest rates (by adding the margin to the loan index), bankers limit how great a change can occur in the actual rate that you pay. These limits, also known as *rate caps,* affect each future adjustment of an ARM's rate following the end of the initial rate.

Periodic adjustment caps limit the maximum rate change, up or down, allowed at each adjustment. For ARMs that adjust at six-month intervals, the adjustment cap is usually 1 percent. ARMs that adjust more than once annually generally restrict the maximum rate change allowed over the entire year, as well. This *annual rate cap* is usually 2 percent.

Finally, almost all adjustables come with *lifetime caps.* You should never take on an ARM without a lifetime cap. These caps limit the highest rate allowed over the entire life of the loan. ARMs commonly have lifetime caps of 5 to 6 percent higher than the initial start rate.

When you take on an ARM, be sure that you can handle the maximum possible payment allowed, should the interest rate on the ARM rise to the lifetime cap.

Locating the Best, Lowest-Cost Lenders

For those of you out there who abhor shopping, we have some bad news. Unless you enjoy throwing away thousands of dollars, you need to shop around for the best deal on a mortgage. Think of it as "dialing for dollars" (or "surfing for dollars," for you Web users).

Whether you do the footwork on your own or hire someone competent to help you doesn't matter. But you must make sure that this comparison shopping gets done.

Suppose that you're in the market for a 30-year, $100,000 mortgage. If, through persistent and wise shopping, you're able to obtain a mortgage that is, for example, 0.5 percent per year lower in interest charges than you otherwise would have gotten, you'll save about $14,000 over the life of the loan (given approximate current interest rates). You can double those savings for a $200,000 mortgage.

Although we encourage you to find the lowest-cost lenders, we must first issue a caution: Should someone offer you a deal that is much better than any other lender's, be skeptical and suspicious. Such a lender may be baiting you with a loan that doesn't exist or one for which you can't qualify, and then you'll get stuck with a higher-cost loan if you don't have time to apply for another mortgage elsewhere.

Shopping on your own

There's no shortage of mortgage lenders in most areas. Although having a large number of options to choose among is good for competition, so many alternatives can also make shopping a headache.

Many different types of companies offer mortgages today. The most common mortgage *originators* (as they're known in the business) are banks, savings-and-loan associations, and mortgage bankers.

"Who cares?" you ask. Well, mortgage bankers do only mortgages, and the best ones offer very competitive rates. Smaller banks and savings-and-loans can have good deals as well. As for the big banks whose names are drilled into your head from advertisements, they usually don't offer the best rates.

As you begin your mortgage safari, you don't have to go it completely alone. If you've done a good job selecting a real estate agent to help you with your home purchase, for example, the agent should be able to rattle off a short list of good lenders and mortgage brokers (see the following section) in the area. Just remember to compare these lenders' loans and rates with those of some other mortgage lenders that you find on your own.

Avoid adjustables with negative amortization

Some ARMs cap the increase of your monthly payment but not the increase of the interest rate. The size of your mortgage payment may not reflect all the interest that you actually owe on your loan. So rather than paying the interest that is owed and paying off some of your loan balance every month, you may end up paying some (but not all) of the interest that you owe. Thus, the extra unpaid interest that you still owe is added to your outstanding debt.

As you make mortgage payments over time, the loan balance you still owe is gradually reduced in a process called *amortizing the mortgage.* The reverse of this process (that is, increasing the size of your loan balance) is called *negative amortization.*

Liken negative amortization to paying only the minimum payment required on a credit card bill. You continue accumulating additional interest on the balance as long as you make only the minimum monthly payment. However, doing this

with a mortgage defeats the purpose of your borrowing an amount that fits your overall financial goals (see Chapter 3).

Some lenders try to hide the fact that an ARM that they're pitching you has negative amortization. How can you avoid negative-amortization loans? Simple — ask!

Also be aware that negative amortization pops up more often on mortgages that lenders consider risky to make. If you're having trouble finding lenders willing to offer you a mortgage, be especially careful.

Last, but not least, realize that many lenders will not put additional financing in the form of second mortgages or home-equity lines of credit behind a negative-amortization loan. They fear that if the negative-amortization loan amount grows too large, it could swallow all the equity in the property.

Otherwise-good real estate agents may send you to lenders that don't necessarily offer the best mortgage interest rates. Some real estate agents may not be up to date with who has the best loans or may not be into shopping around. Others may have simply gotten comfortable doing business with certain lenders or gotten client referrals from said lenders previously.

As you surely know, the Internet offers yet another method for tapping into companies in a particular line of work. In Chapter 11, we offer plenty of advice and recommendations for Web sites that can assist you with mortgage shopping.

Another way to find lenders is to look for tables of selected lenders' interest rates in the Sunday real estate section of the larger area newspapers. However, don't assume that such tables contain the best lenders in your area. In fact, many of these tables are sent to newspapers for free by firms that distribute information to mortgage brokers. Nonetheless, you can use these tables as a starting point by calling the lenders that list the best rates (realizing, of course, that rates can change daily and that the rates you see in the paper may not accurately reflect what's currently available).

INVESTIGATE

Traits of good lenders

Yes, thousands of mortgage lenders are out there. However, not anywhere near that many mortgage lenders are *good* lenders. Real estate agents and others in the real estate trade, as well as other borrowers whom you know, can serve as useful references for steering you toward the top-notch lenders and away from the losers. (To make sure you get unbiased recommendations, ask your agent whether she will be paid a referral fee by any of the lenders being recommended.) As you solicit input from others and begin to interview lenders, seek to find lenders with the following traits:

✔ **Straightforward:** Good loan agents explain their various loan programs in plain English, without using double-talk or jargon. They help you compare their loans with their competitors' loans. Run as fast as you can in the opposite direction from mortgage officers who talk down to you and try to snow you with lots of confusing lingo.

✔ **Approve locally:** Good lenders approve your loan locally. They don't send your loan application to an out-of-town loan committee, where you're transformed from a living, breathing human being into an inanimate loan number. Good lenders use appraisers who are familiar with the local real estate market and have experience appraising the types of properties that are commonly sold locally. Good lenders actively work with you and your agent to get loan approval.

✔ **Market savvy:** Good lenders understand the type of property that you want to buy. Here's another big advantage of local loan approval: No deal-breaking, last-minute loan cancellations unexpectedly arise because

you inadvertently run afoul of some obscure institutional policy.

This type of snafu generally occurs when a mortgage broker tries to find the loan with the lowest interest rate currently being offered anywhere in the universe. Finding the loan is relatively easy. Getting the money, on the other hand, is nearly impossible, because you don't know what bizarre quirks lie buried deep in the loan documents' fine print.

These quirky loans usually apply to absolutely pristine property. For example, an out-of-state lender once approved a loan subject to having all corrective work completed and the house painted inside and out prior to close of escrow. Given that the loan was approved on Monday and the sale was scheduled to close Friday, there was no way that the work could be completed in four days.

✔ **Competitive:** Good lenders are competitive. Don't be afraid to ask the lender that you like best to match the interest rate of the lowest-priced lender you find. At worst, the lender will turn your rate request down. At best, you'll get the lender you want *and* the loan terms you want. Loan rates and charges *are* negotiable.

✔ **Detail-oriented:** Good lenders meet contract deadlines. They approve and fund loans on time. Your agent knows which lenders deliver on their promises and which don't. Talk's cheap. You need action, not empty promises. Missed deadlines may squash your purchase.

If you're a data hound, HSH Associates (800-873-2837; www.hsh.com) publishes, on a weekly basis, lists of dozens of lenders' rate quotes for most metropolitan areas. The initial package, which comes with explanatory booklets, costs $20. If you wish to purchase subsequent updates, those go for $10 each.

Working with a mortgage broker

Mortgage brokers are middlemen, independent of banks or other financial institutions that have money to lend. They can do the mortgage shopping for you.

If your credit history and ability to qualify for a mortgage are questionable, a good mortgage broker can help polish and package your application, and steer you to the few lenders that may make you a loan. Brokers can also assist if lenders don't want to make loans on unusual properties that you're interested in buying. Many lenders don't like dealing with co-ops and tenancies-in-common (see Chapter 8), borrowers with credit problems, or situations where a home buyer seeks to borrow most (90 percent or more) of the value of a property.

Mortgage brokers typically tell you that they can get you the best loan deal by shopping among many lenders. They may further argue that another benefit of using their service is that they can explain the multitude of loan choices, help you select a loan, and assist with the morass of paperwork that's (unfortunately) required to get a loan.

Good mortgage brokers can deliver on most of these promises, and for this service, they receive a cut of the amount that you borrow — typically, 0.5 to as much as 2 percent on smaller loans. Not cheap, but given what a headache finding and closing on a good mortgage can be, hiring a mortgage broker may be just what the financial doctor ordered.

If you're going to work with a mortgage broker, please keep in mind that such brokers are in the business of "selling" mortgages and derive a commission from this work, just as do stockbrokers who sell stock and car salespeople who sell cars. A difference, though, is that the interest rate and points that you pay to get most mortgages through a broker are the same as what you would pay a lender directly. Lenders reason that they can afford to share their normal fees with an outside mortgage broker who isn't employed by the bank. After all, if you got the loan directly from the bank, you would have to work with and take up more of the time of one of the bank's own mortgage employees.

However, some lenders, including those with the lowest rates, don't market through mortgage brokers. And sometimes a loan obtained through a mortgage broker can end up costing you more than if you had obtained it directly from the lender — for example, if the mortgage broker is taking a big commission for himself.

The commission that the mortgage broker receives from the lender isn't set in stone and is completely negotiable, especially on larger loans. On a $100,000 loan, a 1 percent commission amounts to $1,000. The same commission rate on a $300,000 loan results in a $3,000 cut for the broker, even though this three-times-larger loan doesn't take up three times as much of the mortgage broker's time. You have every right to inquire of the mortgage broker what his take is. Don't become overwhelmed with embarrassment; remember, it's your money, and you have every right to know this information! Ask — and don't hesitate to negotiate.

In addition to understanding and negotiating a commission with the mortgage broker, get answers to the following questions when choosing a mortgage broker:

✔ **How many lenders does the broker do business with, and how does the broker keep up to date with new lenders and loans that may be better?** Some mortgage brokers, out of habit and laziness, send all their business to just a few lenders and don't get you the best deals. Ask brokers which lenders have approved the broker to represent them.

✔ **How knowledgeable is the broker about the loan programs, and does the broker have the patience to explain all of a loan's important features?** The more lenders a mortgage broker represents, the less likely the broker is to know the nuances of each and every loan. Be especially wary of a salesperson who aggressively pushes certain loan programs and glosses over or ignores explaining the important points we discuss in this chapter for evaluating particular mortgages.

All the advice that we give for selecting a good lender applies doubly for choosing a good mortgage broker. Some brokers, for example, have been known to push programs with outrageous interest rates and points, which, not too surprisingly, entail big commissions for them. This problem occurs most frequently with borrowers who have questionable credit or other qualification problems.

Also head for cover if your mortgage broker pushes you toward balloon and negative-amortization loans (discussed earlier in this chapter). Balloon loans, which become fully due and payable several years after you get them, are dangerous because you may not be able to get new financing and could be forced to sell the property.

If you're on the fence about using a mortgage broker, take this simple test: If you're the type of person who dreads shopping and waits until the last minute to buy a gift, a good mortgage broker can probably help and save you money. A competent mortgage broker can be of greatest value to those who don't bother shopping around for a good deal or who may be shunned by most lenders.

Loan prequalification and preapproval

When you're under contract to buy a property, having your mortgage application denied (after waiting several weeks) may cause you to lose the property after having spent hundreds of dollars on loan fees and property inspections. Even worse, you may lose the home that you've probably spent countless hours searching for and a great deal of emotional energy to secure. Some house sellers won't be willing to wait or may need to sell quickly. If the sellers have other buyers waiting in the wings, you've likely lost the property.

How could you have avoided this heartache? Well, you may hear some people in the real estate business, particularly real estate agents and mortgage brokers, advocate that you go through mortgage prequalification or preapproval.

Prequalification is an informal discussion between borrower and lender. The lender provides an opinion of the loan amount that you can borrow based solely on what you, the borrower, tell the lender. The lender doesn't verify anything and isn't bound to make the loan when you're ready to buy.

Preapproval is a much more rigorous process, which is why we prefer it if you have any reason to believe that you'll have difficulty qualifying for the loan you desire. Loan preapproval is based on documented and verified information

regarding your likelihood of continued employment, your income, your liabilities, and the cash you have available to close on a home purchase. The only thing the lender can't preapprove is the property you intend to buy because, of course, you haven't found it yet.

Going through the preapproval process is a sign of your seriousness to house sellers — it places sort of a Good Borrowing Seal of Approval on you. A lender's preapproval letter is considerably stronger than a prequalification letter. In a multiple-offer situation where more than one prospective buyer bids on a home at the same time, buyers who have been preapproved for a loan have an advantage over buyers who haven't been proved creditworthy.

Lenders don't charge for prequalification. Given the extra work involved, some lenders do charge for preapproval (perhaps a few hundred dollars). Other lenders, however, offer free preapprovals to gain borrower loyalty. Don't choose a lender just because the lender doesn't charge for preapproval. That lender may not have the best loan terms.

If you do choose to get preapproved with a lender that charges for it, be sure that you're soon going to go through with a home purchase. Otherwise, you'll have thrown good money down the drain.

Even if you plan to shop on your own, talking to a mortgage broker may be worthwhile. At the very least, you can compare what you find with what brokers say they can get for you.

Be aware, though, that some brokers only tell you what you want to hear — that they can beat your best find. Later, you may discover that the broker isn't able to deliver when the time comes. If you find a good deal on your own and want to check with a mortgage broker to see what she has to offer, it may be wise not to tell the broker the terms of the best deal you've found. If you do, more than a few brokers will always come up with something that they say can beat it.

When a mortgage broker quotes you a really good deal (you'll know this if you've shopped a little yourself), ask who the lender is. Most brokers refuse to reveal this information until you pay the few hundred dollars to cover the appraisal and credit report. In most cases, you can check with the actual lender to verify the interest rate and points that the broker quoted you and make sure that you're eligible for the loan. (In some cases, lenders don't market loans directly to the public.)

Should you discover, in calling the lender directly, that the lender doesn't offer such attractive terms to its customers, don't leap to the conclusion that the mortgage broker lied to you. In rare cases, a mortgage broker may offer you a slightly better deal than what you could have gotten on your own.

If the broker was playing games to get your business, charging the broker's up-front fee on your credit card allows you to dispute the charge and get your money back.

Should you apply for more than one mortgage?

When you applied to college or for your last job, you likely didn't apply only to your first choice. You probably had a backup or two or three. Thus, when the time comes to apply for a mortgage, you may be tempted to apply to more than one mortgage lender. The advantage — if one lender doesn't deliver, you have a backup to . . . well, fall back upon.

However, we believe that if you do your homework and pick a good lender with a reputation for low rates, quality service, and playing straight and meeting borrowers' expectations, applying for more than one mortgage isn't necessary on most properties. When you apply for a second loan, you must pay additional application fees and spend more time and effort completing extra paperwork.

Applying to more than one mortgage lender makes more sense in special situations where you run a greater risk for having your loan application denied. The first case is when you have credit problems. Read Chapter 2 to whip your finances into shape before you embark on the home-buying journey; read Chapter 7 for tips on completing your loan application in a way that will make lenders salivate.

The second circumstance under which it makes sense to apply to more than one mortgage lender is when you want to buy a physically or legally "difficult" property. It's impossible, of course, to know in advance all the types of property idiosyncrasies that will upset a particular lender. In fact, both of your authors, earlier in our homeownership days, were denied mortgages because our prospective homes had quirks that a particular lender didn't care for. Minimize your chances for negative surprises by asking your agent and property inspector whether any aspects of the property may give a lender cause for concern.

If you apply for two loans, tell both lenders that you're applying elsewhere. When the second lender pulls your credit report, the first lender's recent inquiry will show up. (Less-than-candid borrowers almost always get caught this way.) Also tell both lenders that you're sincerely interested — just as you would tell all prospective employers.

Chapter 7

Mortgage Quandaries, Conundrums, and Paperwork

In This Chapter

▶ Overcoming common mortgage problems

▶ Handling lower-than-expected appraisals

▶ Completing mortgage forms

*U*nderstanding and selecting a mortgage (the subject of Chapter 6) isn't all that difficult a project after you cut through the jargon and know how to think about your overall financial situation and goals.

Unfortunately, when you apply for a mortgage, obstacles may get in your way. In this chapter, we show you how to glide by these irritating and sometimes not-so-trivial challenges. We also answer your queries about other perplexing (and, in some cases, desirable) alternatives you may have.

In the last section of this chapter, we explain how to complete those dreaded mortgage-application forms.

Conquering Common Mortgage Problems

Few things in life are more frustrating than not being able to have something you really want, especially if you perceive, rightly or wrongly, that most other people you know have it. If you want to buy a home, and you can't finance the purchase, odds are that your dream will have to be put on hold.

Don't despair if obstacles stand in your way. You may have to exhibit a bit more patience than usual, but we've never met anyone who was determined to buy a home who wasn't able to overcome credit or other problems. This chapter shows you how to get the financing you need and deserve!

Insufficient income

Your desired mortgage lender may reject your loan application if you appear to be stretching yourself too thin financially. Although getting angry and sticking pins in your little banker doll is a natural first reaction, you should actually be grateful. Why? Because the lender may be doing you a huge favor by keeping you from buying a home that will prevent you from saving money and achieving other financial goals that may be important to you over time. (For more on this topic, read Chapters 2 and 3 about getting your financial house in order and determining how much home you really can afford.)

If you *know* that you can afford the home that you have your sights set on, here are some keys to getting your loan approved:

✔ **Be patient.** When you have a low income (for example, if you're self-employed and have been deducting everything but the kitchen sink as a business expense), you may need to wait a year or two so that you can demonstrate a higher income.

✔ **Put more money down.** If you make a down payment of 25 to 30 percent or more, some mortgage lenders can approve you for their no-income-verification mortgage loan (in rare cases, they'll do so for 20 percent down). Generally speaking, such mortgages come with higher interest rates than conventional loans, so recognize that you must pay a premium for this type of loan.

✔ **Get a cosigner.** You always knew that you'd hit your parents up again someday for help and favors. If your folks are in good financial shape, they may be able to cosign a loan to help you qualify. A financially solvent sibling, rich aunt, or wealthy pal can do the same.

Be sure to consider the financial and nonfinancial ramifications of having a relative or buddy cosign a loan with you. If you default on the loan or make payments late, you'll besmirch not only your credit history, but also your cosigner's. At a minimum, have a frank discussion about such issues before you enter into such an arrangement, and be sure to write up a loan agreement with your benevolent cosigner.

Debt and credit problems

When you seek to take out a mortgage, lenders examine your credit history, which is detailed in your personal credit report. Lenders also analyze your current debts and liabilities, which you provide on your mortgage application. Your current debts and credit history can produce a number of red flags that may make lenders skittish about lending you money. This section tells you how to deal with the typical problems that concern lenders.

Credit report boo-boos

As you may know, creditors can report your loan delinquencies and defaults to credit bureaus. These blemishes will show up on your personal credit report.

Here's our suggested plan of attack for dealing with such problems:

- ✓ **Be proactive.** If you know that your credit report includes warts and imperfections, write a concise letter to the lender explaining why the flaws are there. For example, maybe you were late on some of your loan payments once because you were out of the country and didn't get your bills processed in time. Or perhaps you lost your job unexpectedly and fell behind in your payments until you located new employment.

- ✓ **Shop around for understanding and flexible lenders.** Some lenders are more sympathetic to the fact that you're human and have sometimes erred. As you interview lenders, inquire whether your previous credit blemishes may pose a problem. You may also consider enlisting the services of a mortgage broker, who may well be more accustomed to dealing with loan problems.

- ✓ **Look to the property seller for a loan.** Property sellers who are interested in playing lender can also be flexible. Surprisingly, some won't even check your credit report. Those who check your credit report may be more willing than banks and other mortgage lenders to forgive past problems, especially if you're financially healthy and strong today.

- ✓ **Fight and correct errors.** Credit reporting agencies and creditors who report information to the agencies make mistakes. Unfortunately, in the financial world you're guilty until you can convince the credit agencies that you're innocent. Start by identifying the erroneous information on your credit report. Should the erroneous information pertain to an account that you never had, tell the credit bureau to examine the possibility that the derogatory information belongs on someone else's report.

  If the bad data *is* for one of your accounts, but a creditor (for example, First Usury Bank, from which you obtained an auto loan) has made an error, you'll likely have to hound such a creditor until it instructs the credit bureau to fix the mistake. To get these sorts of errors corrected, you must be persistent and patient. By law, the credit bureaus are supposed to respond to your inquiry within 30 days. Should you get the runaround from the front-line customer-service representatives you talk to, ask to speak with a supervisor or manager until you get satisfaction. If that technique doesn't work, contact your local Better Business Bureau (see your local phone directory), and file a complaint. You're also allowed to enter a statement of contention on your credit report so prospective creditors, such as mortgage lenders, that pull your credit report can see your side of the story. But your best strategy is to have the disparaging information removed from your credit report.

- ✓ **Get a cosigner.** As we suggest earlier, a cosigner, such as a relative, can also help deal with credit problems that are knocking out your loan application.

- ✓ **Save more, and build a better track record.** If you can continue to rent, buying yourself some more time may do the trick. Why rush buying if lenders avoid you like the plague and reject you or only offer loans with ultrahigh interest rates? Spend a couple of years saving more money and keeping a clean credit record, and you'll eventually have lenders chasing you for your business!

If you're having problems getting approved, sit down with your loan officer, and make a list of the items that you must rectify to get an approval. Instead of trying to guess what's wrong, you'll have a checklist of everything you need to correct.

Excess debt

If you're turned down for a mortgage because of excess debt (such as on credit cards and auto loans), be grateful. The lender has actually done you a favor! Over the long-term, such debt is a serious drag on your ability to save money and live within your income.

Should you have the cash available to pay off some or all of the debt, we emphatically urge you to do so. Mortgage lenders sometimes make this a condition of funding a mortgage, especially when you have significant debts or are on the margin of qualifying for the loan that you desire. If you lack sufficient cash to pay down the debt and buy the type of home you desire, choose among the following options:

- ✓ **Set your sights more realistically.** Buy a less expensive home for which you can qualify for a mortgage.

- ✓ **Go on a financial diet.** Your best bet for getting rid of consumer debt is to take a hard look at your spending (see Chapter 2), and identify where you can make cuts. Use your savings to pay down the debt. Also explore boosting your employment income.

- ✓ **Get family help.** Another potential option is to have your family help you, either by cosigning your loan or by lending or giving you money to pay down your high-interest debt.

Lack of down payment

Saving money in America, where *everything* is considered a necessity at one time or another, can be a chore. Should you lack sufficient money for a down payment, turn to Chapter 3 for suggestions about how to get financing.

Credit (FICO) scores

Lenders generally use a credit scoring system to help them streamline credit application processing. The most commonly used credit scoring system used by mortgage lenders is the FICO score. FICO is short for the company that developed this system — Fair Isaac Corporation.

Higher scores mean that the borrower is far more likely to make timely and complete payments when borrowing money. In other words, such borrowers are the types that lenders prefer making loans to and are generally said to be "low risk."

Credit scores such as the FICO score are determined by using information in your credit report. Because there are three major credit rating agencies (Equifax, Experian, and TransUnion),

you can have a FICO score from each of their reports. (We discuss credit reports and how to obtain them in Chapter 5.)

In the event that you're turned down for a mortgage or other loan, request a copy of your credit report and an explanation from the lender for the specific reasons that you were denied credit. You can improve your credit score over time by addressing lenders' concerns and using the solutions we present elsewhere in this chapter for dealing with common mortgage application problems.

The best defense against being turned down is to examine, understand, and even improve your credit score *before* applying for a mortgage. Please see Chapter 5 for all the details.

Dealing with Appraisal Problems

Your loan application may be sailing smoothly through the loan-approval channels — thanks to your sterling (or at least acceptable) financial condition — and then, all of sudden (like in a Batman and Robin episode):

POW!!! BANG!!! THUMP!!! KABOOM!!!

The property that you've fallen in love with isn't worth what you agreed to pay for it, at least according to the *appraiser* — the person who values property for lenders. You may be shocked, dismayed, and perhaps even frightened that the appraiser has given such a low estimate. What course of action you should take depends upon which of the following three issues caused the low appraisal.

You've overpaid

Appraisals don't often come in lower than the contract's purchase price. When they do, more often than not they're low because you (and perhaps your real estate agent) overestimated what the home is worth. If this is the case, be grateful that the appraiser has provided you a big warning that you're about to throw away money, perhaps thousands of dollars, if you go through with paying the price specified in your purchase contract. It's also possible that the appraised value is low because the home needs a new roof, new foundation, or other major structural repairs. (We cover property inspections in Chapter 13.)

Because you obviously liked the property (after all, you made an offer to buy it), use the appraisal as a tool to either renegotiate a lower purchase price with the seller or get a credit from the seller to do necessary repairs. If the seller won't play, move on to other properties. Also reevaluate your agent's knowledge of property values and motivations — consider finding a new agent if the present agent prodded you into overpaying.

The appraiser doesn't know your area

If you and your agent know local property values and have seen comparable homes that fully justify the price you agreed to pay, it's possible that the appraiser simply doesn't know local property values. One clue that this is the case is if the appraiser doesn't normally appraise homes in your area. Another clue is if the comparable properties that the appraiser chose aren't good, representative comparisons. We get into exactly what is and isn't a comparable property in Chapter 10.

If you have reason to believe that the appraiser may be off base, express your concern to the mortgage lender that you're using. Also, request a copy of the appraisal, which you're entitled to. The lender should be able to shed some light on the appraiser's background and experience with valuing homes in your area. Sometimes, you can have a reappraisal done without an additional charge.

The appraiser/lender is sandbagging you

The least likely explanation for a low appraisal is that your mortgage lender may have come in with a low appraisal to get out of doing a loan that she feels is undesirable. In the business, this trick is called *sandbagging*.

Lenders that use in-house appraisals are best able to torpedo loans that they don't want to make. Why, you may reasonably wonder, would lenders sandbag you on a loan for which they've willingly accepted a loan application? Remember that the eager front-line mortgage person at the bank or the mortgage broker who placed your loan with the lender likely works on commission and isn't the person who makes mortgage-approval decisions at the lending company.

Should you suspect that your loan is being sandbagged, request a copy of your appraisal. If comparable sales data show that the appraisal is low, confront your lender on this issue, and see what she has to say about it. If you get the runaround and no satisfaction, ask for a full refund of your loan application and appraisal fees, and take your business to another lender. You may also consider filing a complaint with the state organization that regulates mortgage lenders in your area.

Those Darn Mortgage Forms

When you finally get to the part of your home purchase where you're applying for a mortgage, you're likely to become so sick of paperwork that you'll yearn for a paperless society. You may be interested in knowing that some lenders (especially online lenders, which we discuss in detail in Chapter 11) are moving to a more computer-driven (and less pen-and-paper-oriented) mortgage-application process. No matter; you're still going to have to provide a great deal of personal and financial information.

In this section, we review the forms that you'll commonly be asked to complete in the mortgage-application process. If you're working with a skilled person at the mortgage lender's firm or mortgage-brokerage firm that you've chosen, that person can help you to navigate most of this dreaded paperwork.

But we know that you probably have some questions about what kinds of information you're required to provide versus information that you don't have to provide. You also may be uncomfortable revealing certain, how shall we say, less-than-flattering facts about your situation, facts that you feel may jeopardize your qualifications for a mortgage. Finally, no matter how good the mortgage person that you're working with is, the burden is still upon you to pull together many facts, figures, and documents. So here we are, right by your side to coach and cajole you along the way.

The laundry list of required documents

Many mortgage lenders provide you an incredibly lengthy list of documents that they require with mortgage applications (see Figure 7-1). One quick look at the list is enough to make most prospective home buyers continue renting!

But don't despair. This list must cover all possible situations, so some of the items won't apply to you. We hope, for example, that you're not simultaneously receiving a diploma, divorcing, being relocated by your employer, and completing bankruptcy papers!

Most of the items on this laundry list are required in order to prove and substantiate your current financial status to the mortgage lender and, subsequently, to other organizations that may buy your loan in the future. Pay stubs, tax returns, and bank and investment-account statements help document your income and assets. Lenders assess the risk of lending you money and determine how much they can lend you based upon these items.

If you're wondering why lenders can't take you on your word about the personal and confidential financial facts and figures, remember that some people don't tell the truth. Even though we know that you're an honest person, lenders have no way of knowing who is honest and who isn't. The unfortunate consequence is that lenders have to treat all their applicants as though they aren't honest.

WHAT TO BRING TO YOUR LOAN APPLICATION

Use the following checklist to be sure that you bring everything you need to make your loan application an easy, hassle-free experience. ORIGINALS ARE REQUIRED UNLESS OTHERWISE STATED.

_____ **Sales Contract** (On the purchase of your new home)

_____ **Original Paystubs For Last 30 Days** (Showing year-to-date earnings, name and Social Security #)

_____ **Most Recent 2 Years Original W-2's**

_____ **Most Recent 2 Years Tax Returns** (With all schedules and signed in blue ink)

_____ **Year-to-Date Profit and Loss Statement and Current Balance Sheet** (If self-employed only)

_____ **Information on Residence History** (For the last 2 years - addresses and dates)

_____ **Coupon Book or Most Recent Statement on All Outstanding Loans and Credit Cards**

_____ **3 Months Bank Statements for All Accounts** (If any recently opened accounts or sizeable deposits, bring documentation to prove the source of the funds.)

_____ **3 Months Statements for IRA/Keogh/401K/Profit Sharing**

_____ **Transcript or Diploma** (If you were a student in the last two years)

_____ **Addresses, Loan Information and Leases (if applicable) on Real Estate You Currently Own**

_____ **Current Landlord's Name, Phone Number and Address or 12 Months Cancelled Checks**

_____ **Copy of Sales Contract** (If you are selling your present home)

_____ **Complete Divorce Papers or Legal Separation Agreement** (If you pay/receive child support or alimony)

_____ **Relocation Agreement** (If you are being transferred into the area)

_____ **Bankruptcy Papers including Schedule of Creditors and Discharge Papers** (If applicable)

_____ **Award Letter and Copy of Most Recent Check** (If you receive Social Security, retirement or disability)

_____ **Pink Slip(s) on Car(s)** (If cars are 5 years old or less)

_____ **Copy of Driver's License and Social Security Card** (FHA only)

_____ **Original Certificate of Eligibility and DD214** (VA only)

_____ **$_____Check for Appraisal and Credit Report Fees**

_____ _____

Figure 7-1:
This is an example of the myriad documents that mortgage lenders ask you to fork over.

Even though lenders require all this documentation, some buyers still falsify information. Worse yet, some mortgage brokers, in their quest to close more loans and earn more commissions, even coach buyers to lie in order to qualify for a loan. One example of how people cheat: Some self-employed people create bogus tax returns with inflated incomes. Although a few people have gotten away with such deception, we strongly discourage this wayward path — it's fraudulent.

Falsifying loan documents is committing perjury and fraud, and isn't in your best interests. Besides the obvious legal objections, you can end up with more mortgage debt than you can really afford. Plus mortgage lenders can catch you in your lies. How? Well, some mortgage lenders have you sign a document (at the time you close on your home purchase or at the time of your loan application) that allows them to request *directly from the IRS* a copy of the actual return you filed with the IRS. *Form 4506* grants the lender permission to get a copy of your tax return. Another document that the lender may spring on you is *Form 8821,* which lenders give to marginal borrowers. This form asks the IRS to confirm specific information and is more likely to be sent in by a lender to verify your financial information as reported for tax purposes (see Figure 7-2). You'll typically get these documents at closing. You can refuse to sign them — but then again, the lender can refuse to make you a loan!

When you can't qualify for a desired mortgage without resorting to trickery, getting turned down is for your own good. Lenders have criteria to ensure that you will be able to repay the money that you borrow and that you don't get in over your head.

Permissions to inspect your finances

In order for a mortgage lender to make a proper assessment of your current financial situation, the lender needs to request detailed documentation. Thus, mortgage lenders or brokers ask you to sign a form (like the one shown in Figure 7-3) authorizing and permitting them to make such requests of your employer, the financial institutions that you do business with, and so on.

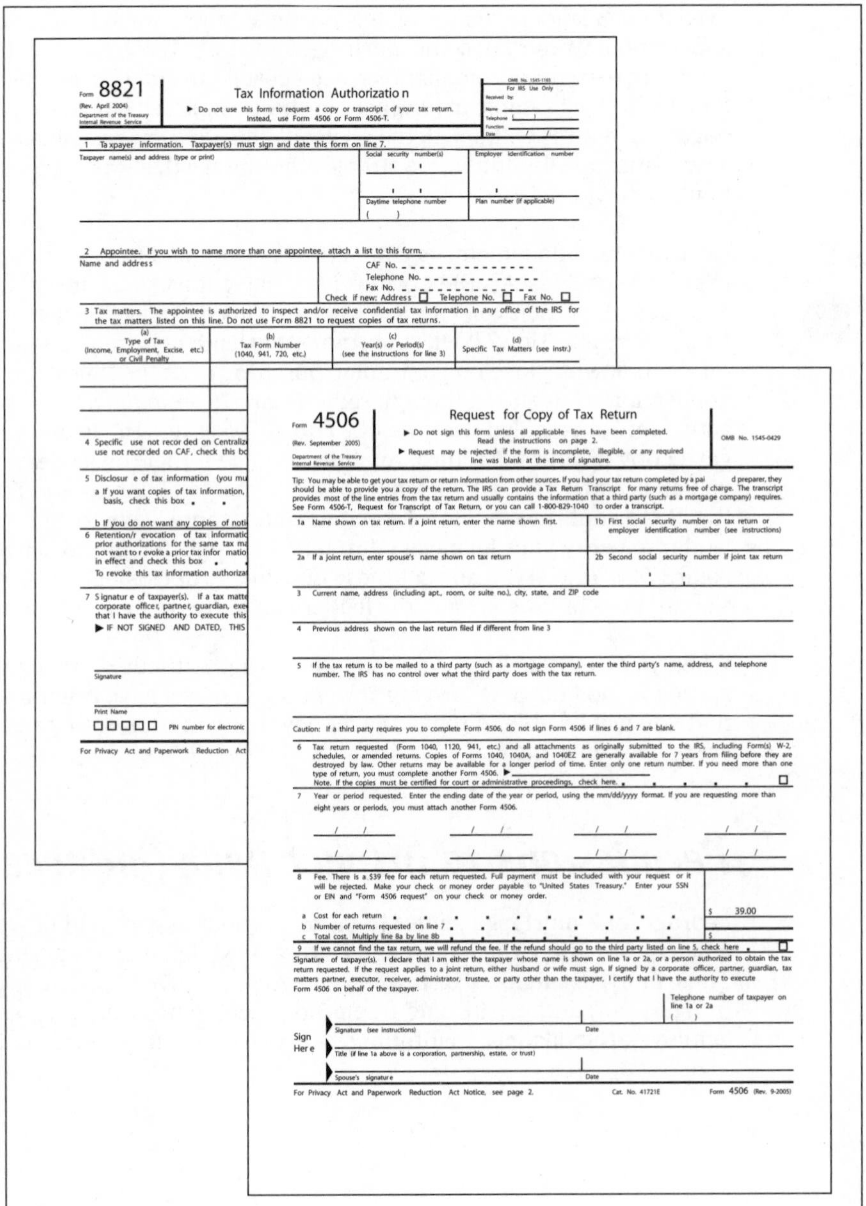

Form 8821
(Rev. April 2004)
Department of the Treasury
Internal Revenue Service

Tax Information Authorization

▶ Do not use this form to request a copy or transcript of your tax return. Instead, use Form 4506 or Form 4506-T.

OMB No. 1545-1165
For IRS Use Only
Received by:
Name
Telephone
Function
Date / /

1 Taxpayer information. Taxpayer(s) must sign and date this form on line 7.
Taxpayer name(s) and address (type or print)
Social security number(s)
Employer identification number
Daytime telephone number
Plan number (if applicable)

2 Appointee. If you wish to name more than one appointee, attach a list to this form.
Name and address
CAF No.
Telephone No.
Fax No.
Check if new: Address ☐ Telephone No. ☐ Fax No. ☐

3 Tax matters. The appointee is authorized to inspect and/or receive confidential tax information in any office of the IRS for the tax matters listed on this line. Do not use Form 8821 to request copies of tax returns.

(a) Type of Tax (Income, Employment, Excise, etc.) or Civil Penalty	(b) Tax Form Number (1040, 941, 720, etc.)	(c) Year(s) or Period(s) (see the instructions for line 3)	(d) Specific Tax Matters (see instr.)

4 Specific use not recorded on Centraliz…
use not recorded on CAF, check this bo…

5 Disclosure of tax information (you mu…
a If you want copies of tax information,…
basis, check this box
b If you do not want any copies of noti…

6 Retention/revocation of tax informatio…
prior authorizations for the same tax ma…
not want to revoke a prior tax informatio…
in effect and check this box
To revoke this tax information authoriza…

7 Signature of taxpayer(s). If a tax matte…
corporate officer, partner, guardian, exe…
that I have the authority to execute this…
▶ IF NOT SIGNED AND DATED, THIS…

Signature
Print Name
☐☐☐☐☐ PIN number for electronic…

For Privacy Act and Paperwork Reduction Act…

Form 4506
(Rev. September 2005)
Department of the Treasury
Internal Revenue Service

Request for Copy of Tax Return

▶ Do not sign this form unless all applicable lines have been completed. Read the instructions on page 2.
▶ Request may be rejected if the form is incomplete, illegible, or any required line was blank at the time of signature.

OMB No. 1545-0429

Tip: You may be able to get your tax return or return information from other sources. If you had your tax return completed by a paid preparer, they should be able to provide you a copy of the return. The IRS can provide a Tax Return Transcript for many returns free of charge. The transcript provides most of the line entries from the tax return and usually contains the information that a third party (such as a mortgage company) requires. See Form 4506-T, Request for Transcript of Tax Return, or you can call 1-800-829-1040 to order a transcript.

1a Name shown on tax return. If a joint return, enter the name shown first.
1b First social security number on tax return or employer identification number (see instructions)
2a If a joint return, enter spouse's name shown on tax return
2b Second social security number if joint tax return
3 Current name, address (including apt., room, or suite no.), city, state, and ZIP code
4 Previous address shown on the last return filed if different from line 3
5 If the tax return is to be mailed to a third party (such as a mortgage company), enter the third party's name, address, and telephone number. The IRS has no control over what the third party does with the tax return.

Caution: If a third party requires you to complete Form 4506, do not sign Form 4506 if lines 6 and 7 are blank.

6 Tax return requested (Form 1040, 1120, 941, etc.) and all attachments as originally submitted to the IRS, including Form(s) W-2, schedules, or amended returns. Copies of Forms 1040, 1040A, and 1040EZ are generally available for 7 years from filing before they are destroyed by law. Other returns may be available for a longer period of time. Enter only one return number. If you need more than one type of return, you must complete another Form 4506. ▶
Note. If the copies must be certified for court or administrative proceedings, check here ☐

7 Year or period requested. Enter the ending date of the year or period, using the mm/dd/yyyy format. If you are requesting more than eight years or periods, you must attach another Form 4506.

8 Fee. There is a $39 fee for each return requested. Full payment must be included with your request or it will be rejected. Make your check or money order payable to "United States Treasury." Enter your SSN or EIN and "Form 4506 request" on your check or money order.
a Cost for each return $ 39.00
b Number of returns requested on line 7
c Total cost. Multiply line 8a by line 8b $

9 If we cannot find the tax return, we will refund the fee. If the refund should go to the third party listed on line 5, check here ☐

Signature of taxpayer(s). I declare that I am either the taxpayer whose name is shown on line 1a or 2a, or a person authorized to obtain the tax return requested. If the request applies to a joint return, either husband or wife must sign. If signed by a corporate officer, partner, guardian, tax matters partner, executor, receiver, administrator, trustee, or party other than the taxpayer, I certify that I have the authority to execute Form 4506 on behalf of the taxpayer.

Telephone number of taxpayer on line 1a or 2a

Sign Here
▶ Signature (see instructions) Date
▶ Title (if line 1a above is a corporation, partnership, estate, or trust)
▶ Spouse's signature Date

For Privacy Act and Paperwork Reduction Act Notice, see page 2. Cat. No. 41721E Form 4506 (Rev. 9-2005)

Figure 7-2: These documents may be waiting to surprise you in the lender's loan papers at closing.

RELEASE OF AUTHORIZATION

I/We hereby authorize ComUnity Lending to verify any information necessary in connection with an F.H.A., V.A., Conventional or Second Trust Deed/Equity Line loan application, including but not limited to the following:

1. *Credit History*
2. *Employment Records*
3. *Bank Accounts*
4. *Mortgage History*

Authorization is further granted to ComUnity Lending to use a photostatic copy of my/our signature (s) below, to obtain information regarding any of the aforementioned items.

APPLICANT (Borrower)   SOCIAL SECURITY NUMBER

APPLICANT (Borrower)   SOCIAL SECURITY NUMBER

CLU/CR

Figure 7-3:
This type of form grants permission to your mortgage lender or broker to verify and document the financial facts of your life.

As we recommend in numerous places throughout this book, you should get, *in writing,* before you agree to do business with a lender, the lender's estimate of what your out-of-pocket expenditures will be in order to close on your home loan. The good news for you is that lenders are required by law to provide, within three days of your application, what's called a *Good Faith Estimate* of closing costs after you've initiated a mortgage with them (see Figure 7-4).

GOOD FAITH ESTIMATE - BORROWER'S SETTLEMENT COSTS

This list gives an estimate of most of the charges you will have to pay at the settlement of your loan. The figures shown, as estimates, are subject to change. The figures shown are computed based on the sales price and financing indicated.
The numbers listed on the left-handed column of this form correspond to the line number on the HUD-1 form, which will be used in conjunction with the settlement of your loan.
THIS FORM DOES NOT COVER ALL ITEMS YOU WILL BE REQUIRED TO PAY IN CASH AT SETTLEMENT; FOR EXAMPLE, DEPOSITS IN ESCROW FOR REPAIRS OR PEST WORK, YOU MAY BE REQUIRED TO PAY OTHER ADDITIONAL AMOUNTS AT SETTLEMENT.

This estimate was prepared for _____ on the date of _____
for the purchase /refi of _____
(property address)

Sales Price / Value	
1st Mortgage	
2nd Mortgage	
Total Financing	(-)
Down Payment	
Financed VA Funding Fee/MIP	
Total Financing including VA Funding Fee / MIP	

NONRECURRING CLOSING COSTS

801	Origination Fee Paid To Lender	%
802	Discount Points Paid To Lender (Govt. Pts.)	%
803	Appraisal Fee	
817	Inspection Fee (442)	
804	Credit Report Fee	
805	Appraisal Review Fee	
806	Document Preparation	
808	Processing Fee Paid To Lender	
809	Underwriting Fee	
905	VA Funding Fee	
810	Courier Fee	
811	Other _____	
813	Flood Certification	
815	Wire Transfer Fee	
816	Warehouse	
1101	Settlement or Closing (Escrow Fee)	
1102	Title Misc. Fees	
1104	(a) Title Insurance Lender's (ALTA)	
1105	(b) Title Insurance Owner's (CLTA)	
1103	Notary Fees	
1201	Recording Fees	
1106	Tax Service Fee	
1301	Pest Inspection	
1202	City Transfer Tax (3.30 x 1,000 of S.P. -split 50-50)	
	Subtotal Nonrecurring Closing Costs	

ITEMS PAID WHILE ACTING AS A BROKER

821	Commission Paid To Broker	%
	Rebate Fee (Premium Pricing and/or Servicing Released Premium) Paid To Mortgage Broker	
825	Processing Fee Paid To Mortgage Broker	
	Subtotal Nonrecurring Closing Costs	

RECURRING CLOSING COSTS OR PREPAID EXPENSES

	_____ Months Taxes	
	_____ Months Insurance	
902	PMI Premium (1st Year)	
	1 Month [ ] PMI 1 Month [ ] MMI	
901*	Interest _____ days	
	Subtotal: Prepaid Expenses	

TOTAL CASH REQUIRED: .TOTAL
Less monies advanced (escrow deposit)
Total cash required at closing

*This interest calculation represents the greatest amount of interest you could be required to pay at settlement. The actual amount will be determined by which day of the month your settlement is conducted. To determine the amount you will have to pay, multiply the number of days remaining in the month in which you settle times $ _____, which is the daily interest charge for your loan.

I hereby acknowledge receipt of a copy of this estimate.

Date: __ / __ / _____   Amended Date: __ / __ / _____

Borrower _____   Borrower _____

Borrower _____   Borrower _____

Prepared By: _____   Prepared By: _____
4/5/93

Type of Program	
P & I @ _____ %	
P/MMI	
P & I (2nd)	
Taxes	
Insurance	
HOA Dues	
Total	

CLU/GFE

Figure 7-4:
Here's an estimated closing-costs worksheet.

The Uniform Residential Loan Application

This is the big enchilada, the whole cannoli, or whatever you want to call it. Mortgage lenders and brokers throughout this vast country use the *Uniform Residential Loan Application* to collect vital data about home purchases and proposed loans. Many lenders use this standardized document, known in the mortgage trade as *Form 1003,* because they sell their mortgages to investors. When mortgage loans are resold, governmental organizations called Fannie Mae and Freddie Mac agree (if the mortgage loans meet federal standards) to guarantee the repayment of principal and interest, which makes it easier for lenders to sell the loans and more desirable for investors to buy them.

Some mortgage lenders may toss you a *Form 1003* and expect you to return it to them completed. Other lenders and brokers help you fill out the form or even go so far as to complete it all for you.

If you let someone fill out the *Uniform Residential Loan Application* on your behalf, know that you're still responsible that the information on the form is accurate and truthful. Also, be aware that in their sales efforts, some mortgage lenders and brokers may invite you to their offices or invite themselves to your home or office to complete this form for you or with you. Although we have no problem with good service, we do want you to keep in mind that you're not beholden or obligated to any lenders or brokers, even if they offer to come over and wash your car and provide you a pedicure! It's your money and your home purchase, so shop around for a good loan or mortgage broker. (Also, keep a copy of all the forms you complete for one mortgage lender to save time should you decide to apply to another lender.)

If, like most people, you take the first whack at completing this form yourself, we trust that you'll find the upcoming sections (in which we walk you through the major items on this application) useful.

1. Type of mortgage and terms of loan

The main items of concern to you in the first section of the application (see Figure 7-5) are the loan amount *(Amount), Interest Rate,* length of the loan *(No. of Months),* and the loan type (fixed rate or ARM). If, at the time that you're applying for your mortgage, you're unsure as to some of these options and what you're going to choose, simply leave the relevant spaces blank.

Your mortgage lender or broker completes the boxes in this section that don't make sense to you — *Agency Case Number* and *Lender Case Number.* Don't fill in these boxes!

I. TYPE OF MORTGAGE AND TERMS OF LOAN					
Mortgage Applied for: ☐VA ☐FHA	☐Conventional ☐USDA/RURAL Housing Service	☐Other (explain):		Agency Case Number	Lender Case Number
Amount $	**Interest Rate** %	**No. of Months**	**Amortization Type:**	☐Fixed Rate ☐GPM	☐Other: (explain): ☐ARM (type):

11. Property information and purpose of loan

Your mortgage lender is curious about why you want to borrow the vast sum of money that you listed in Part I — hence, Part II (see Figure 7-6). In addition to wanting to know the address of the property, the lender wants to know the legal description of the property. The *Legal Description of Subject Property* simply means the block and lot number of the property, which come from the preliminary title report. Your real estate agent, your mortgage lender, and you should each have copies of this report soon after you have a signed purchase agreement.

II. PROPERTY INFORMATION AND PURPOSE OF LOAN					
Subject Property Address (street, city, state & ZIP)					No. of Units
Legal Description of Subject Property (attach description if necessary)					Year Built
Purpose of Loan ☐Purchase ☐Refinance	☐Construction ☐Construction-Permanent	☐Other (explain):	Property will be: ☐ Primary Residence	☐ Secondary Residence	☐ Investment
Complete this line if construction or cnstruction-permit load					
Year Lot Acquired	Original Cost $	Amount Existing Liens $	(a) Present Value of lot $	(b) Cost of Improvements $	Total (a+b) $
Complete this line if this is a refinance loan.					
Year Acquired	Original Cost $	Amount Existing Liens $	Purpose of Refinance $	Describe Improvements ☐ made ☐ to be made Cost: $	
Title will be held in what Name(s)			Manner in which Title will be held	Property will be: ☐Fee Simple ☐Leasehold (show (expiration date)	
Source of Down Payment, Settlement Charges, and/or Subordinate Financing (explain)					

The information you include in the *Purpose of Loan* section tells the lender whether you plan to use the mortgage to buy a home, refinance an existing loan, or build a new home (Construction). The lender also wants to know whether the property is your primary or secondary residence, or an investment property. Your answers to these questions determine which loans your property is eligible for and the terms of the loans. From a lender's perspective, construction loans and investment-property loans are riskier than other loans and generally carry higher interest rates.

You may be tempted (and some mortgage brokers have been, as well) to lie on this part of the mortgage application in order to obtain more favorable loan terms. Be aware that lenders can — and sometimes do — challenge you to prove that you're going to live in the property if they suspect otherwise. Even after closing on a purchase and their loan, lenders have been known to ask for proof that the borrower is living in the property. They may ask you for utility bills (to see whether the bills are in your name), and some lenders have even been known to send a representative around to knock on the borrower's doors to see who is living in the home!

At the time that you apply for your mortgage, you must declare how you will hold title to the property — in other words, how the ownership of the home will be structured for legal purposes. We cover this important decision in Chapter 14.

Mortgage lenders also like to know where your down payment and closing costs are coming from to ensure that this money isn't yet another loan that may burden your ability to repay the money they're lending you. Ideally, lenders want to see the down payment and closing costs coming from your personal savings. Tell the truth — lenders have many ways to trip you up in your lies here. For example, they may ask to see the last several months of your bank or investment-account statements to verify that, for example, a relative didn't recently give you the money.

III. Borrower information

The third part of the *Uniform Residential Loan Application* (see Figure 7-7) is where you get to inscribe your name, rank, and serial number. When you're buying the property with someone else, such as your spouse, you have the added thrill of providing information about the other person, as well.

Figure 7-7:
Part III
says, "So
tell me
about
yourself...."

Borrower	III. BORROWER INFORMATION	Co-Borrower
Borrower's Name (include Jr. or Sr. if applicable)		Co-Borrower's Name (include Jr. or Sr. if applicable)
Social Security Number / Home Phone (incl. area code) / DOB (mm/dd/yyyy) / Yrs. School		Social Security Number / Home Phone (incl. area code) / DOB (mm/dd/yyyy) / Yrs. School
☐Married ☐Unmarried (include / ☐Separated single, divorced, widowed) / Dependents (not listed by Co-Borrower) no. / ages		☐Married ☐Unmarried (include / ☐Separated single, divorced, widowed) / Dependents (not listed by Borrower) no. / ages
Present Address (street, city, state, ZIP) ☐Own ☐Rent ___No. Yrs.		Present Address (street, city, state, ZIP) ☐Own ☐Rent ___No. Yrs.
Mailing Address, if different from Present Address		Mailing Address, if different from Present Address
If residing at present address for less than two years, complete the following:		
Present Address (street, city, state, ZIP) ☐Own ☐Rent ___No. Yrs.		Present Address (street, city, state, ZIP) ☐Own ☐Rent ___No. Yrs.

Yrs. School simply means how many total years of formal schooling you have under your belt. If you graduated from high school, you've had 12 years of schooling. Two- or four-year colleges add that many years on top of the 12. If you were silly enough to go to graduate school, add the number of years that you spent toiling away for those additional scraps of paper to hang on your office or den wall.

Should you leave a short-term residence or job off your application?

Many people who prepare resumes decide to omit positions that they've held for only a short period of time. The reasons vary, but most people do it to make their resumes look stronger and to avoid being perceived as job hoppers.

When you've had gaps in employment, it's better to show the gap than to be caught with your hand in the cookie jar — lenders often ask for the dates of your employment. Don't lie; lenders who catch you in one lie will scrutinize your loan application twice as carefully, looking for more inconsistencies. Lenders don't mind some job hopping.

Another section of the verification-of-employment request, which your current employer receives from the lender, asks what your prospects are for continued employment. The answer to that question is important, too.

In a sense, a mortgage application is like a resume. You want to present your information in its most positive, yet truthful, light.

The lender also wants to know where you've been living recently. (In addition, the company needs to know if your mailing address differs from your home address.)

Lenders are looking for some stability here. Most lenders also request a letter from your landlord to verify that you pay rent on time. If you've moved frequently in recent years, most lenders check with more than your most recent landlord. If your application is borderline, good references can tip the scales in your favor. If you've paid what you owed, and you've paid on time, you have nothing to worry about. If you haven't, you should explain yourself, either by separate letter to the lender or in the blank space on page 4 of the application.

IV. Employment information

Just as mortgage lenders want to know your recent residences, they want to know your recent work history (see Figure 7-8). If you've been in one position for at least the past two years, that's the only position you need to list. Otherwise, you must list your prior employment to cover the past two-year period. Again, the lender is looking for stability, which can help push a marginal application through the loan-approval channels.

If you're a detail kind of person, you may be wondering why the application asks for the monthly income from prior jobs but not your current one. The reason is that you provide the monthly income for your current position in the next section (Part V) of the application.

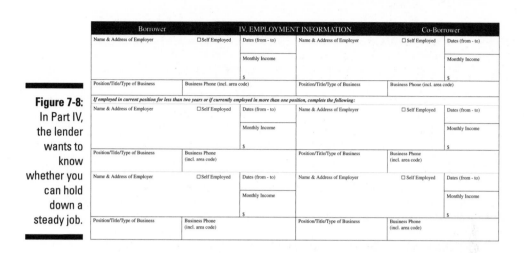

Figure 7-8: In Part IV, the lender wants to know whether you can hold down a steady job.

You may also wonder (and be concerned about) why the lender wants your current and previous employers' phone numbers. Shortly before your loan is ready to close, the lender may call your current employer to verify that you're still employed, but verification of employment is usually done by mail. It is highly unlikely that the lender will call your previous employers.

V. Monthly income and housing expense projections

Part V (see Figure 7-9) makes or breaks many a mortgage application. Here, you list your monthly income, including that derived from investments such as bank, brokerage, and mutual fund accounts. Most people's employment is what qualifies them to borrow money via a mortgage. If your income fluctuates from month to month, simply enter your average monthly income over the past 12 months. (Some lenders use a 24-month average if you're self-employed.)

Figure 7-9: How much do you make, and how much will you spend?

V. MONTHLY INCOME AND COMBINED HOUSING EXPENSE INFORMATION						
Gross Monthly Income	Borrower	Co-Borrower	Total	Combined Monthly Housing Expense	Present	Proposed
Base Empl. Income*	$	$	$	Rent	$	$
Overtime				First Mortgage (P&I)		
Bonuses				Other Financing (P&I)		
Commissions				Hazard Insurance		
Dividends/Interest				Real Estate Taxes		
Net Rental Income				Mortgage Insurance		
Other (before completing, see the notice in "describe other income," below)				Homeowner Assn. Dues		
				Other:		
Total	$	$	$	Total	$	$

* Self Employed Borrower(s) may be required to provide additional documentation such as tax returns and financial statements.

Describe Other Income

Notice: Alimony, child support, or separate maintenance income need not be revealed if the Borrower (B) or Co-Borrower (C) does not choose to have it considered for repaying this loan.

B/C		Monthly Amount
		$

Net Rental Income refers to the difference between your rental real estate's monthly rents and expenses (excluding depreciation). Rental property is property that you've bought for the purpose of renting it out. Therefore, *Net Rental Income* is the profit or loss that you make each month on rental property (excluding depreciation) that you own. If you've recently purchased the rental property, the lender counts only 75 percent of the current rent that you're collecting. When you've held your rental property long enough to complete a tax return, most lenders use the profit or loss (excluding depreciation) reported on your tax return.

Should you have other income sources, such as child support or alimony, list them on the *Other* line, and describe them in the last portion of this section. The more income you can list, the better equipped you are to qualify for a mortgage with the most favorable terms for you.

The *Combined Monthly Housing Expense* area on the right side of this section enables you to tally up your current and proposed housing expenses. If you're currently renting, simply enter your rent in the relevant box. Your proposed expenses refer to what your estimated expenses would be with the purchase of the home that you're expecting to buy. Your mortgage lender or broker can help you complete this important section.

If you're stretching to buy, make sure that the estimates that your lender or broker plugs into the estimated-housing-expense section are reasonable and not inflated. In their efforts to cover their own behinds and to ensure that you don't get in over your head, some mortgage lenders make estimates that are too high. If, for example, the mortgage lender estimates that homeowners insurance will cost you $100 per month, but you already have a quote in hand for good coverage at $80 per month, speak up about the discrepancy.

Should you be precariously balanced on the borderline between qualifying and not qualifying for a loan, lenders will be less inclined to approve your loan if a big difference exists between your current housing expenses and your proposed expenses as a homeowner. Lenders and mortgage brokers refer to people in this situation as subjecting themselves to *payment shock.* If you're in this situation, you should assess whether you can really afford that significant an increase in your monthly housing expenses (see Chapters 2 and 3).

VI. Assets and liabilities

In Part VI (see Figure 7-10), you present your personal balance sheet, which summarizes your assets and liabilities. Your assets are subdivided into liquid (for example, non-retirement account) assets and those assets that are not liquid (such as real estate). *Liquid,* in this example, simply means those assets that you can sell quickly to come up with cold hard cash for a home purchase or some other purpose.

Why so many spaces are allotted to checking and savings accounts puzzles us. If you can't squeeze your other non-retirement holdings in brokerage accounts or mutual funds into the small space provided for *Stocks & Bonds,* use the extra bank-account lines, and explain what you're listing there.

Liabilities are any loans or debts you have outstanding. The more such obligations you have, the more reluctant a mortgage lender will be to lend you a large amount of money.

When you have the cash available to pay off high-cost consumer loans, such as credit card loans and auto loans, consider doing so now. (If you opted for loan prequalification or preapproval, as we discuss in Chapter 6, the lender likely recommended getting rid of these consumer debts at that time.) Such debts generally carry high interest rates that are not tax deductible, and they hurt your chances of qualifying for a mortgage (see Chapter 3 for an explanation of this matter).

Note (at the bottom of the liability column) that you are to list child support and alimony payments that you make, as well as out-of-pocket expenses related to your job if you aren't self-employed. Such monthly expenses are like debts in the sense that they require monthly feeding.

Part VI continues onto page 3 and includes space for the details of rental real estate you already own. If you make a profit from such holdings, that profit can help your chances of qualifying for other mortgages. Conversely, *negative cash flow* (property expenses exceeding income) from rentals reduces the amount that a mortgage lender will lend you. Most mortgage lenders want a copy of your tax return (and possibly copies of your rental agreements with tenants) to substantiate the information you put in this space.

VII. Details of transaction

In Part VII (see Figure 7-11), you detail the terms of your proposed home purchase. The purpose of the first part of this section is to total the cost of the home, including closing costs. After subtracting the expected loan amount, this column arrives at how much money you need to come up with to close on the home purchase. Some prospective buyers find that after they've successfully completed this section, they must go begging to family or borrow more money to close on the purchase.

VI. ASSETS AND LIABILITIES

This Statement and any applicable supporting schedules may be completed jointly by both married and unmarried Co-Borrowers if their assets and liabilities are sufficiently joined so that the Statement can be meaningfully and fairly presented on a combined basis; otherwise, separate Statements and Schedules are required. If the Co-Borrower section was completed about a non-applicant spouse or other person, this Statement and supporting schedules must be completed about that spouse or other person also.

☐ Completed ☐ Jointly ☑ Not Jointly

ASSETS	Cash or Market Value	Liabilities and Pledged Assets. List the creditor's name, address, and account number for all outstanding debts, including automobile loans, revolving charge accounts, real estate loans, alimony, child support, stock pledges, etc. Use continuation sheet, if necessary. Indicate by (*) those liabilities, which will be satisfied upon sale of real estate owned or upon refinancing of the subject property.		
Description				
Cash deposit toward purchase held by:	$			
		LIABILITIES	**Monthly Payment & Months Left to Pay**	**Unpaid Balance**
List checking and savings accounts below		Name and address of Company	$ Payment/Months	$
Name and address of Bank, S&L, or Credit Union				
		Acct. no.		
Acct. no.	$	Name and address of Company	$ Payment/Months	$
Name and address of Bank, S&L, or Credit Union				
		Acct. no.		
Acct. no.	$	Name and address of Company	$ Payment/Months	$
Name and address of Bank, S&L, or Credit Union				
		Acct. no.		
Acct. no.	$	Name and address of Company	$ Payment/Months	$
Name and address of Bank, S&L, or Credit Union				
		Acct. no.		
Acct. no.	$	Name and address of Company	$ Payment/Months	$
Stocks & Bonds (Company name/ number & description)	$			
		Acct. no.		
Life insurance net cash value	$	Name and address of Company	$ Payment/Months	$
Face amount: $				
Subtotal Liquid Assets	$			
Real estate owned (enter market value from schedule of real estate owned)	$			
Vested interest in retirement fund	$			
Net worth of business(es) owned (attach financial statement)	$			
		Acct. no.		
Automobiles owned (make and year)	$	Alimony/Child Support/Separate Maintenance Payments Owed to:	$	
Other Assets (itemized)	$	Job-Related Expense (child care, union dues, etc.)	$	
		Total Monthly Payments	$	
Total Assets a.	$	Net Worth (a minus b) ▶	**Total Liabilities b.**	$

Schedule of Real Estate Owned (If additional properties are owned, use continuation sheet.)

Property Address (enter S if sold, PS if pending sale or R if rental being held for income) ▼	Type of Property	Present Market Value	Amount of Mortgages & Liens	Gross Rental Income	Mortgage Payments	Insurance, Maintenance, Taxes & Misc.	Net Rental Income
		$	$	$	$	$	$
Totals		$	$	$	$	$	$

List any additional names under which credit has previously been received and indicate appropriate creditor name(s) and account number(s):

Alternate Name	Creditor Name	Account Number

Figure 7-10: How much cash and how many assets do you have in reserves for a down payment and closing — and how much do you owe?

VII. DETAILS OF TRANSACTION	
a. Purchase price	$
b. Alterations, improvements, repairs	
c. Land (if acquired separately)	
d. Refinance (incl. debts to be paid off)	
e. Estimated prepaid items	
f. Estimated closing costs	
g. PMI, MIP, Funding Fee	
h. Discount (if Borrower will pay)	
i. Total costs (add items a through h)	
j. Subordinate financing	
k. Borrower's closing costs paid by Seller	
l. Other Credits (explain)	
m. Loan amount (exclude PMI, MIP, Funding Fee financed)	
n. PMI, MIP, Funding Fee financed	
o. Loan amount (add m & n)	
p. Cash from/to Borrower (subtract j, k, l & o from i)	

Figure 7-11:
Time to
calculate
your closing
costs.

VIII. Declarations

Part VIII (shown in Figure 7-12) shouldn't be called *Declarations;* it should be called *Personal Interrogation!*

Questions *a* through *i* (above the dotted line) are potential red flags to lenders. If you answer yes to any of these questions, explain yourself on a separate page or in the blank space on page 4 of the application.

The other questions are important details that lenders need to know. Don't worry; a yes response here won't kill your loan request.

VIII. DECLARATIONS				
If you answer "Yes" to any questions a through i, **please use continuation sheet for explanation.**	**Borrower**		**Co-Borrower**	
	Yes	No	Yes	No
a. Are there any outstanding judgments against you?	☐	☐	☐	☐
b. Have you been declared bankrupt within the past 7 years?	☐	☐	☐	☐
c. Have you had property foreclosed upon or given title or deed in lieu thereof in the last 7 years?	☐	☐	☐	☐
d. Are you a party to a lawsuit?	☐	☐	☐	☐
e. Have you directly or indirectly been obligated on any loan which resulted in foreclosure, transfer of title in lieu of foreclosure, or judgment?	☐	☐	☐	☐
(This would include such loans as home mortgage loans, SBA loans, home improvement loans, educational loans, manufactured (mobile) home loans, any mortgage, financial obligation, bond, or loan guarantee. If "Yes," provide details, including date, name, and address of Lender, FHA or VA case number, if any, and reasons for the action.)				
f. Are you presently delinquent or in default on any Federal debt or any other loan, mortgage, financial obligation, bond, or loan guarantee? If "Yes," give details as described in the preceding question.	☐	☐	☐	☐
g. Are you obligated to pay alimony, child support, or separate maintenance?	☐	☐	☐	☐
h. Is any part of the down payment borrowed?	☐	☐	☐	☐
i. Are you a co-maker or endorser on a note?	☐	☐	☐	☐
j. Are you a U.S. citizen?	☐	☐	☐	☐
k. Are you a permanent resident alien?	☐	☐	☐	☐
l. Do you intend to occupy the property as your primary residence? If "Yes," complete question m below.	☐	☐	☐	☐
m. Have you had an ownership interest in a property in the last three years? (1) What type of property did you own—principal residence (PR), second home (SH), or investment property (IP)? (2) How did you hold title to the home—solely by yourself (S), jointly with your spouse (SP), or jointly with another person (O)?	☐	☐	☐	☐

Figure 7-12:
Time to spill
the beans.

IX. Acknowledgment and agreement

If you haven't been honest on this form, consider Part IX (Figure 7-13) your
opportunity to commit perjury.

You're not off the hook if you had a mortgage broker or other person help
you with this application. Review the answers that they provided before you
sign the agreement. This is the time to ask yourself questions (and to review
your responses) to ensure that you've presented your information in a positive but truthful light.

IX. ACKNOWLEDGEMENT AND AGREEMENT
Each of the undersigned specifically represents to Lender and to Lender's actual or potential agents, brokers, processors, attorneys, insurers, servicers, successors and assigns and agrees and acknowledges that: (1) the information provided in this application is true and correct as of the date set forth opposite my signature and that any intentional or negligent misrepresentation of this information contained in this application may result in civil liability, including monetary damages, to any person who may suffer any loss due to reliance upon any misrepresentation that I have made on this application, and/or in criminal penalties including, but not limited to, fine or imprisonment or both under the provisions of Title 18, United States Code, Sec. 1001, et seq.; (2) the loan requested pursuant to this application (the "Loan") will be secured by a mortgage or deed of trust on the property described in this application; (3) the property will not be used for any illegal or prohibited purpose or use; (4) all statements made in this application are made for the purpose of obtaining a residential mortgage loan; (5) the property will be occupied as indicated in this application; (6) the Lender, its servicers, successors or assigns may retain the original and/or an electronic record of this application, whether or not the Loan is approved; (7) the Lender and its agents, brokers, insurers, servicers, successors, and assigns may continuously rely on the information contained in the application, and I am obligated to amend and/or supplement the information provided in this application if any of the material facts that I have represented herein should change prior to closing of the Loan; (8) in the event that my payments on the Loan become delinquent, the Lender, its servicers, successors or assigns may, in addition to any other rights and remedies that it may have relating to such delinquency, report my name and account information to one or more consumer reporting agencies; (9) ownership of the Loan and/or administration of the Loan account may be transferred with such notice as may be required by law; (10) neither Lender nor its agents, brokers, insurers, servicers, successors or assigns has made any representation or warranty, express or implied, to me regarding the property or the condition or value of the property; and (11) my transmission of this application as an "electronic record" containing my "electronic signature," as those terms are defined in applicable federal and/or state laws (excluding audio and video recordings), or my facsimile transmission of this application containing a facsimile of my signature, shall be as effective, enforceable and valid as if a paper version of this application were delivered containing my original written signature.
Acknowledgement. Each of the undersigned hereby acknowledges that any owner of the Loan, its servicers, successors and assigns, may verify or reverify any information contained in this application or obtain any information or data relating to the Loan, for any legitimate business purpose through any source, including a source named in this application or a consumer reporting agency.

Borrower's Signature X	Date	Co-Borrower's Signature X	Date

Figure 7-13:
Sign here.

X. Information for government monitoring purposes

You may skip Part X (Figure 7-14) if you want to. The federal government tracks the ethnicity and gender of borrowers to see (among other things) whether certain peoples are discriminated against by lenders.

X. INFORMATION FOR GOVERNMENT MONITORING PURPOSES
The following information is requested by the Federal Government for certain types of loans related to a dwelling in order to monitor the lender's compliance with equal credit opportunity, fair housing and home mortgage disclosure laws. You are not required to furnish this information, but are encouraged to do so. The law provides that a lender may not discriminate either on the basis of this information, or on whether you choose to furnish it. If you furnish the information, please provide both ethnicity and race. For race, you may check more than one designation. If you do not furnish ethnicity, race, or sex, under Federal regulations, this lender is required to note the information on the basis of visual observation and surname if you have made this application in person. If you do not wish to furnish the information, please check the box below. (Lender must review the above material to assure that the disclosures satisfy all requirements to which the lender is subject under applicable state law for the particular type of loan applied for.)

BORROWER ☐ I do not wish to furnish this information	CO-BORROWER ☐ I do not wish to furnish this information
Ethnicity: ☐Hispanic or Latino ☐Not Hispanic	**Ethnicity:** ☐Hispanic or Latino ☐Not Hispanic
Race: ☐American Indian or Alaska Native ☐Asian ☐Black or African American ☐Native Hawaiian or Other Pacific Islander ☐White	**Race:** ☐American Indian or Alaska Native ☐Asian ☐Black or African American ☐Native Hawaiian or Other Pacific Islander ☐White
Sex: ☐Female ☐Male	**Sex:** ☐Female ☐Male

To be Completed by Interviewer This application was taken by: ☐Face-to-face interview ☐Mail ☐Telephone ☐Internet	Interviewer's Name (print or type) Interviewer's Signature Date Interviewer's Phone Number (incl. area code)	Name and Address of Interviewer's Employer

Figure 7-14: Big Brother wants to know.

Continuation sheet

Turn over page 3 of the *Uniform Residential Loan Application* to reveal a largely blank page 4. This space is for answers that don't neatly fit elsewhere on the application. Here, for example, you may briefly explain why you've changed jobs so often, justify credit problems, list additional assets and liabilities, or explain why you were arrested for streaking during college. If you have nothing else substantive to reveal, you can simply choose to doodle aimlessly in this space with your favorite crayons! Perhaps you can even start to sketch out the details of your first home-renovation project.

Actually, if you don't have anything to put on page 4, you should draw a diagonal line across it so the lender knows that you saw it and have nothing to say. Be sure to sign at the bottom of this last page as well, even if you don't write anything on it. Many people don't sign — and no wonder, with the Grand Canyon of space between the top of this page and the signature line at the bottom!

Other typical documents

All mortgage lenders and brokers have their own, individualized package of documents for you to complete. Some documents are standard because they are federally mandated. Covering all these forms here is certainly beyond the scope of this book — and most people's attention span. What follows are some of the other common forms that you're likely to encounter from your mortgage lender or broker.

Your right to receive a copy of appraisal

It was not always the case, but you now have the right to receive a copy of the appraisal report. That borrowers didn't always have this right is a bit absurd — after all, you're the one who's paying for the appraisal!

To make sure you know that you have this right, the government requires that mortgage lenders and brokers present you with the document in Figure 7-15.

EQUAL CREDIT OPPORTUNITY ACT
(REGULATION B)

RIGHT TO RECEIVE A COPY OF APPRAISAL

You have the right to a copy of the appraisal report used in connection with your application for credit. If you wish a copy, please write to us at the mailing address provided. We must receive your request no later than 90 days after we notify you of the action taken on your credit application, or you withdraw your application. In your letter you must provide us with your name, the address of the subject property, your current address, and the loan number assigned to your transaction.

I (We) have read and understand the aforementioned conditions regarding my right to receive a copy of our appraisal and acknowledge receipt to a copy of this disclosure.

_____   _____
Applicant   Date

_____   _____
Applicant   Date

Figure 7-15:
Exercise your right to your property's appraisal — ask for a copy.

Despite the fact that the notice tells you to make your request in writing, try making the request verbally to save yourself time. Then, if your request is ignored, go to the hassle of submitting a written request for your appraisal (within 90 days of the rendering of a decision to approve or reject your loan). Appraisals are good to have in your files — you never know when an appraisal may come in handy. At the very least, you can see what properties were used as comparables to yours in order to discover how good or bad the appraisal is.

Equal Credit Opportunity Act

Another form you'll probably see is one that discloses that it is a matter of federal law that a mortgage lender may not reject your loan because of any nonfinancial personal characteristic, such as race, sex, marital status, age, and so forth. You also don't have to disclose income that you receive as a result of being divorced (although we think that doing so is in your best interest because such income may help get your loan approved).

If you have reason to believe that a mortgage lender is discriminating against you, contact and file a complaint with the Department of Real Estate or the government division that regulates mortgage lenders in your state. And start hunting around for a better, more ethical lender.

Part III
Property, Players, and Prices

The 5th Wave   By Rich Tennant

"Mr. Johnson, I think we've found your dream home! By the way, how do you feel about ghosts, ancient burial grounds and curses?"

In this part . . .

1t's time to introduce you to the various types of property you may consider buying and the people you may hire to help you buy a home. In addition to steering you toward winning strategies and winning players, we help you avoid loser properties and, well, losers in general. We provide a crash course on how to distinguish good buys from overpriced turkeys so that you won't overpay (and, in fact, may even get a very good deal) when you purchase your dream home. We close this section with discussing how to harness the powers of the Internet when conducting your home buying research.

Chapter 8

Where and What to Buy

*W*hat's your idea of the perfect car, the perfect job, and the perfect way to spend a day? Would you have said the same things ten years ago? Probably not. Perfection is a moving target — it changes as you change.

Where *the* perfect home is concerned, there's no such thing. For one thing, few people have the financial resources to afford what they think is the perfect home. Even if you're among the fortunate few with bucks to burn, it's still highly unlikely that one home will be perfect for you from birth to earth. The home that's great in your 20s when you're footloose and fancy free probably won't cut it when you're in your 40s if you're married or raising a family. Fast-forward another 20 years to when you're nearing retirement. You may want or need to move to a smaller home that's easier to maintain.

Don't fret. Even though no single home stays perfect forever, this chapter shows you how to profitably achieve sequential perfection in your homes. And because moving is expensive, we also show you how to minimize the number of times you buy and sell.

You probably know someone who's lost money on a house sale. We're sure that you don't plan to be the next victim of a capricious real estate market. Getting a bargain when you buy a home is a fine objective, but don't stop there. Don't you also want your home to appreciate in value while you own it?

The best time to think about how much you'll get for your house when you sell it is before you buy it. Never let your enthusiasm for a house blind you to its flaws. Before you buy, try to look at the property through the eyes of the *next* potential buyer. Anything that disturbs you about the house or neighborhood will probably also bother the next buyer.

We're not suggesting that you should plan to sell your house immediately after buying it. For all we know, you'll live happily ever after in the home you're about to purchase. Then again, an unforeseen life change, such as a job transfer or family expansion, may force you to sell. If that happens, making a nice profit can take some of the sting out of moving day.

Appreciation is handy for a lot more than just increasing your net worth. Given that your home increases in value over time, you may someday find that this *equity* (the difference between market value and the mortgage you owe) can help you accomplish a multitude of important financial and personal goals. You can use the money any way you wish — add to your retirement, help pay your kids' college education, start your own business, or take the Orient Express from London to Venice to celebrate your 25th wedding anniversary. Nest eggs are extremely versatile financial tools — and they're cholesterol free!

In a world filled with uncertainties, no one can guarantee that your home will increase in value. However, buying a good property in a desirable neighborhood tremendously increases your odds of making money. This maxim holds true whether the real estate market is strong or weak when you sell.

Property prices aren't static. They rise and fall due to such factors as the local job market, the supply of and demand for available housing and rental units, interest rates, and annual cycles of strong versus weak market activity. (For more on this subject, turn to Chapter 4.) Most of these things are beyond your control and ability to predict. But this doesn't mean that your financial destiny as a homeowner is a total fluke of fate. On the contrary, you control three important factors that greatly affect your home's value:

- ✔ How much you pay for your home
- ✔ Where your home is located
- ✔ What home you buy

The number-one controllable factor is how much you pay for your home. If you grossly overpay for your house when you buy it, you'll be extremely lucky to make a profit when you sell. That's why we devote Chapter 10 to making sure that you know exactly how to spot well-priced properties and avoid overpriced turkeys.

This chapter focuses on the other two crucial factors under your control: where and what you buy.

Location, Location, Value

If you're wildly wealthy, you can afford to live anywhere you darn well please. The rest of us, however, have somewhat more limited budgets. Even so, unless you're foraging at the bottom of the housing food chain, you'll have many choices on places to spend your money. Where you ultimately decide to buy is up to you.

You've probably already heard that the three most important things you should look for when buying a home are "location, location, location." That axiom is largely true. People buy neighborhoods every bit as much as houses. In good times and bad, folks pay a premium to live in better neighborhoods. Conversely, rotten neighborhoods ravage home values. You'd have trouble selling the Taj Mahal if it were surrounded by junkyards and chicken farms.

But simply stating that the secret of making money in real estate when you buy is "location, location, location" is akin to saying you'll make a fortune in the stock market if you buy low and sell high. It takes more than glittering generalities to make money. You need specifics.

First off, we don't agree that the three most important factors are location, location, location. Besides, we don't see much point in repeating ourselves three times — it's not like you're a complete idiot or something! *Value* — what you get for your money — is important too.

If, for example, everyone knows that Elegant Estates is the *best* neighborhood in town, you'll pay a hefty premium to live there. And although Elegant Estates is currently king of the hill and may stay that way forever, it's also true that this particular neighborhood has no place to go except downhill.

Other neighborhoods, ones that aren't held in such high esteem right now, may eventually improve what they offer home buyers and ultimately experience far greater property-value appreciation. Buying a home in a good location, while important, shouldn't be your sole home-shopping criterion. If you want to buy a home that is a good investment, you must look for good value. We explain how to do that in this chapter.

Characteristics of good neighborhoods

Good neighborhoods, like beauty, are in the eyes of the beholder. For example, being near excellent schools is important if you have young children. If, conversely, you're ready to retire, buying in a peaceful area with outdoor activities may appeal to you, and being next to a noisy junior high school is your nightmare! Neither neighborhood may suit you if you're the footloose and fancy-free type. Your ideal neighborhood is probably a singles' condo complex downtown, so you can be near the action day or night.

Personal preferences aside, all good neighborhoods have the following characteristics:

- ✔ **Economic health:** Nothing kills property values faster than a forest of "For Sale" signs precipitated by corporate layoffs. See Chapter 4 for ways to evaluate the employers and job markets in the various communities where you're contemplating buying a home.

- ✔ **Amenities:** Amenities are special features of a neighborhood that make it an attractive, desirable place to live. Wide streets bordered by stately oak trees, lush green parks, ocean views, quiet cul-de-sacs, parking, and proximity to schools, churches, shopping, restaurants, transportation, playgrounds, tennis courts, and beaches are prime examples of amenities that add value to a neighborhood. Of course, few people can afford to buy in a neighborhood that has all these amenities, but the more of these perks a neighborhood has, the better.

- ✔ **Quality schools:** You may not care how good or bad the local schools are if you don't have school-age children. However, unless you're buying in a remote, retirement, or vacation-type community, you had better believe that when you're ready to sell your house, most prospective buyers with kids will be deeply concerned about the school system. But you should care about the quality of nearby schools for more than just resale value, because good schools produce better kids, and that clearly affects the quality of life in the community. Don't rely on test scores or someone's opinion when assessing school quality; visit the schools and speak with parents and teachers to get a handle on the schools in an area.

- ✔ **Low crime rates:** Most folks today are concerned with crime — and well they should be, given that crime rates in many parts of America are too high. As with schools, don't rely on hearsay or isolated news reports. Communities compile crime statistics, generally by neighborhood. Call the local police department, visit its Web site, or check the town's reference library to get the facts.

- ✔ **Stability:** Some communities are in a constant state of flux. "Out with the old and in with the new" is their motto. Imagine what would happen to property values if a junkyard were replaced by a beautiful park. How about the reverse — an ugly, multistory, concrete parking garage appears where there was once a beautiful park? Check with the local planning department and a good real estate agent for the inside scoop on proposed developments in neighborhoods that you're considering.

- ✔ **Pride of ownership:** A home's cost has no bearing on the amount of pride its owners take in it. Drive through any neighborhood, posh or modest, and you see in a flash whether the folks who live there are proud of their homes. A neighborhood filled with beautifully maintained homes and manicured lawns shouts pride of ownership.

Property values sag when homeowners no longer take pride in their property. Avoid declining neighborhoods that display the red flags of dispirited owners — poorly kept houses, junk-filled yards, abandoned cars on the street, many absentee owners renting houses, high rates of vandalism and crime, and so on. Neighborhood deterioration is a blight that spreads from one house to another.

Selecting your best neighborhood

You may get lucky and find the neighborhood of your dreams right away. You're far more likely, however, to end up evaluating the strengths and weaknesses of several neighborhoods while trying to decide which one to favor with your purchase. If you're on a budget — and most people are — you may have to compromise and make tradeoffs.

Suppose that one neighborhood has the schools you like, the second is closest to your office (which would save you an hour a day commuting), and the third neighborhood is in a town with a delightful beach. They're all good neighborhoods. It's a tough decision.

Following are ways to research and select the best neighborhood *for you.*

Prioritize your needs

Buying a home when you have budgetary constraints involves making tradeoffs. For example, if you want to live in the town with great schools and parks, you'll probably have to settle for a smaller home than you would if you buy in a more average community. When push comes to shove and you have to choose a place to live, you must decide what is most important to you.

Research

As we say earlier in this chapter, in the section "Characteristics of good neighborhoods," you should examine the health of the local economy, area amenities such as parks and entertainment, school quality, and crime rates before you buy a home. So where can you find this wealth of information?

- ✔ **Tap local resources.** Check the local library. The local chamber of commerce is another excellent source of information.

- ✔ **Talk to people who live in the neighborhoods.** Who knows more about a neighborhood than folks who live in it? In addition to asking how they feel about their neighborhood, see what residents say about the other neighborhoods you're considering. If you can spark some neighborhood rivalry, you'll get the dirt about the other neighborhoods' lousy weather, parking problems, unfriendly or snobby owners, and so on. Renters are also a great source of information. Because they don't have a wad of cash invested in a home, renters are generally candid about the short-comings of a neighborhood. Last but not least, drive or walk through the neighborhoods at various times of the day and evening to make sure that their charm stays on 24 hours a day.

✔ **Get days-on-market (DOM) statistics from your real estate agent.** DOM statistics indicate how long the average house in an area takes to sell after it goes on the market. As a rule, the faster property sells, the more likely it is to sell close to full asking price. Quick sales indicate strong buyer demand, which is nice to have when you're ready to sell.

✔ **Get help from a professional.** Ask a real estate agent, lender, or appraiser to compare the upside potential of home values in each neigh-borhood. As Chapter 9 explains, home buying is a team sport. Get an analysis of each neighborhood's present and future property values from full-time real estate people.

Neither real estate agents nor lenders charge for opinions of value. They both, however, have a vested interest in selling you something. Appraisers, on the other hand, have no ax to grind. True, appraisers charge to analyze neighborhood property values and pricing trends. But if you're going to spend hundreds of thousands of dollars for a home, paying an additional few hundred dollars to get an unbiased, professional analysis of a neighborhood's property values may be money well spent.

✔ **Go online.** Several real estate Web sites provide local community data and information. See Chapter 11 for recommended sites and surfing strategies.

Fundamental Principles for Selecting Your Home

Good news. It doesn't matter whether you buy a log cabin, Cape Cod colonial, French provincial, Queen Anne Victorian, or California ranch–style house. You can make money on any property by following three fundamental princi-ples to select the home you buy. As you read the following guidelines, remem-ber that they're not hard-and-fast rules — exceptions do exist.

The principle of progression: Why to buy one of the cheaper homes on the block

An appraiser will tell you that the *principle of progression* states that prop-erty of lesser value is enhanced by proximity to better properties. English translation, please? Buy one of the cheaper homes on the block, because the more expensive houses all around yours pull up the value of your home.

For instance, suppose that your agent shows you a house that just came on the market in a neighborhood you like. At $175,000, it's one of the least expensive homes you've seen in the area. The agent says that the other homes around it would sell for anywhere from $225,000 to $275,000. You start to salivate.

Don't whip out your checkbook yet. Do a little homework first. Find out why this house is so cheap. If the right things are wrong with it, write up the offer. If the wrong things are wrong with it, move on to the next property.

Curable defects

If a house is a bargain because it has defects that aren't too difficult or expensive to correct, go for it. For example, maybe the house is an ugly duckling that just needs a paint job, landscaping, and some other minor cosmetic touches in order to be transformed into a swan. Perhaps it's the only two-bedroom house on the block, but it has a large storage area that you could convert into a third bedroom for not more than $15,000. For $190,000 ($175,000 for the house plus $15,000 to add the bedroom), you're living in a $225,000 to $275,000 neighborhood. Such a deal!

Problems like these are *curable defects* — property deficiencies you can cure by upgrading, repairing, or replacing the defects relatively inexpensively. Painting, modernizing a bathroom, installing new counters and cabinets in the kitchen, and upgrading an electrical system are some examples of curable defects.

Incurable defects

If a house has major problems, it's not a bargain at any price. Who'd want a house located next to a garbage dump? Or what about a *really* ugly home? Just because the seller made a fortune in the sausage business doesn't mean that you (or anyone else) would want to live in a house built in the shape of a giant hot dog. Maybe the house is cheap because a contractor says it's a wreck about ready to fall down, and you'd have to spend at least $125,000 on a new roof, a new foundation, new plumbing, and complete rewiring.

Enormous deficiencies like these are called *incurable defects.* They aren't economically feasible to correct. There's nothing you can do if a house is poorly located. Nor does it typically make sense to pay $175,000 for the hot-dog house so you can tear it down and build a new home (unless that's what comparable vacant lots sell for). By the same token, if you pay $175,000 for the wreck and then pour in another $125,000 on corrective work, you'll have the dubious honor of owning the most expensive house in the neighborhood.

Don't get us wrong. All rehabs aren't bad. We go into more detail about fixer-uppers later in this chapter.

The benefits of renovating cheaper homes

The less expensive houses on the block are also the least risky ones to renovate, thanks to the principle of progression. For example, suppose that you just paid $175,000 for a house that needs a major rehab. Your construction project is located smack-dab in the middle of a neighborhood of $250,000 homes.

The difference between your purchase price and the value of the surrounding homes approximately defines the most you should consider spending on a rehab.

In the preceding example, you should spend no more than $75,000 to bring your home up to the prevailing standard set by the other houses. Of course, this is assuming that you can afford to spend that kind of money (see Chapter 2) and that you have the time and patience to coordinate the rehab work or do it yourself. As long as you improve the property wisely and stay within your budget, you'll probably get most or all the rehab money back when you sell the property.

Use the principle of progression in conjunction with location, location, value. Buying one of the better less-expensive homes in a good neighborhood enhances your likelihood of property appreciation in the years ahead.

The principle of regression: Why not to buy the most expensive house on the block

You guessed it. The *principle of regression* is the economic opposite of the principle of progression.

If you buy the most expensive house on the block, the principle of regression punishes you when you sell. The lower value of all the other homes around you brings down your home's value.

If an evil spirit whispers in your ear that you should buy the most expensive house on the block in order to flaunt your high status in life, go to an exorcist immediately. Don't succumb to the blandishments of the evil spirit unless the probability of losing money when you sell fills you with joy. Satisfy your ego — and make a wiser investment — by purchasing one of the less expensive homes in a better neighborhood.

The most expensive house on the block is also the worst candidate for remodeling. Suppose that you buy a $250,000 home in a neighborhood of $150,000 houses. From an appraiser's perspective, the home already sticks out like a financial sore thumb. Spending another $50,000 to add a fancy new kitchen to what is already the most expensive house on the block further compounds your problem.

That new kitchen almost certainly won't increase your home's value to $300,000. No one can dispute the fact that you spent $50,000 on the kitchen if you have the receipts to prove your expenditures. But folks who buy $300,000 homes generally want to be surrounded by other homes worth as much as, or more than, the one they're buying.

Homes are like cups. When you fill a cup too full, it overflows. By the same token, when you make excessive improvements to your house (based upon sale prices of comparable homes in the neighborhood), the money you spend on the rehab goes down the financial drain. This phenomenon is called *over-improving a property*.

Even if you buy the least expensive house in the neighborhood, you can over-improve it if you spend too much fixing it up. The best time to guard against overimproving your house is *before* you do the work.

If you'll end up with the most expensive house on the block when you finish a project, don't do the project.

The principle of conformity: Why unusual is usually costly

The principles of progression and regression deal with economic conformity. If you want to maximize your chances for future appreciation of the home you buy, your home should also conform in size, age, condition, and style to the other homes in your neighborhood. That's the *principle of conformity*.

This principle doesn't mean that your home has to be an identical clone of every other house on the block. It should, however, stay within the prevailing standards of your neighborhood. For example:

- **Size:** Your home shouldn't dwarf the other houses on the block, or vice versa. If your home is smaller than surrounding houses, use the principle of progression as a guide to bring it into size-conformity with the other houses, and you'll increase your home's value. If, conversely, you have a three-bedroom home in a neighborhood of two- and three-bedroom homes, adding a large fourth bedroom to your house would violate the principle of regression.

✔ **Age:** You almost never see an older home in the midst of a tract of modern new homes. However, every now and then you find a brand-new home incongruously plunked in the midst of older homes. A modern home typically looks out of place in a neighborhood of gracious, older homes. Even if you get a terrific deal on the price, the modern home's lack of conformity with other homes on the block will probably come back to haunt you when you attempt to sell it.

✔ **Condition:** The physical condition of your house has a tremendous impact on its value. Not surprisingly, your home loses value if it's a dilapidated dump compared with the rest of the houses on the block.

Ironically, it's not wise to have your home in far nicer condition than other houses in the neighborhood. Even if your home conforms to all the other houses in size, age, and style, you still overimprove your home if the quality of materials, workmanship, and appliances in your home greatly exceeds the prevailing neighborhood quality standards.

✔ **Style:** The architectural style of the house you buy isn't critical — as long as it conforms to the prevailing architectural style of other homes in the neighborhood. From an investment standpoint, for example, it's not wise to buy the only Queen Anne Victorian in a block filled with Pennsylvania Dutch Colonial houses, or vice versa. Nor should you buy a three-story home when all the surrounding houses are one story high.

Your home doesn't have to be a bland, boring replica of every other house on the block. You can follow the principle of conformity and still express your individuality by the way you landscape, paint, and furnish your home. You know you've done well when people use words like "tasteful" and "exquisite" to describe your home. On the other hand, your decorating motif is a problem if folks refer to your house as "weird" or "eccentric."

Defining Home Sweet Home

What exactly is a home? When you come right down to it, home is an elusive concept. Everyone knows, for example, that home is where the heart is. That's fine and good if you're a romantic but not too helpful if you're a home buyer.

Up until now, we've loosely used the terms "home" and "house" to mean any place where you live or want to live. Under that definition, everything from a studio apartment in Manhattan to a grass hut on a Hawaiian beach qualifies as a home. Now, however, it's time to get precise. We're about to focus on the specific types of property you're most likely to buy: detached homes, condominiums, and cooperative apartments. Each of these options offers homeowners distinct financial and personal advantages and disadvantages that you must understand in order to make a wise buying decision.

Detached residences

If you were raised in a big city, your mental image of home is probably an apartment in a multistory steel-and-concrete building, an attached brownstone, or some other type of row house. If, on the other hand, you grew up in a small town, when someone says "home" you most likely visualize a brick or wood-frame residence with a white picket fence, a garden, and a swingset in the yard.

To distinguish the kind of home you see in areas of abundantly cheap land (and in programs like *Leave It to Beaver*) from condos, co-ops, and other types of property that folks call home, the correct terminology for the white-picket-fence type property is *detached single-family dwelling*. The key operative word is "detached," because such homes aren't attached to any of the surrounding properties. Now that you're properly dazzled by the depth and breadth of our knowledge, we'll just call these "homes" or "houses" like everyone else does.

Detached homes, like cars, come in two basic types: *new* and *used.*

New homes

If you're the type of person who'd never think of buying a used car because you like the new-car smell and don't like buying someone else's problems, you may feel the same way about new homes. They have some very appealing advantages:

- ✔ **A properly constructed new home is built to satisfy today's buyers.** Choosing a new home produced by a reputable builder of high-quality properties gives you the peace of mind of knowing that your home doesn't contain asbestos, lead-based paints, formaldehyde, or other hazardous or toxic substances. Furthermore, you can rest assured that your new home complies with current (and more stringent) federal, state, and local building, fire, safety, and environmental codes. Of course, there's no guarantee that future years won't uncover more hazards!

- ✔ **A properly constructed new home should be cheaper than a used home to operate and maintain.** Operating expenses are minimized because a new home should incorporate the latest technology in energy-efficient heating and cooling systems, modern plumbing and electrical service, energy-efficient appliances, and proper insulation levels. And with a quality new home, your initial maintenance expenses are practically nonexistent because everything is new — roof, appliances, interior and exterior paint, carpets, and so on. Other than changing the light bulbs, what's to fix?

✔ **A properly designed new home won't force you to adjust your lifestyle to its limitations.** On the contrary, new homes have enough wall and floor outlets to accommodate all your high-tech goodies — microwave oven; espresso machine; satellite TV and cable outlets; video recorders; CD and DVD players; hair dryers; electric razors; electric toothbrushes; and home-office gear such as computers, monitors, printers, broadband Internet connections, fax machines, and so on. No unsightly, hazardous tangle of extension cords for you.

New homes are only as good as the developers who build them. Visit several of the developer's older projects. See with your own eyes how well the developments have weathered over the years. Ask homeowners in older developments whether they'd buy another new home from the same developer. See what kinds of problems, if any, they've had with their homes over the years. Inquire whether the builder closed the sale on time and honored all contractual commitments, including the completion of any unfinished construction work, on time. Also find out whether the developer amicably fixed defects that occurred or whether homeowners had to take legal action to get problems corrected. Ask real estate agents how much homes in the developments have appreciated in value over time and how that compares with other homes in the general area.

As you might expect, new homes also have some disadvantages. To wit:

✔ **What you see usually isn't what you get.** You see a professionally decorated, exquisitely furnished, beautifully landscaped model home. You buy a bare-bones, unfinished house where nearly everything — appliances, carpets, window coverings, painting, fireplace finishes, landscaping, and so on — is an extra that isn't included in the base price. Developers often spend tens of thousands of dollars lavishly decorating model homes. Unwary new home buyers can spend small fortunes trying to duplicate the look of model homes. When touring a model home, ask the salesperson to explain exactly what is and isn't included in the no-frills base price.

✔ **Prices are less negotiable.** Developers maintain price integrity to protect the value of their unsold inventory of homes and to sustain appraised values for loan purposes. In fact, a developer who cuts prices is warning you that the project is floundering. Rather than reduce their asking prices, developers bargain with you by throwing in free extras or giving you upgrades (for instance, more expensive grades of carpet, better appliances, or granite kitchen counters instead of Formica) in lieu of a price reduction.

Some developers attract buyers by pricing bare-bones houses very close to their actual cost and then make substantial profits on extras and upgrades. If, upon doing some comparison shopping, you find that these items are outrageously overpriced, don't purchase them from the developer. Instead, buy the bare-bones house, and purchase extras from outside suppliers.

✔ **On a price-per-square-foot basis, new homes are usually more expensive than used ones.** No surprise. Land, labor, and material costs are higher today than they were years ago, when the used homes were built. And don't forget that you're buying a home without any wear and tear.

✔ **New homes in more developed areas are generally built in spots previously considered undesirable or unbuildable.** It's the old "first come, first served" principle. Earlier developments got better sites. Today's developers take whatever land is available — steep hillsides, flood plains, and land located far away from the central business area. Ten or twenty years from now, today's so-called lousy sites will be considered prime areas for new building — it's all relative.

✔ **New homes may have hidden operating costs.** Developments with extensive amenities usually charge the homeowners dues to cover operating and maintenance expenses of common areas such as swimming pools, tennis courts, exercise facilities, clubhouses, and the like. Some homeowners associations charge each owner the same annual fee. Others prorate dues based on the home's size or purchase price — the larger or more expensive your home, the higher your dues. If the development has a homeowners association, find out how its dues are structured and what your dues would be. Also find out what rules (called covenants) govern what you can do with your home as part of the development. Some covenants limit the colors you can use when painting the house, what additions you can make to the property, whether or not you can rent the property, and so on. Although meant to maintain high property values, some of these rules can create problems later as you seek to adapt your property to your changing lifestyle. For more detailed information about the important documents associated with homeowners associations and covenants, be sure to see the section "Attached residences," later in this chapter.

Sometimes, homeowners-association dues are set artificially low to camouflage the true cost of living in the development. When that happens, sooner or later homeowners get slugged with a special assessment to repaint the clubhouse, resurface the tennis courts, or whatever. Make sure that the homeowners association in the neighborhood you're considering has adequate reserves and that its dues accurately reflect actual operating and maintenance costs. Also check to see whether the historic rate of increase in dues has been reasonable and is in line with the current overall inflation rate, which you can probably determine by asking your lender.

✔ **You may have to use the developer's real estate agent to represent you.** Developers always have their own sales staff and their own purchase contracts. Some developers, however, will let you be represented by an outside real estate agent, which is called broker cooperation. Others insist that you use their agent. This is not a negotiable item. If you don't like it, your option is to walk away without buying a home.

If you've fallen in love with a new home, but the developer won't cooperate with outside agents, we recommend that you pay for an independent appraisal to get an unbiased opinion of the home's value. It's also wise to have your contract reviewed by a real estate lawyer of your own choosing. (See Chapter 9 for how to find one and what he can do for you.)

Just because a home is brand spanking new doesn't mean that it's flawless. People build homes. People are human. To err is human — that's why we have the expression *human error.* Moreover, builders work for profit and may be tempted to cut corners to maximize their short-term profits, not to mention that some builders simply aren't very good. Thus, even a brand-new, never-been-lived-in home should be *thoroughly* inspected from foundation to roof by a professional property inspector to discover possible human errors before you purchase it. We cover property inspections in our usual meticulous manner in Chapter 13.

Used homes

Perhaps you're wondering why we classify all homes as being either new or used. Why not "new and old" instead of "new and used"? Because *old* isn't a precise term. How old is old? Is a home built more than 25 years ago old? Or should the cutoff be homes constructed over 50 years ago? If homes built more than 50 years ago are old, what should we call homes built 100 or 200 years ago — decrepit? *Used,* on the other hand, merely means that someone owned the home before you did. (Considering how expensive homes are, you may prefer to call the place you purchase a "previously owned" home. If that makes you feel better, go right ahead.)

Regardless of what you choose to call them, used homes have many commendable features:

- ✔ **Used homes are generally less expensive than new homes.** As a rule, folks who bought houses years ago paid less for their homes than developers charge to build comparable new homes today. Furthermore, at any given time, more used homes are on the market than new homes. Good old competition holds down the price of used homes.

- ✔ **Asking prices of used homes are generally much more negotiable than asking prices of new homes.** Sellers of used homes don't have to protect the property values of an entire development. They typically just want to get their money and move on to life's next great adventure.

- ✔ **Used homes are usually located in well-established, proven neighborhoods.** With a used home, you don't have to wonder what the neighborhood will be like in a few years when it's fully developed. Just look around, and you can see exactly what kind of schools, transportation, shopping, entertainment, and other amenities you have.

✔ **Used homes have been field tested.** By the time you buy a used home, its previous owners have usually discovered and corrected most of the problems that developed over time due to settling, structural defects, and construction flaws. You won't have to guess how well the home will age over the years. You can see it with your own eyes.

No matter how well a home ages, you should still have it thoroughly inspected (inside and out) by qualified professionals before you buy it. The last owners may not have had the time, desire, or money to fix problems. They may also not have been aware of hidden problems. Be sure that the home meets today's building codes; doesn't have environmental, health, or safety hazards; is well insulated; and so on. Never try to save money on home inspections just because the house looks fine to you. The only exception to this stern admonishment is if you yourself happen to be a professional property inspector. (See Chapter 13 for more about home inspections and inspectors.)

✔ **Used homes are "done" properties.** When you buy a used home, you generally don't have to go through the hassle and expense of buying and installing carpets, window coverings, and light fixtures; finishing off the fireplace; planting a lawn; landscaping the grounds; building fences and patios; installing sprinkler systems; and the like. The work is already done (unless the used home is a major rehab project), and everything is generally included in the purchase price.

✔ **Buying a used home may be the only way to get the architectural style, craftsmanship, or construction materials you want.** What if your heart is set on owning an authentic 1800s New England farmhouse or a Queen Anne Victorian? Perhaps you want plaster walls, parquet floors, stained-glass windows, or some other kind of materials or craftsmanship that is unaffordable, if not impossible to find, in new homes. If that's the case, buy a used home.

Like new homes, used homes have some disadvantages:

✔ **Used homes are generally more expensive than new homes to operate and maintain.** Some used homes have been retrofitted with energy-efficient heating and cooling systems. Even so, a used home with 12-foot-high ceilings will always be more expensive to heat than a new home with 9-foot-high ceilings. By the same token, the older a used home's roof, gutters, plumbing system, furnace, water heater, appliances, and so on, the sooner you'll need to repair or replace them.

Before buying a used home, ask the seller for copies of the past two years' utility bills (gas, electric, water, and sewer) so you can see for yourself exactly how much it costs to operate the house. If the utility bills are horrendous, ask your property inspector about the cost of making the house more energy efficient.

✔ **Used homes generally have some degree of functional obsolescence.**
Examples of functional obsolescence due to outdated floor plans or
design features are things like the lack of a master bedroom, one bathroom in a three bedroom house, no garage, inadequate electrical service, and no central heating or air conditioning. How much functional
obsolescence is too much? That depends on you. What we think is
charming, you may consider an uninhabitable disaster. We deal with
extreme functional obsolescence in the fixer-upper section.

✔ **Wonderful used homes are sometimes located in less-than-wonderful
neighborhoods.** You may be attracted to an utterly charming older
home in a lousy neighborhood. Despite how much you think you'd love
living in it, don't forget that you'll have to travel through the undesirable
surrounding area every time you want to get in and out of your dream
house.

Even though you may be able to ignore gang wars and graffiti on every
wall, will prospective buyers be equally tolerant when you're ready to
sell? Remember: "location, location, value." No matter how stunning the
property or how great the deal you're offered on it, don't buy someone
else's problem.

Attached residences

If you can't accept the rules and regulations that would, of necessity, be
imposed upon you by communal living, don't read any further. You're much
too free a spirit to be happy owning an attached residence.

But if you're willing to put up with the constraints of communal living to get
the economic and lifestyle goodies associated with it, read on. You may be
pleasantly surprised.

Condominiums

What type of property offers first-time buyers their most affordable housing
option and gives empty-nesters who own detached homes an ideal lifestyle
alternative for their golden years? If you said "condominiums," go to the head
of the class.

Some folks think that a *condominium* is a type of building. They're wrong.
The kind of building in which a condo is located doesn't matter. Condos can
be apartments in a Chicago high-rise or split-level townhouses in Dallas or
Victorian flats in San Francisco. What makes a condo a condo is the way its
ownership is structured.

The investment value of detached homes

Americans have always had a deep-seated love for detached homes. Like spawning salmon returning to the stream where they were born, many people are inexorably drawn to the same kind of house they grew up in when it's their turn to buy a home. Even if you didn't grow up in a detached home, you may covet one because TV shows and advertisements have drilled into your head that such homes are desirable and a sign of success.

Buyer demand for detached homes makes them good investments. Compared with attached residences, such as condominiums and cooperative apartments, detached homes tend to hold their value better in weak markets and appreciate more rapidly in strong markets. Ask a local real estate agent for a comparison of property-value appreciation in detached versus attached residences, and you'll see what we mean.

First, a quick break for today's foreign-language lesson. In Latin, *con* means "with," and *dominium* means "ownership." Put the two words together, and you get *condominium,* which translates to "ownership with others." You'll definitely dazzle your pals "con" that etymology trivia tidbit.

Suppose that you buy a condo in a Chicago high-rise. You have a mortgage, property taxes, and a fancy deed suitable for framing to prove that you own unit 603, one of 100 condos in that building. So far, owning a condominium is pretty much like owning a detached home that floats in the sky.

When you buy a detached home, an invisible line runs along the border of your property to separate what belongs to you from what belongs to your neighbors. When you purchase a condo, on the other hand, your property line is the interior surfaces (walls, floors, ceilings, windows, and doors) of your unit. In other words, with a condo, you get a deed to the air inside your unit and everything filling it — carpeting, window coverings, and all.

Air and interior improvements aren't all you own. You and the other condo owners in the condominium complex share ownership of the *land* upon which the project is located and the high-rise *building* that contains your individual units. Thus, all of you own a portion of the roof, exterior building walls, and foundation — as well as a chunk of the garage, elevators, lobby, hallways, swimming pool, tennis courts, exercise facilities, and so on. All the parts of the complex beyond the individual units are known as *common areas* because you own them *in common* with all the other condo owners.

If you buy a condo, you automatically become a member of the project's homeowners association. You don't have to attend the meetings unless you want to, but you must pay homeowners-association dues. The dues cover common-area operating and maintenance expenses for everything from staff salaries, chlorinating the pool, lighting the lobby, and garbage collection to fire insurance for the building. A portion of your dues goes into a reserve fund to cover inevitable repairs and replacements such as painting the building occasionally and replacing the roof.

Before buying a condo, find out exactly what percentage of joint ownership you'd have in the entire condominium complex. That amount establishes how much you'll be assessed for monthly homeowners-association dues and what percentage you'll pay of a special assessment that may be imposed on owners to cover unforeseen common-area expenses. It also determines how many votes you'd have in earthshaking matters affecting the complex, such as whether to paint the building aqua or tangerine, whether to repair the existing treadmill in the health club or buy a new one, and so on.

Condominiums use several different methods to establish the ownership percentages. The simplest method is to give each owner an equal share of ownership in the entire development. Thus, each owner has one vote and pays an equal amount of the monthly dues and any special assessments.

If the ownership percentage is based on the size or market value of the condo, people who own the larger or more expensive units have more say in what happens in the complex than do owners of the smaller or less expensive condos. However, the heavy hitters also have accordingly higher monthly homeowners-association dues and pay a larger percentage of special assessments.

Why a condo?

Given their complexity, why do folks buy condominiums? Why doesn't everyone stick to simple, straightforward detached homes? Here's why:

- ✔ **Attached residences increase your buying power.** Compare the price of a two-bedroom condo with a two-bedroom detached single-family dwelling in the same neighborhood. On the basis of livable square footage, condos generally sell for at least 20 to 30 percent less than comparable detached homes. Owning your very own roof, foundation, and plot of land is much more expensive than sharing these costs with a bunch of other owners.

  For some would-be buyers, the choice is either buying a condo that meets their living-space needs or continuing to rent. Economic necessity explains why the path to the American dream for nearly one out of five first-time real estate buyers is condominium ownership. There's buying power in numbers.

- ✔ **Attached residences generally cost less to maintain than detached homes.** Suppose that you're one of 100 condo owners in a Chicago high-rise. Unlike the owner of a detached home, who has to pay the entire cost of maintenance expenses such as installing a new roof or getting an exterior paint job, you can split these maintenance expenses with the other 99 owners. Although replacing the high rise's roof, for example, costs more in absolute terms than replacing the roof of a detached single-family home, the cost per owner should be less. There's economy in numbers.

✔ **Attached residences have amenities that you couldn't otherwise afford.** How many people do you know who own detached single-family homes with tennis courts, swimming pools, and fancy exercise clubs? Most homeowners can't afford expensive goodies like these. But when the cost is shared among all the owners in a large condo complex, the impossible dream is suddenly your hedonistic reality. There's luxury in numbers.

✔ **Attached residences are ideal homes for some empty-nesters.** As you near retirement, you may find yourself rattling around in a detached single-family home like a little ol' pea in a great big empty pod. Perhaps a two-bedroom condo in a building with no maintenance hassles and a doorman who'll forward your mail while you're off on one of your frequent vacations could solve all your problems. There's lifestyle in numbers.

Condo drawbacks

Like detached homes, condos aren't for everyone. Judge for yourself how much the following drawbacks may affect you:

✔ **Condominiums offer less privacy.** Shared walls mean you can hear others more easily. Noise pollution is one of the biggest problems with condos and the one area that prospective condo buyers frequently over-look. Visit the unit at different times of the day and different days of the week to listen for noise. Talk to owners of condominiums in the complex to see whether they're bothered by noise pollution. If possible, spend a few hours or an evening in a unit. Be sure to turn off the easy-listening music that real estate agents may have playing during your tour of the unit.

As a rule, the fewer common walls you share with neighbors, the more privacy you have in your unit. That's one reason corner units sell for a premium. And if your unit is on the top floor, you won't have people walking on your ceiling (unless there's a roof deck, of course). The ulti-mate in condo privacy, if you can afford it, is a top-floor corner unit.

✔ **Condominiums are legally complex.** Prior to buying your condo, you should receive copies of three extremely important documents: a Master Deed or Declaration of Covenants, Conditions, and Restrictions (CC&Rs); the homeowners-association bylaws; and the homeowners-association budget. (See the nearby sidebar, "Condominium docu-ments.") Read these documents from cover to cover.

The CC&Rs, bylaws, and budget are legally binding on all condo owners. Even though they're bulky, bloated, and boring, you must read them very, very, very carefully. If you have questions about what these documents mean, or if you don't understand how they affect you, consult a real estate lawyer. And as long as we're talking about legal stuff, find out from your agent or the homeowners association whether the condominium is either currently involved in litigation or plans to be in the foreseeable future. Lawsuits are expensive.

✔ **Condominiums are financially complex.** As a prospective owner, check the current operating budget. Be sure that it realistically covers building maintenance costs, staff salaries, utilities, garbage collection, insurance premiums, and other normal operating expenses. If the budget is too low, prepare to get slugged with a massive dues increase sooner or later. By the same token, make sure that the budget includes adequate reserve funds to provide for predictable major expenses such as occasional exterior paint jobs and new roofs. How much is adequate? Three to five percent of the condominium's gross operating budget is generally considered a minimally acceptable reserve. If the reserve fund is too low, you're in danger of getting a special assessment in the event of a financial emergency.

We recommend that you review the past several years' operating budgets and financial statements for indicators of poor fiscal management. Here are some red flags to look out for:

- **Frequent, large homeowners-association dues increases.** Dues shouldn't be increasing annually much faster than the current rate of inflation.

- **Special assessments that wouldn't have been necessary if the association had an adequate reserve fund.** When discussing the budget and reserve fund, find out whether any dues increases or special assessments are anticipated in the near future to make up operating deficits or cover the cost of a major project.

- **Too many homeowners who are delinquent in paying their dues.** Operating expenses continue unabated regardless of whether or not all the owners pay their dues.

✔ **Some condominium rules are overly restrictive.** People who live in close proximity to one another need a smattering of rules to maintain order and keep life blissful. Too many rules, however, can turn your condo into a prison. For example, the condominium may have rules specifying what kind of floor and window coverings you must have in your unit, rules regulating the type or number of pets you can have in your unit, rules limiting your ability to rent your unit to someone else, rules forbidding you to make any alterations or improvements to your unit, rules limiting when or how often you can entertain in your unit, and so on. Before you buy, read the CC&Rs and bylaws carefully to find out exactly what kind of usage restrictions they contain. Some of these same restrictions can apply in new detached housing developments, as discussed previously.

If you discover that the condominium (or the new housing development) has restrictions you don't like, don't buy the unit. Trying to modify CC&Rs or bylaws to eliminate restrictions after you've bought a unit is usually an expensive exercise in frustration and futility. We know that you have far better things to do with your life than waste a big chunk of it haggling with condominium associations and their lawyers.

Prudent rental restrictions are good. Ideally, all units in the complex will be owner-occupied. If some owners *occasionally* let friends use their units or rent the units for a week or two while they're on vacation, no big deal. However, if most of the units are owned by absentee investors who rent them to an endless parade of partying strangers, that's bad if you happen to have difficulty sleeping with loud music blaring late at night. You may also have trouble getting a mortgage in a complex with too many renters.

✔ **Brand-new condominium developments have the same advantages and disadvantages as new detached homes, compounded by a condo's added legal and economic complexity.** If you haven't yet read the section about new detached homes earlier in this chapter, now's the time to do so. All our cautionary statements about new detached homes also apply to new condominiums. Like new detached homes, new condo projects are as good or bad as the developers who build them and the lawyers who create them. Because any new project, by definition, doesn't have a track record yet, you must visit earlier projects done by the same developer to see how well they've aged and how satisfied the condo owners are.

Some unscrupulous developers of new condominium projects purposely lowball monthly operating costs to deceive prospective purchasers into thinking that living there will cost less than it really does. These developers pay a portion of the monthly expenses out of their own pockets to keep project costs artificially low. The economic ax falls when the developer turns the project over to the homeowners association, which is soon forced to jack up the dues to cover actual operating expenses. When projected operating costs look too good to be true, they probably are. Compare the new project's projected operating expenses with the actual operating expenses of a comparable established project.

✔ **Where condominium parking and storage are concerned, the obvious isn't.** For example, does your condo deed include a deeded garage or parking space that only you can use, or is parking on a "first come, first served" basis? Are there extra charges for parking, or is parking included in the monthly dues? Are there provisions for guest parking? Is there a parking area for boats or trailers? Do you have a deeded storage area located outside your unit? If so, where is it? If you need even more storage, is any available, and how much does it cost? You're much better off getting answers to these questions before, rather than after, you buy.

✔ **Some older buildings that have been converted from apartments into condominiums have functional-obsolescence problems.** Older buildings frequently have excellent detailing and craftsmanship. However, they also often have outdated heating and cooling systems, and may lack elevators, which are mighty handy if, for instance, you're carrying groceries or suitcases up several flights of stairs. If you're buying a condo in an older building, find out whether utilities are individually metered or lumped into the monthly homeowners-association dues. Does your unit have a thermostat to control its heating and air conditioning, or is the heating and cooling system centrally controlled?

If utilities are included in the monthly dues, other condo owners have no incentive to economize by moderating their use of heat or air conditioning. If you're frugal, you'll just end up subsidizing owners who aren't. By the same token, in a building with central heating and cooling, your climate choices may be limited to roasting in the winter and freezing in the summer. Even if you can live with utility overcharges and personal discomfort, these factors may deter future buyers from purchasing when you try to sell your unit.

✔ **Size can be a problem.** Large condo complexes usually have a cold, impersonal, hotel-like feeling. And as a rule, people who live in large complexes tend not to pay much attention to finances and day-to-day operating details because the homeowners association hires professional property managers to run things for the owners. There are, however, a couple offsetting advantages to owning a condo in a large complex. If, for instance, several owners in a 100-unit complex fail to pay their monthly dues, it's not the end of the world financially. What's more, socially speaking, the odds of regularly running into an owner you detest diminish as the complex increases in size.

Don't buy into a small condominium complex unless you enjoy intimate relations with your neighbors. Carefully size up the other owners. Be sure that they're the kind of folks you can trust to carry their fair share of the load financially and operationally. In a small condo, you actively participate in the homeowners association because you must. Every vote has an immediate impact on your finances and the quality of your life. You don't have to love the other owners. BUT (note the big "but") if some or all of them are the type of people you'll be unable to get along with, don't buy the unit.

TECHNICAL STUFF

Condominium documents

If you're the type of person who only wants to know what time it is, skip this. If, on the other hand, you're fascinated by how watches are made, you'll love this sidebar. It explains how condominiums are created and operated.

A condo project is born when the project developer records the Master Deed or Declaration of Covenants, Conditions, and Restrictions (CC&Rs) in the county recorder's office, which officially makes this information a matter of public record for all the world to see. CC&Rs establish the condominium by creating a homeowners association, stipulating how the condominiums' maintenance and repairs will be handled, and regulating what can and can't be done to individual units and the condominiums' common areas. A similar procedure is sometimes used with new developments for detached housing.

Bylaws keep the condominium functioning smoothly. They describe in minute detail the homeowners association's powers, duties, and operation. The bylaws also cover such nitty-gritty items as how the homeowners-association officers are elected and grant the association the right to levy assessments on individual condo owners.

Last, but far from least, the developer creates a budget. Unlike our government, the condominium's budget can't (theoretically, at least) operate in the red. The current budget establishes how much the condominium expects to spend this year to operate and maintain itself. Condo owners also receive an annual statement of income and expenses showing precisely how last year's dues were spent and spelling out the condominium's current financial condition.

After reading the disadvantages of condo ownership, you may think that only a fool would buy a condo. Not true. We know plenty of content condo owners who'd never consider buying a detached dwelling. In our attempt to protect you, we sometimes go a little overboard on the cautionary side of things. We do so with your best interests at heart.

Condominiums make the most sense for folks who don't want operating and maintenance hassles (remembering that you'll still have the *expense*), want to maximize their bang for the buck spent on living space, and don't need a private yard. Buying a condo for a few years while you save enough money to purchase a detached home usually doesn't make economic sense. Given the expenses of buying and selling a condo, combined with its probable lack of decent appreciation, you're probably better off waiting to buy a detached home if you think you can do so within five years.

Cooperative apartments

The two most common types of attached residences are condominiums and cooperative apartments, which are usually called co-ops. You can't tell which is which by looking at the building or individual units. Like condominiums, what makes a co-op a co-op is its legal status.

Condos need to be inspected, too

When you buy a condo, you must inspect the entire building — not just your unit. As Chapters 9 and 13 explain, you need a professional property inspector on your real estate team because the structural and mechanical condition of a property greatly affects its value. What's the condition of expensive common-area components such as the roof, heating and cooling systems, plumbing and electrical systems, elevators, foundation, and the like? Are amenities such as tennis courts, swimming pool, and health facilities in good shape? Because you're buying part of all the common areas in addition to your individual unit, you need a professional's opinion of the entire complex's condition.

Check the building's soundproofing by asking other owners whether they're bothered by noises emanating from units above, below, or beside their unit. The building has a ventilation problem if you can smell other people's cooking odors in your unit or the hallways. If you discover that expensive repairs or replacements are needed, and the condominium's reserve fund doesn't have anywhere near enough money to cover the anticipated costs, don't buy a unit in this complex. Sooner or later, the owners will be hit with a special assessment and/or a big dues increase.

You'll be delighted to know that most of the pros and cons of condominium ownership also apply to co-ops, so you don't have to read a ton of new stuff. (If you haven't read the previous section on condos, do so now.) In the following sections, we just focus on the three ways in which condos and co-ops differ: the definition of legal ownership, management, and your financing options.

Definition of legal ownership: Deed versus stock

When you buy a condo, you get a deed to your unit. When you buy a co-op, you get a stock certificate (to prove that you own a certain number of shares of stock in the cooperative corporation) and a *proprietary lease,* which entitles you to occupy the apartment you bought. The corporation owns the building and has the deed in its name as, for example, the 10 West 86th Street Corporation. Thus, you're simultaneously a co-owner of the building and a tenant in the building you co-own.

In most cooperatives, shares are allocated based on a how big a unit is and what floor it's on. Thus, a top-floor apartment usually has more shares than a ground-floor unit of the same size. The more shares you have, the greater your influence in the co-op, because each share gives you one vote. Unfortunately, power has a price. Your pro-rata share of the cooperative's total maintenance expenses is based on the number of shares you own in the corporation. If you own a great many shares, your monthly expenses will be disproportionately high. And when you're ready to sell, your unusually high monthly expenses may reduce your unit's value.

Buying and selling co-ops is often challenging

Buying and selling co-ops is usually a lot more difficult than buying and selling condos. Most cooperatives stipulate that individual owners can't sell or otherwise transfer their stock or proprietary leases without the express consent of either the board of directors or a majority of owners.

Prospective buyers generally must provide several letters of reference regarding their sterling character and Rock of Gibraltar creditworthiness. In addition, they may have to submit to a personal grilling by the board of directors. Given that the owners live in close proximity to one another and depend upon one another financially, having the ability to screen out party animals, deadbeats, and the like is reasonable as long as that power isn't misused to unfairly discriminate against buyers.

Even so, some buyers find the approval process extremely intrusive and strenuously object to giving strangers their financial statements. The approval process also tends to slow the sale of co-op units on the market.

Owning a co-op is a two-edged sword. As a co-op owner, you have much more control over who your neighbors will (or won't) be than do condo owners. Unfortunately, that control cuts both ways. When you try to sell your unit, people you consider perfect buyers may be turned down by the co-op because your neighbors think that the prospective buyers would entertain too much or can't carry the load financially. Giving up the right to sell your co-op to the highest bidder may be too high a price to pay for the right to choose your neighbors.

Management: Homeowners association versus board of directors

If you've always fantasized about being the chairman of the board, here's your chance: Buy a co-op apartment, and work your way up the corporate ladder. Because your unit is in a building owned by a corporation, it's governed by a board of directors elected by you and the other owners. Nomenclature aside, just like the homeowners association in a condominium, the board of directors is responsible for the cooperative's day-to-day operations and finances.

Financing your purchase

Securing a mortgage to purchase your co-op may be difficult. Many lenders flat-out refuse to accept shares of stock in a cooperative corporation as security for a mortgage. Conversely, some co-ops absolutely won't permit any individual financing over and above the mortgage the corporation has on the building as a whole. These co-ops believe that one proof of creditworthiness is your ability to pay all cash for your unit.

Unless you're richer than Midas, don't buy a co-op if only one or two lenders in your area make cooperative-apartment loans. Odds are you'll pay a higher interest rate due to the lack of lender competition and lender concerns about the greater risks of co-ops. Worse yet, what if these lenders stop making co-op mortgages, and no other lenders take their place? You won't be able to sell your unit until you find an all-cash buyer (and they're few and far between) or until you have the financial resources to lend the money yourself to the next buyer.

Finding a Great Deal

If you're like most people, you're cursed with champagne taste and a beer budget. The homes you hunger for cost far more than you can afford. To buy one of these dream homes, you'd either have to get a really, really good deal or win the lottery.

Good deals *are* out there. The trick is knowing where to find them and how to evaluate them. Don't waste time looking at perfect houses if you're searching for a deal. People pay premium prices for perfection. The houses you find great deals on are imperfect properties — houses with either physical or financial problems. The deal you're offered is an inducement to tackle the problem. Whether the deal is ultimately better for you or for the seller is the question.

In Chapter 4, we discuss strategies for getting a good buy in any type of housing market. In the rest of this chapter, we cover special property situations that may be good deals or pigs in a poke.

Finding a fixer-upper

Fixer-uppers are rundown houses with physical problems. Real estate agents generally refer to fixer-uppers euphemistically as "needing work" or "having great potential."

Fixer-uppers aren't very popular in sluggish real estate markets. Most buyers in such markets don't want to put up with the hassle or financial uncertainties associated with doing a major rehab. They prefer to buy houses in move-in condition. Such a house is a safe but passive investment. Because its potential has already been fully realized, the new owner can't do anything to significantly increase its value.

A fixer-upper, on the other hand, offers potentially larger rewards to folks who have the vision to see beyond the mess that is to the wonderful home that could be. A fixer-upper buyer must also have the financial resources and courage to tackle the risks. If you fit that profile, here's what you may be able to look forward to after you've transformed your ugly duckling into a swan:

- You'll be living in a nicer home and a better neighborhood than you'd otherwise have been able to afford.

- Instead of buying a home decorated in someone else's idea of good taste, your home will be done the way you like it.

- You may have increased your home's fair-market value in excess of your out-of-pocket expenses for improvements you made.

For example, if you're handy, you can add thousands of dollars of value to a fixer-upper by doing labor-intensive jobs such as painting, wallpapering, and landscaping yourself. Sweat equity can pay big dividends.

If, like us, you're mechanically challenged, forget sweat equity. It's less frustrating and cheaper in the long run to earn money doing what you do best and then using some of that money to hire competent contractors to do what *they* do best. Poor workmanship is a false economy; it looks awful and reduces property values. Doing the project well the first time is easier, faster, and ultimately less expensive than doing it badly yourself and then paying someone else to fix your mess. If you're one of those rare people who can do quality work yourself, by all means try your hand at it — just be realistic about the required time and costs.

Some fixer-uppers are easy to spot. They look like classic haunted houses — peeling paint, shutters falling off, overgrown yard, and so on. Things don't get any better on the inside. These houses may need everything from a good cleaning to electrical system and plumbing overhauls.

Other fixer-uppers, however, are much more subtle. Some older houses, condos, and co-ops, for example, may look fine at first glance but have functional obsolescence. They're livable, but they need improvements, such as adding master bedrooms, bathrooms, or garages, and upgrading their electrical systems to bring them up to today's more rigorous housing standards.

Digging for a diamond among the dumps

Finding the right fixer-upper isn't a matter of luck. On the contrary, it takes persistence, skill, and plain hard work. You spend lots of time tromping through properties; invest more precious time evaluating promising fixer-uppers that ultimately don't make sense economically; and then, just when you're ready to give up, you finally discover a diamond in the rough that you end up buying.

Here's how to separate diamonds from dumps:

- ✔ **Read this book.** Everything you need to know is here. Pay special attention to the topics covered in this chapter (good neighborhoods; principles of progression, regression, and conformity; and used homes and condos), Chapter 10 (accurately determining fair market value so you don't overpay), and Chapter 13 (property inspections). Also, be sure that you can financially afford all the necessary outlays after the purchase for the fix-up work (see Chapter 2).

- ✔ **Inspect the heck out of the fixer-upper before you buy it.** Every property should be carefully inspected prior to purchase (see Chapter 13). Fixer-uppers need even more scrutiny so that you know precisely what you're getting yourself into. Your purchase offer must be conditioned upon your approval of the property inspections and satisfactory resolution of corrective work issues you discover. You can find these clauses in Chapter 12.

✔ **Get contractors' bids for structural repairs and renovations.** You can use contractors' bids as a negotiating tool to get a corrective-work credit or lower sales price from the sellers for structural repairs such as termite-damage repairs and a new roof. You should also get cost estimates for renovations such as bathroom modernization, new kitchen appliances and cabinets, central heating, and anything else required to bring the property up to date.

If the bids and cost estimates you receive indicate that you'd end up with the most expensive house on the block, don't do the project. Fix-up work has three iron laws:

- It's always more disruptive than you expected.

- It always takes longer to finish than you planned.

- It always costs more than you estimated.

So if estimated fix-up costs would make the property the most expensive house on the block, by the time the work is finally completed, the actual costs will make it the most expensive house in the state!

Getting a loan is usually difficult if the cost of anticipated corrective work repairs exceed 3 percent of the property value, which is always the case with major fixer-uppers. However, a good real estate agent should know which lenders in your area specialize in fixer-upper loans. Given that one such lender finds you creditworthy and your project feasible, that lender may give you a mortgage to buy the property *and* a construction loan to make the improvements.

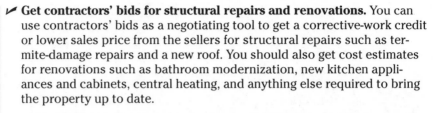

Structural repairs versus renovations

Work done on fixer-uppers falls into two broad categories: structural repairs and renovations. *Structural repairs* are changes you make to a property to bring it up to local health and safety standards. Such work can include foundation repairs, roof replacements, new electrical and plumbing-system installations, and so on — things that cost big bucks but add relatively little value to property. Ideally, you can get a credit from the seller to do some, if not all, of the necessary structural repairs. The less you have to take out of your pocket for corrective work, the more you have to spend on renovations.

Renovations increase a fixer-upper's value by modernizing the home. Remodeling an old kitchen, installing a second bathroom, and adding a garage are a few examples of major structural renovations that make your home more functional, more pleasant to live in, and more valuable when you sell it.

Cosmetic renovations (painting, carpeting, landscaping, and the like) also add value with far less expense and aggravation. The ideal fixer-uppers to buy are ones that look awful but simply need cosmetic fixes to look their best.

Final thoughts on fixer-uppers

Feeling somewhat overwhelmed by the risks associated with fixer-uppers is normal. Now you understand why most home buyers avoid them. They fear being sucked into a bottomless bog that utterly disrupts their lives and totally devours their savings. Rent *Mr. Blandings Builds His Dream House* and *The Money Pit* at your local video store to preview what may be in your real estate future!

Most novice home buyers, especially first-time buyers, woefully underestimate the time and cost required to fix up homes. When all is said and done, nearly all people find that it would have cost them the same or less to buy a more finished home and avoid the headaches of doing or coordinating the renovations. Some folks have ended up in financial ruin and even divorced over the stresses of such renovations.

If you like challenges and are willing to do a ton of extra detective work, remember these tips to maximize your chances of succeeding with a fixer-upper:

- Buy in the best neighborhood you can afford.
- Buy one of the cheaper houses on the best block.
- Make sure that the renovations will more than pay for themselves in increased property value.
- Make sure that the purchase price is low enough to allow you to do the corrective work and renovations without turning your property into the most expensive house on the block.

If the real estate gods play fair and square, whoever buys the exquisitely *finished* home you transformed from a dump will pay a bonus for your farsightedness to see the fixer-upper's potential, for your audacity to tackle the financial risk, and for your stamina to put up with the chaos and filth of a rehab. If (and only if) you select wisely, negotiate the price wisely, and renovate wisely, you'll enjoy years of blissful living in the wonderful home you created — and ideally make a fine profit to boot when you sell it.

Taking over a foreclosure

To get a mortgage, you give the lender the right to take your home away from you and sell it to pay the balance due on the mortgage if you:

- Don't make your loan payments
- Don't pay your property taxes
- Let your homeowners insurance policy lapse
- Do anything else that financially endangers your home

The legal action to repossess a home and sell it is called a *foreclosure*.

Every year, hundreds of thousands of homes end up in foreclosure. These foreclosures often result from misuse of consumer credit. In other cases, however, people fall on hard times — they lose a job, experience unexpected healthcare costs, suffer a death in the family, or go through a divorce.

You may have heard stories about people who got good deals buying foreclosures far below the property's appraised value. And in fact, some people who buy foreclosed property luck out. But for every lucky winner, there are many more people who don't profit or who actually lose money buying foreclosures.

Buyer beware — foreclosures are generally legal and financial cesspools. Unless you have an expert on your team who will guide you through the entire foreclosure process from beginning to end, don't even think about buying a foreclosure.

If you buy a foreclosed home, you'll most likely also buy the previous owner's problems. Here's a list of risks to ponder:

- ✔ **Physical:** Some homeowners react to the emotional devastation of a foreclosure with a scorched-earth attitude of "If we can't have it, we'll make darn sure that nobody else wants it." Before leaving, they take appliances, light fixtures, cabinets, sinks, toilets, and anything else of value. In extreme cases, they break windows, pour concrete down kitchen and bathroom drains, rip wiring out of walls, uproot shrubs, cut down trees, and do anything else they can think of to trash the property. What if you're the high bidder for a sabotaged house at an auction of foreclosed properties? Lucky you.

  Lenders usually won't let you inspect foreclosed properties prior to their auction. Nor can you make your offer to purchase subject to getting a loan. The risk of buying a property that you can't first inspect greatly exceeds the possible reward.

- ✔ **Financial:** Depending on which state the house is located in, a foreclosure can take anywhere from four months to over a year to complete. Suppose that you get what appears to be a good deal from people who are actually selling partway through the foreclosure process to avoid the stigma of foreclosure. What if these people lie about how much they owe on their mortgage and property taxes? What if they don't tell you about unrecorded mortgages, court judgments, or federal and state tax liens (outstanding tax bills) hanging over the house? One guess who's liable for debts secured by the property. Lucky you.

- ✔ **Possession:** Suppose that after buying a foreclosure at an auction, you visit your new home and discover that the previous owners are still living in it with their last remaining possession — a shotgun. They have no intention of leaving peacefully. Who do you think will have the pleasure of evicting them? Lucky you.

Back-on-the-market properties

When a house listed for sale receives an acceptable offer, the sellers usually tell their agent not to actively market the property or solicit other offers while they work with the buyers to satisfy the contract's terms and conditions of sale, such as property inspections and financing. If such a property comes back on the market (*BOM,* in real estate lingo), it means that the deal fell apart.

Property comes back on the market for many reasons. Perhaps the buyers couldn't qualify for a loan or got cold feet. Maybe the lender didn't think the house was worth as much money as the buyers were willing to pay for it and wouldn't approve their request for a loan. The far and away most common reason deals fall through, however, is that the buyers and sellers couldn't agree on how to handle the corrective work discovered during the inspections.

Ironically, the castle that all the buyers coveted when it was the newest listing on the market may turn into a "that old thing" pumpkin when it returns. Suddenly, suspicious buyers wonder what's wrong with the house. Real or imagined, that stigma of being a problem property repels a lot of people. They don't want to buy a house that someone else rejected. As a result of reduced buyer enthusiasm, BOM homes often sell for a lower price the second time around.

Don't categorically reject a house that comes back on the market. Find out why it's BOM. If the problem is related to property defects, ask the sellers to show you copies of the inspection reports. Given that the problems are correctable and that you can negotiate a good deal, the sellers' misfortune could be your good fortune. Sellers who've had a deal implode are frequently more willing to realistically negotiate on price and terms with the next buyer. If you apply the principles we cover in the fixer-upper section of this chapter, you could turn a BOM into a great deal.

Given possible sabotage by the previous owner, buying a foreclosure is never *entirely* safe. The least risky way to purchase one is to buy directly from a lender who got title to the property because no one bought it at auction. Here's why:

- ✔ Any recorded or undisclosed mortgages, court judgments, or tax liens on the house are either removed from the property or at least revealed to you prior to your purchase.

- ✔ You can — absolutely must, in fact — have the house minutely scrutinized by professional property inspectors. Where foreclosures are concerned, you have to find out whether the previous owner left any hidden surprises for you.

- ✔ The price and terms of sale are negotiable. Even though foreclosures are normally listed at their appraised value, lenders may make allowances for corrective work by either reducing the price or giving you a credit to do the work. They'll also, as a rule, offer attractive loan terms (low cash down payments, no loan fees, below-market interest rates) to get rid of these blighted properties quickly. After all, they're in the loan business — not property management.

Think long and hard before buying a foreclosure. Even if you purchase one directly from a lender, you may be buying a house permeated from foundation to roof by shattered dreams. Such a house probably hasn't been given the best of care. Do your homework carefully, have the property thoroughly inspected, and understand *fully* what you're getting yourself into before you buy.

Pooling Your Resources: Ad Hoc Partnerships

As home prices have escalated in many densely populated parts of the country, so has the frequency of unrelated people forming ad hoc partnerships to buy houses. These couples aren't necessarily romantically involved. On the contrary, they're usually folks who decide that a good way of turning the American dream of owning a home into reality is to join forces as partners.

Types of residential partnerships

One type of ad hoc partnership, known as *equity sharing,* involves outside investors who don't live in the property. The investor provides cash to buy a house, which the other partner lives in while the property (ideally) appreciates in value. After a specified period of time — say, five years — the partner who lives in the house has the option either to buy out the investor's share of the property or to sell the house and split the proceeds.

With *live-in partnerships,* the other type of residential ad hoc partnership, all partners live together in the jointly purchased property. By pooling their income and cash for a down payment with a significant other, friend, or relative, these individuals get a place to call home; a tax shelter; and, if the real estate gods are willing, a profit when they eventually sell and go their separate ways.

Live-in partnerships are the real estate version of Siamese twins. People who live in ultraclose proximity to their partners every day have a personal relationship that is far more intense than in an equity-sharing partnership.

We've seen live-in partnerships that turned out wonderfully. As time passed, the partners became even closer friends than they were before buying the house. Most live-in partnerships, however, are no more than marriages of convenience that the partners suffer through solely to reap economic benefits. Bickering about things like whether to patch a leaky roof or get a new one, who left the sink full of dirty dishes (again!), whether to paint the living room purple or gold, and who gets the backyard for a party next Saturday can strain even the best of relationships.

Structuring a successful partnership

Too many partnerships end up on the rocks unnecessarily. Why? The partners didn't anticipate problems related to co-ownership that arose. Ironically, most of these problems are foreseeable and avoidable. Proper planning prevents problems.

Before forming a residential partnership, you can do two things to greatly increase your odds for success:

- ✔ **Give it a trial run.** If you're considering a live-in partnership, we recommend that you live with your prospective partner for at least six months before buying a home together. You may discover that you have a major compatibility problem — for example, you may go to bed each night by nine, and your roomie may love to party into the wee hours of the morning. Ditto if you, Felix, insist on having everything in its place, and your partner-to-be, Oscar, uses the floor for a closet. Imagine the delights of co-ownership if you always pay your bills by the first of the month, and your partner's favorite sport is a spirited game of duck-the-bill-collector.

- ✔ **Put it in writing.** We also recommend having a lawyer who handles residential real estate partnerships prepare a written partnership agreement as soon as possible. Don't reinvent the wheel; let an experienced lawyer guide you and your prospective partner through the foreseeable "what ifs" of every partnership.

The partnership from hell

Unfortunately, partnerships occasionally turn into unmitigated disasters. Irv's sad tale illustrates some pitfalls of residential partnerships.

Irv and Sid, good pals for almost 25 years, bought a condo together. Irv used money inherited from his mother for the condo's down payment and closing costs. Sid, who had a much higher income than Irv but no cash, lived in the condo as his principal residence. Sid covered the monthly mortgage payments, property taxes, and homeowners-association dues, and also paid rent to Irv.

It was a perfect partnership. Sid got the tax deductions he needed, plus 25 percent of the appreciation when the condo sold. Sid's rent payments gave Irv a good return on the cash he'd invested, and he'd get the lion's share of the condo's appreciation when it sold. Irv and Sid were delighted with their arrangement.

All went well for nearly a year. Then, without warning, Sid filed bankruptcy.

Irv's rent payments stopped, of course. What's more, the bankruptcy court put a lien on the condo to tie up Sid's assets — and inadvertently tied up Irv's money as well. Worst of all, Irv and Sid didn't have a written partnership agreement describing their 75/25 equity split. Without something in writing, Irv was unable to prove this fact to the court's satisfaction.

Ideally, you should have the agreement drawn up well before you make an offer to purchase. Why the rush? To make sure that you and your partner understand precisely how the partnership operates and what your responsibilities to each other are. The agreement should cover important issues such as the following:

- ✔ **Financial arrangements:** This section of the agreement deals with the economics of buying, maintaining, and selling the property. It also specifies the tax deductibility of mortgage interest and property taxes for each partner if the partnership involves unequal financial contributions.

  What happens if, for example, your partner suddenly dies or goes bankrupt? How you take title in the property is critical. (We cover this important issue in Chapter 14.) Should the partners in a live-in partnership give each other first right of refusal to buy the partner's share before it can be sold to an outsider? Planning for the unexpected sure beats reacting to a crisis. Your agreement must have equitable provisions for terminating the partnership.

- ✔ **Dispute resolution:** What if you and your partner come to blows on a critically important issue like whether to plant daisies or roses along the side of the house? If only two partners are involved, how do you break tie votes? Anticipate disputes. Even the best of friends occasionally disagree. That's a fact of life. Provide a method (such as mediation or arbitration) to resolve the problems you can't work out between yourselves.

- ✔ **Game plan:** If you and your partner intend to improve the property you purchase by, for example, remodeling the kitchen or converting a pair of flats to condominiums, your partnership agreement should be as specific as possible regarding the intended scope of work, project timing, cost, and so on. Plan now to prevent arguments later.

Never rush into a partnership — the economic consequences of a mistake may be devastating. Carefully weigh the pros and cons. Then get everything in writing with help from a lawyer experienced in covering all the "what if" situations just in case everything doesn't turn out as wonderfully as you hope.

Chapter 9

Assembling an All-Star Real Estate Team

*W*inston Churchill once characterized the former Soviet Union as "a riddle wrapped in a mystery inside an enigma." Churchill's apt description applies equally well to the home-buying process. If you're like most folks who are looking for a home, you're not an expert on property values, financing, or tax and real estate law. And when your life savings are on the line, ignorance isn't bliss. Not understanding what's involved in the process of buying a home can cost you big bucks and make you unhappy with the home that you ultimately purchase.

How can you find your way through the convoluted maze of constantly changing real estate market conditions, local laws, regulations, and tax codes? Where can you sign up for a crash course in home values? Even if you have the aptitude, how will you find the time to become an expert in so many fields?

One way around these problems is to do nothing. You can't get into trouble if you're lying in a corner, curled tightly into the fetal position. Of course, the downside of doing nothing is that nothing gets done. You can never buy a home using this method.

Reading *Home Buying For Dummies,* 3rd Edition is a far more dynamic course of action. This book shows you how to become a smart home buyer. However, this book can't do everything for you.

Understanding the theory of property values and knowing what your dream home is actually worth are two very different things. Similarly, reading about home buying isn't a slam-dunk guarantee that you'll become an expert home buyer — there's no substitute for years of practical experience in the field. You also need some experts on your side. Don't worry. We explain how to find competent experts who can help you buy a home and who won't charge you an arm and a leg for that help.

The Team Concept

Time and time again, we've seen smart people blunder into horrible situations while buying a home. More often than not, what got them into trouble was ignorance of something that they (or their advisors) should have known but didn't.

Strangely enough, knowing everything yourself isn't important. What is important is having good people on your team — people who know what you need to know so that they can help you solve the problems that invariably arise.

Lining up the players

You don't have to become an instant expert in home values, mortgages, tax and real estate law, title insurance, escrows, pest-control work, and construction techniques in order to play the home-buying game well. You can choose to hire people who have mastered the skills that you lack. Home buying is a team sport. Your job is to lead and coach the team, not play every position. After you've assembled a winning team, your players should give you solid advice so that you can make brilliant decisions.

If cost were no object, you'd hire every competent expert you could get your hands on. But because you probably don't have an unlimited budget, you need to determine which experts are absolutely necessary and which tasks you can handle yourself. In this chapter, we explain which experts are generally worth hiring and which ones you can pass on. Ultimately, of course, you must determine how competent or challenged you feel with the various aspects of the home-buying process.

Here's a thumbnail sketch of the possible players on your team:

  ✔ **You:** Always remember that you're the most important player on your team. In nearly every home purchase, something goes wrong — one of your players drops the ball or doesn't satisfy your needs. You have every right to politely, yet forcefully, insist that things be made right.

Remember that you hire (and pay) the players on your team. They work for you. Bad players may see things the other way around — they'd like to believe (and want you to believe) that they're in charge. They may try to manipulate you to act in their interests rather than yours. Don't tolerate this. You're the boss — you can fire as well as hire.

✔ **Real estate agent:** Because the home you're about to buy is probably the largest single investment you'll ever make, you must have someone on your team who knows property values. Your agent's primary mission is to help you find your dream home, tell you what the home is worth, and negotiate for it on your behalf.

✔ **Real estate broker:** Every state issues two kinds of real estate licenses: a salesperson's license and a broker's license. People with broker's licenses must satisfy much tougher educational and experience standards. If your real estate agent is not an independent broker or the broker for a real estate office, he (or she) must be supervised by a broker who is responsible for everything that your agent does or fails to do. In a crisis, your transaction's success may depend upon backup support from your agent's broker.

✔ **Lender:** If you can't pay, you can't play. And because most folks can't pay all cash for their homes, you probably need a loan to buy your dream house. A good lender offers competitively priced loans and may even be able to help you select the best type of loan from the financial minefield of loan programs available today.

✔ **Property inspector:** A house's physical condition greatly affects its value. Your dream home should be thoroughly inspected from roof to foundation before you purchase it; to ensure that you actually get what you think you're buying.

✔ **Escrow officer:** Mutual distrust is the underlying rule of every real estate deal. You and the seller need a neutral third party, an escrow officer, who handles funds and paperwork related to the transaction without playing favorites. The escrow officer is the home-buying game's referee.

✔ **Financial and tax advisors:** Before you buy a home, you should understand how the purchase will fit into the context of your overall financial situation. You should address the issues of what your financial goals are and, given those goals, how much house you can afford. In Chapter 2, we explain how to do that.

✔ **Lawyer:** You may or may not need a lawyer on your team, depending on your contract's complexity, where your dream home is located, and your personal comfort level. The purchase agreement you sign when buying a home is a legally binding contract. If you have any questions about your contract's legality, put a lawyer who specializes in real estate law on your team.

Odds are you won't win the game unless you have a winning team. But remember that your players are *advisors* — not decision makers. You're the boss and decision maker. The buck stops with you. After all, it's your money on the line.

Avoiding gratuitous advice

We'll say it again: Buying a home is a team sport. Successful transactions result from the coordinated efforts of many people — agents, brokers, lenders, property inspectors, escrow officers, tax advisors, and lawyers. Each player brings a different set of skills to the game and should make an important contribution to your team.

As long as your experts stick to what they know best, everything goes smoothly. Whenever one of your experts invades another expert's turf, however, war breaks out with a bang.

Unsolicited opinions related to property values are an example of one devastating type of gratuitous advice. Such opinions are usually volunteered by tax advisors or lawyers during a review of your transaction. Lawyers and tax advisors don't know property values. Making a lowball offer based on their bad advice, no matter how well intentioned, could blow the deal on your dream home.

Incredibly, some buyers foolishly *solicit* gratuitous advice in a misguided attempt to save a few bucks. "Why," buyers ask themselves, "hire a CPA for tax advice if we can get free tax advice from our agent? Why pay for legal advice from a lawyer if our escrow officer will give us free opinions about the best way for us to take title to our home?"

Why? Because if you're lucky, free advice from the wrong expert is worth exactly what you pay for it. Zip. Zero. Nada. Nothing.

If you're *unlucky,* free advice can be very expensive. The IRS, for example, shows no mercy if you make a mistake based upon faulty advice. Ironically, this type of mistake usually ends up costing you far more than a lawyer or tax advisor would have charged you for correct advice.

Given the adverse consequences of bad advice, *good* experts don't offer guidance that they aren't qualified to give. If asked, they categorically refuse to give such advice. Instead, they redirect their clients to the proper experts. Good experts are wise enough to know what they don't know and humble enough to admit it. On a more selfish level, they don't want to get sued by their clients for giving lousy advice.

Beware of experts who offer you gratuitous advice outside their fields of expertise.

Reeling in a Real Estate Agent

"What's it worth?"

The wrong answer to this question can cost you *big* bucks! Worse yet, there's no simple answer to this deceptively simple question, because home prices aren't precise. As Chapter 10 explains, home prices can't be reduced to a math problem where 2 plus 2 reassuringly equals 4 now and forevermore. Home prices aren't fixed — on the contrary, they slither all over the place.

REMEMBER

Houses sell for *fair market value,* which is whatever buyers offer and sellers accept. Fair market value isn't a specific number; it's a price *range.*

Suppose that you make an offer on a house worth about $150,000. If the seller has a better agent than you do, and you're desperate to buy, you may end up paying $160,000. On the other hand, if you're in no hurry to buy, and your agent is a good negotiator, you may be able to buy the home for $140,000. Home sale prices are often directly related both to the agent's knowledge of what comparable houses have sold for and to the agent's negotiating skills. Of course, other factors (such as the buyer's and seller's motivation, needs, and knowledge) are also important.

A good agent can be the foundation of your real estate team. An agent can help you find a home that meets your needs, negotiate for that home on your behalf, supervise property inspections, and coordinate the closing. Agents often have useful leads for mortgage loans. A good agent's negotiating skills and knowledge of property values can save you thousands of dollars.

Some people think that "good agent" is a contradiction in terms. These folks will tell you that all agents have a hidden agenda: to make people buy more expensive homes than they can afford in order to fatten agents' commission checks.

Some agents *may* try to pressure you to buy sooner rather than later (and to pay more than you should) in order to fatten their own commissions. And unfortunately, many well-intentioned-but-inept agents are also out there. In this chapter, we explain how to avoid the bad agents — and how to sift through the masses of mediocre agents — in order to narrow the field down to good agents who are worthy of their commissions.

Types of agent relationships

Say that you've been working with an agent named Al who has been showing you property for several months. Yesterday, you finally found a home you like. The house seemed well priced, but you told Al to make a lowball offer anyhow. (What the heck. Everybody knows that prices are negotiable. If the sellers don't like the price, let them make a counter offer.) But what if your agent blew your cover? Suppose that Al told the sellers all your innermost secrets — such as how much cash you have for a down payment and how much you're *really* willing to pay for the house. Now the sellers can beat you at your own game. If you discover what Al did to you (many victimized buyers don't), you'd undoubtedly feel hurt, betrayed, and pretty darn angry. You'd ask Al just whose side he's on.

The answer to that question has changed somewhat over the years. In decades past, buyers thought that they had agents who represented *them*. But in fact, they didn't. Back then, all agents were legally bound to be either agents or sub-agents *of the seller*.

Subagents, also called *cooperating agents,* work with one another through membership in a *Multiple Listing Service* (MLS). Agents use the MLS to promote their own real estate listings, and such agents offer to share their commissions with agents from other offices who actually sell the listed properties. As subagents of the seller, MLS participants are obliged to get top dollar for the sellers' properties.

Unfortunately, most buyers didn't know that the very agents who were working with them were actually representing the interests of the sellers. And the law didn't require agents to tell buyers which party they (the agents) actually represented before preparing offers on behalf of their buyers.

Times have changed somewhat. Some states (such as California) have adopted improved consumer-protection laws. These states passed laws that force agents to give both buyers and sellers a written disclosure regarding their duties as agents. The laws then allow buyers and sellers to select which type of relationship they want to have with their agents.

Home buyers and sellers can have three different types of relationships with real estate agents. We explain *dual agency* in the sidebar "Dual agency and conflicts of interest." The other possible relationships are both types of *single agency,* which is when the agent represents only one of the two parties in the transaction:

✓ **Seller's agent:** In this form of single agency, the agent works solely for the seller.

✓ **Buyer's agent:** In this type of single agency, the agent works only for the buyer. A buyer's agent isn't an agent of the seller even if the buyer's agent gets a portion of the commission paid by the seller.

Although single agency is an improvement over the old system, buyer's agents still suffer from the conflict of interest inherent in getting a commission that is tied to a percentage of the amount that a buyer spends for a property.

Dual agency and conflicts of interest

In certain transactions, an agent represents both the seller and the buyer. This type of representation is called *dual agency*.

Dual agency is the most confusing form of agency. Most people think that dual agency means that the exact same agent represents both the buyer and the seller. Such a situation is possible, but it is highly unusual and even more inadvisable. One agent can't possibly represent your best interests as a buyer and the seller's best interests at the same time.

In a more common kind of dual agency, the sale of a particular property involves two different agents who both work for the same real estate broker. Suppose that Sam Seller decides one sunny Sunday to list his house for sale with Sarah, an Acme Realty agent. Sarah smiles as she signs the agreement to represent Sam as the seller's exclusive agent.

Simultaneously, Betty Buyer bumps into Bob, who's also an Acme Realty agent, at a Sunday open house. Betty likes Bob's style and asks him to represent her exclusively as a buyer's agent. Bob enthusiastically agrees.

So far, so good. Sam has Sarah, his exclusive agent. Betty has Bob, her exclusive agent. Things get complicated later that afternoon when Bob shows Betty Buyer the house Sarah just listed for Sam Seller. Betty is bedazzled. She loves the house and tells Bob to write up an offer on it immediately.

When Betty decided to make an offer on Sam's house, the agency relationships that Betty and Sam had with their respective agents changed.

Like it or not, Sarah suddenly represented both Sam and Betty. Similarly, Bob became the agent of both Betty and Sam.

Why? Even though two different agents are involved, both agents work for the same real estate broker, Acme Realty. As soon as Bob started to work on Betty's offer, Acme Realty represented the seller and the buyer of the same property. That's dual agency.

Dual agency probably won't be a problem if you end up working with an agent in a small office that has only a few agents. The odds that you'll buy a home listed by one of the other agents in your agent's office are slim. However, if the agent that you select works for a large brokerage operation with multiple offices and thousands of agents (such as Coldwell Banker), your odds of having to deal with dual agency skyrocket.

As a buyer, you must be on guard for two potential problems when confronted with dual agency. First, make sure that your agent isn't sharing confidential information with any other agents at her real estate company. Second, watch out for agents who push their own company's listings because selling an in-house listing generates higher commissions for them.

Most states permit dual agency relationships as long as the agency status is disclosed to both the sellers and the buyers in advance, and both parties agree to it. Undisclosed dual agency can be used as grounds to have a purchase agreement revoked and usually permits the injured parties to seek recovery against the real estate agents.

In rare cases, buyer's agents don't accept money from sellers. Instead, a buyer signs a contract to work exclusively with a buyer's agent, and the buyer pays the agent a retainer that is applied toward the fee owed when the buyer's agent finds the buyer a home. Depending on the contract provisions, the retainer may or may not be returned to the buyer if the buyer's agent fails to find the buyer a satisfactory property to purchase.

Here's a way to have the best of both worlds with a buyer's agent. This technique removes the buyer's agent's incentive to get you to spend more, yet it keeps you from paying a fee if you don't buy a home. Offer your buyer's agent a lump-sum commission plus a bonus if, *and only if,* the agent gets you a better buy. For example, if the agent typically receives 3 percent of a home's sale price, and you expect to buy a home for approximately $200,000, offer the agent a flat $5,000 commission plus an additional $100 bonus for every $1,000 below $200,000 the agent reduces the price for you, up to a maximum $6,000 commission.

Is your agent your ally or your enemy? Because laws regarding an agent's legal responsibility vary from state to state, it's important that you know how the game is played in your state. Be sure that you determine who your agent represents before you begin working together.

How agents get paid

Real estate brokerage is an all-or-nothing business. As a rule, agents are paid a commission only when property sells. If the property doesn't sell, agents don't get paid.

This payment method can create a conflict of interest between you and your agent. The payment method won't create a conflict of interest with *good* agents, because good agents put your best interests in front of their desire to get paid. You know that you're working with a bad agent, however, if the agent is more interested in quickly closing the sale and having you pay top dollar than in diligently educating you and getting you the best possible deal.

Allow us to answer your burning questions about real estate commissions:

- ✔ **How much do real estate agents get in commissions?** Commissions are calculated as a percentage of the sale price. Depending on local custom, commissions on homes usually range from 4 to 7 percent of the sale price.

- ✔ **Who pays the commission?** Typically, sellers. After all, sellers get money when property sells. Buyers rarely have much money left after making the down payment for their dream home and paying loan charges, property-inspection fees, homeowners-insurance premiums, moving costs, and the other expenses of purchase noted in Chapter 3. Because commission is part of the sales price, however, the effective cost of the commission comes out of both the buyer's and seller's pockets.

✔ **Are commissions negotiable?** Absolutely. *Listing agreements* (the contracts that property owners sign with brokers to sell property) and purchase agreements usually state that commissions aren't fixed by law and may be negotiated between sellers and brokers.

✔ **How is the commission distributed?** Suppose that a house sells for a nice, round $200,000. Assuming a 6 percent commission rate, the sale generates a $12,000 commission. That's a lot of money. At least it would be if it all went to one person, but commissions don't work that way as a rule.

Usually, the commission is divided in half at the close of escrow. The *listing broker,* who represents the sellers, gets half ($6,000, in our example) of the commission, and the other half ($6,000) goes to the *selling broker,* who represents the buyers.

If the selling or buying agent works for a broker, the broker typically gets a portion of the commission. The brokerage firm typically takes 30 to 50 percent of the commission, which leaves the agent 50 to 70 percent. In some firms, such as RE/MAX, agents pay a fixed monthly fee to their brokerage firm and end up keeping 80 to 90 percent of the commissions they bring into the firm. Agents who work on their own as independent brokers, of course, don't have to split their commissions with anyone.

Buying without an agent

You may see a For Sale by Owner (also known as a FSBO — pronounced fiz-bo) or two during your home search. The sellers may even be friends, neighbors, or work colleagues. Because no real estate agent is involved on the selling side of a FSBO transaction, the sellers don't have to pay a commission. That shaves big bucks off their expenses of sale.

If the FSBO home meets your needs, and you found it yourself, you may rightfully wonder whether you need an agent to complete the deal. After all, if the sellers don't have to pay your agent's commission, they should be willing to sell you the home at a lower price.

Some home buyers have successfully purchased their dream homes without an agent. Others have made big boo-boos that way.

If you're a novice, using an agent usually makes sense. Consider the additional value that an agent brings to the transaction beyond finding you the property — such as negotiating; estimating market value; and helping coordinate property inspections, contingency removals, seller disclosures, financing, opening escrow, and myriad other details.

You may also consider asking an agent to represent you for less than the standard 3 percent commission because you found the property yourself. If you decide not to use an agent, consider hiring an attorney by the hour to review the contract and handle the transaction's important legal details.

Where an agent's time goes

Some people think that real estate commissions are disproportionately large relative to the amount of work that agents do. That's a polite way of saying that agents are grossly overpaid.

Justifying a good agent's commission is easier if you understand what we call The Iceberg Theory. As you probably know, 90 percent of an iceberg's bulk is hidden underwater. You can't tell how big an iceberg is by the portion you see floating above the waterline. By the same token, you can't tell how much time agents spend working for you. Good agents spend at least nine hours working behind the scene for every hour spent in the presence of their clients.

Unfortunately, most buyers and sellers don't know this. Buyers and sellers think that commissions are excessive, given the relatively few hours they actually see their agents working for them.

Unlike lawyers and other professionals who bill clients by the hour, real estate agents don't itemize the time spent on a transaction from start to finish. If they did, you'd have a much better idea of where your agent's time goes.

Good real estate agents typically spend around 20 hours a week touring new properties and checking up on houses that have been on the market a while in order to see which houses are still available and which have had offers accepted on them. Agents do this legwork, week in and week out, to keep themselves current regarding what's on the market and how property values are changing.

After you select an agent, she starts targeting houses you may want to buy. Good agents screen several properties for each one they eventually show you, saving you the time of doing the screening yourself. Your agent spends time playing phone tag with listing agents, trying to get instructions about how to show properties, and scheduling showings. Then she spends more hours with you, touring houses and searching for your elusive dream home.

Once you've found your dream home, your agent spends time preparing an offer to purchase, presenting the offer, and negotiating counter offers with the seller's agent regarding the price and terms of sale. After the offer is accepted, a good agent spends more hours helping you with such things as securing a mortgage; coordinating transaction details with the seller's agent; providing information and paperwork to the escrow officer; going through the home with your various property inspectors; and reviewing mandated local, state, and federal disclosure statements from the sellers.

Characteristics of good agents

Good agents can be male or female, and they come in a wide assortment of races, colors, creeds, and ages. All good agents, however, have the following characteristics that are beneficial to buyers:

✔ **Good agents educate you.** Your agent knows the home-buying process and carefully explains each step so that you *always* understand what's happening. Agents should be patient, not pushy. A good agent *never* uses your ignorance to manipulate you.

✔ **Good agents don't make decisions for you.** Your agent *always* explains what your options are so that *you* can make wise decisions regarding your best course of action.

✔ **Good agents tell you when they think that adding other experts (inspectors, lawyers, and the like) to your team is advisable.** Experts don't threaten a good agent. The agent's ego should always be secondary to the primary mission of serving you well.

✔ **Good agents voluntarily restrict themselves geographically and by property type.** Your agent has ideally learned that trying to be all things to all people invariably results in mediocre service. Different communities can have radically different market conditions, laws, and restrictions. (For more information, see the sidebar "Agents who work outside their areas of expertise are dangerous.")

✔ **Good agents are full-time professionals, because serving you properly is a full-time job.** To reduce the financial impact of changing jobs, many people begin their real estate careers as part-timers, working as agents after normal business hours and weekends. That's fine for the agents, but not you.

One of the first questions you must ask any agent you're considering working with is "Are you a full-time agent?" Just as you wouldn't risk letting a part-time lawyer defend you, don't let a part-time agent represent you.

✔ **Good agents have contacts.** Folks prefer doing business with people they know, respect, and trust. You can use your agent's working relationships with local lenders, property inspectors, lawyers, title officers, insurance agents, government officials, and other real estate agents. Good agents will refer you to highly skilled service providers who offer competitive pricing.

Watch out for duplicitous agents with hidden agendas. Instead of referring you to the best possible service providers, these agents limit their recommendations to people who refer business to them or pay them a referral fee.

✔ **Good agents have time.** Agents earn their living selling time, not houses. Success is a two-edged sword for busy agents. An agent who is already working with several other buyers and sellers probably won't have enough surplus time to serve you properly. Occasional scheduling conflicts are unavoidable. But if you often find your needs being neglected because your agent's time is overcommitted, get a new agent.

Agents who work outside their areas of expertise are dangerous

Many pitfalls await unwary buyers who trust agents who work outside their areas of expertise. Although extreme, here's a real-life example of a disaster caused by an agent who specialized in property located in Sonoma, a peaceful suburban town about 40 miles north of the city of San Francisco.

The Sonoma agent represented her friend in the purchase of a small apartment building located in San Francisco. The buyer planned to convert the apartments to condominiums and then sell the condos individually at a profit.

Unfortunately, the Sonoma agent knew nothing about San Francisco's strict rent-control law or its equally strict condo-conversion ordinance. The intent of these laws is to discourage people from converting lower-rent apartments to upscale condos.

Had the building been converted to condos, the total proceeds from individual sales would've been less than the price the buyer had originally paid for the building, due to the restrictive nature of these two laws. The agent's negligence ultimately led the buyer to lose $125,000 when she later resold the building.

This agent not only made the mistake of working in "foreign territory," but also failed to recommend that the buyer put a local real estate lawyer on her team to advise the buyer about these legal issues. The buyer could have sued her agent for malpractice. She didn't, because the agent was her "friend."

With friends like that, the buyer didn't need any enemies. If the Sonoma agent had been a true friend, she'd have referred the buyer to a good San Francisco agent.

Agents who go out of their area of geographical or property expertise do so because they're either greedy or just too darn inept to know better. Whatever the reason, avoid such agents like the plague.

Selecting your agent

Now that you know the glittering generalities of a hypothetical good agent, you're ready to get down to the nitty-gritty specifics of choosing an agent of your very own. We strongly recommend that you interview at least three agents before selecting the lucky one.

Finding referral sources

If you have trouble finding three good agents to interview, here are some referral sources:

- ✔ **Friends, business associates, and members of religious, professional, and social organizations to which you belong:** In short, anyone you know who's either house hunting or who owns a home in your target neighborhood can be a source of agent referrals. Don't just ask for names; find out why these folks liked their agents.

✔ **Your employer:** The company you work for may have a relocation service that you can consult.

✔ **Professionals in related fields:** Financial, tax, and legal advisors can be good agent-referral sources.

✔ **The agent who sold your previous home:** If you're a homeowner who's moving into a new area, ask the agent who sold you your home to recommend a good agent in that area. Good agents network with one another.

✔ **Sunday open houses:** While you're investigating the houses, check out the agents. These agents have already proved (by their open-house activity) that they work the neighborhood in which you want to buy.

Don't take any referral, even if it's from the Pope, as gospel. Most people who give referrals have limited or outdated experience with the recommended agent. Furthermore, the person making the referral is probably not a real estate expert.

Requesting an activity list

After you've identified at least three good agents, the fun begins. To avoid a misunderstanding, tell each agent that you plan to interview several agents before you select the one you'll work with. Ask each agent to bring to the interview a list of *every* property the agent listed or sold during the preceding 12 months. This list, called the *activity list,* is an extremely powerful analytical tool.

Here's what the activity list should include and how you should use the list during the interview:

✔ **Property address:** Addresses help you zero in on the agent's geographical focus. See for yourself exactly how many properties the agent sold and listed in your target neighborhood(s). Eliminate agents who are focused outside your area *and* agents who have no geographical focus.

✔ **Property type (house, condo, duplex, other):** You can use this information to determine whether the agent works on the kind of property you intend to buy. If, for example, an agent specializes in condos, and you want to buy a detached single-family home, you may have a problem.

✔ **Sales price:** Does the agent handle property in your price range? An agent who deals in *much* more or less expensive property than you expect to buy may not be the right agent for you. If, for example, you plan to spend $150,000, and the least expensive house the agent sold in the past year cost $300,000, you have a mismatch. Such agents probably won't spend much time on you because they have bigger fish to fry.

- ✔ **Date of sale:** Sales activity should be distributed fairly evenly through-out the year. If it isn't, find out why. A lack of recent sales activity may be due to illness or marital problems that may reduce the agent's effectiveness.

- ✔ **Whom the agent represented — seller or buyer:** Seasoned agents work about half the time with buyers and the other half with sellers. Newer agents primarily work with buyers. Avoid agents who work primarily with sellers. These agents generally lack either the interest or aptitude to work effectively with buyers.

- ✔ **Total dollar value of property sold during the preceding 12 months:** Comparing the three agents' grand-total property sales is a quick way to measure each agent's individual activity and success. There are, how-ever, other equally important factors to consider when selecting your agent. You don't necessarily want a "top producer." These agents get to the top by listing and selling large quantities of property. They usually don't have the time or patience to do the hand-holding and education you may need, especially if you're a first-time buyer.

- ✔ **Name and current phone numbers of sellers/buyers:** You'll use this later to spot-check references.

Words whisper; actions thunder. The activity list transforms cheap chatter into solid facts. Good agents willingly give you their lists and encourage you to check client references. Bad agents don't want you talking to their unhappy victims. Eliminate from consideration any agent who won't give you a comprehensive activity list — she is trying to hide either a lack of sales or unhappy clients.

Interviewing agents

Begin each interview by spending a few minutes analyzing the agent's activity list. After you've finished reviewing the list and had time to organize your thoughts, get answers to the following questions:

- ✔ **Are you a full-time agent?** You should have asked this before inviting the agent to be interviewed. If you forgot, do it now. Don't work with part-time agents.

- ✔ **Whom do you represent?** This gets back to the fundamental question of agency. Is the agent representing you exclusively, or is he a dual agent who represents both you and the seller? Be sure that you know exactly whom your agent represents at all times.

- ✔ **What can you tell me about your office?** Discuss office size, staff sup-port, market specialization, and reputation. See whether the agent's broker is knowledgeable, is available to you if necessary, and is a good problem-solver. In a crunch, your transaction's success (or failure) could depend upon the quality of backup support that you and the agent receive.

Don't put too much weight on the size of the agent's office. Some excellent agents work as sole practitioners, and other excellent agents prefer the synergism and support services of a huge office. Although larger offices tend to have more listings, no one office ever has a monopoly on the good listings. Quality of service is more important than quantity of agents or listings.

✔ **How long have you been an agent?** You want an agent who keeps learning and growing. After five years in real estate, a good agent has five years' experience, whereas a mediocre agent has one year's experience five times. Time in the saddle is, by itself, no guarantee of competence.

✔ **Do you have a salesperson's license or a broker's license?** An agent must satisfy more rigorous educational and field-sales experience requirements to get a broker's license. Many fine agents have only a salesperson's license throughout their entire careers. Although a broker's license isn't a guarantee of excellence, good agents often obtain a broker's license to improve their professional skills and to give themselves an advantage in agent-selection situations.

✔ **Do you hold any professional designations? Have you taken any real estate classes recently? What do you read to keep current in your field?** Taking continuing-education courses and reading to stay abreast of changes in real estate brokerage are good signs. So is obtaining professional designations, such as the GRI (Graduate, Realtor Institute) and CRS (Certified Residential Specialist) designations through the National Association of Realtors' study programs. However, credentials in and of themselves are no guarantee of competence or ethics.

✔ **What is your understanding of my home-buying needs?** You've probably already told the agent what type of property you want to buy, the neighborhood you'd like to live in, and how much you can spend. See whether the agent remembers what you said. If the agent doesn't remember, watch out. You need an agent who listens carefully to what you say.

✔ **What do you think of the other two agents (name them) whom I'm interviewing?** To encourage frankness, assure the agents that you won't repeat what they say to you. Good agents don't build themselves up by tearing down other agents. If all three agents are good ones, you won't hear any derogatory comments. However, if one of the agents (or the agent's firm) has a bad reputation in the real estate community, the other two agents should tell you. Good or bad, the reputations of your agent and the agent's office rub off on you.

✔ **How many other buyers and sellers are you currently representing?**
If, for example, the agent holds three listings open every weekend and is
working with six other buyers to boot, where do you fit in? Although
some scheduling conflicts are inevitable, you shouldn't have to contort
your life to fit the agent's schedule. A good agent has time to accommodate your schedule.

✔ **Do you work in partnership with another agent or use assistants?**
Some agents team up with another agent to handle buyers and sellers
jointly. If this is the case, you must interview both agents. Other agents
delegate time-consuming detail work to their assistants so they themselves can focus on critical points in the transaction. If an agent relies on
such assistants, be sure that the assistants are qualified and that you
understand exactly how and when during the buying process the agent
will work directly with you. You don't want to hire an agent only to find
that you end up working most of the time with her assistant — whom
you can't stand.

✔ **Is there anything I haven't asked about you or your firm that you
think I should know?** Perhaps the agent is planning to change firms or
is leaving next week to take an 80-day trip around the world. Maybe the
agent's broker is going out of business. *This is the make-sure-that-I-find-
out-everything-I-need-to-know-to-make-a-good-decision question.*

Checking agents' references

Here's your chance to profit from other people's mistakes, which is infinitely
preferable to goofing up yourself. You should have activity lists with the
names and phone numbers of every buyer and seller that the agents represented during the past 12 months. You can pick and choose the people you
want to call, rather than being restricted to a highly selective list of references who think that these agents are God's gift to real estate.

What's to prevent agents from culling out their worst transactions? Nothing.
However, the more deals they delete, the less activity they have to show you —
and the worse they look when you compare the agents' overall sales activity.

Suppose that each agent gives you a list containing 50 transactions. Assuming
one buyer or seller for each transaction, 50 clients per agent times three
agents interviewed equals 150 phone calls. You'd be on the phone forever!

Good news. You don't have to call each and every client to check references.
You can get a pretty darn accurate picture of the agents by making as few as
six calls per agent.

Here's a fast, easy way to get a representative sampling of client references:

1. **Because you're a buyer, ignore all references from sellers.**

   Doing so probably slices the list in half.

2. **Zero in on people who bought property similar in price, location, and property type to what you want to buy.**

3. **Call two of those representative buyers who purchased a home about 12 months ago, another two buyers who bought 6 months ago, and two buyers whose escrows closed most recently.**

   By spreading references over the past year, you can find out whether the agent's level of service has been consistently good.

Now that you've identified which buyers to call, here's what to ask when you have them on the phone:

✔ **Is the agent trustworthy? Honest? Did the agent follow through on promises?** Your agent can't be even the tiniest bit untrustworthy, dishonest, or unreliable. A negative answer to any of these questions is the kiss of death.

✔ **Did the agent have enough time to serve you properly? Was the agent available as required to fit your schedule?** Occasional scheduling conflicts are okay. Frequent conflicts are absolutely, flat-out unacceptable.

✔ **Did the agent explain everything that happened during the buying process clearly and in sufficient detail to satisfy you?** What one person thinks is sufficient detail may not be nearly enough information for another. You know which type of person you are — question agent references accordingly.

✔ **Did the agent set realistic contract deadlines and meet or beat them?** "Time is of the essence" is a condition of every real estate contract. Contract time frames for obtaining a loan, completing property inspections, and the like are extremely important and must be strictly adhered to, or the deal will go belly-up. Good agents prepare well-written contracts with realistic time frames and then ensure that all deadlines are met on or before the due dates.

✔ **Do the words *self-starter, committed,* and *motivated* describe the agent?** No one likes pushy people. But if you're under pressure to buy quickly, the last thing you want is a lethargic agent. You shouldn't have to jab your agent periodically with an electric prod to make sure that he's still breathing. Find out how energetically the agent in question is prepared to work.

✔ **Who found the home you bought — you or the agent?** This question is a double check of the agent's market knowledge. Good agents not only know what's already on the market, but also know which houses will be coming on the market soon. You shouldn't have to find the house you buy — that's your agent's job.

✔ **Did the agent negotiate a good price for your home?** See whether the agent's buyers *still* think that they got a good deal. Good agents are frugal when spending their clients' money. Good agents use their knowledge of property values and their negotiating skills to make sure that their clients pay the fair market value or less for the homes that they buy. People who bought homes six months or a year ago can tell you how well their purchase prices have stood the test of time.

✔ **Would you use the agent again?** This is the ultimate test of customer satisfaction. If someone says "no," find out why not. The negative answer may be due to a personality conflict between the buyer and the agent that won't bother you. On the other hand, the negative answer may reveal a horrendous flaw that you haven't yet discovered in the agent.

✔ **Is there anything I haven't asked you about the agent or the agent's office that you think I should know?** You never know what you'll find out when you ask the famous catch-all question.

Making your decision

After analyzing all three agents' sales activity, interviewing the agents, and talking to their buyers, you have most of the facts you need to make an informed decision. Here are three final considerations to help you select the paragon of virtue that you need on your real estate team:

✔ **Will you be proud having the agent represent you?** People who deal with your agent will form opinions of you based upon their impressions of your agent. You can't afford to have anyone on your team who isn't a highly skilled professional.

✔ **Do you communicate well with the agent?** Good agents make sure that you completely understand everything they say. If you can't understand your agent, you're not stupid — the agent is a poor communicator.

✔ **Do you enjoy the agent's personality?** Home buying is stressful, even for the coolest of cucumbers. You'll be sharing some extremely intense situations with your agent. Working with an agent you like may transform the home-buying process from a horrible experience into an exciting adventure — or at least a tolerable transaction.

Getting the most from your agent

After working so hard to find a great agent, it would be a shame to inadvertently ruin the relationship. Good buyer/agent relationships aren't accidental. Such relationships are based upon pillars of mutual loyalty and trust that develop over time.

Poor relationships, conversely, result from misconceptions of how the game is played. Some buyers act in what they think is their best interest, but they end up unintentionally harming themselves.

More isn't always better

One common fallacy is thinking that five agents are five times better than one agent. The theory sounds so logical. If you work with agents from a variety of offices, you can get better market coverage and first peek at the new listings that each office puts on the market. The more agents you work with, the better your chances of quickly finding your dream home.

Things don't work that way in the real world. When smart agents first meet you, they will probably ask whether you're working with any other agents. These agents are trying to find out how much you know about the market (so they won't waste time showing you houses that you've already seen) and learn what you didn't like about the properties that you saw.

One good agent can quickly show you every home on the market that meets your price, neighborhood, size, and condition specifications. If none of the houses is what you want, good agents keep looking until the right home hits the market. Good agents don't limit their searches to houses listed by their offices. They investigate anything even remotely similar to what you want, regardless of which office listed the property. Whether you work with one agent or one hundred, you'll see the same houses.

Agents know that they won't get paid if you don't buy. That risk comes with the job. What agents hate is losing a sale after months of hard work because they called you shortly *after* another agent called you about the same house. That risk is unnecessary. You're free, of course, to work with as many agents as you wish. In fact, working with more than one agent makes sense if you're looking for a home in more than one geographic area. Don't be surprised, however, if good agents in the same area opt out of a horse race. Their odds of getting paid for their work increase dramatically when they spend their time on buyers who work exclusively with them. Loyalty begets loyalty.

The risk of playing the field is rarely worth the reward. One loyal agent totally committed to finding you a home is infinitely better than five agents working for you as a last resort because they consider you just marginally better than Benedict Arnold. Like marriages, the best buyer/agent relationships are monogamous.

Your agent isn't the enemy

Another fallacy is viewing your agent as your adversary. True, you don't want to tell your innermost secrets to a loose-lipped agent who'll blithely blab them to the seller or seller's agent. Some buyers think that the less their agent knows about them, the better. Such buyers believe that after agents know why they want to buy and how much cash they have, the agents will somehow magically manipulate them into spending far more than they can afford to spend for the home they eventually buy.

Not true. Good agents ask such questions because they need to be sure that you're financially qualified in order to avoid wasting your time and theirs by showing you properties that you can't afford. If your agent knows that you're under deadline pressure to buy, she'll give your house hunt top priority.

Good agents won't betray your trust. They know that if they take care of you, the commission takes care of itself. If you can't trust your agent, don't play cat-and-mouse games — *get a new agent*.

Ironically, smart agents fear you as much as or more than you fear them. They know that you have the power to make or break their careers. If they please you, you'll be a source of glowing referrals for them. If they upset you, you'll tell everyone you know about the bad job they did.

Use the immense power of potential referrals to manage your relationship with the agent. If your agent does a lousy job, don't get mad — tell the world every gory detail of your rotten experience. Nothing ruins an agent's career faster than dissatisfied clients.

Bagging a Broker

Selecting a broker is easy. When you choose an agent, your agent's broker goes along for the ride. It's a package deal.

If your transaction rolls merrily along from the time your offer is accepted to the close of escrow, you'll probably never meet the broker. But if the engine begins to misfire and the wheels start coming off, one guess who you'll turn to for a quick repair job. Brokers are the invisible grease in problematic transactions.

All states issue two markedly different types of real estate licenses: one for salespeople (agents) and one for brokers. Agents who have broker's licenses must satisfy much more stringent educational and experience standards than agents with a salesperson's license do.

Your agent may have either type of license. Broker licensees have the option either to operate independently or to work for another broker. An agent who has a salesperson's license, on the other hand, *must* work under a broker's direct supervision so that you have access to the broker's higher lever of expertise should you need it.

When Harry Truman was president, he had a sign on his desk that read "The buck stops here." Like Truman, good brokers don't pass the buck. Here are some of their other characteristics:

- ✔ **Excellent reputation:** The broker's image, good or bad, will be obvious from comments that you hear while checking agent references. You want the seller, lender, and all other people involved in your transaction working with you because of your broker's reputation, not in spite of it. Buying a home is hard enough without the added burden of having to overcome guilt by association. If an agent's references disparage the agent's broker, dump the agent.

- ✔ **Extensive business relationships:** Good brokers develop and maintain relationships with the people whom their office deals with — other brokers, lenders, title officers, city officials, and the like. This preexisting reservoir of goodwill is yours to use when the going gets rough. Brokers with strong business relationships can work near-miracles for you in a crisis.

- ✔ **Strong problem-solving skills:** Participants in real estate transactions sometimes get highly emotional. When your life savings are on the line, you may occasionally lash out at your agent and the other players. Someone has to resolve the resulting quarrels and misunderstandings. That someone is the broker.

The broker's job is to help solve your problems. Call your broker into the game if your agent is stymied by a tough problem or if you're having trouble with your agent. Everything your agent does or fails to do is ultimately the broker's responsibility.

Landing a Lender

Everyone thinks that buying a home is likely to be the largest single purchase you'll ever make. Unless you're an all-cash buyer, however, everyone is wrong. Here's why.

Suppose that your dream home's purchase price is $250,000. You make a 20 percent cash down payment of $50,000 and get a $200,000 fixed-rate loan at 7.5 percent interest from your friendly lender. Over the next 30 years, you conscientiously repay the loan with payments of about $1,400 a month. (We show you in Chapters 3 and 6 how to crunch these numbers for yourself.)

Your 360 monthly loan payments total approximately $500,000. If you originally borrowed $200,000, the additional $300,000 you paid is interest on your loan. Total interest charges *exceed* your home's purchase price!

If you can't pay, you can't play. You need a good lender on your team to transform you from a home looker into a homeowner. By finding the right lender, you can save yourself big bucks over the life of the loan.

No one loan is right for everyone. A person fresh out of college who's struggling to buy a condo with 5 percent cash down has vastly different loan requirements than an older, cash-rich couple who put 50 percent cash down on a retirement cottage by using equity from the sale of their previous house.

Generations ago, finding the right loan was easy. You could get any kind of mortgage you wanted, as long as it was a 30-year, fixed-rate loan. All home loans were basically the same except for minor variations in loan fees and interest rates.

Street-smart versus book-smart

Book-smart people have theoretical knowledge. They know only what should happen in a perfect world based upon what they've read. You're getting book-smart right now.

Street-smart people, conversely, know how things work in the real world. They learned the hard way through years of hands-on, practical experience. A good real estate broker is one of the most street-smart people on your home-buying team.

People learn very little from uneventful, routine transactions; they're like flying a plane on autopilot. Street smarts come from the sweaty-palm deals. Fortunately, most agents have only one or two of these gut-wrenching messes each year. When these turbulent transactions occur, the broker takes control of the plane, so to speak.

Because the broker participates directly or indirectly in every deal the office handles, your broker's practical experience is directly related to the number of agents in the office. A broker who manages a 25-agent office, for example, gets 25 years' of real estate experience per calendar year. Any broker who can survive five years of handling all the office's truly terrible transactions becomes a superb problem-solver out of sheer necessity.

Those kinder, gentler days of yesteryear are long gone. Today, you're confronted by a bewildering array of fixed- and adjustable-rate mortgage (ARM) programs. In Chapter 6, we take the mystery out of securing a mortgage and selecting a lender.

Procuring Property Inspectors

A home's price is directly related to its physical condition. Homes in top shape sell for top dollar. Fixer-uppers sell at greatly reduced prices because whoever buys them must spend money on repairs to get them back into pristine condition.

Even if you're a rocket scientist, you can't know how much work a house may need just by looking at it. You can't see whether the roof leaks, the electrical system is shockingly defective, the plumbing is shot, the furnace's heat exchanger is cracked, the chimney is loose, or termites are feasting on the woodwork. Invisible defects like these cost major money to repair.

Because you don't want to inadvertently become the owner of a home with such expensive hidden problems, you need property inspectors on your team. None of the other players on your team — including real estate agents, lenders, and brokers — is qualified to advise you about a house's physical condition or the cost of necessary corrective work. In Chapter 13, we cover everything you need to know about property inspections and selecting property inspectors.

Even though a home isn't quite as complicated as a space shuttle, it still has plenty of expensive systems that can go haywire. "Saving" money by forgoing inspections just because a home appears to be in good condition is a false economy. The vast majority of home problems aren't visible. Never buy a house that hasn't been thoroughly inspected from foundation to roof by a qualified inspector of your own choosing.

Electing an Escrow Officer

One common denominator crops up in most every real estate deal: mutual distrust. As a buyer, would you give the sellers your hard-earned money before every single condition of the sale is satisfied? Not likely. If your positions were reversed and you were the seller, would you give the buyers the *title* (ownership) to your house before you got their money? No way.

Deals would grind to a halt without something to bridge the gulf of mutual buyer-and-seller distrust. Even the simplest transaction involves myriad details that must be resolved to everyone's satisfaction before the sale can be completed. That's why real estate, like other team sports, has a referee.

Your *escrow officer* is the referee who keeps the game civilized. Strictly speaking, escrow officers aren't on anyone's team — they're neutral. They act as a disinterested third party for buyers and sellers without showing favoritism to either party.

After you and the seller have a signed contract, all the documents, funds, and instructions related to your transaction are given to the escrow holder specified in your purchase agreement. We cover this process, known as *opening an escrow,* in detail in Chapter 14.

Buyers and sellers often select the escrow holder based upon the recommendation of their real estate agents. Depending on where the property you're buying is located, local custom dictates whether your escrow is handled by a lawyer, bank, real estate broker, or the firm that issues the title-insurance policy.

Escrow fees range from a few hundred dollars to several thousand dollars and are based on your property's purchase price. Once again, local custom usually determines whether the buyer or the seller pays for the escrow or whether the escrow fees are split fifty-fifty. However, as we discuss in Chapter 12, this item is often negotiable.

Finding (Or Forgoing) Financial and Tax Advisors

The real estate game is played with real money — your hard-earned cash. You've likely scrimped, saved, and done without in order to get the cash for your down payment. When you sell your house someday, its equity will probably be a major chunk of your net worth. Either way, buying or selling, you have big bucks on the line.

A home purchase has an enormous impact on your personal finances. Before you buy a home, you need to understand how a home purchase will fit within the context of your overall finances and your other goals. Be sure to read Chapters 2 and 3, which deal with these important issues.

Some experts give wrong advice

Ray wasn't very sophisticated about tax advisors when he moved to San Francisco. Several people whom Ray worked with suggested that he use their tax advisor. He selected her based on their recommendations (plus the fact that her office was only two blocks away from his).

Ray knew he'd made a mistake when he went over to her office to review the tax return she'd prepared for him. Ray asked her how she had arrived at the itemized deductions for auto expenses and professional training. In both cases, they were much higher than the totals of the receipts Ray had given her.

She explained that these higher deductions reduced his tax bite and said no one would question the deductions because they were within acceptable IRS guidelines. Ray still didn't understand her concept of deducting more money than he had spent.

Ray's tax advisor rather impatiently went through the tax return again, speaking more slowly and using smaller words the second time. She concluded by saying he shouldn't worry about what she'd done because everyone overstates expenses.

Ray knew that she was speaking English because he recognized nearly all the words, but they seemed to be bouncing off his forehead without penetrating his brain. He was getting more and more frustrated. His tax advisor was getting later and later for her next appointment. In desperation, she finally gave Ray the return and sent him home like a schoolboy to "think it over."

He did.

Ray decided the problem wasn't that he was stupid. The problem was that he'd been given unethical advice. In her zeal to save Ray money, the tax advisor had falsified Ray's deductions. That falsification was wrong. Worse, it was illegal. Ray solved the problem by getting a new tax advisor.

Never blindly follow the advice of experts because you're in awe of their expertise. Experts can be just as wrong as ordinary mortals.

You can elect to hire a financial advisor, but most such titled advisors aren't set up to handle home-buying questions objectively. The reason: Financial advisors stand to gain financially from the advice they render. Many so-called financial consultants get commissions from the investments they sell you. If this is the case, how motivated will they be to advise you to use your cash to buy a home instead of an investment from them?! Advisors who manage money on a fee (or a percentage) basis have the same conflict of interest.

If you're going to hire an advisor, use one who works by the hour and doesn't have a vested interested in your home-buying decision. Few financial advisors work on this basis. Although tax advisors are more likely to work on this basis, they tend to have a narrower-than-needed financial perspective. A competent tax advisor may be able to help you structure the home's purchase to maximize your tax benefits. For most transactions, however, a tax advisor is unnecessary.

If you want to hire a financial or tax advisor, interview several before you select one. Check with your agent, banker, lawyer, business associates, and friends for referrals. As is the case with selecting your agent, you should get client references from each tax advisor and call the references.

Here's what to look for in a good financial or tax advisor:

- ✔ **Is this a full-time job for the advisor?** The realm of personal finances and taxes is too vast for you to trust a part-timer. You need the services of a full-time professional.

- ✔ **Does the advisor speak your language?** Good advisors can explain your financial alternatives in simple terms. If you don't understand exactly what the tax advisor is saying, ask for clarification. If you still don't understand, get another tax advisor. (See the sidebar "Some experts give wrong advice.")

- ✔ **Is the advisor objective?** Hire someone who works solely by the hour and doesn't have a vested interest in the advice he gives you about when to buy and how much to spend.

- ✔ **What is the advisor's fee schedule?** Hourly fees vary widely. Don't pick someone strictly on a cost-per-hour basis. An advisor who's just beginning to practice, for example, may charge only half as much as one with 20 years' experience. If the rookie takes four hours to do what the old pro does in an hour, which advisor is more expensive in the long run? Furthermore, the quality of the seasoned veteran's advice may be superior to the quality of the novice's advice.

- ✔ **Is the tax advisor a Certified Public Accountant (CPA) or Enrolled Agent (EA)?** These professional designations indicate that the tax advisor has satisfied special education and experience requirements and has passed a rigorous licensing exam. A CPA does general accounting and prepares tax returns. An EA focuses specifically on taxation. Only CPAs, EAs, and attorneys are authorized to represent you before the IRS in the event of an audit.

- ✔ **Does the tax advisor have experience with real estate transactions?** Tax practice, like law or medicine, is an extremely broad field. The tax advisors that IBM uses (for example) are undoubtedly wonderful, but IBM's tax advisors aren't necessarily the best ones for you. You need a tax advisor whose clients have tax problems like yours.

The best advisors in the world can't do much to change the financial and tax consequences of a transaction *after* the deal is done. If you're going to consult advisors, do so *before* you make significant financial decisions. Plan your financial and tax situation instead of reacting to the consequences after the fact.

Looking for Lawyers

Lawyers are like seat belts: You never know when you may need them. Your deal is rolling merrily along when out of nowhere — slam, bam, wham — you hit a legal pothole and end up in Sue City.

That real estate purchase agreement you sign is meant to be a legally binding contract between you and the seller. If you have any questions about the legality of your contract, get a lawyer on your team *pronto*. No one else on the team is qualified to give you legal advice.

Here's what determines whether you need a lawyer on your team:

- **The location of the property you're buying:** In states such as California, lawyers rarely work on deals that involve only filling in the blanks on a standard, preprinted purchase agreement that has been previously reviewed and approved by members of the bar association. In other states, such as New York, however, lawyers routinely do everything from preparing purchase contracts to closing the escrow. Your agent will know the role that lawyers need to play in your locale.

- **The complexity of your transaction:** You need a lawyer any time you get into a situation that isn't covered by a standard contract. Unless your agent is also a lawyer, she isn't qualified to do creative legal writing. Complicated issues, such as those that frequently arise from partnership agreements between unrelated people who buy property together, and the complex legal ramifications of taking title to your home should be handled by a lawyer. (We get into partnership agreements in Chapter 8 and taking title in Chapter 14.)

- **When no agent is involved:** Say that you're buying a home that's being offered for sale directly by the owner. If neither you nor the seller has an agent, get a lawyer to prepare the contract and have the lawyer do the work that an agent would normally handle. Eliminating an agent doesn't eliminate the need for disclosures, inspections, contingency removals, and myriad other details involved in the home-buying process.

- **To sleep at night:** You may have the world's easiest deal. Still, if you'd feel more comfortable having a lawyer review the contract, your peace of mind is certainly worth the cost of an hour or two of legal time.

Selecting your lawyer

If, for whatever reason, you decide that you need a lawyer, interview several before making your selection. Law, like medicine, is highly specialized. A corporate attorney or the lawyer who handled your neighbor's divorce isn't the best choice for your real estate team. Get a lawyer who specializes in residential real estate transactions. Your agent and broker are excellent referral sources because they work with real estate lawyers all the time in their transactions.

A good lawyer:

- ✔ **Is a full-time lawyer and licensed to practice law in your state:** Of course.

- ✔ **Is local talent:** Real estate law, like real estate brokerage, is extremely provincial. The law varies not only from state to state, but also from one area to another within the same state. Rent-control laws, condominium-conversion statutes, and zoning codes, for example, are usually passed by city or county governing agencies. A good local lawyer knows the laws and has working relationships with people who administer the laws in your area.

- ✔ **Has a realistic fee schedule:** Lawyers' fees vary widely. A good lawyer gives you an estimate of how much it will cost to handle your situation. As with financial and tax advisors, the experience factor comes into play. Seasoned lawyers generally charge higher hourly fees than novice lawyers, but seasoned lawyers also tend to get a lot more done in an hour than inexperienced lawyers can. A low rate is no bargain if the novice is learning on your nickel.

- ✔ **Has a good track record:** If your case may go to trial, find out whether the lawyer has courtroom experience. Some lawyers don't do trial work. Then ask about the lawyer's track record of wins versus losses. What good is a lawyer with a great deal of trial experience if that lawyer has never won a case?

- ✔ **Is a deal-maker or a deal-breaker (whichever is appropriate):** Some lawyers are great at putting deals together. Others specialize in blowing them out of the water. Each skill is important. Good deal-makers, however, aren't always equally good deal-breakers, and vice versa. Depending on whether you want the lawyer to get you out of a deal or keep it together, be sure that you have the right type of lawyer for your situation.

If your lawyer's *only* solution to every problem is a lawsuit, you may be in the clutches of a deal-breaker who wants to run up big legal fees. Find another lawyer!

- ✔ **Speaks your language:** Good lawyers explain your options clearly and concisely without resorting to incomprehensible legalese. Then they give you a *risk assessment* of your options in order to help you make a sound decision. For example, the lawyer may say that your first course of action will take longer but will give you a 90 percent chance of success, while the faster option gives you only a 50 percent chance of prevailing.

Getting the most out of a lawyer

Whoever said that an ounce of prevention is worth a pound of cure must have been thinking of lawyers. A two-hour preventive consultation with your lawyer is infinitely better than a two-month trial that could take place just because you "saved" money by avoiding a consulting fee.

If you're not sure whether you'll need a lawyer, Chapter 12 contains a clause you can put in your contract to get out of any deal that isn't approved by your lawyer. You don't actually need to get a lawyer if you use this clause; it just gives you the option to have the contract reviewed later by a lawyer if you wish.

Good lawyers are strategists. Given adequate lead time, they can structure nearly any deal to your advantage. Conversely, if you bring wonderful lawyers into the game after the deal is done, all they can do is damage control. The best defense is a good offense.

Beware of the *legal awe* factor. Some people hold lawyers in awe because their word is viewed as law. Disobey lawyers, they think, and you'll go to jail. Baloney. Don't blindly follow your lawyer's advice. If you don't understand the advice or if you disagree with it, question it. You may be correct, and the lawyer may be wrong. Lawyers are every bit as fallible as everyone else.

Chapter 10

What's It Worth?

*Y*ou see a home for sale. The asking price is $249,500. Is that charming cottage a steal or an overpriced turkey?

If you don't have the faintest idea, don't worry. That's normal. Most buyers don't know property values when they start hunting for a home. To become an *educated buyer,* you need to take time to familiarize yourself with property values.

When Ray began his real estate career, he spent dozens of hours each week looking at houses. Like all new agents, his appetite for property was boundless and indiscriminate — big houses, tiny condos, old property and new, houses in pristine condition or fixer-uppers, uptown, downtown, and midtown. If it had a roof and a For Sale sign, Ray toured the property inside and out.

Why? The best way to learn property values is to eyeball as many houses as possible and then monitor them until they sell. That's how agents educate themselves.

You don't need to see every house in town to get educated. A good agent can accelerate your learning curve by playing the real estate version of show-and-tell. You have to tour only houses that meet your specific wish list for budget, style, size, and neighborhood. After seeing no more than a dozen houses comparable to your dream home, you should be an educated buyer.

Don't be surprised if you're utterly confused after a day spent looking at property for sale. When you see six or seven houses in rapid succession, it's challenging to remember which one had the wonderful kitchen and which one had the huge backyard with a swingset. To make your property tours most productive, follow these tips:

✔ **Take notes.** You'll probably get a listing statement (those one-page, house-for-sale advertisements/marketing pieces), brochure, or Multiple Listing Service fact sheet describing each property you visit. To help you remember the house, make notes directly on your information sheet regarding distinguishing features such as a sunken living room, a crazy floor plan, or a location near a commuter rail stop.

✔ **Review the tour.** After you've finished for the day, discuss the houses you saw with your real estate agent (if you have one). If your memory is fuzzy about a property or two that you visited, your agent can ideally fill in the details.

✔ **Save the info sheets.** As you'll see when you read the "Determining Fair Market Value: Comparable Market Analysis" section later in this chapter, sale prices are mighty important negotiating tools. Ask your agent (or the listing agent, if you don't have an agent) to tell you when a house you toured sells and how much it sold for. Mark the sale price and date of sale on your info sheet for future reference.

The Three Elusive Components of Worth

Oscar Wilde said a cynic is someone who knows the price of everything and the value of nothing. In the real estate game, neither *cost* nor *price* is the same as *value*. When you understand what these words mean and how they differ, you can replace emotion with objectivity when looking at houses and during price negotiations after you finally make an offer. Out-facting people usually beats trying to out-argue them.

Value is a moving target

Value is your opinion of what a particular home is worth to you, based on how you intend to use it now and in the future. Value isn't carved in stone. On the contrary, it's pretty darn elusive.

For one thing, opinions are subjective. We, your humble authors, may think that we resemble Robert Redford and Paul Newman. You, on the other hand, are of the opinion that we look like Boris Karloff and Bela Lugosi — in full monster makeup. No harm done, as long as we all realize that a big difference exists between subjective opinions and objective facts.

Furthermore, *internal factors* — things related to your personal situation — have a sneaky way of changing over time. Suppose that you currently place great value on a home with four bedrooms and a large, fenced-in backyard. The home must be located in a town with a good school system. Why? Because you have young children.

Uneducated buyers are inadvertent liars

Ray has only to look into a mirror to see the perfect prototype of a lying, uneducated buyer. Like all buyers, Ray honestly believed he was telling his agent the truth when he and his sweet wife, Annie B., began looking for a home in the wine country about 50 miles north of San Francisco. When they first met their agent, Beverly Mueller, Ray wasted no time establishing the ground rules of the house hunt.

"We don't need the Taj Mahal," Ray told Beverly. "I'm in the real estate army, not a civilian like your other buyers. Trust me when I tell you that $300,000 is the flat-out, absolute, upper limit of what we'll spend."

"I understand, Ray. We'll only look at places under $300,000," Beverly said.

And look they did. Over the next several months, Beverly showed them every house in their price range on the market in the Sonoma Valley. Ray and Annie rejected each and every one. Either they liked the land and hated the house, or vice versa. They were ready to give up when they got lucky.

Ray and Annie found Woodpecker Haven, the home they ended up buying in Glen Ellen, thanks to Karen and Herman Isman, friends of theirs who were also working with Beverly. Karen and Annie drove from San Francisco to Glen Ellen together to see a house that Beverly thought the Ismans would like. It was love at first sight — not for Karen, for Annie.

Why hadn't Beverly shown Ray and Annie the house? Because its asking price was $390,000 — far more than the $300,000 ceiling Ray imposed. Beverly's mistake was believing what Ray told her when they first met.

Why did Ray lie? He didn't intend to. Had he and Annie found what they wanted for less than $300,000, Ray would've been telling the truth. Only after three months of looking at property did it become clear that what Ray and Annie wanted to spend and what they wanted to live in were totally out of whack with market reality.

Many buyers hit the same wall sooner or later during their education process. Ray and Annie belatedly realized that they had to make trade-offs — either reduce their expectations to fit their budget or expand their budget until it satisfied their expectations.

That was when they became educated buyers. They were finally realistic enough to make tough decisions.

What Ray and Annie experienced happens to most people. For example, you ruefully decide that either the swimming pool or the family room has to go because you can't afford a home that has both and still buy in the neighborhood you like. Or perhaps you opt to keep your wish list intact and buy in a slightly less wonderful neighborhood. Something has to give when you're forced to confront reality.

The other alternative is expanding your buying power. Much as you'd like the security of a 30-year fixed-rate loan, you decide to get an adjustable-rate mortgage instead because the ARM allows you to qualify for a bigger loan. Much as you'd like to buy without financial assistance from your parents, you swallow your pride and ask them for a loan. Again, something has to give.

Groucho Marx once said he'd never belong to any club that would have him as a member. Paraphrasing Groucho, most folks would rather not settle for the house they can afford if, by stretching themselves a bit, they can buy their dream home.

Twenty years from now, when the kids are grown and have moved out (you hope!), you may decide to sell the house. Why? Because you no longer need such a big home. Neither the house nor the school system changed — what changed were internal factors regarding your use for the property and thus its value to you.

External factors are things outside your control that affect property values. If your commute time is cut in half because mass-transit rail service is extended into your neighborhood after you buy your home, your home's value may increase. If a garbage dump is built next door to you, you'll have a big problem getting top dollar for your house when you sell it.

The law of supply and demand is another external factor that affects value. If more people want to buy than sell, buyer competition drives home prices up. Conversely, if more people want to sell than buy, home prices drop. See Chapter 4 for a complete explanation of all the factors that influence home prices.

Cost is yesterday

Cost measures past expenditures — for example, what the sellers paid when they bought their house. What the sellers originally paid or how much they spent fixing up the house after they bought it doesn't mean diddlypoo as far as a house's present or future value is concerned. That was then, and this is now.

For example, when home prices skyrocketed in most parts of both coasts during the latter half of the 1990s and into the 2000s, some buyers accused sellers of being greedy. "You paid $400,000 seven years ago. Now you're asking $850,000," they said. "If you get your price, you'll make an obscenely large profit."

"So what?" sellers replied compassionately. "If you don't want to pay our modest asking price, move out of the way so those nice buyers standing behind you can present their offer." In a hot seller's market, people who base their offering price on what sellers originally paid for property waste everyone's time.

However, the market doesn't always go in the same direction forever. In the early 1990s, for example, prices had declined in many areas. Sellers would've been ecstatic to find buyers willing to pay them what they'd paid five years earlier, when home prices peaked.

Price is what it's worth today

Sellers have *asking prices* on their houses. Buyers put *offering prices* in their contracts. Buyers and sellers negotiate back and forth to establish *purchase prices.* Today's purchase price is tomorrow's cost. Is the purchase price a good value? That depends.

You may get a bargain if you find a house owned by people who don't know property values or who must sell quickly due to an adverse life change such as divorce, job loss, or a death in the family. Folks who don't have time to sit around waiting for buyers willing to pay top dollar usually take a hit when they sell. Time is the seller's enemy and the buyer's pal.

If, however, you must buy quickly to relocate for a new job or to get your kids settled before school starts, watch out. You could overpay because you don't have enough time to search for a good deal.

Cost is the past, price is the present, and value (like beauty) is in the eyes of the beholder. What the sellers paid for their house years ago, or what they'd like to get for it today, doesn't matter. Don't squander your hard-earned money on an overpriced house to satisfy a seller's unrealistic fantasy.

Fair Market Value

Natural disasters aside, every home will sell at the right price. That price is defined as its *fair market value* (FMV) — the price a buyer will pay and a seller will accept for the house, given that neither buyer nor seller is under *duress.* Duress can come from life changes such as major health problems, divorce, or sudden job transfer, which put either the buyers or sellers under pressure to perform quickly. If appraisers know that a sale was made under duress, they raise or lower the sale price accordingly to more accurately reflect the house's true fair market value.

Fair market value is more powerful than plain old *value.* As a buyer, you have an opinion of what the house is worth to you. The sellers have a separate, not necessarily equal (and probably higher), opinion of their home's value. These values are opinions, not facts. You can't bank opinions.

Unlike value, fair market value is fact. It becomes a fact when buyers and sellers agree upon a *mutually acceptable price.* Just as it takes two to tango, it takes a buyer and a seller to make fair market value. Facts are bankable.

"Can't sell" versus "won't sell"

Two weeks of extraordinarily heavy winter rain undermined the soil of a subdivision in the Anaheim Hills area of Los Angeles. After this drenching, homes in the 25-acre development began slipping downhill at the rate of about 1 inch a day.

Home foundations and swimming pools cracked. Streets and sidewalks buckled. Local authorities finally ordered everyone in the subdivision to evacuate their homes until the ground stabilized.

Unlike most frustrated sellers we know, these folks really *couldn't* sell their homes. Forces of nature beyond their control reduced their houses' value to zero. Other than salvage value, no market exists for unintentionally mobile homes.

Fortunately, most homeowners who claim that they "can't" sell their houses don't have this problem. They aren't disaster victims whose homes are suddenly rendered valueless by an act of God. On the contrary, they have buyers galore for their houses, as well as scads of lenders who'd make loans to those buyers.

If nothing is wrong with their houses, what's the problem? The homeowners. The problem isn't that they *can't* sell. These homeowners *won't* sell.

As long as homeowners choose not to accept what buyers are willing to pay for their houses, they won't sell — and those houses will remain on the market at their inflated asking prices. It's a self-fulfilling prophecy. As a prospective home buyer, beware of such greedy, unrealistic sellers.

When fair market value isn't fair — need-based pricing

Whenever the real estate market gets all soft and mushy, many would-be sellers feel that fair market value isn't fair at all. "Why doesn't our house sell?" they ask. "Why can't we get our asking price? It's not fair."

Don't let your highly developed sense of fair play make a sucker out of you. Sellers frequently confuse "fair" with "impartial." Despite its friendly name, fair market value isn't a warm, cuddly fairy godmother. On the contrary, it can be heartless and cruel. Need isn't a component of fair market value. Fair market value doesn't care about any of the following:

✔ How much the sellers need because they overpaid for their house when they bought it

✔ How much the sellers *need* to recover the money they spent fixing up their house after they bought it

✔ How much money the sellers *need* to pay off their loan

✔ How much money the sellers *need* from the sale to buy their next humble abode: Buckingham Palace

Here's why a seller's *need-based pricing* doesn't enter into fair market value. Suppose that two identical houses next door to each other are listed for sale. One house was purchased for $32,000 three decades ago. The other house sold a couple years ago for $320,000, soon after home prices peaked in the area. The first home has no outstanding loan on it. The other still has a big mortgage.

Bill and Mary, who own the house purchased two years ago, *need* more money than Ed, owner of the house purchased 30 years ago. After all, they paid ten times as much as Ed for their house, and they owe the bank big bucks to pay off their mortgage.

Because the houses are basically identical in size, age, condition, and location, they have the same fair market value. Not surprisingly, they both sell for $275,000. That gives Ed a nice nest egg for retirement but barely pays off Mary and Bill's mortgage. Fair? Ed thinks so. Bill and Mary don't.

Fair market value is brutally impartial. It is what it is — not what buyers or sellers want it to be.

Median home prices versus fair market value

Some folks think that median sale prices for homes indicate fair market values. They don't.

Organizations such as the National Association of Realtors, the chamber of commerce, and private research firms generate *median sale-price statistics* by monitoring home sales in a specific geographic region such as a city, county, or state. One function of these organizations is to gather market-research data on home-sales activity.

There's nothing magical about the *median sale price.* It's simply the midpoint in a range of all the home sales for a reporting period. Half the sales during the reporting period fall above the median, and half fall below it. The median-price home, in other words, is the one exactly in the middle of the prices of all the houses that sold.

When this book went to press, the median sale price of a home in America was about $220,000, which tells you that half the homes in America sold for more than $220,000, and half sold for less than $220,000. Unfortunately, all you know about this hypothetical median-price home is its price.

You don't know how many bedrooms or baths the median-price home has. Nor do you know how many square feet of interior living space the house has, how old it is, or whether it has a garage or a yard. You don't even know where this elusive median-price house is located, other than that it's somewhere in the United States.

If median-price information is so vague, why bother with it? Because it tells you two important things:

✔ **Price trends:** If the median price of a home in America was $140,000 five years ago and is $220,000 now, you know home prices in general are rising. You don't know why median prices are going up, just that they are.

✔ **Price relativity:** If the median-price home in Yakima, Washington, sells for $185,000 versus $550,000 for the median-price Honolulu home, you know that you'll get a much bigger bang for your housing buck in Yakima. Honolulu has many excellent qualities, but cheap housing isn't one of them.

Median-home-price statistics make interesting reading, but they aren't any more accurate for determining specific home values than median-income statistics are for determining how much you'll earn from your next employer. You need much more precise property-value information before you invest a major chunk of your life's savings in a home.

Chapter 3 can help you determine how much you can afford to spend on a home. You can find some Web sites in Chapter 11 that you can use to locate affordable areas by comparing median home prices on a town-by-town and neighborhood-by-neighborhood basis. When median-price statistics indicate that home prices are rising or falling sharply in an area, find out why by reading and talking to players on your real estate team, such as your agent.

Determining Fair Market Value: Comparable Market Analysis

Believe it or not, houses are like Red Delicious apples. Most houses are green and need more time on the real estate tree before they are ready to pick. A few are ripe for picking right now. The trick is knowing which is which, because houses don't turn red as they ripen.

That's one reason you must understand fair market value and know the asking prices and sale prices of houses comparable to the one you want to buy. Smart home buyers know which houses are green and which are ripe.

The basics of a helpful CMA

The best way to accurately determine a home's fair market value is to prepare a written *comparable market analysis* (CMA). A competent real estate agent can and should prepare a CMA for a home that you're interested in before you make your purchase offer. Every residential real estate office has its own CMA format. No matter how the information is presented to you, Tables 10-1 and 10-2 show you what good CMAs contain.

Table 10-1		Sample CMA — "Recent Sales" Section				
Address	*Date Sold*	*Sale Price*	*Bedrm/Bath*	*Parking*	*Condition*	*Remarks*
210 Oak	04/30/06	$390,000	3/3	2 car	Very good	Best comp. Approx. same size and cond. as dream home (DH), slightly smaller lot. 1,867 sq. ft. $209/S.F.
335 Elm	02/14/06	$368,500	3/2	2 car	Fair	Busy street. Older baths. 1,805 sq. ft. $204/S.F.
307 Ash	03/15/06	$385,000	3/3	2 car	Good	Slightly larger than DH, but nearly same size and condition. Good comp. 1,850 sq. ft. $208/S.F.
555 Ash	01/12/06	$382,500	3/2.5	2 car	Excellent	Smaller than DH, but knockout renovation. 1,740 sq. ft. $220/S.F.
75 Birch	04/20/06	$393,000	3/3	3 car	Very good	Larger than DH, but location isn't as good. Superb landscaping. 1,910 sq. ft. $206/S.F.

These are facts. The CMA's "Recent Sales" section helps establish the fair market value of 220 Oak — your *dream home* that is currently on the market — by comparing it with *all* the other houses that:

| ✔ Are located in the same neighborhood

| ✔ Are approximately the same age, size, and condition

| ✔ Have sold in the past six months

These houses are called *comps,* which is short for *comparables.* Depending on when you began your house hunt, you probably haven't actually toured all the sold comps. No problem. A good real estate agent can show you listing statements for the houses you haven't seen, take you on a verbal tour of the properties, and explain how each one compares with your dream home.

Communicating well with your agent about subjective terms such as *large, lots of light, close to school,* and so on is critically important. You must understand precisely what the agent means when using such terms. Conversely, your agent must understand precisely what you want, need, and can afford.

If you and your agent were to analyze the sale comps in our example, you would find that houses comparable to the home you want to buy — 220 Oak, in Table 10-2 — are selling for slightly over $200 per square foot. Putting the sale prices into a price-per-square-foot basis makes comparisons much easier. As you can see in Table 10-2, anything that's way above or below the norm really leaps out at you.

Table 10-2		Sample CMA — "Currently for Sale" Section				
Address	*Date Listed*	*Asking Price*	*Bedrm/ Bath*	*Parking*	*Condition*	*Remarks*
220 Oak (Dream Home)	04/25/06	$395,000	3/3	2 car	Very good	Quieter location than 123 Oak, good detailing, older kitchen. 1,880 sq. ft. $210/S.F.
123 Oak	05/01/06	$399,500	3/2	2 car	Excellent	High-end rehab. & priced accordingly. Done, done, done. 1,855 sq. ft. $215/S.F.
360 Oak	02/10/06	$375,000	3/2	1 car	Fair	Kitchen & baths need work, no fireplace. 1,695 sq. ft. $221/S.F.

Address	Date Listed	Asking Price	Bedrm/ Bath	Parking	Condition	Remarks
140 Elm	04/01/06	$379,500	3/3	2 car	Good	Busy street, small rooms, small yard. 1,725 sq. ft. $220/S.F.
505 Elm	10/31/06	$425,000	2/2	1 car	Fair	Delusions of grandeur. Grossly overpriced! 1,580 sq. ft. $269/S.F.
104 Ash	04/17/06	$389,500	3/2.5	2 car	Very good	Great comp! Good floor plan, large rooms. Surprised it hasn't sold. 1,860 sq. ft. $209/S.F.
222 Ash	02/01/06	$419,500	3/2	1 car	Fair	Must have used 505 Elm as comp. Will never sell at this price. 1,610 sq. ft. $261/S.F.
47 Birch	03/15/06	$409,000	4/3.5	2 car	Good	Nice house, but over-improved for neighborhood. 2,005 sq. ft. $204/S.F.
111 Birch	04/25/06	$389,500	3/3	2 car	Very good	Gorgeous kitchen, no fireplace. 1,870 sq. ft. $208/S.F.

The "Currently for Sale" section of the CMA compares your dream home (in this case, 220 Oak) with neighborhood comps that are *currently on the market.* These comps are included in the analysis to check price trends:

- ✔ **If prices are falling:** Asking prices of houses on the market today will be lower than sale prices of comparable houses.

- ✔ **If prices are rising:** You'll see higher asking prices today than for comps sold three to six months ago.

If you've been looking at houses in a specific area for a while, you've probably been in all the comps currently on the market in that area. You don't need anyone to tell you what you've seen with your own eyes. However, you do need an agent's help to compare the comps you've seen with comps you haven't seen, because the houses sold before you began your house hunt.

As Table 10-2 shows, your dream house appears to be priced very close to its fair market value based on the actual sale price of 210 Oak (in Table 10-1). Given that 220 Oak has 1,880 square feet, it's worth $392,920 at $209 per square foot. Factually establishing property value is easy once you know how.

Your CMA must be comprehensive. It should include *all* comp sales in the past six months and *all* comps currently on the market. Getting an accurate picture of fair market values is more difficult if some parts of the puzzle are missing, especially in a neighborhood where homes don't sell frequently.

Like milk in your refrigerator, comps have expiration dates. Lenders usually won't accept houses that sold more than six months ago as comps. Their sale prices don't reflect current consumer confidence, business conditions, or mortgage rates. As a general rule, the older the comp, the less likely that it represents today's fair market value.

Six months is generally accepted as long enough to have a good cross section of comp sales but short enough to have fairly consistent market conditions. But six months isn't carved in stone. If a major economic calamity occurred three months ago, for example, six months is too long for a valid comparison. Conversely, if homes in a certain area rarely sell, you may need to examine comparable sales that occurred more than six months ago.

Sale prices are always given far more weight than asking prices when determining fair market value. Sellers can ask whatever they want for their houses; asking prices are sometimes fantasy. Sale prices are always facts — they indicate fair market value. The best proof of what a house is worth is its sale price. Don't guess. Analyze the sale of comparable homes. Be sure that the comparable sales information factors in price reductions or large credits given for corrective work repairs (for example, a $5,000 credit from the sellers to the buyers to replace a broken furnace).

The flaws of CMAs

CMAs beat the heck out of median-price statistics for establishing fair market values, but even CMAs aren't perfect. We've seen people use exactly the same comps and arrive at very different opinions of fair market value. Discrepancies creep into the CMA process if you blindly compare comps without knowing all the following details of the subject properties:

✓ **Wear and tear:** No two homes are the same after they've been lived in. Suppose that two identical tract homes are located next door to each other. One, owned by an older couple with no children or pets, is in pristine condition. The other, owned by a family with several small kids and several large dogs, resembles a federal disaster area. Your guess is as good as ours when figuring out how much repairing the wear-and-tear damage in the second house will cost. A good comparable analysis adjusts for this difference between the two homes.

✔ **Site differences within a neighborhood:** Even though all the comps are in the same neighborhood, they aren't located on precisely the same plot of ground. How much is being located next to the beautiful park worth? How much will you pay to be seven minutes closer to the commuter-train stop? These value adjustments are a smidge less precise than brain surgery.

✔ **Out-of-neighborhood comps:** Suppose that in the past six months, no homes were sold in the neighborhood where you want to live. Going into another neighborhood to find comps means that you and your agent must make value adjustments between two different neighborhoods' amenities (schools, shopping, transportation, and so on). Comparing different neighborhoods is far more difficult than making value adjustments within the same neighborhood.

✔ **Noncomp home sales:** What if five houses sold in the neighborhood in the past six months, but none of them were even remotely comparable in age, size, style, or condition to the house you want to buy? You and your agent must estimate value differences for three- versus four-bedroom homes, old versus new kitchens, small versus large yards, garage versus carport, and so on. If the home you want has a panoramic view, and none of the other houses has any view at all, how much does the view increase the home's value? Guesstimates like these don't put astronauts on the moon.

These variables aren't insurmountable obstacles to establishing your dream home's fair market value. They do, however, greatly increase the margin of error when trying to determine a realistic offering price. You can minimize pricing problems created by these variables if you and/or your agent actually tour comparable homes inside and out.

A valid comparison of your dream home to the other houses is impossible if you and your agent have only read about the comps in listing statements or seen them on a Web site. Here's why:

✔ **Most listing statements are overblown to greater or lesser degrees.** You don't know how exaggerated the statement is if you haven't seen the house for yourself. You may consider the "large" master bedroom tiny. That "gourmet" kitchen's only distinction may be an especially fancy hot plate. The "sweeping" view from the living room may exist only if you're as tall as Michael Jordan. Of course, you won't know any of these things if you only read the houses' puff sheets instead of visiting them in person.

- ✔ **Floor plans greatly affect a home's value.** Two houses, for example, may both be approximately the same size, age, and condition, yet vary wildly in value. One house's floor plan flows beautifully from room to room; the rooms themselves are well proportioned, with high ceilings. The other house doesn't work well because its floor plan is choppy and the ceilings are low. You can't tell which is which just by reading the two listing statements.

- ✔ **Whoever controls the camera controls what you see.** Remember when viewing those stunning color photos or video footage of a house being advertised on a Web site that you're permitted to see only what the person who took the pictures wants you to see. You certainly won't get a peek at less desirable things, such as worn areas on the living-room carpet or graffiti sprayed on the garage door of the house next door.

Eyeball. Eyeball. Eyeball. *Eyeballing* — personally touring houses and noting important details both inside and out with your own eyes — is the best way to decide which houses are true comps for your dream home.

Getting a Second Opinion: Appraisals versus CMAs

If you're in no rush to submit an offer, and you're the suspicious type, you can double-check the opinion of value that you and your agent arrived at before making an offer on your dream home. You can pay several hundred dollars to get a professional appraisal of the house.

Getting an *unbiased* second opinion of value is always reassuring. An appraiser won't tell you what you want to hear just to make a sale. The appraiser isn't trying to sell you anything. Whether you buy the house or not, the appraiser gets paid.

Unfortunately, the fact that the appraiser charges a fee regardless of whether you buy the house cuts both ways. Suppose that you and the sellers can't reach an agreement on price and terms of sale because the sellers are deluded. Even if your offer isn't accepted, you still get a bill from the appraiser. Paying for appraisals or property inspections before your offer is accepted generally isn't wise.

If you think a professional appraisal is vastly superior to your agent's opinion of value, think again. A good agent's CMA is usually as creditable as an appraisal. Conversely, if a professional appraisal is vastly superior because your agent is a lousy judge of property values, you should get a better agent.

In any given geographical area, appraisers usually don't eyeball nearly as many houses as agents who concentrate on that area. Appraisers aren't lazy; they use their time in other ways.

Formal appraisals are time consuming. An appraiser inspects the property from foundation to attic, measures its square footage, makes detailed notes regarding everything from the quality of construction to the amount of wear and tear, photographs the house inside and out, photographs comps for the house being appraised, writes up the appraisal, and so on. Agents can tour 15 to 20 houses in the time it takes an appraiser to complete one appraisal.

Because touring properties is so time consuming, because good agents are already doing the legwork, and because it's usually impossible to tour a home after the sale has been completed, appraisers frequently call agents to get information about houses the agents listed or sold that may be comps. No matter how good an agent's description of the house is, however, personally touring the property is still best. Any appraisal's accuracy is reduced somewhat whenever the appraisal is based on comps the appraiser hasn't seen.

Agents also call one another about houses they haven't seen, so don't think that appraisers are the only ones who dial for info. However, remember that you're relying upon your agent's local market knowledge to help you determine what a home is worth. If your agent hasn't seen most of the comps used in your CMA, get an agent who knows the market.

Unless you're pretty darn unsure about a property's value and willing to spend the money whether the deal goes through or not, don't waste money on a precontract appraisal.

Why Buyers and Sellers Often Start Far Apart

The average buyer may be brighter than the average seller. How else can you explain why buyers are generally so much more realistic about property prices?

It's not as though there are two different real estate markets: an expensive one for sellers and a cheap one for buyers. Sellers have access to exactly the same comps buyers do. Yet buyers' initial offering prices tend to be far more realistic than sellers' initial asking prices. Why? Figure 10-1 may offer some insight into that question.

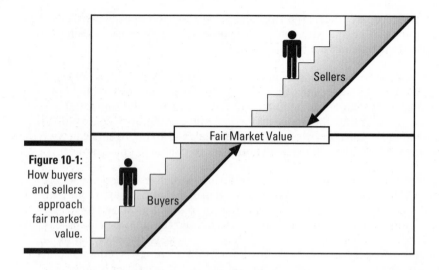

Some people believe that the selfish interests of buyers and sellers force them to approach a house's fair market value from opposite directions. Buyers bring their offering price *up* to fair market value because they don't want to overpay. Sellers ratchet their price *down* to fair market value because they hate the thought of leaving any money on the table.

That's logical but simplistic. This reasoning still doesn't explain why many sellers initially tend to be so much more unrealistic than buyers.

The better you understand the warped thought processes of these sellers, the better you can handle their unreasonable objections to your eminently fair offer. To that end, here are the common causes of absurdly high asking prices.

Inept agents

Just because *you* used the information in Chapter 9 to select a great agent doesn't mean that everyone will. In fact, many people do a rotten job of picking an agent.

Perhaps the sellers' agent is an incompetent boob who doesn't know anything about property values. Those poor misguided sellers didn't put a smart asking price on their house because their agents gave them lousy advice.

When your agent discovers that the other agent is inept — either by the poor quality of the comps that the sellers' agent used to establish the asking price or by reputation (these things get around in the real estate brokerage community) — what can you do? That depends.

Bidding wars

When house sellers select an agent, the interviewing process may go awry. Bidding wars often develop among the agents competing to list the sellers' house for sale. The concept of fair market value is the bidding war's first victim. If you try to buy such a house, you could be the second victim. Here's what happens when the sellers interview agents:

"Thanks for giving me an opportunity to list your lovely house, Mr. and Mrs. Seller," the first agent says. "As you can see by reviewing the CMA, my fair market value analysis indicates that eight houses sold in your neighborhood in the past six months. Three of them were significantly larger than yours, so they can't be used as comps. The five houses comparable to yours in size, age, location, and condition sold in the range of $350,000 to $370,000. Based on their sale prices, I recommend an asking price of $375,000."

Now the second agent strikes. "Who cares what the comps indicate? Your house is painted a particularly attractive shade of turquoise, and your lawn is greener than the lawns of any of those other houses. I suggest starting with a nice, round asking price of $400,000."

Agent Three knows that he probably won't get the listing unless he outbids the other two agents. "Our firm's Internet marketing program is incredibly successful," he says, oozing confidence. "Through our relocation service and Internet referrals, we'll undoubtedly be able to find a buyer who'll be willing to pay $425,000."

This technique of successive agents giving ever-higher property valuations is known as *buying a listing.* Sellers, when confronted by the choice of market reality versus fantasy, often succumb to fantasy. They rationalize their decision by telling themselves that the highest bidding agent has the most faith in their house.

That's horse-hockey. If the sellers in this example select the highest bidder, it's because that agent dazzled them with the extra $50,000 they'd get by selecting him to sell their house. He told them what they wanted to hear. Greed triumphed over reason.

So who wins the bidding war? Not the folks who own the house. If their asking price has no basis in the real world, you won't purchase it. Neither will any other educated buyer.

How can you avoid becoming the victim of a bidding war? You know what we're going to say. Trust the comps to tell you what the house is worth. If the sellers won't listen to reason, move on. Comps don't fantasize. Neither should you.

If the house has been on the market for a month or two, and the sellers are open to reason, your agent's brilliant comps will prevail over their agent's fantasy pricing. The sellers will grasp the concept of fair market value and either gratefully accept your offer or make a modest counter offer because your offering price is so logical, realistic, and fair.

You have a problem, however, if their house just came on the market. The sellers probably won't believe anything you and your agent say about the asking price being too high. They'll discount your opinion of their house's fair market value because they suspect that you're trying to steal their home. They'll be nearly as suspicious of a formal appraisal done by your hand-picked appraiser.

Time cures overpricing by inept agents. The longer the house stays on the market without selling, the more the sellers will doubt their own and their agent's opinion of value.

If the sellers' house isn't priced to sell, and they won't listen to reason, move on to the next house on your list. No telling how long the sellers will take to get smart. Don't put your life on hold waiting for them to wise up. They may be very slow learners.

Unrealistic sellers

Some sellers get excellent pricing advice from agents — and choose to ignore it. Sellers attempting to sell without an agent often make the same mistake — they opt for the ever-popular need-based pricing method (described earlier in this chapter) to set their asking price.

Sellers need time to accept that buyers don't care how much they paid for their house, how much they spent fixing it up, or how much they need to buy their next home. The sellers are stuck with these problems. The buyer isn't.

Unless an overpriced house has been on the market long enough to bring the sellers back to reality, move on. Most sellers aren't open to reason until they've tried their price for a couple of months or feel external pressure to sell. Trying to reason with such sellers prematurely is like trying to teach a pig how to whistle. Your time is wasted, and the pig gets upset.

Spotting overpriced turkeys

Many agents show buyers overpriced houses, but their intention is not to sell these houses. One of the tactics that smart agents adopt early in their careers is using OPTs (overpriced turkeys) to graphically demonstrate the value of well-priced homes.

Suppose that an agent shows you a three-bedroom, two-bath house with a price tag of $299,500 and then takes you to an even more attractive four-bedroom, three-bath home in the same neighborhood _with the same asking price_. The agent doesn't have to say another word — the difference between price and value is glaringly obvious. The OPT makes the sale.

Here's another way to spot OPTs: They get lots of showings but no offers.

Chapter 11

Tapping the Internet's Best Resources

. . . .

In This Chapter

▶ Honing in on helpful information

▶ Starting to shop

▶ Knowing what to be careful about

. . . .

*N*o other personal financial transaction provokes more financial and emotional anxiety than buying a home. Most of us rightfully feel huge trepidation when buying something with upward of six digits in its sticker price. You have to confront deciding how much to spend, selecting a good real estate agent, negotiating on a property, choosing a mortgage, and handling the myriad closing details — all of which are mysterious, jargon-filled, and fraught with commission-hungry salespeople. (Ditto for the headaches when it comes time for you to sell.) Add in some time pressure for a job relocation or impending birth of a child (or two), and you have a surefire recipe for psychological stress.

Enter the Internet. In this chapter, we highlight how you can use the Internet to make yourself a more informed consumer and your home search more effective. We name names and recommend for your consideration the best sites that we've come across. We also warn you about common pitfalls that you may encounter online.

Finding Useful Information

The number of real estate Web sites vastly exceeds those good enough to warrant a bookmark. In this section, we give some pointers so that you can quickly head in the right direction when you start your search.

Bypass traditional search engines

Don't waste your time using traditional search engines — a method in which you explore (search) the Internet by looking for Web sites that contain information that matches the keyword or phrase you entered into the search engine. At one widely used search engine, for example, when we entered "Santa Rosa, CA real estate" into the search engine, the results list showed more than 2 million Web sites!

Web site owners do whatever they can to get their Web sites to show up near the top of a particular Web search. Let us simply say that you won't necessarily find the best sites or the best companies among the first listing from a given Web search. Unless you're seeking a specific site — such as the Web site for the Santa Rosa public schools — our advice is to skip search engines.

Get your feet wet at Realtor.com

Given the sheer number of sites to choose among, the best place to start your realty Web surfing is a comprehensive site that includes useful residential real estate resources, as well as plenty of listings of houses for sale.

Our top pick for the best residential real estate Web site is www.realtor.com, sponsored by the National Association of Realtors (NAR). In previous editions of this book, this site wasn't worthy of such high praise, but now it is — thanks to continued improvements.

Realtor.com has well over 2 million listings of houses for sale from hundreds of Multiple Listing Services (MLS) around the country. Most listings are quite detailed and usually include a map so that you see approximately where the property is located. Increasing numbers of listings also include multiple photos, and some include a "virtual tour." Because this is the official Web site of the NAR, though, don't expect to find any For Sale by Owner listings here. Obviously, the goal of this site is to provide some resources to prospective home buyers (and sellers) in the hope of connecting you with a real estate agent. However, you may use this site as you wish without providing any personal details or making a commitment to any agent.

This site also sports some useful resources in your search for a specific town and neighborhood by accessing community statistics including demographic data, public-school information, crime statistics, and even helps you begin the mortgage-shopping process.

Our chief complaint with this Web site is the ubiquitous ads. The good news, however, is that you can tap into this site's vast resources without having to commit to buy anything or work with anyone pitching his services.

Read quality real estate news

You must be careful when surfing the Web in general and especially when searching for useful, objective, and quality real estate information and perspectives. Here are a couple sites we recommend for keeping up with the latest real estate developments, as well as continuing to add to your burgeoning real estate knowledge:

- ✔ **DeadlineNews.com** (www.deadlinenews.com)**:** Crackerjack real estate writer Broderick Perkins, who wrote for The San Jose Mercury News for 16 years, operates this site. In addition to articles on regional and national real estate issues, DeadlineNews.com includes extensive coverage of California's sometimes nutty and always fascinating real estate markets.

- ✔ **InmanNews.com** (www.inman.com)**:** Although this site has some articles of interest to real estate consumers, most of this site's content appeals to people actively involved in real estate–related fields. You will, however, find numerous real estate columnists, including veteran syndicated columnist Robert Bruss.

Discover more at these sites

Several other top real estate and government organizations offer useful information through their Web sites. So how do you know where and what to look for? Of course, we're going to tell you! Here are our top picks:

- ✔ **The Federal Emergency Management Agency** site (www.fema.gov) can help you see where various disasters (such as earthquakes, tornadoes, and floods) are most likely to strike, and provides helpful educational resources on such topics as flood insurance and disaster preparation and prevention. The site also points you to useful resources should you or your loved ones need help someday.

- ✔ **The American Society of Home Inspectors** (www.ashi.org) can help you find an ASHI-certified inspector and teach you more about the home-inspection process (which we cover in Chapter 13). You'll also find information and links to a variety of timely consumer protection issues, such as Consumer Product Safety Commission recalls and notices, water testing, and septic systems.

- ✔ **The U.S. Department of Housing and Urban Development Housing** (www.hud.gov) has an extensive Web site that includes HUD and other government agency listings of homes for sale. The site also has an excellent section for people with disabilities and their housing needs.

Discrimination complaints (either as a buyer or renter) can be submitted to HUD. Bring your best reading glasses — the type size on this site is microscopic in places!

✔ **The U.S. Department of Commerce's Bureau of Economic Analysis** (www.bea.doc.gov) has a treasure trove of state and local area economic data. If you want to review data to get more comfortable with the economic health of communities in which you may buy a home, this is the site for you!

Doing Some Preliminary Shopping

Our favorite thing about using the Internet as a tool for hunting real estate is that you can quickly get an overview of what's going on. When it's convenient in your schedule, you can surf from Web site to Web site without salespeople pressuring you. Home buyers can use the Internet to compare one community with another in such areas as school test scores, weather, and crime statistics. You can research many aspects of the buying process, including home prices, real estate agents, property inspectors, mortgages, and movers without ever leaving your easy chair. With the click of a mouse, the Internet can instantaneously whisk you *anywhere* in the world *any time* of the day or night. And you can expect to save money, too, because the Web is supposed to cut out middlemen and their extra costs.

One thing we do want you to remember regarding the Internet is this: Seeing is believing. Sitting in front of your computer screen in your current living quarters is simply no substitute for pounding the pavement and touring neighborhoods and properties. You can't talk to people you run into on the street, chat with school officials, or experience the quality and friendliness of local store owners through your computer.

Surveying homes for sale

Perhaps the Internet's greatest contribution to the home-buying process is the ability it gives you to peruse many listings of homes for sale at your convenience. Especially if you're contemplating an out-of-state move and want a general idea of what you can get for your money, accessing home listings online is invaluable. The screening abilities of many sites with home listings sure beats scouring classified ads for a given area to find, say, all the houses in a particular community with at least three bedrooms and central air conditioning for under $300,000.

Most real estate agents today will set you up to automatically receive e-mail updates of newly listed homes for sale that meet specific criteria (for example, at least 3 bedrooms, at least 2,000 square feet, and so on). Just beware of agents lazily using this instead of their personal eyeballing of properties and contacting you with precise feedback about given properties for sale that may meet your needs.

If you're not ready to work with an agent, start your home-search process on www.realtor.com, which allows you to search for homes that meet specific criteria.

For smaller communities not well covered through real estate listing Web sites, try tracking down a small-town newspaper, which you can do through the Newspaper Association of America's Web site (www.newsvoyager.com). A small-town paper can be an excellent source to discover what's going on in the area you're considering for your home purchase.

If you're serious about actually buying a home you see promoted online, please be aware that what you see isn't always what you can get. Even though one of the supposed virtues of the Internet is how up to date it is, that is often *not* the case with sites listing homes for sale. As syndicated real estate columnist Robert Bruss said in one of his columns, "My experience has been that most of these home listing Web sites contain outdated or incomplete listings, which can be a waste of time."

Sifting school information

Even if you don't have school-age children of your own, you should investigate what's going on with local schools in areas where you're considering buying a home. If you do have school-age children, you should be even more motivated to collect information to assist you with the all-important decision as to where to live.

School information sites that we like include www.greatschools.net, www.schoolmatch.com, www.psk12.com, and www.schoolmatters.com. These sites can be useful starting points for collecting basic information about public schools in a given area. These sites typically offer some free content as well as other information and data for a fee. You can also see how a particular school and district compare with those in the rest of the nation. In addition, state departments of education often have useful (although cumbersome-to-access) data on public schools. (Also check out www.neighborhoodscout.com for useful school information along with other community data.)

Please remember, of course, that getting data from a Web site is no substitute for visiting a school and talking to parents, administrators, and teachers. These latter steps take extra time and energy but often help folks make important decisions based upon more complete information.

Perusing "best places" to live

Whenever a job relocation or family change prompts a move, it can raise the question "Where's the best place to live?" What's best, of course, is in the eyes and desires of the beholder. One financial magazine, for example, claimed that Moorestown, N.J., is the best place to live. With all due respect to that lovely town and the people who call it home and enjoy it, we urge you not to accept any publication's or any person's rating of the supposed best place to live as being applicable to your situation.

Neighborhood Scout (`www.neighborhoodscout.com`) is a terrific site that allows you to select customized search criteria to find the best places that meet your needs. If you don't wish to customize, you can begin your search with preset search criteria (which you may later modify) designed to appeal to common home-buying populations such as "Families with Children" or "Retirement Dream Areas."

The Internet is a selling tool

It may seem odd for us to include a tip about selling a house that you have yet to purchase. But sooner or later, most folks end up selling for one reason or another.

When it comes time to sell your home, many house sellers are tempted to cut real estate agents — and their typical 6 percent commission — out of the picture. Web sites have made surprisingly little headway in helping consumers bypass agents by doing a For Sale by Owner — known in the trade as a FSBO.

Some sites offer scaled-back real estate agent services for a reduced commission. The communities typically served by such services tend to have higher-cost homes. Think of these realty brokers as discount brokers. With the reduced level of service comes a lower price. One site

trumpets: "Sell with us and pay only 4.5 percent." To that we say, when it comes time to sell your house, should you choose to hire an agent, hire the best one you can, and negotiate the commission. You can have a great agent and a competitive commission to boot. Pick up a copy of the latest edition of our companion book, *House Selling For Dummies,* to find out how.

Although the Internet is supposed to threaten middlemen and their profit margins, that doesn't seem to be happening so far with the residential real estate buying and selling process. The fact that FSBO Web sites haven't really taken off is noteworthy. Remember — there's no substitute for pounding the pavement. Nothing, including the Internet, beats actually seeing a home and the surrounding environment in person.

Familiarizing yourself with financing options

An increasing number of online mortgage brokers and lenders provide rate quotes and offer to help you find a low-cost loan. The interactive features of some sites allow you to compare the total cost of loans, including points and fees, under different scenarios such as how long you keep the loan and what happens to the interest rate on adjustable-rate mortgages. Interpreting these comparisons, however, requires a solid understanding of mortgage lingo and pricing. The worst sites are little more than glorified advertisement listings of mortgage lenders who have paid a fee to be on the site.

Among mortgage Web sites, E-Loan (www.eloan.com) is our favorite. E-Loan offers loans from dozens of mortgage lenders and useful tools for comparing the cost of various loans. For those mortgage shoppers unsure of what type of loan they desire, loan consultants are available through a toll-free phone number. Through the site, you can check on the status of a pending loan. A caution about this site: Like most others, it has a simplistic affordability calculator that uses traditional lender's criteria (down-payment amount, income, monthly debt payments, mortgage interest rate) in determining the mortgage amount you can supposedly afford.

This site, like most other mortgage sites, is best used to research the current mortgage marketplace rather than to actually apply for a loan. The reason: Mortgage lending is still largely a locally driven business that varies based upon the nuances of a local real estate market. Lynnea Key of Lynnea Key Realty in San Francisco says "I've had some near disasters with Internet sites located out of the area that don't understand the local market here, where we've had multiple offers and overbids. I've had clients have to scramble at the last minute for a local lender. In multiple-offer situations, when I represented a prospective buyer, some listing agents are uneasy with mortgage preapproval letters from an Internet site." (We discuss preapproval in Chapter 6.)

Mortgage data tracker and publisher HSH Associates (www.hsh.com) provides tons of information and data on mortgages and other types of loans through its Web site. If you're in the market for an adjustable-rate mortgage (ARM), you can check out the history of the interest-rate movements of various ARM indexes used so that you can see how quickly or slowly each index adjusts to overall changes in interest rates. The site also boasts many useful articles and links on a variety of mortgages and selected home issues, such as environmental hazards in the home.

Fannie Mae, the company that backs most local mortgage lenders through guaranteeing loans that meet its stringent credit criteria, also has useful consumer information on its www.homepath.com site. For example, you can search for lenders that offer particular mortgages such as Fannie 97, a mortgage that requires only a 3 percent down payment and allows for lower income qualification. You'll also find excellent background information on Fannie Mae's reverse-mortgage programs, which help older homeowners tap their home's equity, as well as listings of foreclosed homes for sale.

The Drawbacks of Searching for Houses in Cyberspace

The reality of real estate Web sites often falls short of what you may expect. The following sections tell you what to watch out for.

Conflicts of interest

Sadly, most Web sites are hardly bastions of objectivity or free of commercialism. On the contrary, Internet sites often have an ax to grind or an agenda to push. They generally derive most, if not all, of their revenue from advertising. Thus, whenever you're online, always be on guard as to whether something is featured or promoted because it's truly best or because a company or individual paid the owner of the Web site to be brought to your attention.

Consider what Yahoo! did to its real estate section since the previous edition of this book was published. In the past, when users searched for properties on Yahoo!, they were generally able to easily obtain listings for properties that met their search criteria. Now, unfortunately, the listings are bare bones both in number as well as content, thanks to a "relationship" forged between Yahoo! and Prudential Real Estate. In order to see more listings, users must agree to a lengthy terms-of-use agreement that includes the following gems. For example: "I hereby grant the independently owned and operated Prudential Real Estate franchisee ("Prudential Real Estate") my express written consent to engage in unsolicited communications with me for a period of up to 18 months."

If you think agreeing to the terms of use enables you to see all the properties meeting your search criteria, think again. The agreement states, "I understand that Prudential Real Estate will limit the number of properties displayed to me in response to my search requests based upon Prudential Real Estate's sole determination of the reasonable number of properties appropriate to be displayed in response to a single search request, given existing market conditions, total number of matching listings in the MLS database compilation, and other 'reasonable use' restrictions deemed appropriate by Prudential Real Estate, which may vary from market to market and from time to time."

And if you want to see a property, the terms of use state, "I agree that I will not attempt to contact the seller of any property that I have identified by using Prudential Real Estate's website and that I will not attempt to enter onto any such property except through an appointment arranged by an agent or employee of Prudential Real Estate."

Bankruptcies

Most Web sites operated for commercial purposes will fail (as is the case with most small businesses in general). You should be careful when choosing to do business with any online company, especially smaller ones, those new to the real estate field, or those on the verge of running out of cash.

Misleading home-valuation tools

Be careful when using the home-valuation tools that purport to help you determine the fair market value of a home or size up the fairness of your property taxes. You can find these tools on many general-interest real estate Web sites, as well as on sites such as Domania.com. As a rule, these sites don't give you the kind of information you need to find and evaluate truly comparable properties. And they almost always end up being a referral resource for real estate agents who pay the site a fee for the referrals.

Now, with the click of your computer mouse, you can visit a multitude of Web sites that offer addresses, sale dates, and sale prices for houses that sold in recent years. You can do searches of towns where you may want to live by specific property, by street, or by price range. (*Note:* Not all communities' house-sales data can be found on such sites — in fact, public reporting of such information is prohibited in certain areas.)

These Web sites encourage prospective home buyers to use their invaluable sale price data to find areas they can afford and to determine what a particular house is worth. Existing homeowners can supposedly use the information to appeal unfairly high property-tax assessments.

If this sounds too good to be true, read Chapter 10 immediately to see the right way to value a home! Who cares whether 123 Main Street sold for $275,000 in April of last year? You need a lot more than an address, a sale price, and date of sale to value a home properly. What about little details like size, age, condition, yard size, and so on?

Untrustworthy mortgage calculators

There's usually a significant difference between the amount the ubiquitous online mortgage calculators say you can borrow and how much you can actually *afford* to borrow. The dollar amount that a lender or online calculator comes up with is based solely on the ratio between your expected housing payments and income. Although this may satisfy a lender's concern that you won't default on a loan, such a simplistic calculation ignores your larger financial picture: how much (or little) you have put away for other long-term financial goals, such as retirement or college education for your children.

Take a hard look at your budget and goals before deciding how much you can afford to spend on a home; don't let some slick, Java-based calculator decide this for you.

Slow surfing

The speediness of your online connection greatly determines the efficiency of and your satisfaction with your Web-surfing experience. In many communities, among the fastest Internet connections are DSL — Digital Subscriber Line — connections and cable-modem connections (offered by a local cable television company). Compared with traditional dial-up (56K) computer modems, such services load Web pages far faster; especially important with real estate Web sites, which are generally cluttered with advertising. Another benefit of these faster Internet connections is that because they're always connected, you don't have to go through the tedious and time-consuming process of logging on (and sometimes incurring busy signals) every time you want to check your e-mail or surf the Internet. Of course, these speedy connections aren't free, so you have to consider whether the $40 or so per month is worth it. For small-business owners for whom time is money and for home computer users who spend a lot of time on the Internet, high-speed Internet services are worth this cost.

Part IV
Making the Deal

The 5th Wave   By Rich Tennant

"The paperwork for your mortgage seems to be in order. Now, if we can tap a vein for your signature we'll be all set."

In this part . . .

Play ball! When you've done all your preliminary homework, you're ready for this part. Here's where we show you how to negotiate a super deal and how to get your home inspected from roof to foundation so that you know whether it's in perfect shape or riddled with expensive defects. Because you can't close the purchase until you get homeowners insurance, we explain what, where, and how to buy the coverage you need. Finally, we describe some of the legal and tax ramifications of your purchase along with ways to make sure that your deal closes smoothly and without unnecessary costs.

Chapter 12

Negotiating Your Best Deal

*W*hen it comes to buying things, most Americans are lousy negotiators. Negotiation isn't part of our culture. We've been conditioned for generations to be docile buyers who pay whatever price is marked on a can of beans or a TV set. Instead of negotiating with someone eyeball-to-eyeball to drive down the price, at best we comparison-shop to find the store with the lowest price. (And many time-starved people don't even do that.)

Sure, we can negotiate when our back is to the wall. We haggle over expensive things like cars and dicker with the boss for a raise, but doing so makes us uncomfortable. We walk away from these encounters with the nagging suspicion that we came out on the short end of the deal — that someone else could've done better.

Realizing our nation's discomfort with negotiating, some car dealers have taken the haggling out of buying a car. Instead of using high-pressure sales tactics, these dealers post a sales price on the car — the *no-dicker sticker*. That's their price; take it or leave it. If you take it, you probably won't get the lowest price, but some people think that's a fair trade-off in order to avoid the unpleasantness of negotiating.

You won't find no-dicker stickers on homes. On the contrary, generally everything from the purchase price to the date that escrow closes is negotiable. Given today's high home prices in most of the densely populated parts of the United States, buying a home is the ultimate in high-stakes negotiating. Good negotiators come out of a home purchase smiling. Bad negotiators take it in the wallet.

"Good" depends upon your perspective

Brace yourself. You may be shocked by the sellers' response to your offer to buy their home. From your perspective, you made a really good offer. They, on the other hand, may think your offer stinks.

Here, for example, is the perspective of first-time buyers who just blew their budget to smithereens making a $210,000 offer for a home listed at $239,000: "Honey, I'm so nervous. Do you think the sellers will accept our offer? I know their home costs a lot more than we planned to spend, but you know as well as I do that it's the best place we've seen in four months of looking. What's taking them so long to get back to us? The suspense is killing me."

And here's the perspective of the retired couple who got their $210,000 offer: "Calm down, dear. Your face is beet red. Remember your blood pressure. I'm sure that nice young couple didn't mean to insult us. And no matter what you say, I can't believe that they think we're doddering old fools who don't know how much our house is worth. They probably made the best offer they could. Please don't throw it away."

Two entirely different takes on the exact same offer. Buyers generally think that they're paying too much. Sellers usually think that they're giving their house away. When you're playing for real money, these conflicting perceptions fuel emotional fires that heat up the negotiating process.

Following the tips in this chapter will give you the negotiating advantage you so richly deserve throughout the home-buying process. And of course, these tips make getting the keys to your dream home faster, easier, and less expensive.

Understanding and Coping with Your Emotions

Emotion is an integral part of home buying. Real estate transactions are emotional roller-coaster rides for everyone involved.

Sometimes, like San Francisco fog, emotion drifts into transactions so quietly that you hardly notice it. More often, however, it thunders into deals like a herd of elephants.

Examining the violent forces at work

Consider the violent forces acting upon you during the home-buying process:

- ✔ **You're dealing with people at their most primal level.** Shelter, food, and security are the three most basic necessities of life. Home is where the heart is. Your home is your castle. People become vicious when their homes are threatened. Speaking of primal urges, now you know why looking for a home is called house hunting.

✔ **You're playing for large amounts of real money.** Whether this is your first home or your last, it's probably the largest purchase you've ever made. How much you pay for a home isn't the issue. When significant amounts of real money are at risk, the emotional intensity for you and the seller is just as great, whether the house you buy costs $250,000 or $2.5 million.

✔ **You're probably going through a life change.** Buying a home would be plenty stressful if you had to deal with only seeking shelter and spending tons of money. Throw in a life change (such as marriage, divorce, birth, death, job change, or retirement), which is often the motivation to purchase a home, and you've created an emotional minefield.

Because eliminating emotions from a home purchase is impossible, the next-best thing to do is to recognize and manage them. By all means, share your concerns and frustrations in a productive way with your spouse or a friend who has purchased a home or, better yet, with a good therapist! Bottling up emotions isn't healthy or possible — the longer you stew, the worse the likely explosion is going to be. But the worst thing you can do is vent your frustrations and fears at other people in the transaction — especially the sellers. The folks who do the best job of controlling and properly directing their emotions generally end up getting the best deals.

Controlling yourself

Here are five techniques you can use to control your emotions during the home-buying negotiations:

✔ **Put the transaction in perspective.** Which is worse: a failed home purchase or failed open-heart surgery? No matter how badly things go with your real estate transaction, keep reminding yourself that this isn't a life-or-death situation. Tomorrow is another day. The sun will rise again, roses will bloom again, birds will sing again, and children will laugh again. Life goes on. If worst comes to worst, the deal may die, but you'll live on to find another place that you can call home.

✔ **Don't let time bully you.** Most life changes have predictable time frames. You have plenty of advance notice on marriages, births, retirements, and the like. Don't put yourself under needless pressure by procrastinating or by creating unnecessary, self-imposed deadlines. Allow yourself enough time to buy a home. Allocate time properly, and it will be your friend rather than your enemy.

✔ **Maintain an emotional arm's length.** Keep your options open. Be ready to walk away from a potential house purchase if you can't reach a satisfactory agreement with the sellers on price and terms. Mentally condition yourself to the prospect that the deal may fall through. Houses are like buses: If you miss one, another will come along sooner or later.

✔ **Accept uncertainty as a part of your transaction.** Much as you'd like to know everything about a property before making an offer on it, the game is played with incomplete information. You always have far more questions than answers at the beginning of a transaction. Don't worry; you'll be fine as long as you know what things you need to find out and get the answers in a timely manner during your transaction.

✔ **Stay objective.** Use a comparable market analysis (CMA) to factually establish the fair market value of the home that you want to buy (see Chapter 10). A good real estate agent can help you use this information to prepare an equitable offer. If you don't plan to use an agent, consider working with a real estate lawyer. Having someone to buffer you from your unavoidable emotional involvement is helpful if your composure starts to slip. Just make sure that you work with professionals who are patient, not pushy, and who are committed to getting you the best deal.

First things first

Early in Ray's career, he worked with a buyer who insisted upon having every question about a house answered before he'd submit an offer to purchase it. He wanted to structure a flawless offer. Because Ray didn't know any better, he went along with the plan. They spent several weeks fine-tuning the offering price by checking comparable home sales and getting quotes from contractors to do the necessary corrective work that had been discovered during the inspections ordered by a previous prospective buyer.

Unfortunately, Ray and the buyer got a hard lesson in accepting uncertainty because they'd overlooked one tiny detail; Ray's "buyer" didn't have a signed offer on the house. The seller got tired of their dithering around, endlessly gathering information, and sold the property to someone else.

If you're smart, you'll do what the successful buyer of this home did: Make a deal first.

Condition your offer upon getting all your questions answered while you have the house "tied up" with a contract.

That way, if everything goes well, you end up the proud owner of a wonderful home. If, however, you can't get a loan, or you don't like the findings of the inspection reports, you can either renegotiate the deal or bail out of the transaction and move on to a more promising home. In the meantime, however, you've removed the property from the competition by getting your offer accepted.

Don't waste time getting answers to secondary questions until you answer the primary question: Can you and the seller agree on price and terms of sale? Failure to go for the commitment wastes time and money, and may cause you to lose the property.

The Art of Negotiating

Is negotiating like water or ice? If you said "water," go directly to the head of the class.

Negotiating is fluid, not rigid. There is no one-size-fits-all *best* negotiating strategy that you can use in every home-buying situation. Good negotiators adjust their strategy based upon a variety of factors, such as:

- How well priced a property is
- How long it's been on the market
- How motivated the sellers are
- How motivated you are
- Whether you're dealing from a position of strength (a buyer's market) or weakness (a seller's market)

Good negotiators, however, apply a few basic principles to every situation. If you understand these principles, you can greatly increase the odds of getting what you want.

Being realistic

Good negotiators understand that facts are the foundation of successful negotiation. If you want to become a good negotiator, you must see things as they are, rather than as you want them to be. Wishful thinking makes bad negotiation.

What's wishful thinking? A common wish in a rising real estate market, for example, is that you can pay yesteryear's price for today's home. Perhaps you saw a similar house offered for sale at a much lower price six months ago. You ignore the fact that prices have increased since then, which eliminates your chance of buying a home today at the old price. Another common (and generally unrealistic) wish is that you can afford to buy a home similar to the one that you were reared in.

How do you eliminate wishful thinking? By replacing fantasy with facts. Unfortunately, that's easier said than done, because we all inevitably get emotionally involved when we negotiate for something that we intensely desire. Even though that emotional involvement is part of human nature, allowing emotion to seep into a negotiation can cost you dearly.

The importance of objectivity

Unlike you and the seller, good real estate agents don't take things personally. The seller's agent, for example, won't be offended if your agent tells her that you hate the emerald-green paint in the kitchen and the red flocked wallpaper in the den. Your agent, by the same token, won't blow his cork if the seller's agent says that your offer is ridiculously low.

Agents find it easy to be objective. After all, they're not the ones who spent three long weekends painting the kitchen or months looking for just the right wallpaper to put in the den. Neither is it their life's savings on the negotiating table.

Good agents listen to what the market says a house is worth. They don't allow distracting details (such as how much the seller paid for the house ten years ago or how little you can afford to spend for it today) to confuse negotiations. As you know if you've read Chapter 10, no correlation exists between these need-based issues and the current fair market value of a home.

Some folks think that agents have calculators for hearts. Not true. The good agents know that if they aren't coldly realistic about property values, the home won't sell, and they won't get paid.

The red flags in agent negotiations

If you follow our advice in Chapter 9 when selecting your real estate agent, you'll choose one who's a good negotiator.

Doing a lousy job of selecting an agent can cost you big bucks. Bad agents don't know how to determine fair market values; as a result, you may pay too much for your home. And why should the bad agent care? After all, the more you pay, the more your agent makes, because agents' commissions are typically a percentage of the purchase price. If your agent pushes you to buy and can't justify the offering price by using comparable home sales, fire your agent, and get a good one.

Good negotiators avoid making moral judgments. As long as the seller's position isn't illegal, it's neither immoral nor unfair. It's simply a negotiating position. Of course, agents are human. Sometimes, even the best agents *temporarily* lose their objectivity in the heat of battle. You know that this has happened if your agent gets red in the face and starts accusing the other side of being unfair.

If your agent snaps out of the funk quickly, no problem. On the other hand, if your agent can't calm down, you've lost your emotional buffer. Agents who lose their professional detachment are incapable of negotiating well on your behalf.

Fact versus opinion

You and the sellers can use exactly the same facts (that is, recent sale prices of comparable houses) and yet reach entirely different opinions of fair market value. As we point out in Chapter 10, although houses may be comparable in terms of age, size, and condition, no two homes are identical after they've been lived in.

Furthermore, even though all the houses used in the comparable market analysis are in the same neighborhood, *site differences* (that is, proximity to schools, better view, bigger yard, and the like) usually affect individual property values. Last but not least, even though all the comparable houses were sold during the previous six months, property values can be affected by changes in mortgage rates and consumer confidence.

For example, your agent thinks that 123 Main Street, which sold two months ago for $280,000, is the best comparable *(comp)* for the house that you're trying to buy. The seller's agent agrees that it's a good comp but points out that this house has a two-car garage, whereas 123 Main Street has only a one-car garage. Your agent says that 123 Main Street has a larger kitchen with a breakfast nook and is two blocks closer to the park. The seller's agent says that the property you are considering has higher-quality kitchen cabinets and a new refrigerator, and is three blocks closer to the bus stop.

And so it goes. Everyone agrees on 123 Main Street's sale price and date of sale. These are *facts.* They're the same no matter who looks at them.

But how much value does a second garage space add to the home that you want to buy? Is being closer to the bus stop worth more to you than proximity to the park? Is an eat-in kitchen more or less valuable to you than fancy kitchen cabinets and a new refrigerator? The answers to these questions are *opinions* that are based on your value judgments. Another person would probably value the amenities somewhat differently.

Pricing isn't 100 percent scientific at this level of scrutiny. No two buyers are alike. Each buyer has different needs and, due to those differing needs, will reach different conclusions regarding opinions of value.

No matter how satisfying it may be to go on an emotional rampage with your agent about the seller's utter lack of good taste, market knowledge, or scruples, getting angry won't get you the house. If your agent can't maintain a level head, ask your agent's broker (see Chapter 9) to negotiate for you, or get another agent.

Examining your negotiating style

Finding two people who have exactly the same negotiating style is as unlikely as finding two identical 200-year-old houses. All negotiating styles, however, boil down to variations on one of these two basic themes:

- ✔ **Combative (I win, you lose):** These negotiators view winning only in the context of beating the other side. To them, negotiation is war. They take no prisoners.

> ✔ **Cooperative (we both win):** These negotiators focus on solving problems rather than defeating opponents. Everyone involved in the transaction works together to find solutions that are satisfactory to both sides.

Which negotiating style is better? That depends on the kind of person you are, what your objectives are, and how much time you have.

Most folks opt for cooperation because they know that the world is round — what goes around nearly always comes back either to haunt you or to help you. Why fight battles in some weird game of mutually assured destruction if you can peacefully work together as allies to solve your common problems?

Combative negotiation is tolerated in a strong buyer's or seller's market. The operative word is *tolerated.* People grudgingly play an "I win, you lose" game when they have no alternative. However, in a balanced market that favors neither buyers nor sellers, combative negotiators are usually told, "I won't play your stupid game because I don't like your style."

Cooperative negotiation, on the other hand, works well under all market conditions because its goal is to scratch everyone's itch. We all enjoy winning and hate losing. People sometimes cry when they're defeated. Problems, on the other hand, never cry when they're solved.

Brute force versus style

Ray knows a real estate agent who's a superb technician. He is brilliant at determining a home's fair market value; writes flawless contracts; understands financing; and stays current on real estate laws, rules, and regulations. Technically, he's impeccable.

Unfortunately, he has no compassion. He's coldly perfect himself and expects equal perfection from everyone else. He is an ultra-hardball negotiator who neither gives nor expects mercy from his opponents. Some of his own clients don't even like him, but they all respect him because they know that he'll fight ruthlessly on their behalf.

Other agents hate working with this agent *because* he's such a brutal negotiator. They deal with him only when they have absolutely no alternative. If he represents a buyer in a multiple-offer situation, for example, his buyer's offer won't be selected if the selling agent can find any way to work with another buyer whose agent is less combative.

Ray Jones, a San Francisco agent who died several years ago, was this agent's exact opposite. Jones lacked technical polish, but he was kind, fair, and generous, and made folks smile with their hearts. His clients and other agents adored him. In a multiple-offer situation, his buyer's offer was either accepted or at least counter-offered, if possible. He made buying a home fun.

Think carefully when selecting an agent to represent you. People do business with you for only two reasons: because they have to or because they want to. The right agent can give you a negotiating advantage. The ruthless negotiator may make sense for buyers who are in no hurry to buy and who desire to get a good deal on a property. For others, such a piranha could be bad news.

Unfortunately, some people are born competitors. The only cooperation they understand is the cooperation of a team that is working together to defeat its opponents. If you're a cooperative negotiator, here are two ways to protect yourself from combative negotiators:

- **Try switching them from combative to cooperative by finding ways you both can win.** Shift their emphasis from beating you to solving the problem. "You want to sell. I want to buy. How can we do it?"

- **If that fails, deep-six the deal.** If you keep negotiating, born competitors will strip the money from your bank account and the flesh from your bones. They confuse concessions with weakness. If, for example, you offer to split the difference, they'll take the 50 percent you give them as their just due and then go for the rest. They won't be happy until they thrill to a victory that is enhanced by your unconditional defeat. Life's too short to subject yourself to this kind of punishment. No matter how strong a seller's market you must contend with, you can find sellers who are cooperative negotiators — if you try.

Negotiating with finesse

Skillful negotiators get what they want through mutual agreement — not brute force. Brute force is crude, rude, ugly, and decidedly unfriendly. Here are some concepts that you may find useful for negotiating with finesse:

- **Phones are for making appointments.** Never, never, never let your agent or lawyer present an offer or attempt to negotiate significant issues over the phone. Saying no over the phone is too easy for the sellers. Even if they agree with everything you want, they may change their minds by the time they actually have to sign the contract.

- **Oral agreements are useless.** In our society, we have *written* contracts because people have notoriously selective memories. If you want your deal to be enforceable in a court of law, put everything about it in writing. Get into the habit of writing short, *dated* MFRs (Memos for Record) of important conversations (such as "June 2 — lender said we'd get 7.5 percent mortgage rate," "June 12 — sellers want to extend close of escrow a week," and so on). Put these notes into your transaction file, just in case you need to refresh your memory. Heed the immortal words of Samuel Goldwyn: "A verbal agreement isn't worth the paper it's written on."

- **Deadline management is essential.** Real estate contracts are filled with deadlines for things like contingency removals, deposit increases, and (of course) the close of escrow. Failure to meet deadlines can have dreadful consequences. Your deal could fall apart — you could even get sued. Most deadlines, however, are flexible — if you handle them correctly.

Suppose that you just found out that completing the property inspections will take longer than anticipated. *Immediately* contact the sellers to explain the reason for the delay and then get a *written* extension of the deadline. Reasonable delays can usually be accommodated if properly explained and promptly handled.

The Negotiating Process

Negotiation is an ongoing process — a series of steps without a neatly defined beginning and end. Think of water flowing.

Each step in the negotiating process begins by gathering information. After you read this book, you'll understand the various aspects of buying a home. Then you can translate your information into action that generates more information that in turn leads to further action. And so it goes, until you're the proud owner of your dream home.

One way to begin the first action phase is to get your finances in order, get preapproved for a loan, and select an agent to work with you through the next information-gathering phase. You and your agent then investigate various neighborhoods and tour houses so that you know what's on the market. You also figure out the difference between asking prices and fair market values. After you know what houses are really worth, you're ready to focus on the specific neighborhood that you want to live in and begin seriously searching for your dream home.

Making an offer to purchase

After you find your dream home, you're ready for the next action step in the negotiating process: making an offer to purchase. No standard, universally accepted real estate purchase contract is used throughout the country. On the contrary, purchase contracts vary in length and terms from state to state and, within a state, from one locality to another.

We include the California Association of Realtors' *Residential Purchase Agreement* in Appendix A so that you can see what a well-written, comprehensive residential real estate contract looks like. When you're ready to write an offer, your real estate agent or lawyer should provide a suitable contract for your area.

Real estate contracts are revised quite often due to such things as changes in real estate law and mandated seller disclosure requirements. A good agent or lawyer will use the most current version of the contract. Check the contract's revision date (usually noted in the bottom-left or -right corner of each page) to make sure you're not using a form just slightly newer than the *Declaration of Independence.*

A carelessly worded, poorly thought-out offer can turn what should be a productive negotiation into an adversarial struggle between you and the sellers. Instead of working together to solve your common problem (that is, "you want to buy, and they want to sell — how can *we* each get what *we* want?"), you get sidetracked by issues that can't be resolved so early in the negotiating process.

Although buying a home can be a highly emotional experience, good offers defuse this potentially explosive situation by replacing emotion with facts. Buyers and sellers have feelings that can be hurt. Facts don't. That's why facts are the basis of successful negotiations.

All good offers have three things in common:

- ✔ **Good offers are based upon the sellers' most important concern: a realistic offering price.** You shouldn't pull the offering price out of thin air. Instead, base your offering price on houses (comparable to the seller's house in age, size, condition, and location) that have sold within the past six months. As Chapter 10 explains, sellers' asking prices are often fantasy. Actual sale prices of comparable houses are facts. Focus on facts.

- ✔ **Good offers have realistic financing terms.** Your mortgage's interest rate, loan-origination fee, and time allowed to obtain financing (explained in the upcoming section on contingencies) must be based upon current lending conditions. Some offers get blown out of the water because a buyer's loan terms are unrealistic. *Focus on facts.*

  If you've been prequalified or, better yet, preapproved for a loan (see Chapter 6), you or your agent should stress that advantage when you present your offer. This proves to the sellers that you're a creditworthy buyer who's ready, willing, and financially able to purchase their house.

- ✔ **Good offers don't expect a blank check from the sellers.** Unless property defects are glaringly obvious, neither you nor the sellers will know whether any corrective work is needed at the time that your offer is initially submitted. Under these circumstances, it's smart to use property-inspection clauses (explained in the next section) that enable you to reopen negotiations regarding any necessary corrective work *after* you've received the inspection reports.

  Remember that negotiation is an ongoing process. After the *action* of having your offer accepted, your property inspectors gather *information.* After they've determined what is actually required in the way of corrective work, you and the sellers can renew your negotiations *(action)* armed with hard facts *(information).* This sequence beats wasting time and energy by arguing with the sellers about the cost to complete corrective work before any of you know the precise number of dollars needed to do the repairs. *Focus on facts.*

If the sellers agree with the price and terms contained in your offer, they'll sign it. Their agent should give you a signed copy of the offer immediately. When you actually receive a copy of the offer signed by the sellers, you have what's called a *ratified offer* (that is, a signed or accepted offer). This doesn't mean that you own the house or that it has been sold. All you can say for now is that a sale is pending.

Leaving an escape hatch: Contingencies

Even though the sellers have accepted your offer, it should contain extremely important escape clauses known as contingencies, which you cleverly built into the contract to protect yourself. A *contingency* is some specific future event that must be satisfied in order for the sale to go through. It gives you the right to pull out of the deal if that event fails to happen. If you don't remove a contingency, the sale falls apart, and your deposit money is usually returned.

These two contingencies appear in nearly every offer:

- ✔ **Financing:** You can pull out of the deal if the loan specified in your contract isn't approved.

- ✔ **Property inspections:** You can pull out of the deal if you don't approve the inspection reports or can't reach an agreement with the sellers about how to handle any necessary repairs.

Other standard contingencies give you the right to review and approve such things as a condominium's master deed, bylaws, and budget, as well as a property's title report. You can, if you want, make the deal contingent upon events such as your lawyer's approval of the contract or your parents' inspection of the house. As a rule, no *reasonable* contingency will be refused by the seller.

Don't go overboard with contingencies if you're competing for the property with several other buyers. Sellers, especially in strong real estate markets, don't like offers with lots of contingencies. From their perspective, the more contingencies in an offer, the more likely the deal is to fall apart. You must delicately balance the need to protect yourself with the compelling need to have your offer accepted. Keep your contingency time frames realistic but short. Resolve as many simple questions as possible before submitting the offer. For instance, if your parents insist on seeing the property you want to buy before they'll loan you money for a down payment, take them through the home before making your offer to eliminate that contingency.

If you're considering making your offer subject to the sale of another house (such as the one you're living in now), don't do so if you're in a bidding war with other buyers. Check out the section "Negotiating from a position of weakness," later in this chapter, for reasons why including this type of contingency could cost you the house you're bidding on.

Here's a typical loan contingency:

> Conditioned [the magic word] upon buyer getting a 30-year, fixed-rate mortgage secured by the property in the amount of 80 percent of the purchase price. Said loan's interest rate shall not exceed 7.5 percent. Loan fees/points shall not exceed 2 percent of loan amount. If buyer can't obtain such financing within 30 days from acceptance of this offer, buyer must notify seller in writing of buyer's election to cancel this contract and have buyer's deposits returned.

If you want to see a more detailed financing contingency, read paragraph 2 of the California Association of Realtors' purchase contract in Appendix A of this book. We cover property inspections in Chapter 13.

The purchase agreement you sign is meant to be a legally binding contract. As we say in Chapter 9, it's wise to put a lawyer on your team immediately if you have *any* concerns about the legality of your contract. Even if you don't have a lawyer when you sign the contract, including the following clause in your offer may be prudent if you have legal questions:

> Conditioned upon my lawyer's review and approval of this contract within five days from acceptance.

Using this clause doesn't mean you actually have to hire a lawyer. It does, however, give you the option of having the contract reviewed later by a lawyer if you wish. By the way, good contracts provide space to write in additional terms and conditions. In the California Association of Realtors' contract, it's paragraph 25.

Include a provision in your contract that specifically states that contingencies must be removed in writing. Doing so should eliminate confusion between you and the sellers regarding whether a contingency has been satisfied. See paragraph 14 of the California Association of Realtors' contract (in Appendix A) for one way to handle this.

What good is a ratified offer filled with escape clauses? Well, a ratified offer (riddled with escape clauses or not) ties up the property. You don't have to worry about the owners selling the property to someone else while you're spending time and money inspecting it.

First get an agreement on the price and terms of sale — *then* get answers to all your other questions.

Getting a counter offer

It's highly unlikely that the sellers will accept your offer as it's originally written. Even if they love your offering price, they'll probably tweak your offer here and there to make it acceptable to them. Sellers use *counter offers* to fine-tune the price, terms, and conditions of offers they receive.

You'll be relieved to know that counter-offer forms are far less complicated than offer forms. Take a look at the California Association of Realtors' *Counter Offer* in Figure 12-1, for example, and you'll see that it's only a one-page form.

Suppose that you offer $275,000 for a home that you like, and you ask to close escrow 30 days after the sellers accept your offer. Because they had the house listed at $289,500, the sellers think that your offering price is a mite low. Furthermore, they need six weeks to relocate.

Instead of rewriting your entire offer, they give you a counter offer. It states that they're willing to accept all the terms and conditions of your offer except that they want $285,000 and six weeks after acceptance to close escrow.

The ball's in your court once again. You don't mind a six-week close of escrow, but you don't want to pay more than $280,000, so you give the sellers a *counter-counter offer* to that effect.

Now only one bone of contention remains: the price. The sellers come back to you with a *firm* $284,000. You grudgingly respond at $281,000 and instruct your agent to make it clear to the sellers that you won't go any higher. Two can play the *firm* game. Negotiations now resemble the trench warfare of World War I.

If you really want the home, this phase of the game can be nerve-racking. You worry about another buyer making the sellers a better offer and stealing the house away while you're trying to get the price down that last $3,000. The sellers are equally concerned that they'll lose you by pushing too hard for the final $3,000. You don't want to pay a penny more than you have to. The sellers don't want to leave any money on the table.

You and the sellers are tantalizingly close to agreement on price. Your offering price and the sellers' asking price are both factually based upon recent sales of comparable houses in the neighborhood. So why the deadlock? Because sometimes the same facts can lead to different conclusions (see the sidebar "Fact versus opinion," earlier in this chapter).

An equitable way to resolve this type of impasse is to split the difference fifty–fifty. If the sellers in our example use this technique, they'll come back to you with a $282,500 offer — down $1,500 from their *firm* asking price of $284,000 and up $1,500 from your *firm* offering price of $281,000. The mutual $1,500 concession equals less than 1 percent of the home's fair market value based on a $282,500 sale price. That's pinpoint accuracy in a real estate transaction.

Splitting the difference won't work in all situations. It is, however, a fair way to quickly resolve relatively small differences of opinion (a few percent or less of the home's price) so you can make a deal and get on with your life.

CALIFORNIA
ASSOCIATION
OF REALTORS®

COUNTER OFFER No. _____

For use by Seller or Buyer. May be used for Multiple Counter Offer.

(C.A.R. Form CO, Revised 10/04)

Date _____, at _____ , California.

This is a counter offer to the: ☐ California Residential Purchase Agreement, ☐ Counter Offer, or ☐ Other _____ ("Offer"),

dated _____, on property known as _____ ("Property"),

between _____ ("Buyer") and _____ ("Seller").

1. **TERMS:** The terms and conditions of the above referenced document are **accepted subject to the following:**
   A. Paragraphs in the Offer that require initials by all parties, but are not initialed by all parties, are excluded from the final agreement unless specifically referenced for inclusion in paragraph 1C of this or another Counter Offer.
   B. Unless otherwise agreed in writing, down payment and loan amount(s) will be adjusted in the same proportion as in the original Offer.
   C. _____
   _____
   _____
   _____
   _____
   _____
   D. The following attached supplements are incorporated into this Counter Offer: ☐ Addendum No. _____
   ☐ _____   ☐ _____

2. **RIGHT TO ACCEPT OTHER OFFERS:** Seller has the right to continue to offer the Property for sale or for other transaction, and to accept any other offer at any time prior to notification of acceptance, as described in paragraph 3. If this is a Seller Counter Offer, Seller's acceptance of another offer prior to Buyer's acceptance and communication of notification of this Counter Offer, shall revoke this Counter Offer.

3. **EXPIRATION:** This Counter Offer shall be deemed revoked and the deposits, if any, shall be returned unless this Counter Offer is signed by the Buyer or Seller to whom it is sent and a Copy of the signed Counter Offer is personally received by the person making this Counter Offer or _____ who is authorized to receive it, by 5:00PM on the third Day After this Counter Offer is made or, (if checked) by ☐ _____ (date), at _____ AM/PM. This Counter Offer may be executed in counterparts.

4. ☐ **(If checked:) MULTIPLE COUNTER OFFER:** Seller is making a Counter Offer(s) to another prospective buyer(s) on terms that may or may not be the same as in this Counter Offer. Acceptance of this Counter Offer by Buyer shall **not** be binding unless and until it is subsequently re-Signed by Seller in paragraph 7 below and a Copy of the Counter Offer Signed in paragraph 7 is personally received by Buyer or by _____, who is authorized to receive it, by 5:00 PM on the third Day after this Counter Offer is made or, (if checked) by ☐ _____ (date), at _____ AM/PM. Prior to the completion of all of these events, Buyer and Seller shall have no duties or obligations for the purchase or sale of the Property.

5. **OFFER: BUYER OR SELLER MAKES THIS COUNTER OFFER ON THE TERMS ABOVE AND ACKNOWLEDGES RECEIPT OF A COPY.**
   _____ Date _____
   _____ Date _____

6. **ACCEPTANCE: I/WE** accept the above Counter Offer **(If checked** ☐ **SUBJECT TO THE ATTACHED COUNTER OFFER)** and acknowledge receipt of a Copy.
   _____ Date _____ Time _____ AM/PM
   _____ Date _____ Time _____ AM/PM

7. **MULTIPLE COUNTER OFFER SIGNATURE LINE:** By signing below, Seller accepts this Multiple Counter Offer. NOTE TO SELLER: Do NOT sign in this box until after Buyer signs in paragraph 6. (Paragraph 7 applies only if paragraph 4 is checked.)
   _____ Date _____ Time _____ AM/PM
   _____ Date _____ Time _____ AM/PM

8. (_____/_____) (Initials) **Confirmation of Acceptance:** A Copy of Signed Acceptance was personally received by the maker of the Counter Offer, or that person's authorized agent as specified in paragraph 3 (or, if this is a Multiple Counter Offer, the Buyer or Buyer's authorized agent as specified in paragraph 4) on (date) _____ at _____ AM/PM. **A binding Agreement is created when a Copy of Signed Acceptance is personally received by the maker of the Counter Offer, or that person's authorized agent (or, if this is a Multiple Counter Offer, the Buyer or Buyer's authorized agent) whether or not confirmed in this document. Completion of this confirmation is not legally required in order to create a binding Agreement; it is solely intended to evidence the date that Confirmation of Acceptance has occurred.**

The copyright laws of the United States (Title 17 U.S. Code) forbid the unauthorized reproduction of this form, or any portion thereof, by photocopy machine or any other means, including facsimile or computerized formats. Copyright © 1986-2004, CALIFORNIA ASSOCIATION OF REALTORS®, INC. ALL RIGHTS RESERVED.

THIS FORM HAS BEEN APPROVED BY THE CALIFORNIA ASSOCIATION OF REALTORS® (C.A.R.). NO REPRESENTATION IS MADE AS TO THE LEGAL VALIDITY OR ADEQUACY OF ANY PROVISION IN ANY SPECIFIC TRANSACTION. A REAL ESTATE BROKER IS THE PERSON QUALIFIED TO ADVISE ON REAL ESTATE TRANSACTIONS. IF YOU DESIRE LEGAL OR TAX ADVICE, CONSULT AN APPROPRIATE PROFESSIONAL.

This form is available for use by the entire real estate industry. It is not intended to identify the user as a REALTOR®. REALTOR® is a registered collective membership mark which may be used only by members of the NATIONAL ASSOCIATION OF REALTORS® who subscribe to its Code of Ethics.

SURE TRAC
The System for Success®

Published and Distributed by:
REAL ESTATE BUSINESS SERVICES, INC.
a subsidiary of the California Association of REALTORS®
525 South Virgil Avenue, Los Angeles, California 90020

Reviewed by _____ Date _____

EQUAL HOUSING OPPORTUNITY

CO REVISED 10/04 (PAGE 1 OF 1) Print Date

COUNTER OFFER (CO PAGE 1 OF 1)

Figure 12-1:
A typical counter-offer form.

Reprinted with permission, CALIFORNIA ASSOCIATION OF REALTORS®. Endorsement not implied.

The Finer Points of Negotiating

A perfectly balanced market that favors neither buyer nor seller is rare. The market is almost always in a state of flux. As a result, the playing field usually tilts toward the buyer or seller.

Negotiating when the playing field isn't level

President Lyndon Johnson was a consummate politician. He'd cajole, promise, arm-twist, flatter, pressure, sweet-talk, threaten, jawbone, wheedle, bully, or horse-trade other politicians into supporting his legislation.

The late president's negotiating skills were legendary. Once, when accused of using somewhat-unethical tactics to get the votes required to pass one of his Great Society programs, LBJ just shrugged. "Sorry you feel that way, son," he supposedly said. *"All I ever wanted was my unfair advantage."*

In a perfect world, you'd always have an unfair advantage. Unfortunately, the world is imperfect. No matter how good you are as a negotiator, sooner or later you'll have to negotiate from a position of weakness. The trick in these circumstances is to give yourself every possible advantage.

Buyer's and seller's markets

In the late 1980s, many California home buyers complained bitterly about sellers taking unfair advantage of them. Given the frenzied seller's market at that time, it wasn't unusual for owners of a well-priced house to receive multiple offers on it while their agent was still nailing up the For Sale sign. (Slight exaggeration, but you get the point.) Five years later, the hobnailed boot was on the other foot. Instead of a supply–demand imbalance, there was a demand–supply imbalance. The anguished screams now came from sellers who were complaining about buyers taking unfair advantage of *them*.

The party in the weaker position always characterizes the market as "bad." Because you're a seeker of wisdom and truth, don't kid yourself. The market is, in reality, neither good nor bad. The market is impersonal. The market is the market. Moaning and groaning about unfair market dynamics won't help you if you're caught in a seller's market any more than complaining helps sellers caught in the viselike grip of a buyer's market.

Negotiating from a position of weakness

Newly listed homes that are priced to sell often generate multiple offers in a seller's market. But even when the market isn't a seller's market, a well-priced, attractive new listing may draw multiple offers.

Unless you absolutely *must* have a particular home and price is no object, be careful about entering a bidding war. Such auctions can drive the price of a home above its fair market value. That situation is great for the seller, but it is financially deadly for you. We don't want you to overpay.

If you really want a home, and you know that other offers will be made, here's how to improve your chances of winning in a multiple-offer situation:

- ✔ **Use comparable sales data to predetermine the upper limit of what you'll pay.** Don't get caught up by the excitement of a bidding war and let your emotions override your common sense. Be sure that you've read Chapter 10, and you know how to determine fair market value. Set no matter what limits on the amount that you'll bid. Otherwise, you could grossly overpay.

- ✔ **Put yourself in the sellers' position.** The sellers don't care how long you've been looking for a home or how little you can afford to pay. Faced with several offers, sellers select the offer that gives them the best combination of price, terms, and contingencies of sale. Find out what the sellers' needs are before making your offer. Their self-interest invariably prevails.

  A high purchase price isn't the only way to sweeten a deal. If you have the money, make an extra-large (25 or 30 percent or more of the purchase price) down payment so the sellers know that your loan will surely be approved. Or you could offer to let the sellers rent back their house for a month or two after the close of escrow (see Chapter 14) or give the sellers an extra-long close of escrow so they have plenty of time to find another home. You could also offer to buy the home "as is" so the sellers won't have to pay for any corrective work. If you do this, however, make your offer contingent upon your approval of inspection reports so you can get out of the deal if the house needs too much work.

- ✔ **Make your best offer initially.** Buyers who win bidding contests, in the words of Civil War General Nathan Bedford Forrest, get there "firstest with the mostest." If you want the house, don't hold back in a multiple-offer situation: You may never get a second chance to make your best offer.

- ✔ **Get preapproved for a loan.** Informed sellers worry about the financial strength of prospective buyers. They don't want to waste their time on buyers who can't qualify for a loan. All other things being equal, if you're preapproved for a loan (see Chapter 6), you should prevail over buyers whose financial status is in doubt. And if you've been preapproved for a loan, you'll know that *you* aren't wasting your time and money on a house that you may not qualify to buy.

- ✔ **Don't make your offer subject to the sale of another house.** As discussed earlier in this chapter in the section on contingencies, if you own a house that you *must* sell in order to get the down payment for your new home, you're in trouble. You'll most likely be competing with other buyers who don't have that limitation. The sellers have enough problems selling their house without worrying about whether you can sell yours. Why should they take your offer if they can accept one without a subject-to-sale contingency in it? Offers made subject to the sale of another house get no respect in a multiple-offer situation.

✔ **If you must sell in order to buy, put your old house on the market before seriously looking for a new home.** Ideally, you'll have a ratified offer on your old house before making an offer to buy a new place. Then, even with a subject-to-sale clause, your negotiating position will be much stronger. And you won't waste time worrying about how much money you'll have when and if your house sells. Stipulate a long close of escrow on the old house and the right to rent it back for several months after the sale so that you'll have adequate lead time to buy your new home.

Spotting fake sellers

Why would anyone want to be a fake seller? That some people would knowingly waste their time and money on an exercise in futility is absurd.

The key word is *knowingly.* All sellers start out thinking that they're sincere. As the quest for a buyer continues, however, circumstances ultimately prove that some sellers are phony.

Fake sellers cleverly mimic genuine sellers. Like real sellers, counterfeit sellers sign listing agreements, have For Sale signs in their yards, advertise in newspapers, and have open houses on Sundays. They outwardly appear to be the real McCoy. If you don't know how to detect fake sellers, you'll waste your precious time, energy, and money by fruitlessly negotiating to buy a house that isn't really for sale.

Identifying bogus sellers is ridiculously easy once you know how. Here are five simple tests that you can use to spot the fakes.

Are the sellers realistic?

The number-one reason that houses don't sell is that they have unrealistic asking prices. When people categorically state that they "can't" sell a grossly overpriced house, they expose themselves as fakes. What they're actually saying is that they refuse to accept the market's opinion of what their house is worth. People who won't listen to reason aren't sellers — they're property owners masquerading as sellers.

Real sellers may *inadvertently* overprice their homes initially. Unlike fake sellers, however, they eventually wise up. They know that they have a problem if they get no offers (or only lowball offers). Authentic sellers accept the relevance of using recent sales of comparable houses in the neighborhood to establish their house's fair market value. Genuine sellers are realistic.

Sometimes, homes sell for more than the asking price

Amy was a buyer who knew precisely what she wanted. Her dream home didn't have to be large. It did, however, need a light and airy feeling, a gourmet kitchen, nice views, a beautiful garden, and a garage. She'd been house hunting a long time because she refused to settle for anything less than her dream home.

Amy had a good agent. When a house that met all of Amy's specifications was listed at $295,000, Amy and her agent were waiting at the front door on the first day that the house was opened for inspection.

They weren't alone. The home was mobbed with drooling buyers and agents. Everything about the property, including its finely honed price, was flawless. The house was definitely priced to sell.

The listing agent told everyone that offers would be accepted in two days. Given the high level of buyer interest, Amy's agent knew that there would be multiple offers. She suggested that Amy could probably beat the competition by offering $5,000 over the asking price. Based on the sale price of comparable houses in the

neighborhood, the agent said the home was priced at (or perhaps slightly below) its fair market value. If all the other offers came in right at full asking price, Amy's $300,000 offer would stand out from the crowd.

Amy refused. Why, she reasoned, spend an extra $5,000 if she didn't have to? A full-price offer certainly wouldn't insult the sellers. If that wasn't enough money, Amy was sure that the sellers would give her a counter offer.

She was wrong. The sellers didn't counter any of the many offers they received. Instead, they simply accepted the highest offer, which wasn't Amy's.

Amy took a calculated risk. She could've been right. In fact, we've seen multiple-offer situations in which not one of the offers was close to full asking price. Multiple offers are no guarantee that a house will sell at or over its asking price.

Each situation is different and must be evaluated on its own merits. And don't forget to look at the comparable sales data.

Are the sellers motivated?

Most folks don't sell their homes to generate commissions for real estate agents. Sellers are usually motivated by a life change, such as wedding bells, a job transfer, family expansion, retirement, or a death in the family. Perhaps the sellers are in contract to buy another home but can't complete the purchase until their house sells. Or their house may be in foreclosure. Real sellers always have a motive for selling.

In dire situations, such as an impending foreclosure or divorce, sellers often instruct their agents not to tell anyone why they're selling. If possible, however, find out why the house is being sold *before* making your offer. Knowing the sellers' motivation allows you to shape your offer's terms (that is, quick close of escrow, letting the sellers rent back the house after the sale, and the like) to fit the sellers' circumstances.

Lack of motivation is a gigantic red flag. If the sellers or their agent say that they're testing the market, run as fast as you can in the opposite direction. Unmotivated sellers aren't.

Do the sellers have a time frame?

Deadlines make things happen. Seller deadlines are often established by such things as when the twins are due, when school starts, when they have to begin new jobs in another city, when the escrow is due to close on the new home that they're buying, and so on. Authentic sellers always have a deadline within which they must complete their sale.

Time is a powerful negotiating tool. If you aren't under pressure to buy, and the sellers must sell immediately (if not sooner), time is your pal and their enemy. Conversely, if you have less than four weeks to find a place to live before the kids start school, the watch is on the other wrist. Ideally, you know the sellers' deadline, but they don't know yours. Most real negotiation occurs at the 11th hour, 59th minute, and 59th second of a 12-hour deadline.

You could be in deep trouble if you have a deadline and the sellers don't. If you reveal this information to the sellers, they may use your deadline to beat you to a pulp. Beware of procrastination. Don't let time bully you — and keep your deadlines to yourself.

Are the sellers forthright?

Genuine sellers are disarmingly candid about their house's physical, financial, and legal status. They know that withholding vital information endangers the sale and may lead to a lawsuit. Early disclosure of possible problems, on the other hand, gives everyone the lead time required to solve them. Real sellers don't have a "buyer beware" mindset.

If you keep getting nasty surprises, you're working with fake sellers. Straightforward folks have only one defense against devious sellers who are playing an expensive, and possibly even devastating, game of *I've Got a Secret.* Terminate the transaction.

Are the sellers cooperative?

Real sellers look for ways to make transactions go more smoothly. They work with you to solve problems rather than waste time trying to figure out who's to blame if something goes wrong. Genuine sellers have a let's-make-it-happen attitude. They're deal-makers, not deal-breakers.

Inconsistent behavior is a red flag. If the sellers suddenly start missing contract deadlines or become strangely uncooperative, they may have lost their motivation to sell. Perhaps the wedding was postponed or the new job fell through. Whatever the reason, people sometimes switch from being real sellers to being fakes in midtransaction. Find out why the sellers are acting strangely as soon as you notice the change, and you may be able to head off the problem. If you ignore the danger signs, you'll never know what hit you when the deal blows up in your face.

Lowballing

A *lowball* offer is one that is far below a property's actual fair market value. An example of a lowball offer is a $150,000 offer on a house that's worth every penny of $200,000.

Who makes lowball offers? Sometimes, it's a graduate from one of those scuzzy, get-rich-quick real estate seminars. Another lowball offer may come from somebody who is bottom-fishing for sellers in dire financial distress. More often, however, lowballing is a negotiating tactic used by people who state categorically, "No one ever pays full asking price. You always have to start low to end up with a fair price."

Those statements aren't true, of course. When you do your homework, you know the difference between well-priced properties and overpriced turkeys. (See Chapter 10 for a brush-up.)

Why lowballing is usually a bad idea

As we discuss earlier in this chapter, lowballing a well-priced house breaks the first rule of a good offer: Make a realistic offering price based upon the sale price of comparable houses. Because skillful negotiators understand both sides of the issue, imagine that you're the seller of a house that is priced as close as humanly possible to its fair market value.

Several days after your house goes on the market, you receive an offer with an absurdly low purchase price. After the vein in your neck stops pounding, what conclusions can you form about the lowballing buyers?

- ✔ **Taken in the best possible light, the buyers obviously haven't done their homework regarding comparable home sales.** Because they're grossly ignorant about fair market value, why should you try to educate them?

- ✔ **Maybe the buyers think that you don't know what your house is really worth and are trying to exploit your ignorance.** (That vein starts throbbing again.)

- ✔ **Perhaps the buyers are trying to steal your house based upon a mistaken impression that you're desperate to sell.** There's a name for critters that prey on misfortune: *vultures.*

None of these conclusions is at all favorable. As a seller, you'd probably make one of the following responses to buyers who lowballed your well-priced house:

- ✔ **Let the buyers know that their offer is totally unacceptable by having your agent return it with a message that you wouldn't sell your house to them if they were the last buyers on earth.** Why make a counter offer to people who are either idiots or scoundrels?

- ✔ **Make a full-price counter offer.** To show your contempt for the buyers, you'll hardball them on each and every term and condition in their offer. (Two can play this game.)

Buyers who lowball a well-priced property listed by sellers who can wait for a better offer destroy any chance of developing the mutual trust and sense of fair play upon which cooperative negotiation is based. Bargaining is fine, but you must find a motivated seller and not aim too low. Starting at 25 percent below what the home is worth generally won't work unless the seller is desperate.

When low offers are justified

There's a huge difference between submitting an offer that's at the low end of a house's fair market value and lowballing. Suppose that you offer $280,000 for a home listed at $299,500. You base your offering price on the fact that comparable houses in the neighborhood recently sold in the $280,000-to-$295,000 price range. You're at the low end of the range of fair market values. The sellers are at the high end. You're both being realistic.

If your offer is based on actual sales of comparable houses, it won't insult the seller. Such a low offer will, however, spark lively debate as both of you attempt to defend your respective prices. Coming in on the low side of a property's fair market value is fine as long as you have plenty of time to negotiate and reason to believe that the seller is motivated.

In situations like the preceding one, your best bet is to have an encyclopedic comparable market analysis and an agent who has *personally* eyeballed all the comps. Follow the guidelines that we discuss in Chapter 10.

A low offer is justified only when it isn't a *lowball* offer. Ironically, some sellers provoke low offers by their unwise pricing. These sellers insist on leaving room to negotiate in their price because they "know" that buyers never pay full asking price.

Sound familiar? This practice, unfortunately, becomes a self-fulfilling prophecy. When buyers who know property values make an offer on an overpriced house, their initial offering price is usually on the low side to give themselves room to negotiate. What goes around, comes around.

Suppose that a house's fair market value is $300,000. If the sellers put this house on the market at $360,000 so they'll have a 20-percent negotiating cushion, and you offer $240,000 for the same reason, you and the sellers start out $120,000 apart. It takes a heap of extra negotiating to bridge a gap that big.

Don't play their silly game unless you have time to squander. Make your initial offer at the low end of the house's fair market value, and see how the sellers respond to it. If they refuse to accept the hard evidence of recent comparable home sales in the neighborhood, don't waste valuable time trying to educate them. They aren't sellers yet — they're property owners masquerading as sellers. If you want the house, bide your time. Don't make your move until they wise up and lower their price, or their agent puts the word out that they're motivated sellers who won't turn down any reasonable offer.

Negotiating credits in escrow

Putting a "let's sell it" price on a house isn't always enough to get the house sold, especially in a buyer's (weak) market. Sellers often find that they have to give buyers money in the form of seller-paid financial concessions in order to close the deal. The two most common concessions are for nonrecurring closing costs and corrective work.

Nonrecurring closing costs

Some sellers come right out and tell you that they'll pay your nonrecurring closing costs if doing so will help put a deal together. *Nonrecurring closing costs* are one-time charges for such things as your appraisal, loan points, credit report, title insurance, and property inspections. If you've read Chapter 3, you know that we're talking big bucks here. Closing costs can amount to 3 to 5 percent of the purchase price.

Even if the sellers don't offer to pay your nonrecurring closing costs, asking for this concession as one of the terms in your offer *usually* won't hurt. Two general exceptions to this rule are when it's a seller's (strong) market or when you're in a multiple-offer situation.

Here's how the credit works. Say that you've signed a contract to buy a $250,000 house. You have $55,000 in cash, and the escrow officer has just told you that you'll have nonrecurring closing costs totaling 4 percent ($10,000) of the purchase price.

About now, you may be wondering, "Why not just reduce the purchase price to $240,000 instead of asking the sellers for a $10,000 credit?" After all, the sellers' net proceeds of the sale are the same either way, and simply reducing the purchase price is less complicated. Not to mention that because property taxes are often based on the purchase price, a lower purchase price will probably cut your annual tax bite.

The reason: If you're short of cash, as most buyers are, a credit is more help-ful than a price reduction. If you have to pay $10,000 in closing costs, you won't have enough cash left to make a 20 percent ($48,000) down payment on your $240,000 home. With less than 20 percent down, your monthly loan costs increase because you have to pay a higher interest rate on your mort-gage plus private-mortgage-insurance costs. Neither will you have any cash left over for emergencies. Under these circumstances, you'd probably decide to buy a less-expensive house.

Contrast that scenario with paying $250,000 for the house and getting a credit from the sellers for nonrecurring closing costs. After putting 20 percent ($50,000) cash down to get the loan with the lowest interest rate, you still have $5,000 in the bank thanks to the $10,000 credit. The credit makes the deal happen.

If you have plenty of cash, get a price reduction rather than a credit. In most areas, the lower your purchase price, the lower your annual property taxes. Just be aware that most agents will lobby for the credit because a price reduction cuts into their commissions.

Corrective work

Typically, neither you nor the sellers know how much, if any, corrective work is needed when you submit your offer. Therefore, purchase contracts have provisions for additional negotiations regarding corrective work credits *after* all the necessary inspections have been completed.

If the property inspectors find that little or no corrective work is required, you have little or nothing to negotiate. Suppose, however, that your inspec-tors discover the $250,000 house you want to buy needs $25,000 of corrective work for termite and dry-rot damage, foundation repairs, and a new roof. Big corrective-work bills can be deal killers.

Seeing is believing. We strongly recommend that you and the seller's agent be present, if possible, during property inspections so that you both actually see the damage. And when you receive the inspection reports, use them as nego-tiating tools. Give the sellers copies of the reports for them to review before you meet with them to negotiate a corrective work credit.

This is the moment of truth in most home sales. Sellers usually don't want to pay for the corrective work. Neither do you. The deal *will* fall through if this impasse can't be resolved.

At this point in the negotiations, it's critical that the sellers realize that the value of their house has just been reduced by the cost required to repair it. If comparable houses with no termite or dry-rot damage, with solid foundations, and with good roofs are selling for $250,000, the sellers' house is worth only $225,000 in its present condition. Given its reduced value, an 80 percent loan is $180,000 — not $200,000 based on a $250,000 fair market value. If you can borrow only $180,000, and the sellers refuse to reduce the selling price from $250,000 to $225,000, you have to drop out of the deal.

The sellers may refuse to pay for repairs found by inspectors that you have hired. The sellers may question the impartiality or validity of your inspection reports and order their own inspections to verify or refute yours. The sellers may even threaten to pull out of the contract if you don't back off on your demands.

Sellers who try to punish the messenger are usually making a big mistake. You didn't bring the damage with you when you came, and (luckily for you) you won't take it with you when you go. Like it or not, the sellers are stuck with it. If they drive you away, they may still have a legal obligation to tell other buyers what you've discovered. That disclosure will probably lower the price that any future buyer will pay for their house. All things considered, working things out with you will probably be faster (and no more expensive) than waiting for another buyer.

Lenders also participate in corrective-work problems. They get copies of inspection reports when borrowers tell them that a serious repair problem exists, when their appraisal indicates a property obviously needs major repairs, or when the purchase contract contains a credit for extensive repairs. Whenever the property's loan-to-value ratio exceeds 80 percent, lenders actively help buyers and sellers resolve corrective-work problems.

You can solve repair problems in a variety of ways:

- ✔ **Ideally, the sellers leave enough money in escrow to cover the required corrective work with instructions for the escrow officer to pay the contractors as their work is completed.** This strategy has several advantages. You can supervise the work to be sure that it's done properly by contractors of your choice. The sellers don't have to suffer through having the work done while they're living in the house, and they don't have to incur any liability for the workmanship. Last but not least, the lender knows that the work will be done.

- ✔ **Alternatively, the lender withholds a portion of the full loan amount in a passbook savings account until the corrective work has been completed.** In cases involving major corrective work, the lender may refuse to fund the loan until the problems have been corrected.

- ✔ **The sellers may give a credit for corrective work directly to buyers at the close of escrow.** Lenders usually don't approve of this approach, because it raises uncertainties about whether the corrective work will actually be completed. If it isn't, the security of the lender's loan is impaired.

You can make the sellers feel better by offering to get competitive bids on the work from several reputable, licensed contractors. As long as the lowest bidder will do a quality job in a timely fashion, you and the sellers benefit. This additional effort on your part shows the sellers that you don't want to get rich off their misfortune. All you want is what you thought you were buying in the first place: a well-maintained home with a good foundation and a roof that doesn't leak. Empathy is an excellent negotiating tactic.

Chapter 13

Inspecting and Protecting Your Home

Given how much houses cost today, it's idiotic not to have the home you plan to purchase carefully inspected before buying it. Skipping inspections to save a few bucks (relatively speaking) could be the most expensive mistake you ever make. Think of your biggest fiscal fiasco ever. Multiply it by a hundred. That gives you some idea of the magnitude of the boo-boo you may make if you buy a home without first having it *thoroughly* inspected from foundation to roof.

Why are we so obsessed about property inspections? According to a study commissioned by *The Wall Street Journal* and conducted by housing economist Robert Sheehan, approximately two out of every five houses have at least one major defect. If the odds were two out of five that you'd get hit by a car the next time you walked across the street, you'd be pretty darn careful to inspect oncoming traffic before crossing!

Conducting Thorough Inspections

A home's physical condition greatly affects its value. You'd feel horrible if you paid top dollar for a home that you thought was in tip-top shape and discovered after you bought it that the house was riddled with expensive defects. Yet unless you're a professional property inspector, you probably won't have the faintest idea how much corrective work a house needs simply by looking at it.

Believe it or not, buying homes was even riskier a generation ago. The prevailing attitude then was extremely simple: "Buyer beware."

Today, fortunately, the situation has improved. Most states (but certainly not all) now require that sellers and real estate agents make full, immediate disclosure to prospective buyers of all *known* mechanical, structural, and legal problems associated with owner-occupied residential property. If this trend continues, the time may come when the warning shifts to "Seller and real estate agent beware." (Real estate agents also have liability if they fail to disclose a known problem about a property.)

Don't let your guard down. Even though the real estate market is a tad more consumer friendly than it used to be, don't be lulled into a false sense of complacency. *Latent defects* — hidden problems that sellers and their agents don't know about the home you're buying — can get you into a heap of budget-busting trouble after you complete your purchase.

If you haven't read Chapter 12 yet, take a quick look at the section about negotiating either a corrective-work credit or a price reduction. You can see how to use property inspections so that they pay for themselves many times over.

All properties should be inspected

Overinspecting a house is much better than underinspecting it. Suppose that you spend $350 to have the home you want to buy completely inspected by a qualified inspector, and you find out that nothing is wrong with it. Did you waste your money? Nope. You can sleep soundly, knowing that your home doesn't need any corrective work.

If, conversely, you skip the inspection to save $350 and later discover that your house needs $35,000 worth of repairs, you end up spending $100 in repairs for every dollar that you "saved." Such a deal! You might as well "save" money by not putting coins into parking meters and consider walloping parking tickets a normal driving expense!

Here's a list of properties that *must* be inspected prior to purchase:

✔ **Used houses:** You're most likely to order inspections if your "new" home is someone else's used house. Obviously, the older the house, the greater the likelihood that you'll find defects in its mechanical and structural systems.

✔ **New houses:** Even if you're buying a newly constructed, never-been-lived-in home, having it thoroughly inspected is wise. Just because the building is new doesn't guarantee that it was built properly. Believe it or not, brand-new houses often have construction flaws, sometimes major ones. Some home builders are not competent, or they cut corners to save some money and boost their profits.

- ✔ **Condominiums:** You need an inspection before buying a condominium. Don't forget that when you buy a condo, you're also buying into the entire building in which your condo is located (see Chapter 8). As a co-owner of the building, you must pay your proportional share of the cost for corrective work required in common areas, such as the roof, heating system, or foundation.

- ✔ **Townhouses, cooperative apartments, and all other forms of co-ownership property:** See the preceding bullet point about condominiums. Shared ownership doesn't get you off the hook. You still need property inspections.

All properties need inspecting. Period. Inspect detached residences, attached residences, single-family dwellings, multifamily dwellings, condos, co-ops, townhouses, and anything else that has a foundation and a roof. If you're spending big bucks for a property, protect your investment by having it inspected.

The two types of defects: patent and latent

Property defects come in two general categories: patent and latent. *Patent defects* are right out in the open for the world to see. You don't need a professional property inspector to point out glaringly obvious stuff like water stains on the ceiling, cracks in the wall, or a flooded basement. You do, however, need a trained professional to tell you whether these defects are signs of major problems or merely inconsequential blemishes.

Latent defects can be even more financially devastating than patent defects because they're hidden. Like playing a high-priced game of hide-and-seek, you must find latent defects or literally pay the consequences.

Latent defects are out of sight — behind walls or concealed in inaccessible areas under the house and up in the attic, away from casual observation. Faulty wiring, termite damage, a cracked heat-exchanger in the furnace, and health- and safety-code problems (such as lead in the water pipes and asbestos insulation) are some examples of latent physical flaws.

Legal blemishes, such as zoning violations and fraudulent title claims, illustrate another kind of latent defect that only experts can detect.

Patent-defect red flags

You don't have to be a professional inspector to give property a basic once-over. Even the rankest amateur can check the water pressure and turn on water faucets to see whether they leak. Flipping light switches on and off and flushing the toilets to find out whether they work properly are easy but effective tests. Open the refrigerator to see whether it's cold inside. Turn on the stove's heating elements to see whether they get hot. You may be surprised how many defects you discover with these simple tests.

By the same token, you can spot the danger signs of possibly serious structural problems even if you've never had any special training, as long as you know what to look for as you walk through a property. Although we advocate that you hire a professional property inspector, here's a list of red flags that even a mechanically challenged home buyer should be able to spot:

- ✔ **Cracks:** Check the property's foundation, interior walls, exterior retaining walls, fireplace, chimney, concrete floors (basement, garage, and the like), and sidewalk for large cracks. Any crack that you can stick a pencil into is a large crack. Watch for vertical cracks on any walls and long horizontal or diagonal cracks on exterior walls.

- ✔ **Moisture:** Look for water stains on ceilings, walls, and floors. Feel basement walls for dampness. Sniff out the source of moldy smells. Check for drainage problems inside and out by looking for standing water. A sump pump in the basement or garage is a red flag waving to get your attention.

- ✔ **Stickiness:** All doors (exterior, interior, garage, and cabinets) and windows should open and close easily.

- ✔ **Looseness:** You shouldn't be able to see daylight around windows, doors, or skylights.

- ✔ **Unevenness:** Floors shouldn't slope, and walls shouldn't bulge.

- ✔ **Insects:** If the house you're buying is made of wood or wood and stucco, it may have problems with wood-destroying insects or organisms. Mud tubes along a house's foundation or in its basement are a sign of termite infestation. Look carefully at those areas of the property that come into contact with the earth — foundation, decks, garage, and fencing — for signs of decayed or rotted wood.

- ✔ **Slides:** Check hillsides immediately behind the property to see whether they have netting on them or show evidence of recent earth or mud slides.

Before you have the property inspected, discuss any red flags you discover with your property inspector. Let the pro check them out to see whether they're major problems or only relatively minor flaws that you can quickly and inexpensively correct. A sticking front door, for example, can indicate either that the house has expensive foundation problems or simply that the door absorbed moisture because it wasn't properly sealed.

Types of property inspections

What inspections should you get to protect your investment? That depends on what area of the country you live in, how the building in question is constructed, and what you plan to do to the property after buying it. Here are the three most common types of inspections — which we recommend be done *after* you have an accepted offer to purchase but *before* removing your inspection contingencies (so that you're able to negotiate the correction of problems discovered by the inspections, as we recommend in Chapter 12):

✔ **Prepurchase interior- and exterior-components inspection:** No matter whether you're buying a wood-frame cottage in the country or an urban condo in a 20-story steel-and-concrete building, you need a complete inspection of the property's interior and exterior. The inspection should cover such areas as the roof and gutters, plumbing, electrical work, heating and cooling systems, insulation, smoke detectors, kitchen, bathroom, and foundation. The inspection should also point out health, safety, and environmental hazards. This type of inspection usually takes several hours to complete and costs $300 to $600, depending upon how large the property is and the inspection's length and degree of detail.

Don't be surprised if the property inspector recommends additional inspections. Good property inspectors are generalists who are trained to spot red flags. Like doctors who are general practitioners, good property inspectors refer their clients to specialists, such as roofers, structural engineers, and pest-control inspectors, if they discover a problem beyond their scope of expertise. Property inspectors know that you can't make good decisions unless you have the best possible information.

✔ **Pest-control inspection:** Warm climates, such as in the South and West, are a mixed blessing. You're not the only one who loves warm, balmy weather. So do termites, carpenter ants, powder-post beetles, dry rot, fungi, and other wood-munching infestations or infections. If these are a problem in your area, you also need a pest-control inspection. These inspections generally cost $150 to $400.

Pest-control inspections are very limited in scope — the inspectors check for property damage caused only by wood-destroying insects (infestations) and organisms (infections, such as dry rot and fungi). Although homes made of wood or wood and stucco are the wood destroyers' primary targets, even brick homes aren't safe. If you get a pest-control inspection, it should be in addition to your prepurchase interior- and exterior-components inspection — not in lieu of it.

✔ **Architect's or general contractor's inspection:** You need an architect or a general contractor on your team if you're buying a fixer-upper; intending to do corrective work; or planning a major property renovation, such as adding rooms or installing a new bathroom. The architect or general contractor can tell you whether what you want to do is structurally possible and meets local planning codes for such things as height restrictions and lot coverage. This inspector can also give you time and cost estimates for the project.

Architects and general contractors usually don't charge for their initial property inspection because they're hoping to get your business. Although these people provide a valuable service, take their reports with a grain of salt. Don't expect them to give you a completely objective assessment as to whether you should buy the property, because they'd probably love to do the work for you.

Inspecting inspectors

Unfortunately, some people who anoint themselves "home inspectors" have neither the background nor the training to do proper prepurchase home inspections. To compound the problem, most states don't certify, license, or regulate home inspectors. If you have a clipboard, a pickup truck, and a good "houseside manner," you too can be a home inspector nearly anywhere in the country.

Worse yet, some contractors inspect houses and then do the corrective work that they discover during their own inspections. That situation ought to start a red flag waving in your mind. Unscrupulous contractors can — and do — manipulate this conflict of interest to their advantage by finding and creating work for themselves.

One way around this problem is to hire someone who only does inspections. A growing number of property inspectors are exactly that: professional property inspectors, not contractors. This distinction is more than just semantic. Performing property inspections requires a special expertise that not all contractors, engineers, and architects have.

Professional property inspectors are specifically trained to do inspections and only inspections; they make their living solely from inspection fees. They don't do corrective work, which eliminates the temptation to find unnecessary corrective work during their inspections.

Selecting your inspector

How can you find a qualified home inspector? Ask friends and business associates who've recently bought homes whom they used for their property inspections. Get a list of home inspectors from a real estate agent. Be careful, though, of inspectors who are popular with agents — that popularity *may* stem from not killing too many deals by going easy on their inspections. Also check the Yellow Pages of your local phone book under "Building Inspection Services" or "Home Inspection Services." If several sources recommend the same inspector, you've probably found a good one.

Just because someone has a diploma issued by an organization with an impressive name doesn't mean that individual is a qualified property inspector. Unfortunately, some "professional" associations' only criterion for membership is the ability to pay an initiation fee and annual membership dues. No matter how fancy the diploma, don't be fooled by what could be a meaningless piece of paper.

The *American Society of Home Inspectors* (ASHI) is a professional association of independent home inspectors. Just because an inspector is an ASHI member doesn't guarantee that you'll get a good inspection, but it certainly increases the likelihood that you'll be working with a qualified professional. You can't just plunk down a membership fee and join. All ASHI-certified members have performed at least 250 property inspections and have passed two written proficiency exams as a prerequisite of membership. ASHI members must also adhere to ASHI's standards of practice, continuing-education requirements, and code of ethics. To find members in your area, call ASHI at 800-743-2744 or visit its Web site at `www.ashi.org`.

We recommend that you interview several property inspectors prior to hiring one. Here are questions to help you select the best inspector:

- ✔ **Are you a full-time, professional property inspector?** Only one answer is acceptable: yes.

- ✔ **What can you tell me about your company?** Discuss the company's size and how long it has been in business.

- ✔ **Do you carry errors-and-omissions insurance?** Errors-and-omissions insurance covers the possibility that a property inspection could miss some problems. If an inspector makes an error that costs you big bucks, errors-and-omissions insurance can help make amends.

- ✔ **How many inspections do you personally perform each year?** Although the average number of inspections varies from area to area, active inspectors usually conduct between 150 and 400 inspections per year. Find out whether the inspector works primarily in the area in which the property you want to have inspected is located and is thus familiar with *local* codes, *local* regulations, and *local* problems (such as floods, mud slides, earthquakes, tornadoes, and the like).

- ✔ **Do you hold any special licenses or certifications?** Property inspectors usually have a background in some related field, such as construction, engineering, architecture, electricity, plumbing, or insurance-claim adjusting. This diversity adds extra insights to their inspections. Membership in ASHI or another trade association for property inspectors indicates at least a minimal knowledge of home-inspection procedures.

✔ **What is the scope of your prepurchase inspection?** Make sure that the inspection covers *all* the property's major structural and mechanical systems, inside and out, from foundation to roof. Anything less is unacceptable.

✔ **How long will your inspection take?** Time actually spent at the site is an important consideration. This inspection isn't a race. It usually takes two or three hours to *thoroughly* inspect a condo or a home of average size.

✔ **What type of report will I receive?** Verbal reports, like verbal contracts, are worthless. A boilerplate, checklist-type report is only marginally better. You must have a detailed description of your specific property's mechanical and structural condition. You need a narrative report, written in plain English, that clearly explains the implications of its findings.

Get sample reports from each inspector that you interview. The best way to see whether a company writes good reports is to read one so that you can draw your own conclusion. Figure 13-1 features a superficial inspection report; we include an example of a thorough inspection report in Appendix B so that you know what a good inspection report looks like.

✔ **Do you mind if I tag along during your inspection?** Mind? On the contrary, good inspectors insist that you be present during the property inspection.

✔ **Will your report include an estimate of the cost to do your recommended corrective work?** This is a trick question. If the inspector says yes, don't use the inspector. Good professional property inspectors do only inspections. They don't do corrective work. Neither do they solicit business for their friends. Good inspectors help you establish repair costs by referring you to three or four reputable contractors, roofers, electricians, and other repair people that you can contact for corrective-work quotes. Because there's usually more than one way to fix a defect, you have to decide how best to deal with a problem after you've consulted the appropriate repair people.

✔ **How much does your inspection cost?** Unfortunately, this is generally the first question that buyers ask when shopping for a property inspector. This is no time to be penny wise and pound foolish. Watch out for unrealistically low, "this week only" promotional fees that new inspectors may offer. Don't let green inspectors practice on you. Quality inspections cost more than quickie, one-size-fits-all, checklist inspections, because they're worth a lot more. Ultimately, because fees charged by good inspectors are usually pretty much the same (because of competitive pressure), you'll probably end up using the correct criteria to select your inspector: compatibility and competence.

✔ **Would you mind if I call some of your recent customers for references?** Good property inspectors are happy to give you names and phone numbers of their satisfied customers. Bad inspectors may balk at providing references or direct you to people they know will say something positive about them. Be sure to check at least three references in the town where the property is located per inspector. Ask the references whether, after close of escrow, they discovered any major defects that their inspector missed and whether they'd use their inspector again.

INSPECTION REPORT

NAME _____ ADDRESS _____ DATE 8 /29/

COMMERCIAL /RESIDENTIAL /INCOME   FLOORS IN USE 3   NUMBER OF UNITS 3

DESCRIPTION: *Wood Frame Stucco Front*

BASEMENT/SUB-STRUCTURE	EX	GD	FR	PR
FOUNDATION				X
SILL PLATE				
WALLS/STUDS				
COLUMNS				
GIRDERS		X		
SUB-FLOOR		X		
FLOOR JOISTS				
SEISMIC BRACING				

INTERIOR	EX	GD	FR	PR
LATH & PLASTER		X		
SHEETROCK		X		
FLOORS:				
KITCHEN		X		
BATHROOM(S)			X	
GENERAL AREA		X		
DOORS		X		
STAIRS/HANDRAIL		X		

EXTERIOR	EX	GD	FR	PR
SIDING			X	
TRIM		X		
CAULKING				
FLASHING				
DRAINAGE/SLOPE				X
EARTH CLEARANCE				
PORCHES		X		
STAIRS			X	

PLUMBING	EX	GD	FR	PR
COPPER		X		
GALVANIZED				
MIXED				
DRAINS				
VENTS			X	
FIXTURES				
MAIN SERVICE - WATER				
MAIN SERVICE - GAS				

ROOF	EX	GD	FR	PR
TAR & GRAVEL			X	
ASPHALT SHINGLE				
ROLL ROOFING				
WOOD SHINGLE/SHAKE				
GUTTERS		X		
DOWNSPOUTS				X

HEATING SYSTEM	EX	GD	FR	PR
GRAVITY		X		
FORCED AIR				
SPACE:		X		
GAS				
ELECTRIC				
MIXED				

ELECTRICAL	EX	GD	FR	PR
110 ___ 220 ✓				
FUSES ___ BREAKERS ✓		X		

WATER HEATER	EX	GD	FR	PR
GAS		X		
ELECTRIC				
SIZE 50 GAL		X		

COMMENTS: 1) *Romex wire running exposed in upper closet.*

2) *Wall fire protection is missing in closet behind heater*

3) *Caulk is missing from kitchen sink*

BY. _____

SIGNED: _____

Figure 13-1: This is an example of the type of superficial inspection report that you don't want to waste your money on. For an example of a good inspection report, see Appendix B.

Seeing and reading are infinitely better than just reading

You, your agent, and the seller's agent should join the inspector during the property inspection. Reading even the finest of inspection reports is, at best, a mediocre substitute for being at the property and looking at the defects with your own eyes. This may be your best opportunity to question the inspector about the ramifications of a defect and discuss various ways to correct problems. By seeing and talking about the defects, you gain a better understanding of why some defects are no big deal to fix, whereas others cost megabucks to repair.

From a negotiating standpoint, the sellers are more likely to accept the inspection report's findings if their agent was present when the inspection was performed. They'll know that the defects are real — their agent actually saw the defects and can point them out to the sellers before they get a copy of the inspection report. They'll know that a skilled professional inspected their house — not some stooge that you hired to defame their property so that you could swindle them out of their hard-earned money. They'll know that even if they drive you away by hardballing you on the corrective work, they'll still be stuck with the problem of selling a defective house.

Even if the house is in perfect condition, you should know where certain things are. If you attend the inspection, your inspector can show you where to find important stuff like the furnace, water heater, and circuit breakers. The inspector should also show you where the emergency shutoff valves for the house's gas, electric, and water systems are. By attending the inspection, you'll learn much more about the house's care and maintenance than you'd ever pick up by reading the inspection report.

If it's flat-out impossible to be at the inspection because you're stuck in another city or must be at a command-performance business meeting, make sure to have someone you trust (your agent, a relative or friend, or someone equally trustworthy) at the inspection to act as your eyes and ears. Ask your surrogate to make an audiotape or videotape recording of the inspection, which you can use to supplement the inspection report. Watching a videotape is not as good as personally being there, but it sure beats just reading a report. You can also call the inspector if you have questions about the report.

Last but not least, pay attention. Don't bring along a gaggle of kids, relatives, friends, business associates, painters, carpet suppliers, plumbers, electricians, or contractors who'll distract you from the job at hand: learning everything you can about the property that you want to buy. Focus on the inspection.

Optimizing your inspection

Here are guidelines for getting the biggest bang out of the bucks that you invest in a prepurchase property inspection:

✔ **Always make your offer to purchase a house subject to your review and approval of the inspection reports.** Doing so gives you the opportunity to either negotiate a credit or price reduction for corrective work that is discovered during the inspections or, if you wish, get out of the deal. We cover this subject extensively in Chapter 12.

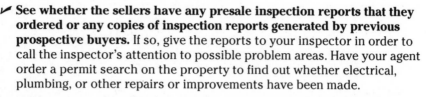

✔ **See whether the sellers have any presale inspection reports that they ordered or any copies of inspection reports generated by previous prospective buyers.** If so, give the reports to your inspector in order to call the inspector's attention to possible problem areas. Have your agent order a permit search on the property to find out whether electrical, plumbing, or other repairs or improvements have been made.

Suppose that the sellers give you a presale inspection report that they ordered just before putting their house on the market. It says that their house is in perfect condition. You could save money by relying on their report instead of getting your own. Should you? No way. Never let the fox tell you how things are in the henhouse. Always pay for your own inspection by an inspector of your own choosing.

✔ **Read your property inspector's report carefully.** If you don't see some defects listed in the report that your inspector specifically mentioned during the inspection, call the inspector to find out why. By the same token, don't be the least bit shy about calling your inspector to get a detailed explanation of *anything* you don't completely understand in the report.

✔ **To minimize the cost of corrective repairs, get bids on the job from several reputable, licensed contractors.** Never try to save money by using unlicensed contractors to do the work without permits. Doing so is usually illegal, can create health and safety problems, and can adversely affect your home's resale value. Many states require that house sellers disclose to prospective purchasers the fact that work on the house was done without permits. If your state doesn't mandate this type of disclosure now, it probably will by the time that you're ready to sell your house.

✔ **Use your property inspector during the contractor bidding process.** If the contractors have questions regarding items discussed in the inspection report, refer them to the report's author for clarification. For an additional fee, some property inspectors will help you evaluate bids you receive to do the corrective work.

Prepurchase property inspections are intended to give you a factual basis for negotiating the correction of big-ticket defects — not to nickel-and-dime sellers over credits for stained carpets and worn curtains. If your new home is someone else's used house, let your *offering price* reflect the home's reduced value due to normal wear-and-tear cosmetic defects.

If your agent or the seller offers to pay for a *home warranty plan* or *home protection plan* (that is, a service contract that covers some of your home's major systems and appliances), it wouldn't be gracious of you to turn down a freebie. Never accept such a plan in lieu of an inspection, however, and don't buy this type of plan for yourself. After spending $250 or so for the plan, you pay an additional $25 to $50 deductible each time

> you need someone to come out and look at a problem. Furthermore, these plans significantly limit how much they pay to correct major problems. Hiring a professional property inspector to inspect the home diligently and uncover all existing problems so that you can negotiate their correction with the sellers is a better way to spend your money.

Don't expect your inspections to eliminate all future maintenance problems. In time, the garbage disposal will break. All roofs leak eventually. When these things happen, it isn't part of some hideous plot to defraud you.

Anything in your home that can break or leak will break or leak, sooner or later. Repairs come with homeownership. After closing on your home purchase, normal upkeep is your responsibility — not the sellers'. They'll have repairs of their own to make to their new home.

Insuring Your Home

Nobody likes to spend money for insurance. But if something could cause you a financial catastrophe, you should insure against that risk. The point of insurance is that you spend a relatively small amount of money to protect against losing a great deal of money. For example, if your home burns to the ground and it's not insured, you could be out tens (if not hundreds) of thousands of dollars.

You shouldn't waste money insuring potentially small-dollar losses. Suppose that you mail a package that contains a gift worth $50. If the postal service loses it, you'll be bummed, but the loss won't be a financial catastrophe for you. You shouldn't waste your money on such insurance.

Here are the types of insurance that you do need to have in place *before* you purchase your dream home.

Homeowners insurance

When you buy a home, most lenders require that you purchase homeowners insurance. Even if you're one of those rare people who can buy a home with cash without borrowing money, you should carry homeowners coverage. Why? First, your home and the personal property (furniture, carpets, audio equipment, computers, china, and the like) in your home would cost a small fortune to replace out of your own pocket.

Second, your home can lead to a lawsuit. If someone were injured or killed in your home, you could be sued for tens or hundreds of thousands of dollars, perhaps even a million dollars or more.

The following sections tell how to get the homeowners coverage that you need.

The cost of rebuilding

If your home is destroyed, which most frequently happens from fires, your insurance policy should pay for the cost of rebuilding your home. The portion of your policy that takes care of this loss is the *dwelling coverage* section of the policy. The amount of this coverage should be equal to the cost of rebuilding the home that you own. The cost to rebuild should be based on the square footage of your home. Your policy's dwelling coverage amount should not be based on what you paid for the home or the amount of your mortgage. If you're buying a condominium or cooperative apartment, examine the coverage that your building's homeowners association carries.

Get a policy that includes a *guaranteed replacement cost* provision. This provision ensures that the insurance company will rebuild the home even if the cost of construction is more than the policy coverage. If the insurance company underestimates your dwelling coverage, the company has to eat the difference.

Ask the insurers that you're speaking with how they define *guaranteed replacement cost coverage* — each insurer defines it differently. The most generous policies, for example, pay for the full replacement cost of the home, no matter how much the replacement ends up costing. Other insurers set limits — for example, they agree to pay up to 120 percent of your policy's total dwelling coverage.

Lawsuit protection

Liability insurance protects you against lawsuits arising from bad things that happen to others while they are on your property. Suppose that a litigious passerby happens to slip on a banana peel that was left on your driveway. Or perhaps your second-floor deck collapses during a beer fest, and someone breaks a leg or two.

Carry enough liability insurance to protect at least two times the value of your assets. Although the chances of being sued are remote, remember that if you are sued, the financial consequences can be staggering. In fact, if you have substantial assets (worth more than a couple hundred thousand dollars, for example) to protect, you might consider what's called an *umbrella,* or *excess-liability policy.* Bought in increments of $1 million, this coverage adds to the liability coverage on your home and car(s). Check for such policies with your home and auto insurers.

Personal property protection

On a typical homeowners policy, the amount of personal property coverage is usually set at about 50 to 75 percent of the amount of dwelling coverage. If you're a condominium or cooperative apartment owner, however, you'll generally need to choose a specific dollar amount for the personal property coverage that you want.

Some policies come with *personal property replacement guarantees* that pay you for the replacement cost of an item rather than for the actual value of a used item at the time that it's damaged or stolen. If this feature isn't part of the standard policy sold by your insurer, you may want to purchase it as a *rider* (add-on provision), if such a rider is available.

If you ever need to file a claim, having documentation of your personal property helps. The simplest and fastest way to document your personal effects is to make a videotape of your belongings. Alternatively, you can maintain a file folder of receipts for major purchases and make a written inventory of your belongings. No matter how you document your belongings, be sure to place this documentation somewhere outside your home (and not in the vegetable garden). A list or video isn't going to do you much good if it's in your home and goes up in a puff of smoke during a fire or is irreparably damaged in a horrendous flood!

Where to get good coverage inexpensively

As with other types of insurance and other financial products, you must shop around. But we know that you have better things to do with your time than shop, so here's a short list of companies that are known for offering high-quality, low-cost policies:

- ✔ **AMICA:** Call the company at 800-242-6422 for information. Although AMICA customers generally give the company high ratings, AMICA's prices are sometimes on the high side.

- ✔ **Erie Insurance:** This company does business primarily in states in the Midwest and Mid-Atlantic. Check your local phone directory for agents who sell Erie Insurance policies or call 800-458-0811 for a referral to a local agent.

- ✔ **GEICO:** Call the company for specifics at 800-841-3000.

- ✔ **Liberty Mutual:** Check your local phone directory for agents who sell Liberty Mutual's policies.

- ✔ **Nationwide Mutual:** Check your local phone directory for agents who sell Nationwide Mutual's insurance.

✔ **State Farm:** Check your local phone directory for agents who sell State Farm insurance.

✔ **USAA:** Insurance through USAA is available to military officers and their family members. Call the company for specifics and to see whether you qualify (800-531-8080).

You may have access to more specific information for your state. Many state insurance departments, which you can locate through the state government listings in your phone book, conduct surveys of insurers' prices and tabulate any complaints received. We also include information about some helpful Web sites in Chapter 11.

As you shop around, ask about special discounts for such things as homes with a security system or smoke-detection system, discounts for people who have multiple policies with the same insurer, and senior discounts.

Other catastrophes to insure against

Depending upon where the home you buy is located, it may be subjected to earthquakes, floods, hurricanes, mud slides, tornadoes, wildfires, or other bad stuff. Standard homeowners policies don't protect against all these vagaries, so you must secure additional riders.

Thousands of communities around the country are at risk for floods. Hence, if you live in one of these areas, you need to purchase a flood-insurance rider. Check with prospective homeowners insurance providers. The federal government flood insurance program (800-638-6620; www.fema.gov/nfip) can provide background information on the types of policies available through private insurance companies.

Earthquakes are another risk to insure against. In addition to California, parts of the Midwest (and even parts of the East Coast) have active fault lines.

Ask people in the area that you're considering moving to what the local risks are. The U.S. Geologic Survey (check your local phone directory; www.usgs.gov) and the Federal Emergency Management Agency (800-358-9616; www.fema.gov) offer maps showing, respectively, earthquake and flood risks. Be aware, and be informed.

Because the cost of earthquake and flood coverage is based on insurance companies' assessments of the risks of both your area and your property type, you should *not* decide whether to buy these riders based upon only your perception of how small a risk a major quake or flood is. The risk is already built into the price.

You may be able to pay for much of the cost of earthquake or flood insurance by raising the deductibles on the main parts of both your homeowners insurance and the other insurance policies that you carry. Remember — you can more easily afford the smaller claims than the big ones. If you think that flood or earthquake insurance is too costly, compare the costs of the coverage with the expense that you will incur to completely replace your home and personal property. Buy this insurance if you live in an area that has a chance of being affected by these catastrophes.

Title insurance

Fast-forward to a time several months after you've closed escrow on the purchase of your dream home. Suppose that we ask you to prove to us that you actually own the home.

"No problem," you say. You go to the safe deposit box where you keep all your important documents and pull out the fancy deed that the recorder's office mailed to you a couple weeks after you completed your purchase.

Sorry. That deed isn't proof positive.

For example, a man and his "wife" signed a deed that transferred the title to their house to another couple. A few weeks later, the buyers were shocked to find that their deed wasn't valid because the real wife's signature had been forged. In fact, the real wife didn't even know that her husband had sold the property.

Title risks

In theory, you can go down to the local county recorder's office and find out who owns any piece of property in the county simply by checking the public record. In fact, all sorts of irregularities in the history of the various people who have owned the property since it was originally constructed can affect a property's title — irregularities that are difficult or impossible to find, no matter how diligently you comb the public records.

Here are some causes of these hidden risks to titles:

- ✔ **Secret spouses:** A seller may claim to be single when, in fact, he or she is secretly married in another state. Or perhaps the seller was divorced in a community-property state where, through marriage, one spouse obtains a legal interest in property held individually by the other spouse. Whatever the reason, sometimes a present or former spouse no one knew about will show up out of the blue and file a claim against the property. This explains why title-company representatives are so infernally curious about your marital status. They must know whether you're single, married, divorced, or widowed in order to keep ownership records accurate.

- ✔ **Undisclosed heirs:** When property owners die without wills, probate courts must decide who their rightful heirs are. Court decisions may not be binding on heirs who weren't notified of the proceeding. Even when there's a will, probate courts must sometimes settle questions concerning the will's interpretation. Undiscovered heirs sometimes magically appear and claim that they now own the property in question.

- ✔ **Questionable competency:** Minors and people adjudged to be mentally incompetent can't enter into binding contracts unless their court-appointed guardians or conservators handle the transaction. If, for example, the seller was a minor or was mentally incompetent when a deed was signed, the transaction may be voidable or invalid.

✔ **Goofs:** This is a highly technical, catchall category for human errors. It covers everything from clerks who overlook liens recorded against property (liens for unpaid federal and state income taxes or local property taxes, for example) and other important documents while doing title searches, to surveyors who incorrectly establish property boundaries. Honest mistakes create many title problems.

✔ **Forgery and fraud:** As was the case with the fake wife, sellers are sometimes fraudulently impersonated. By the same token, signatures can be forged on documents. Escrow officers demand identification (that is, a photo ID, such as a driver's license issued within the past five years or a current passport) to *establish beyond a shadow of a doubt that you are who you claim to be.*

✔ **Name confusion:** A lot of title problems result from people having names similar (or identical) to the buyer's name or seller's name. Even though you prove that you are who you claim you are, you also have to prove who you *aren't.* If you have a fairly common last name, you'll probably have to fill out a Statement of Information to help the title company distinguish you from other people with names like yours. If you have an ordinary name like Brown, Chen, Garcia, Gonzalez, Johnson, Jones, Lee, Miller, Nguyen, Williams, or the ever-popular Smith, expect to be asked to complete a Statement of Information.

What type of information is requested in a Statement of Information? You (and your spouse if you're married) will have to provide your full name, Social Security number, date and year of birth, birthplace, date and place of marriage (if applicable), residence and employment information, previous marriages, and the like. This information will be used to differentiate good old honest you from the legions of ne'er-do-wells out there with names similar to yours.

What title insurance does

Many people who buy homes spend hundreds of dollars for title insurance without really understanding what they're getting for their money. *Title insurance* assures homeowners and mortgage lenders that a property has a marketable *(valid)* title. If someone makes a claim that threatens your ownership of the home, the title insurance company protects you and the lender against loss or damage, according to the terms and provisions of your respective title insurance policies.

Most of your title insurance premium pays for research to determine who legally owns the property that you want to buy and to find out whether any unpaid tax liens or judgments are recorded against it. Because title companies do a good job of eliminating title risks *before* folks buy property, only about 10 percent of the premium goes toward indemnifying homeowners against title claims *after* the close of escrow.

The title insurance premium that you pay at close of escrow is the one and only title insurance premium that you'll have to pay *unless you refinance your mortgage*.

Title insurance deals with your risk of loss from *past* problems (such as unpaid property-tax liens or forgery in the chain of title) that *may* exist at the time that your policy is issued. Because your policy covers the past, which is a fixed event, you pay only one title-insurance premium *as long as you keep your original mortgage*.

If you refinance your mortgage, you'll have to get a new title-insurance policy to protect the lender from title risks (such as income-tax liens or property-tax liens) that may have been recorded against your property between the time your previous policy was issued and the date of the refinance. If you refinance your loan, ask the title company whether you qualify for a *refinance rate* on the new title-insurance policy. Most title companies will give you a big premium reduction — as much as 30 percent off their normal rates — if your previous policy was issued within five years of the new policy's issuance date.

Two kinds of title insurance

As a homeowner, you have a choice of two different kinds of *owners* title insurance. Depending on the extent of the coverage that you desire, you can either get a standard-coverage policy or an extended-coverage policy.

As you'd expect, *a standard title-insurance policy* is less expensive than an extended policy because its coverage is more limited. Standard policies are limited to certain off-record risks (such as fraud in the chain of title, defective recordings, and competency) plus *recorded* (at the local county recorder's office) mechanic's liens, tax assessments, judgments, and other property defects that a search of public records can uncover.

Extended title-insurance policies cover everything that standard policies do, plus they provide expanded coverage for off-record risks that could be discovered through an inspection of the property or by making inquiries of people in actual possession of the property, as well as defects such as *unrecorded* (never recorded at the county recorder's office) mechanic's liens, leases, or contracts of sale. Only an extended title-insurance policy would've protected the homeowners in the faulty-land-survey and kitchen-fire examples in the sidebar "Actual examples of title-insurance problems."

Title-insurance costs vary greatly, depending upon the geographic area in which your home is located, the home's purchase price, and the type of coverage that you get. In addition to the owners policy that we recommend you purchase to protect your investment, you'll need to buy a policy to protect the mortgage lender against loss on the loan amount.

Actual examples of title-insurance problems

Folks usually don't pay much attention to title insurance when they're buying a home. Most people get title insurance only because the lender won't give them a mortgage if they don't have it. But home buyers are mighty glad to have such a policy when a title problem rears its ugly head.

For example, a woman spent close to $10,000 to remodel an existing carport and shed and to build a fence along her property line after obtaining her neighbor's permission. So far, so good. Everything was fine for the woman until her neighbor sold his place several years later. The new owners had their property surveyed and discovered that her carport, shed, and fence extended about 2 feet onto their land. Instead of tearing everything down, which was the woman's first impulse after getting the bad news, she decided to file a claim on her title-insurance policy.

The title company discovered that she was the victim of a faulty land survey. It solved the problem by buying from her new neighbors an *easement in perpetuity* to use the land that she had improved so that she could leave everything (carport, shed, and fence) exactly where it was.

Another example involves a couple whose kitchen was destroyed by fire. The county building department said that to rebuild it, the couple would have to remove a preexisting carport that extended into a 5-foot lot setback. The previous owners had gotten all the necessary permits that were required to build the carport, but the local zoning laws had changed since the time the carport was built in 1970.

The clever couple knew what to do. They called their friendly title-company representative. After investigating their problem, the title company paid a contractor $5,000 to remove the carport. The title company also paid the couple $19,000 to compensate them for the reduced value of their property because it no longer had covered parking.

In some Eastern states, title companies are barred from doing title searches. If that prohibition exists in your area, you'll have to use a lawyer to handle your title search and escrow. In either case, shop around to see who offers the best combination of competitive premiums and good coverage.

Local custom and practice determine who usually pays for title insurance. In some parts of the country, custom dictates that the buyer pays for it. In other areas, however, the seller pays the title insurance premium, or buyers and sellers split the cost fifty-fifty. As we point out in Chapter 12, the payment for title insurance is a negotiable item. Regardless of local custom, if you're in a strong buyer's market, the sellers may offer (or you could ask them) to pay your title-insurance costs in order to put the deal together. If, conversely, you're bidding against several other buyers for a particularly desirable house, you'd be smart to sweeten your offer by paying for title insurance, even though local custom prescribes that sellers pay for it.

Chapter 14

It Ain't Over Till the Weight-Challenged Escrow Officer Sings

The big day draws near. Soon, if all goes well, you'll plunk down the balance of your down payment, sign on the dotted line, and pick up the keys to your dream home.

For most people, the final throes of buying a home involve elephantine incertitude, high anxiety, and flop sweats. You, however, are *not* most people. The tips you find in this chapter will soothe your fevered brow, smooth the yellow brick road to success, and make the endgame downright pleasant and enjoyable.

An Escrow Is a Good Thing

As soon as possible after you and the seller have a *ratified offer* (that is, a signed contract), all funds, documents, and instructions pertaining to your transaction should be delivered to a neutral third party: the *escrow holder* designated in your purchase agreement. The act of giving these funds, documents, and instructions to the escrow holder constitutes the *escrow*. Depending on the local custom in your area, a lawyer, an escrow firm, or a title company may handle the escrow. Buyers and sellers generally select an escrow holder based on recommendations from their agents. However, as with other companies you choose to do business with in your home-buying transaction, know that escrow fees and service quality vary.

Real estate deals are often characterized by mutual distrust. You and the seller need someone that both of you can trust to hold the stakes while you two meet to work through all the resolved and unresolved details in your contract. The *escrow holder* (also known as the *escrow officer*) is your referee — a neutral third party who shouldn't show any favoritism to either you or the seller.

Know thy escrow officer

Your escrow officer is responsible for preparing and reviewing papers related to the transfer of *title* — a legal document that stipulates ownership of the property. This includes getting them properly signed, delivered, and made a matter of public record; complying with your lender's funding instructions; ordering a title search (explained in Chapter 13); and accounting to you and the seller for your respective money. The escrow officer handles the nitty-gritty paperwork and money details.

When the escrow is opened, your contract will probably be filled with loopholes known as *contingencies* or *conditions of sale*. For example, your contract should be written so that you can get out of the deal if you don't approve the property inspection reports, if the seller can't give you clear title to the property, or if you can't get a loan. The escrow officer's job is to receive and follow your instructions. Don't instruct the escrow officer to give your money to the seller until you are *fully* satisfied that the seller has performed under the contract. Chapter 12 goes into great detail about contingencies.

Ideally, your escrow will go smoothly from start to close. If, however, the escrow officer ever gets conflicting instructions from you and the seller or lender, the escrow will stop dead in its tracks until the argument is resolved. What kind of conflicting instructions? Disputes about whether or not the purchase price includes an item of personal property (that is, a refrigerator, a fireplace screen, light fixture, and the like) are always popular. So are disagreements about whether corrective work should be done prior to or after close of escrow.

Our friend Kip Oxman, a most excellent real estate attorney and broker, has a great saying that works wonders in dispute-resolution situations: "When all else fails, RTC." You can find the answers to most controversies if you **R**ead **T**he **C**ontract. The real estate purchase agreement included in Appendix A is an example of an extremely explicit contract that is intended to eliminate ambiguity.

Good escrow officers are worth their weight in gold in times of crisis when the shouting, tears, and threats of lawsuit begin. At moments like this, often only the escrow officer's incredible patience and crisis-mediation skills keep deals glued together.

Give yourself an unfair advantage by humanizing your escrow. Either call or visit your escrow officer at her office to introduce yourself. Ask whether she needs any additional information to make the escrow go faster and smoother. Some questions your escrow officer may ask include the following: What's your middle name? Where can you be reached during the day? What's your insurance agent's name and phone number? What's your Social Security number (so your deposit can be placed in an interest-bearing account)? A little consideration and respect now will do wonders for you later if the escrow hits a rough patch.

Cover all the bases

To avoid truly horrible surprises, pay particular attention to the following three areas.

Closing costs

If you have a nice, orderly, sequential mind, you've undoubtedly read the preceding 13 chapters and know that we have a detailed itemization of closing costs in Chapter 3. If you're the kind of person who loves to skip around and sample random chapters that strike your fancy, we suggest that you read that section now, or the following tips won't make as much sense.

As soon as possible, get a rough idea of how much money you'll have to come up with at the close of escrow. Immediately after opening escrow, ask the escrow officer to prepare a statement of your estimated closing costs. Even though it may take several weeks to get actual costs for inspection fees, repair-work credits, homeowners insurance premiums, and the like, at least you'll have a preliminary number that you can fine-tune as additional information becomes available. Having the knowledge available in this preliminary statement beats getting hammered by unexpected closing costs a couple of days before the close of escrow.

Estimate the closing expenses on the high side. Overestimating expenses and finding, when actual costs come in, that you won't need as much money to close as you first expected is ideal. The sooner you put a box around your closing costs, the better. Don't react to the situation — control it.

If, like most folks, you must put additional money in escrow just prior to the close of the transaction, use a cashier's check or a money order, or have your funds wired directly to the escrow to prevent delays. Be sure you stay on top of your bank to ensure that the wire is expedited, because banks sometimes drop the ball. Personal checks take time to clear. Credit cards don't cut it in escrows. If you have questions regarding what constitutes *good funds,* ask your escrow officer well in advance of the close of escrow. If your money is out of town, for example, in a high-yielding money-market fund (such as is recommended in Chapter 3), check with your investment company about how you can wire money from your account to the escrow company.

Preliminary title report

Shortly after escrow is opened, you should receive an extremely important document: the *preliminary title report* (or *prelim*) from your title company. This report shows who currently owns the property that you want to buy, as well as any money claims (such as mortgage liens, income-tax judgments, and property-tax assessments) that affect the property. Last but not least, the preliminary title report shows third-party restrictions and interests, such as condominium covenants, conditions, and restrictions (CC&Rs) and utility-company or private easements, that limit your use of the property.

Your contract should be contingent upon your review and approval of the preliminary title report. Look it over carefully. Ask your agent, escrow officer, title-company representative, or lawyer to explain anything in the report that you don't understand. Don't be shy — there's no such thing as a dumb question.

As per the purchase contract, you should have the right to *reasonably* disapprove of certain claims or restrictions that you don't want on the property and to ask the owner to clear them prior to the close of escrow. For example, asking the seller to pay off all debts secured by liens and judgments against the property is reasonable. Asking the seller of a condo to remove the CC&Rs would be unreasonable because, as noted in Chapter 8, the CC&Rs are an integral part of the property.

A preliminary title report is *not* title insurance. You can find more on the distinction between title insurance and a preliminary title report in the title-insurance section of Chapter 13.

Final closing statement

You may believe that the most important piece of paper you get when escrow closes is the deed to your new home. From an accounting standpoint, however, the most important piece of paper is the final closing statement that you get from the escrow officer on the day that your escrow actually closes.

If you think of the escrow as a checking account, the final closing statement is like your checkbook. The final closing statement records all the money related to your home purchase that went through the escrow as either a credit or a debit:

✔ **Credits:** Any money that you put into escrow (such as your initial deposit and down payment) appears as a credit to your account. You may also receive credits from the seller for such things as corrective-work repairs and property taxes. And, of course, your loan is a credit.

✔ **Debits:** Funds paid out of escrow on your behalf are shown as debits. Your debits include modest and not-so-modest expenses, such as what you graciously paid the seller for your dream home, loan fees, home-owners-insurance premiums, and property inspection fees.

You meet with your escrow officer several days before close of escrow to sign the loan documents and other papers related to your home purchase. At that time, you'll receive an estimated closing statement detailing what your closing costs will be if the escrow closes as scheduled. Check the estimated closing statement *extremely* carefully, line by line and from top to bottom, to be absolutely certain that it accurately reflects your credits and debits.

Escrow officers are human — they sometimes make mistakes. So do other participants in the transaction who may have given the escrow officer incorrect information. And guess what — when mistakes turn up, whose favor do you think they are in? Probably not yours! It's your money on the table. Pay attention to detail. Review the closing statement, and question whatever isn't clear or correct. You need not determine at the time you sign the loan documents precisely what is wrong with the closing statement. Take it home with you, and continue inspecting it and asking the various parties to the transaction to clarify anything you don't understand about it.

The final closing statement is extremely important. Keep a copy for your files — it will come in handy when the time comes to complete your annual income-tax return. As detailed in Chapter 3, some expenses (such as loan origination fees and property-tax payments) are tax deductible. Furthermore, the closing statement establishes your initial tax (cost) basis in the property. When you're ready to sell your property, you may owe capital-gains tax on any profit you've made by selling the property for more than your cost basis (see Chapter 17 for more details).

'Tis the season: December escrows

As a rule, December is a slow month for home sales. A week or two before Thanksgiving, most buyers switch their attention from houses to holidays and family gatherings, and those buyers typically don't get back onto the home-buying track until around Super Bowl Sunday in late January.

Here are two reasons that you may decide to buck the trend:

✔ **Bargain hunting:** When the other buyers drop out of the market, you're the only game in town for sellers who must move soon or stubborn sellers who foolishly waited too long to get realistic about their asking price. If they must sell, sellers instruct their agents to put the word out that they're willing to deal. The magic phrase is "Bring us an offer." If you're a lowballer looking for a deal, now's the time to make your move.

✔ **Tax deductions:** What you get doesn't matter — what does matter is what you get to keep. Buying a home in December gives you tax deductions that you can use to reduce your federal and state income taxes in that calendar year. As we discuss in Chapter 3, owning a home gives you physical shelter and tax shelter. On your income taxes, you can, for example, write off your loan origination fee (points), mortgage interest, and property taxes that you pay prior to December 31.

Escrows are perverse creatures under even the best of circumstances. They're proof positive of Murphy's Law, which states that whatever can go wrong will — and *always* at the worst possible time. Experienced escrow officers know that nasty surprises can rear their ugly heads whenever you least expect them.

The list of potential surprises is unpleasantly long: missed deadlines, title glitches, problems paying off existing loans, changes in your loan's terms, insufficient funds to close escrow, funds not wired as promised, and so on.

December escrows are particularly perverse. Partying zaps your strength and reduces your effectiveness. People forget to sign papers before leaving on vacation. December 31 is an immutable deadline if you want to close this year for tax purposes. If you end up with a late December escrow, here are some things you (and your real estate agent) should do to make sure that you meet your deadline:

✔ **Stay in touch with your lender.** Lenders need copious documentation to substantiate loan applications. Be sure that your lender has all the required documents as soon as possible. Lenders say that lack of follow-up on loan-document verification is the number-one cause of escrow delays. In Chapter 7, we provide an extensive checklist of items, such as W-2s, tax returns, bank statements and so on, that your lender may need you to provide to verify the information on your loan application.

✔ **Don't leave any blank spaces on your loan application.** Draw a line through any section that doesn't apply to you. If you leave a section blank, the lender may assume that you forgot to complete it. And make a photocopy of everything that you submit in case the originals get lost or you need to refer to the documents when the lender questions something you wrote.

✔ **Stay in touch with your escrow officer.** Don't let your file get buried in a pile of pending escrows stuck on the corner of your escrow officer's desk. You or your agent should check with the escrow officer periodically to make sure that things are going smoothly.

✔ **Be available to sign your loan documents.** You may have only 24 to 48 hours after your loan package arrives at the escrow office to sign the documents and return them to the lender. A delay could cost you the loan.

✔ **If you're leaving town for the holidays, tell your agent, lender, and escrow officer well in advance of your departure.** You can usually make special arrangements to close your escrow — no matter where you are — as long as people have advance warning and know how to reach you. The key to success is keeping everyone posted.

✔ **Check the calendar.** Many offices are open only till noon on Christmas Eve and New Year's Eve. When Christmas Day and New Year's Day fall on Saturday or Sunday, office hours can really get crazy. Some businesses and public offices close on the preceding Friday, others close on the following Monday, and still others close on both Friday and Monday in order to give their employees a four-day holiday. Be sure to check the holiday office schedule of your agent, lender, escrow officer, and so on. Don't let a holiday office closing derail your deal.

✔ **Allow time between when you'd like to close and when you must close.** Give yourself maneuvering room to resolve last-minute problems that inevitably appear when you least expect them. Don't schedule your closing on the last business day of the year. You'll have no margin for error if you need to close by year's end.

Follow through

Engagements are to weddings what escrows are to buying houses. Just as wedding bells don't always ring for everyone who gets engaged, all open escrows don't end in home purchases.

Many escrows could've been saved by applying a fundamental principle of winning tennis: Follow through. Tennis pros know that there's more to the game than simply making contact with the ball. Pros continue their swing "through the ball" after they hit it, because they know that the last part of the stroke is as important as the initial contact with the ball. If they don't follow through properly, the ball won't end up where they want it to go.

And so it is with real estate deals. Buyers, sellers, and agents often say that a house has been *sold* when the purchase contract is signed. *Not true!* Nothing was sold. The buyer and seller merely ratified an offer. *Big difference!*

If you want to actually buy and move into the home — that is, close your escrow — everyone involved in your transaction must follow through on all the details. You won't be the proud owner of your dream house until the weight-challenged escrow officer sings!

How You Take Title Is Vital

One of the most important decisions that you can make when buying a home is how you take title in the property. If you're unmarried, your choices are simpler because you take title as a sole owner. When two or more people co-own a property, however, the number of ways to take title multiplies dramatically.

How title is held is critically important. Each form of co-ownership has its own rainbow of advantages, disadvantages, tax consequences, and legal repercussions. You shouldn't make this decision in haste at an escrow office while signing your closing papers. Unfortunately, that's what usually happens.

What's the best form of co-ownership for you? That depends on your circumstances. Here are some forms of co-ownership and the advantages of each type.

Joint tenancy

Suppose that you and your spouse buy a house together as joint tenants. When your spouse dies 20 years from now, ownership of the house automatically transfers to you without going through probate. This feature of joint tenancy co-ownership is known as the *right of survivorship*.

Joint-tenancy benefits don't stop there. You also get a *stepped-up basis* on your spouse's half of the house. This stepped-up basis may save you big bucks on the capital-gains tax that you'll have to pay if you ever sell the house.

Here's how a stepped-up basis works. Say that you and your spouse paid $180,000 for the house when you bought it. Immediately after your spouse's death, the house is appraised at $300,000.

Your new cost-of-the-home basis for tax purposes is $240,000 ($90,000 for your half-share of the original purchase price, plus $150,000 for your spouse's half of the house at date of death) because no capital-gains tax applies to your spouse's $60,000 of appreciation in value.

Even though we used a married couple in our example, you need not be married to use joint tenancy co-ownership. However, a minimum of two people must co-own.

Community property

Only married couples can take title as community property. Compared with joint tenancy, an advantage of community property co-ownership is that both halves of your house get a stepped-up basis upon the death of your spouse. This gives you even bigger tax savings.

Using the same figures as the joint-tenancy example, as the surviving spouse, your cost basis is the full $300,000. Capital-gains tax is forgiven on every penny of appreciation in value between the date of purchase and your spouse's death.

Another advantage of community property co-ownership is the ability to will your share of the house to whomever you wish. Because of the right of survivorship, this choice isn't possible when title is held as joint tenants.

Tenants-in-common or partnerships

Holding title as tenants-in-common or in the form of a partnership doesn't give you a stepped-up basis upon the death of a co-owner. This creates an obvious disadvantage from a tax standpoint.

Offsetting legal advantages exist, however, for unrelated persons who take title either as tenants-in-common or as a partnership. Under these forms of co-ownership, you generally have the right to will or sell your share of the property without permission of the co-owners. Furthermore, co-owners don't have to have equal ownership interests in the property — a nice feature for people who just want a small piece of the action.

Getting help drafting an agreement

If you're smart — and we know that you must be, or you wouldn't be reading this book — you and your co-owners should have a formal written agreement, prepared by a real estate lawyer, to cover situations likely to arise while you jointly own the property. (***Note:*** Such agreements are generally used and advisable when partners purchasing a property are not a married couple). Here's a recap of key provisions to include in your written agreement (you can find more on these items in the partnership section of Chapter 8):

✔ Provisions to buy out a co-owner who has to sell when the other owners want to keep the property

✔ Provisions to prorate maintenance and repair costs among co-owners with unequal shares in the property

✔ Provisions to resolve disputes regarding such things as what color to paint the house

✔ Provisions for penalties if a co-owner can't cover his or her share of loan payments or property taxes

The preceding information is not intended to be your definitive guide to the subtleties of real property title vesting. This chapter merely points out the most important issues that you should consider. Don't make a decision of this magnitude in haste, especially if your situation is unusual or complicated. In addition to deciding how to hold title, you should consider estate-planning issues, such as wills and potential trusts (see Chapter 2 to find out more).

Getting Possessive

The day your escrow closes is legally confusing. You don't own the home when the day begins at 12:01 a.m., but you're the owner of record when the day ends at midnight. Sometime during the day, the escrow officer gives the seller your money, notifies you that the deed has been recorded, and officially announces that you're now the proud owner of your dream home. Congratulations!

Moving day

When can you actually take possession of your home and move into it? That depends on the terms of your contract. Look at paragraph 3 of the sample purchase contract in Appendix A to see an example of a Closing and Occupancy clause that specifies date and time of possession and delivery of keys from seller to buyer. Here are your usual options:

✔ **Move in the same day that escrow closes.** This is fine if the sellers have already moved out. If, however, the sellers haven't moved yet and don't want to deliver possession until they're absolutely, 100 percent certain that escrow has closed, you have a logistical problem. For two moving vans to occupy exactly the same driveway at exactly the same time borders on the impossible. Moving into a house while someone else is moving out is something you'll never attempt more than once. There are easier ways to go crazy.

✔ **Move in the day after escrow closes.** We recommend this alternative if the sellers won't deliver possession until escrow closes. Let the sellers have the day that escrow closes as their moving day. After all, the sellers are still the owners until title transfers. Moving day is stressful, even under the best of circumstances. Why create unnecessary stress for yourself by trying to move in as the sellers are leaving?

After the sellers vacate, but before your movers bring your belongings into the house, check your new home carefully for damage that may have been caused by the sellers' movers. When movers are involved, accidents can happen. We cover this problem in the next section.

Whether you move into your home the day that escrow closes or the following day, you start paying for utilities and homeowners insurance effective the day that escrow closes. Don't forget to coordinate phone installation and resumption of utility services, if necessary, with the proper companies a couple of weeks prior to the scheduled close of escrow.

✔ **Move in after a seller rent-back.** Sellers may remain in their house for several weeks after escrow closes while waiting to get into their new home. In that case, the buyer signs a separate *rent-back agreement* with the sellers, which becomes part of the purchase contract. The rent-back agreement covers such things as who pays for utilities and maintenance, what happens if property damage occurs, how much rent the sellers pay you, and what the penalties are if the sellers don't vacate the property on the date specified in the rent-back.

It's customary for the sellers to pay rent equal to what you're paying for principal and interest on your mortgage, plus property taxes and insurance, so that you don't have out-of-pocket expenses on what you pay to own the house during the term of their rental. The amount equaling *principal, interest, taxes,* and *insurance* (known as PITI) is prorated on a per-day basis from close of escrow until the sellers vacate. Suppose that PITI is $50 per day, and the sellers expect to be out three weeks after escrow closes. You both instruct the escrow officer to hold *four* weeks' PITI in escrow to give you a cushion if the sellers encounter a delay in moving into their new place. When the sellers actually move out, you and the sellers jointly instruct the escrow officer to pay you PITI for the actual rental period and to refund to the sellers the unused portion of funds held in escrow.

If the home you're buying is vacant, you may be tempted to ask for permission to start fixing the house up before close of escrow. After all, painting or waxing floors, for example, is much easier and faster when the house is empty. *Don't do it.* If the deal falls through, you've spent your time and money fixing up someone else's house. If the house catches fire, you don't have insurance to cover your losses. The risk exceeds the reward. Instead, allow some time to do these tasks *after* escrow closes and *before* moving in.

Final verification of condition

Read the Final Verification of Condition clause in paragraph 15 of the California Association of Realtors' purchase contract (Appendix A). If your state's contract doesn't have this type of clause in it, instruct your agent or lawyer to write such a clause into your contract. Nearly all contracts also have something like paragraph 25 (Other Terms and Conditions) just for this type of supplement to the contract.

We urge you to inspect the property a few days (ideally, the day) before escrow closes to be sure that the property is still in the same general condition that it was in when you signed the contract to buy it. What if the sellers knocked a big hole in the kitchen wall during a wild party? What if they forgot to water the lawn, and it turned into a rock garden? What if a sinkhole appeared smack-dab in the middle of the driveway? The "what ifs" are endless.

You'll probably find that everything is fine. But if it isn't, you can order the escrow officer to stop the escrow while you resolve the problem. Such an action always gets the seller's and real estate agent's attention. If you and the seller can't work out a mutually satisfactory solution, you may have to kill the deal. Killing the deal is better than buying a problem.

Coping with Buyer's Remorse

Many home sellers are convinced that they left the family jewels on the table when they sold their houses. The notion that they "gave their house away" is called *seller's remorse*. Seller's remorse is painful, but it generally departs within a month or two after the sale. Sellers are lucky to have such an uncomplicated dementia.

If you're like most buyers, you'll experience the flip side of this nasty psychosis. *Buyer's remorse* is the sinking feeling that you paid way, way, waaaay too much for your new home.

Unfortunately, buyer's remorse is much more complex than seller's remorse. Buyer's remorse is compounded by many other anxieties — that you're getting the world's worst mortgage, that the bottom will fall out of property values in the years after you buy a home, that you'll lose your job, that your health will fail, and that your faithful dog will die.

We're here to help you deal with fear of overpayment. Those other anxieties are absolutely normal reactions to the uncertainties most of us *initially* experience. They *will* go away. If it makes you feel any better, nearly all home buyers are traumatized by the same concerns while purchasing a home.

In time, you'll discover (as we and millions of others who have gone before you did) that you have a fine mortgage, property values are stable, your continued employment is secure, your health is great, and so is your dog's. Don't take our word for this. Do a little dialing for dollars to verify that you got a good loan, check the help-wanted ads for jobs like yours, discuss property values with neighbors, get a physical examination, and take your dog to the vet.

So what about the fear that you're paying waaaay too much? If the real estate gods love you, you'll get a light case of buyer's remorse that you can treat by taking a couple of aspirin. Some buyers, however, are so ravaged by it that they try to break their contract.

You can't deal with buyer's remorse until you accept it for what it is: raw, naked fear. You're afraid that you're overpaying for the house. That fear tears some buyers apart. The symptoms of typical, fear-driven buyer's remorse are easy to spot. After you've signed the contract to buy your dream home, you do one or more of the following:

- ✔ **Read ads in the real estate section of your local newspaper even more intently than you did before you signed the contract.** You're searching for similar or nicer houses with lower asking prices. (You forget that most houses read a lot better in ads than they eyeball when you tour them.)

- ✔ **Spend Saturday and Sunday touring open houses.** Reading ads isn't enough for you. You pound the pavement, looking for better buys than you got. Seeing, after all, *is* believing. (Speaking of seeing, you may see the remorseful sellers making the rounds of the same houses that you're looking at, trying to find less-nice properties with bigger asking prices.)

- ✔ **Discuss your purchase with friends, neighbors, business associates, and the guy standing behind you while you wait in line to buy movie tickets.** You ask anyone and everyone whether they think that you're paying too much, even though 99.9 percent of the people that you talk to don't have a clue about property values for homes similar to yours. (You accept as gospel any wild guess they make that confirms your suspicions.)

After going through these exercises *during* escrow and for a couple of months *after* the purchase (until you're emotionally and physically exhausted), you'll probably discover that your fears are groundless. Nothing's wrong or unusual about your concerns. What is wrong is letting these fears gnaw away at you secretly instead of openly confronting them.

Facts defeat fear. The faster you get the facts you need, the less you'll suffer.

As Chapter 10 explains, a home can have more than one correct price. Pricing and negotiation are arts, not precise sciences. Don't beat yourself up with *asking* prices. You're okay as long as your home's *purchase* price is in line with the *sale* prices of comparable houses.

If you follow the principles we cover in this book, you'll be just fine! Unlike many home buyers, you know how to get your finances in order before you buy, and you know how to determine what you can really afford to spend on a home. You know how to find a great neighborhood, a great property, a great mortgage, a great agent, and a great property inspector. You can spot an overpriced turkey and a good value. You know about property inspections and negotiating for repair of property defects. You know how to avoid nasty people and property surprises.

Knowledge is power. After you've assimilated the advice in this book, you'll be extremely powerful. You have nothing to fear. Go for it!

Part V
The Part of Tens

The 5th Wave   By Rich Tennant

"Oh, I think we absolutely did the right thing by purchasing this house, but Frank has got a bad case of buyer's remoras."

In this part . . .

This part includes information on the ten financial musts after you buy, ten things to know when investing in real estate, and ten things to consider when selling your house.

Chapter 15

Ten Financial "To Do's" After You Buy

*A*lthough it may have seemed that the day would never come — here you are, a *homeowner*. A homeowner — can you believe it? Go ahead and pinch yourself!

Perhaps you're already correcting your friends who ask how it feels to be a homeowner. Most new owners say, "Well, the bank owns more of the house than I do." Actually, you own 100 percent of the property — you just owe the mortgage lender a bucketload of money! Trust us when we say that although it may seem like a lot of money now, it won't seem that way decades from now. You'll be glad then that you decided to buy rather than continue renting. What you owe today, you'll ideally own free and clear in 30 years, if not sooner.

If you think that the hard part is over after you buy a home, you may be in for a surprise. Moving probably wasn't a picnic, but moving is just the beginning of your quest to transform your new slag-heap into a beauteous home.

As a new homeowner, you must sidestep the many solicitations that will be winging your way. Unfortunately, when you buy a home, you end up on a zillion or so mailing lists because your home purchase is a matter of public record. Some communities even publish home sales (complete with buyer and seller names and purchase price) in the local newspaper, for goodness' sake!

This chapter can help you become a financially happy new homeowner and can help you avoid the pitfalls to which many new homeowners before you have fallen prey.

Stay on Top of Your Spending and Saving

After you buy and move into your home, if you're like most new homeowners, your furniture and other personal possessions seem to take on an even shabbier tinge than before. And because you're now living in the property, you soon discover aspects of it that you don't like as much as when you were looking at it from the outside as a prospective buyer. This is another bitter bite of *buyer's remorse,* a common affliction of new home buyers that we discuss in Chapter 14.

Most home buyers can find unlimited furniture, appliances, and remodeling projects that quickly exhaust the incomes of even the rich and famous. Because of these spending temptations, more than a few home buyers end up not saving any of their hard-earned incomes. Some new homeowners even end up building credit card (and other high interest) consumer debt because their spending outstrips their income.

Feeling a squeeze in the budget when you buy a home is perfectly normal. After all, your housing expenses are probably higher than they were when you were renting. But that's all the more reason that you need to take a lean-and-mean approach to the rest of your budget and spending (see Chapter 2). You can also make your home more energy efficient by doing some simple things such as adding insulation and installing water-flow restrictors in faucets and showerheads. Also, use your home-inspection report to identify other opportunities for improvement.

Don't neglect saving toward important financial goals, such as retirement. And take your time transforming your new home into a veritable palace. Rejoice and take solace in the fact that you have a roof over your head, a warm and comfortable place to sleep, and adequate living space — things that many people around the world can only dream about.

Consider Electronic Mortgage Payments

Mortgage lenders want to be paid and to be paid on time. And you want to pay them on time. Late payments can cost you dearly — many mortgages have stipulations for penalties equal to 5 percent of the amount of the mortgage payment if your payment is late. If your payment is one whole month late, a 5 percent penalty works out to an annualized interest rate in excess of 60 percent! Even being one day late can trigger this penalty. (And you thought that credit card debt was costly to carry at 18 percent!) Late charges also show up as *derogatories* on your credit report.

Sign up for your mortgage lender's automatic-payment service to have your mortgage payment zapped electronically from your checking account to the lender on the same day each month. If your mortgage lender doesn't offer this service, establish it yourself through one of the many home-banking services, such as CheckFree (800-297-3180; www.checkfree.com), or through bill-payment software such as Quicken or Microsoft Money.

Rebuild Your Emergency Reserve

Most people clean out their emergency reserve (and then some) in order to scrape together enough cash to close on their home purchase. Ideally, you should have ready and available an emergency cash reserve equal to at least three months' worth of living expenses. If your employment is unstable, and you lack family to lean on financially in a pinch, aim for six months' worth of living expenses. Keep the emergency money in a high-yielding money-market mutual fund (see Chapter 3).

As with saving money to accomplish other important financial goals, rebuilding your emergency reserve requires you to go on a financial diet and spend less than you earn. Easier said than done, especially with all the tempting things to spend money on for your home. Avoid the malls, mail-order catalogs, and home-improvement stores until you're back on an even keel!

Ignore Solicitations for Mortgage Insurance

Soon after you move into your home — often within a matter of just weeks or months — your mailbox will flood with solicitations offering you mortgage life insurance and mortgage disability insurance. Most of the solicitations come from your mortgage lender, but other solicitations may come from insurance firms that picked up on the publicly available information revealing that you recently bought your home.

The fundamental problem with these insurance policies is that given the amount of insurance protection offered, such policies are usually grossly overpriced and don't provide the right amount of benefits. The size of your mortgage shouldn't necessarily determine the amount of life and disability insurance protection that you carry. If you need life insurance protection because you have dependents who rely on your income, it's generally wise to buy low-cost, high-quality term insurance. Likewise, if you're dependent on your income, make sure that you have proper long-term-disability insurance coverage. See Chapter 2 to find out more about satisfying your insurance needs.

Ignore Solicitations for Faster Payoff

Another type of solicitation that you may receive extols the virtues — thousands of dollars in interest savings — that you can reap if you pay your mortgage off faster. For a monthly fee, these services offer to turn your annual 12-monthly-payment mortgage into 26 biweekly payments, each of which is half of your current monthly payment. Thus, you'll be making 13 months' worth of mortgage payments every year instead of 12. Doing so will usually shave about 8 years off the repayment schedule of a 30-year mortgage.

These services have two problems. First, you're paying the service money for paying off your mortgage faster — something you can do without the service and its fees. Second, paying off your mortgage faster than necessary may not be in your best interest.

The question to ask yourself is what you would do with the extra money each month if you didn't pay off the mortgage faster. If you'd spend it on something frivolous that would provide only fleeting, superficial enjoyment, paying off your mortgage faster is probably a better use of the money. Likewise, if you're an older (or otherwise risk-averse) investor, you're unlikely to earn a high enough rate of return by investing your money to make it worth your while not to pay off your mortgage faster.

On the other hand, if you could instead put more money away into a tax-deductible retirement account, paying off your mortgage faster may actually cost you money rather than save you money. Neither is it wise to pay down your loan if doing so leaves you cash poor. Suppose that you lose your job and take several months to find a new one. Or suppose that your home needs a new roof, and you don't have the cash to pay for it. You should have at least three to six months' worth of living expenses in some readily available place such as a money-market fund. If you don't, you may have to use high-interest-rate (and not tax-deductible) credit cards to pay for unexpected expenses.

Consider Protesting Your Tax Assessment

In most communities, real estate property taxes are based upon an estimate of your home's value. If home prices have dropped since you bought your home, you may be able to appeal your assessment and enjoy a reduction in the property taxes that you're required to pay.

Contact your local assessor's office to inquire into the local procedure for appealing your property taxes. Generally, the process involves providing comparable sales data in writing to the assessor to prove the reduced value of your home. If you need help with this exercise, contact the real estate agent who sold you the home. Just be aware that your agent may want to make you feel as though your home hasn't decreased as much in value in order to make you (and perhaps himself) feel better. Explain that you're trying to save money on your property taxes and need comps that sold for less than you paid for your house. See Chapter 10 if you need a quick refresher on establishing property values.

Refinance If Interest Rates Fall

In Chapters 6 and 7, we explain how to select a magnificent mortgage and provide many tips for getting the best mortgage deal you can. But after you're into the routine of making your mortgage payments, if you're like most people, staying on top of strategies to keep your mortgage costs to an absolute minimum is probably as high on your priority list as flossing your teeth three times a day.

Keep an eye on interest rates. Please see the mortgage shopping resources we recommend in Chapter 6, as well as some Web sites we recommend in Chapter 11 to efficiently assist you with that task. As you may already know, interest rates — like the weather — change. If interest rates decrease from where they were when you took out your mortgage, you may be able to refinance your mortgage and save yourself some money. *Refinancing* (as described in Chapter 6) simply means that you take out another new (lower-cost) mortgage to replace your old (higher-cost) one.

If rates have dropped at least one full percentage point since you originally took out your loan, start to contemplate and assess refinancing. The key item to calculate is how many months it will take you to recoup the costs of refinancing (loan fees, title insurance, and the like). Suppose that your favorite mortgage lender tells you that you can whack $150 off your monthly payment by refinancing. Sounds good, huh? Well, not so quick there, Poindexter. First, you won't save yourself $150 per month just because your payment drops by that amount — don't forget that you'll lose some tax write-offs if you have less mortgage interest to deduct.

To figure how much you will really reduce your mortgage cost on an after-tax basis, take your tax rate (as delineated in Chapter 3) and decrease your monthly payment savings you expect from the refinance by that amount. If you're a moderate-income earner, odds are that you're in the 28 percent tax bracket. So if your mortgage payment would drop by $150, and if you were to reduce that $150 by 28 percent (to account for the lost tax savings), your savings (on an after-tax basis) would actually be $108 per month.

Now, $108 per month is nothing to sneeze at, but you still must consider how much refinancing the loan will cost you. If the refinancing costs total, for example, $6,000, it will take you about 56 months ($6,000 divided by $108) to recover those costs. If you plan on moving within five years, refinancing won't save you money — it will actually cost you money. On the other hand, if it costs you just $3,000 to refinance, you can recover those costs within three years. If you expect to stay in your home for at least that long, refinancing is probably a good move.

Keep Receipts for All Improvements

Sooner or later, you will spend money on your home. You should track and document some of what you spend money on for tax purposes in order to minimize the capital gain that you may owe tax on in the future. *Capital gain* simply means the difference between what you receive for the house when you sell it less what it cost you to buy the house — with one important modification. The IRS allows you to add the cost of improvements to the original cost of your home in order to calculate what's known as your *adjusted-cost basis*.

Capital Gain = Net Sale Price – (Purchase Price + Capital Improvements)

For example, if you buy your home for $225,000, and over the years, it appreciates so that (after paying the costs of selling) your net selling price is $350,000, your capital gain is $125,000. Remember, though, that the IRS allows you to add the value of the capital improvements that you make to your home to your purchase price.

Capital improvement is money you spend on your home that permanently increases its value and useful life — putting a new roof on your house, for example, rather than just patching the existing roof. So if you made $10,000 worth of improvements on the home you bought for $225,000, your capital gain would be reduced to $115,000. Money spent on maintenance, such as fixing a leaky pipe or replacing broken windows, is not added to your cost basis (see Chapter 3 for more details).

Before you sell your home, please be sure to understand the tax consequences of such a transaction. As we discuss in Chapter 17, many homeowners are eligible to shelter a large chunk of their home's capital gain from taxation when the time comes for them to sell.

Ignore Solicitations to Homestead

Another pitch that you, as a new homeowner, may get in the mail is one offering to homestead your home if you pay the friendly firm anywhere from $50 to $100. *Homesteading* means protecting some of your home's equity from lawsuits. A firm may offer to file the appropriate (and quite simple) legal document to protect a portion of your home's equity from lawsuits.

If you live in a state where you need to take action to secure your homestead exemption, by all means do so. Just call the recorder's office, and ask how to do it. The process is simple (and, in some states, unnecessary) and not worth paying a firm to do for you.

Take Time to Smell the Roses

Okay, so it's a cliché. But too often, people work, work, work to afford a home and don't take the time to enjoy life, family, and friends (or even their home). If you buy a home that's within your financial means, and you're resourceful and thrifty with your spending in the years that you live in it, your home shouldn't dictate your finances and your need to work. You should own the home. It shouldn't own you.

No one (that we're aware of) has ever said on her deathbed that she wished that she had spent more time toiling away at work (and, therefore, less time with family, with friends, and for herself) so that she could spend more money on her home.

Chapter 16

Ten Things to Know When Investing in Real Estate

Both owning a home and paying down the mortgage on your home over the years should create *equity* — the difference between what your home is worth and what you owe on it. Even if the unlikely happens and your home doesn't appreciate in value, you'll build equity as you pay down your mortgage. More than likely, however, your home will also appreciate in value over the years that you own it.

Your home, then, is an investment. You can use the equity in your home in future years for a variety of important purposes, including (but not limited to) helping finance your retirement, pay for educational costs, and fund frivolous and fun things such as traveling. In addition to owning your home, you can invest in real estate in other ways. In this chapter, we include our top ten tips and things you should know if you're going to invest in real estate.

If you want to invest in real estate or stocks, bonds, mutual funds, small businesses, and the like, first invest your time in finding out what makes such investments tick and in learning how you can make informed decisions that fit with your personal financial situation and goals. Pick up a copy of the latest editions of Eric's *Investing For Dummies, Real Estate Investing For Dummies,* and *Mutual Funds For Dummies* to find out more about investing.

Real Estate Is a Solid Long-Term Investment

During the 1990s, many people got swept up in the euphoria of a booming U.S. stock market. Year after year, the market cranked out easy double-digit returns for investors. We sometimes hear stories of people who made small fortunes because they happened to buy into the right stock at the right time. Meanwhile, in many parts of the country, real estate prices rose little by comparison. So it seemed to some people, including media pundits, that real estate was yesterday's good investment.

Home values in all locations have always gone through up-and-down cycles. However, the long-term trend is up, and the rises usually are far greater than the subsequent declines. (Stocks, as you may know, go through similar and often more violent cycles — witness the major stock market decline in the early 2000s.) So if you have a long-term (ideally, a decade or more) investing-time horizon, you should do just fine if you invest in real estate. The average annual returns are comparable with those enjoyed by long-term stock market investors. The best time to buy a house is always a decade ago. A decade from now, today's prices may look dirt cheap.

Real Estate Investing Isn't for Everyone

If you're an impatient, busy person, investing in real estate probably isn't going to be an ideal investment. For one thing, locating, negotiating, and closing on property can take a big chunk of your time if you want to buy good property at a good price. Then there's the chore (and the time sinkhole) of managing the property — you're responsible for everything from finding tenants to keeping the building clean and in good working order. Your stock and mutual fund investments won't call you in the middle of the night to fix a plumbing problem, but your tenants may!

Even if you have the time to invest in real estate, you may also consider some other important aspects of your personal financial situation. As we discuss in Chapter 2, taking advantage of tax-deductible retirement accounts is vital to your long-term financial health and ability to retire. Buying investment real estate can prevent you from saving adequately in retirement accounts. Saving for your down payment can hamper your ability to fund these retirement accounts. And most of the properties that you buy will require additional out-of-pocket money in the early years.

REITs Are Good If You Loathe Being a Landlord

If you want to place some money in real estate but don't like the thought of being a landlord, consider *real estate investment trusts (REITs)*. REITs are managed by a company that pools your money with that of other investors to purchase a variety of investment real estate properties that these trusts manage.

REITs trade on the major stock exchanges, and some mutual funds also invest in REITs. Among the better REIT mutual funds to consider are the following:

- ✔ CGM Realty: 800-345-4048; www.cgmfunds.com

- ✔ Cohen & Steers Realty Shares: 800-437-9912; www.cohenandsteers.com

- ✔ Fidelity Real Estate Investment Portfolio: 800-544-8888; www.fidelity.com

- ✔ T. Rowe Price Real Estate Fund: 800-638-5660; www.troweprice.com

- ✔ Vanguard REIT Index Fund: 800-662-7447; www.vanguard.com

Don't Invest in Limited Partnerships

You should avoid real estate limited partnerships that are sold through securities brokerage firms. Securities brokers, often operating under the misleading titles of *financial consultant* or *financial advisor,* love to sell limited partnerships because of the hefty commissions that limited partnerships pay to the broker. The broker's take can range as high as 10 percent or more. Guess where this money comes from? If you said, "Out of my investment dollars," go to the head of the class!

In addition to the fatal flaw that only 90 cents on the dollar you invest actually go to work for you in the investment, broker-sold limited partnerships typically carry hefty annual operating fees ranging from 2 to 3 percent. So when you add it all up (or, we should say, after all these commissions and fees are subtracted from your hard-earned dollars), limited partnerships are destined to be poor investments for you.

Avoid Timeshare Condos and Vacation Homes

Another way that smart people lose a great deal of money when investing in real estate is through involvement in timeshare condominiums and vacation homes. The allure of both of these purchases is having a place to which you can escape for fun and relaxation.

With a timeshare, you're essentially buying the ownership of one week's use of a condominium. Suppose that, for this privilege, you pay a one-time fee of $7,000.

Although $7,000 may not sound like a lot, if one week costs $7,000, buying the entire year's rights to use the timeshare condo comes to more than $350,000. However, buying a similar condo in the area may set you back only about $125,000! So you're paying a *huge* markup on your week's ownership because of the costs of selling all those weeks and the need for the timeshare distributor to make a profit. (And you'll be on the hook as well for your share of the annual maintenance fees of a couple hundred dollars or more.)

A far better idea is to rent a condo that someone else owns — it's cheaper than owning, you can go to a different resort area each year (ski, beach, whatever), and you'll have no ownership and managing headaches. Or you could buy a condo outright, rent it out to others throughout the year, and then rent another one for yourself for the week or two or whatever each year when you plan to take a vacation.

Another chilling thought: Timeshare condominiums are nearly impossible to sell. As we say in Chapter 8, the best time to think about selling a property is *before* you buy. Real estate is a relatively illiquid form of investment anyhow — why freeze your money solid in a timeshare condo?

Vacation homes present a different problem. Most people who purchase a vacation home use it for only a few weeks during the year. The rest of the time, the property is left vacant, creating a cash drain. Now, if you're affluent enough to afford this luxury, we're not going to stand in your way and discourage you from owning more than one home. But many people who buy vacation homes aren't wealthy enough to afford them.

Before you buy a vacation property, examine your personal finances in order to determine whether you can still save enough each month after such a purchase to achieve your important financial goals, such as paying for higher education for your children or building your retirement nest egg. If you do buy a vacation home, consider buying a property that you can rent out during most of the time that you're not using it.

Residential Properties Are Your Best Investment Option

If you're going to invest in real estate, residential property is generally your safest and wisest investment:

- ✔ First, such types of real estate are probably the most familiar to you because you've lived in (and perhaps bought) such properties already.

- ✔ Second, residential property should be easier for you to manage and deal with on an ongoing basis. (Be sure that you're knowledgeable about current rent-control laws — if any — in your community and how they affect the property you may buy.)

Don't forget that with landlording comes lots of responsibilities and occasional tricky situations. That's why we strongly recommend that you consult a good local real estate lawyer if you have *any* questions about the legality of buying or operating your rental property. We discuss legal beagles in Chapter 9.

Commercial or retail real estate has many financial and legal nuances that you probably haven't dealt with (and probably don't want to deal with). Business real estate also tends to be more volatile in value because it is more easily overbuilt, and the number of businesses, unlike the population of people in a locale, can shrink more quickly during poor economic conditions. We're not saying that you should never try investing in this more-complicated type of property, but it's better for you to learn to swim in a backyard pool before leaping straight into a shark-infested sea.

Consider Fixer-Upper Income Property

Residential property that has curable defects (see Chapter 8) can be a good investment for people who can manage the repair and rehabilitation of the property. You must buy such property at an absolute-rock-bottom price. To an investor, fixer-uppers can provide an income stream from rentals, as well as an appreciation in the value of the property that can result from bringing the property back to its highest and best use.

Before you try your hand at buying and fixing up a property, talk to people in your local area who have already done so. Real estate agents and tax advisors can probably refer you to other like-minded investors. Ask these investors to explain all the work involved, what surprises they confronted, and whether they would make similar purchases again if they'd known what they do now.

Consider Converting Small Apartment Buildings to Condos

In real estate markets like those in densely populated urban areas, buying a multiunit building and converting the units to condominiums can be extremely profitable. To make such a transformation succeed, you need a good real estate agent who knows the value of apartments as condos and a good real estate lawyer. You also need a wise contractor who can help you estimate the costs of the work and the challenges involved in securing proper building permits.

As we recommend for those contemplating buying fixer-uppers, before you try to buy a multiunit building and attempt to convert it to condos, talk to other investors who have already done so. Also speak with your town's planning and building permit departments to see what sort of regulatory red tape awaits you. If the property is under rent control, be sure your lawyer investigates the ramifications of getting permission to do a condo conversion, which may include requirements such as giving a lifetime lease to handicapped and older tenants living in the building.

Consider the Property's Cash Flow

When you're considering the purchase of real estate for investment purposes, you must crunch some numbers. You don't need to remember any calculus (or even any high-school algebra) to do these calculations — basic addition, subtraction, multiplication, and division will do.

In order to decide how much a specific property is worth (as a prospective buyer) and in order to understand the financial ramifications of your ownership of that property, calculate what's called the property's *cash flow*. You determine cash flow by summing the rental income that a property brings in on a monthly basis and then subtracting all the monthly expenses, such as the mortgage payment, property taxes, insurance, utility expenses that you (as the landlord) pay, repair and maintenance costs, advertising expenses, 5 percent (or more) vacancy factor, and so on. Be realistic ,and add up all the costs. If the current owners of the property you're buying are using it as investment real estate, ask the sellers for a copy of *Schedule E* (Supplemental Income and Losses) from their income-tax return.

Your Rental Losses Are Limited for Tax Purposes

If you purchase rental property that produces a negative cash flow, you should know before you buy whether you can claim that loss on your personal income-tax return. If you're a high-income earner — making more than $100,000 per year — your ability to deduct rental losses may be limited. If you're a really high-income earner — making more than $150,000 per year — you may not be able to deduct any of your rental losses.

Chapter 17

Ten Things to Consider When Selling Your House

. . . .

In This Chapter

▶ Deciding whether to sell

▶ Pricing it right

▶ Choosing an agent

▶ Planning for after the sell

. . . .

*O*nce you own a home, the odds are extraordinarily high that someday you will sell it. People who live their entire lives in their first home are rare. (Eric's maternal grandparents accomplished this extraordinary feat — living more than six decades in the same home!)

Selling a house is generally somewhat less complicated than buying one. But just because selling a house may be easier than buying one doesn't mean that most people sell their houses properly.

If word gets out that you're considering selling your house, real estate agents will be attracted to you like hungry mosquitoes to the one person on a desert island. And when you sell a house, the IRS and state tax authorities may be waiting with open wallets to attempt to take a chunk of your profits, especially if you don't take the time to understand tax laws and how to make them work for you before you sell. So in this chapter, we advise you about some important issues that you should weigh and ponder before you sell. And if you do decide to sell, we want you to do the best possible job of selling your house and avoiding the tax man (legally). In addition to reading this chapter, when it comes time to sell, check out our companion book: *House Selling For Dummies.*

Why Are You Selling?

Start with the basics. If you're contemplating selling, consider whether your reasons for selling are good ones. For example, who wouldn't like to live in a larger home with more amenities and creature comforts? But if you hastily put your home on the market in order to buy a bigger one, you may be making a major mistake. If your next, more expensive home stretches you too far financially, you may end up in ruin.

When you need to relocate for your job, or when you have had a major life change, moving may be a necessity. Even so, you should weigh the pros and cons of keeping your property versus selling. Start this analytic process by reading the rest of this chapter.

Can You Afford to Buy the Next Home?

If you want to buy a more costly property, such a move is known in the real estate business as *trading up*. Doing an honest assessment of whether you can really afford to trade up is imperative. As we say in Chapter 3, no mortgage lender or real estate agent can objectively answer that question for you. Based on your income and down payment, the lender and agent can tell you the *most* that you can spend. They can't tell you what you can *afford* to spend and still accomplish your other financial and personal goals.

One of the biggest mistakes that trade-up home buyers make is overextending themselves with debt to get into a more expensive property. The resulting impact on their budgets can be severe — no money may be left over for retirement savings, for educational expenses, or simply for having fun. In the worst cases, people have ended up losing their homes to foreclosure and bankruptcy when they suffered unexpected events, such as job losses or the deaths of spouses who had inadequate insurance.

Before you buy your next home, go through the same personal-finance exercises we advocate in Chapters 2 and 3. Get a handle on what you can really afford to spend on a home. Unless your income or assets have increased significantly since the time that you purchased your last home, you probably can't afford a significantly more expensive property. The most important issue for people to consider is how spending more money each month on a home will affect their ability to save for retirement.

What's It Worth?

When you're ready to sell your house, you'd better have a good understanding of what it's worth. You (and your agent, if you're using one to sell your house) should analyze what comparable properties are currently selling for in your neck of the woods. For a discussion about comparable market analysis, see Chapter 10.

Listing agreements cover service, not sale

A *listing agreement* is *not* a contract between you and a real estate agent to sell your house. A listing agreement isn't a contract of sale — it's a personal service contract. It has nothing to do with actually transferring your property to buyers. It only authorizes a broker to act as your agent in finding people who'll buy your house.

Two basic promises appear in listing agreements. Your broker promises to do his or her best to find buyers for your house. You agree to pay your broker a commission if the broker finds buyers who are ready, willing, and able to purchase your house under the price and terms of the listing agreement.

Here is where things get tricky: Although the listing doesn't technically obligate you to sell your house, in rare circumstances you may still be required to pay your broker a commission if he finds a buyer willing to purchase under the price and terms of the listing agreement and you, for some trivial reason such as not liking the buyer's pet pug, suddenly decide not to sell. If, on the other hand, you decide not to sell because the job you were offered is no longer available, it's highly unlikely you'd have to pay a commission.

However, if the broker produces an offer that doesn't meet the price and terms of the listing agreement, you don't have to accept it and, therefore, don't owe him a commission — no matter how much time, energy, and money he has spent on your behalf. Selling a house isn't the same as playing horseshoes. Close doesn't count in real estate brokerage.

Avoid signing a listing agreement that commits you to working exclusively with a broker for more than three months. If the broker does a good job and needs to renew the listing because your house hasn't sold yet, you can renew or extend the listing. If, conversely, the broker does a lousy job, you have to suffer for only three months.

If you need to sell your house without wasting a ton of time and energy, do what smart retailers do: Price it to sell. We're not advocating that you give your property away, so to speak, but we are suggesting that you avoid inflating your asking price to a point far above what the sales of comparable houses suggest that your house is worth.

You may be tempted, particularly when you're in no great hurry to sell, to grossly overprice your house in the hope that an uneducated buyer may pay you more than the property is really worth. The danger in this strategy is that you won't find a fool who will part with all that money for your overpriced property, and no one else will bid on it. Then, as you lower the price closer to what the house is really worth, prospective buyers may be wary of buying your property because of the extended length of time that it's been on the market. In the end, you may have a hard time getting 100 percent of what your house is really worth.

Have You Done Your Homework to Find a Good Real Estate Agent?

When most people are ready to sell their houses, they enlist the services of a real estate agent. Good agents can be worth their commission if they know how to prepare the property for sale, market it, and get it sold for top dollar. Unlike when you're a home buyer, your interests as a seller are aligned with a good agent's interests — the more you sell the property for, the more you net from the sale, and the more the agent gets paid.

Given how much homes actually cost (and how much they cost to sell and buy), you owe it to yourself to have a good agent representing you in the sale of your house. Be sure that the agent you select isn't currently listing so many other properties for sale that the agent lacks enough time to properly service your listing. Also, the agent you worked with when you bought the home isn't necessarily the best agent to hire when you sell it. Different steps and expertise are required to sell (rather than buy) a house.

Do You Have the Skills to Sell the House Yourself?

Although some property owners possess the skills and time needed to sell a house themselves, most don't. The carrot that may entice you to sell a house yourself is the avoidance of the 5 to 7 percent sales commission that agents will ask for before they attempt to sell your property. Don't forget, however, that half of this commission goes to a buyer's agent. Because most buyers work with agents (partly because the agents' services appear to be at no cost to the buyers), you'll potentially save yourself only 2.5 to 3.5 percent of the final selling price of your property by selling it without an agent on your side.

Whether or not you sell the house yourself, interview several agents who've demonstrated that they know your neighborhood as a result of listing and selling properties in the area, and ask them to prepare a comparable market analysis for your house. Base your asking price on what comparable properties have sold for in the past six months. If you're shopping for an agent, also ask each one for an activity list of all the houses that he has sold over the past 12 months so that you can obtain references from property sellers who have worked with each agent.

Have You Properly Prepared the House for Sale?

The real work of selling a property begins before you ever formally place it on the market for sale or allow the first prospective buyer through the front door. Prepare your house for sale both inside and out. At a minimum, you should do the sort of cleanup work that you do before your parents (or perhaps the in-laws) visit — you know, scrambling around the house cleaning *everything* up (or at least tossing it under beds and into closets!).

But you have more to do than just running a vacuum (after you pick up the laundry from the floors) and washing the dishes. Have some good but brutally honest friends and prospective agents walk through the house with you to point out defects and flaws that won't cost you an arm and a leg to fix (for example, repairing leaky faucets or painting areas in need of new paint). Don't be defensive — take good notes! You should generally avoid major projects, such as kitchen renovations, room additions, and the like. Rarely will you get a high enough additional sales price to compensate you for the extra costs (and headaches) of these major projects (not to mention for the time that you spend coordinating or doing the work).

Do You Understand the House's Hot Buttons?

People don't buy homes — they buy a *hot button,* and the rest of the home goes with it. Hot buttons vary from home to home. Dynamite kitchens or baths, fireplaces, views, and gardens are often buyer turn-ons. Location is the hot button for people who *must* live in a certain neighborhood.

How can you determine your house's hot buttons? Think back to what appealed to you when you bought it. What you liked then will probably be the same hot buttons that will appeal to the next buyers. After you've identified the hot buttons, emphasize them in your listing statement, multiple-listing description, and newspaper ads. Successful sellers know what the buyers will buy before they begin the marketing process.

What Are the Financial Ramifications of Selling?

Before you sell your house, you should understand the financial consequences of the sale. For example, how much money will you spend on fix-up work? How much should you be netting from the sale in order to afford your next home?

Unless you want to and can afford to be the proud owner of two homes, we advocate selling your current house before you commit to buying another. You can ask for a long close of escrow and a rent-back, if necessary, so that you have time to close the sale of your next home without camping out on the street. Be sure about these things upfront so that you won't have nasty surprises along the way or after you sell.

Do You Know the Rules for Capital-Gains Taxes on the Sale of a House?

Under current tax laws, most house sellers enjoy a significant tax break. Specifically, a large amount of *capital gains,* or profits, on the sale of a home are excluded from tax: up to $250,000 for single taxpayers and $500,000 for married couples filing jointly. (See Chapter 15 for information about calculating your profit.)

To qualify for this capital-gains exclusion, the seller must have used the house as her principal residence for at least two of the previous five years. You can use the exclusion no more than once every two years.

These newer house-sale laws replaced the previous rules relating to capital gains on the sale of a house. Thus, house sellers can no longer "roll over" profits from the sale of one home into the purchase of a more expensive one in order to avoid taxation. Gone also is the requirement to be 55 years of age or older to get a special $125,000 exclusion on profits.

For the vast majority of house sellers out there, the new laws are a boon. Most people's house-sale profits don't come anywhere near the new exclusion limits, and many will benefit from the repeal of the age restriction. However, there are some homeowners out there, especially those who live in higher-cost areas and who have owned their homes for many years, whose gains exceed the $250,000 or $500,000 limits and who have lost the ability to roll these profits over into a higher-priced home. If they sell, they will owe tax on whatever profits exceed their applicable exclusion limits.

Part VI
Appendixes

"Well, I inspected the house, and the trap doors, secret passages, and subterranean dungeon are all okay, but I'd look into caulking around the snake pit."

In this part . . .

Don't let the word *appendix* scare you. This part includes such priceless goodies as a sample of a comprehensive purchase contract, an example of an excellent inspection report, and a glossary chock-full of the many less-than-intuitive terms tossed around in the real estate business.

Appendix A

Sample Real Estate Purchase Contract

•••

*B*ecause a real estate purchase contract is a legal document, your real estate agent or lawyer should provide you the appropriate contract form for your area and help you fill it out. As a rule, these contracts range from somewhat complex to quite complex and sometimes convoluted. Most purchase contracts include a warning that says something like this:

"This is more than a receipt for money. It is intended to be a legally binding contract. Read it carefully."

Heed the warning!

Purchase contracts vary in length, complexity, and terms from state to state and, within a state, from one locality to another. This appendix includes a sample of the California Association of Realtors' real estate purchase contract. We chose California's contract because it's one of the most comprehensive residential real estate contracts around.

Blank spaces are open invitations to confusion (at best) and deception (at worst)! Giving someone a contract with blank spaces above your signature is like giving someone a signed blank check. They can fill in whatever they want over your signature, and you may have to pay. *Do not leave any spaces blank on your contract.*

Another important thing to check is the contract's *revision date* — usually located in the bottom-left or -right corner of the page. Be sure that you're working on the most recent version of the purchase contract.

See Chapter 12 for a more in-depth discussion of real estate purchase contracts.

CALIFORNIA
ASSOCIATION
OF REALTORS®

CALIFORNIA
RESIDENTIAL PURCHASE AGREEMENT
AND JOINT ESCROW INSTRUCTIONS
For Use With Single Family Residential Property — Attached or Detached
(C.A.R. Form RPA-CA, Revised 10/02)

Date _____, at _____, California.
1. **OFFER:**
   A. **THIS IS AN OFFER FROM** _____ ("Buyer").
   B. **THE REAL PROPERTY TO BE ACQUIRED** is described as _____
      _____, Assessor's Parcel No. _____, situated in
      _____, County of _____, California, ("Property").
   C. **THE PURCHASE PRICE** offered is _____
      _____ Dollars $ _____
   D. **CLOSE OF ESCROW** shall occur on _____ (date)(or ☐ _____ **Days** After Acceptance).
2. **FINANCE TERMS:** Obtaining the loans below **is a contingency** of this Agreement unless: **(i)** either 2K or 2L is checked below; or **(ii)** otherwise agreed in writing. Buyer shall act diligently and in good faith to obtain the designated loans. Obtaining deposit, down payment and closing costs **is not a contingency**. Buyer represents that funds will be good when deposited with Escrow Holder.
   A. **INITIAL DEPOSIT:** Buyer has given a deposit in the amount of . . . .$ _____
      to the agent submitting the offer (or to ☐ _____), by personal check
      (or ☐ _____), made payable to _____
      which shall be held uncashed until Acceptance and then deposited within **3** business days after
      Acceptance (or ☐ _____), with
      Escrow Holder, (or ☐ into Broker's trust account).
   B. **INCREASED DEPOSIT:** Buyer shall deposit with Escrow Holder an increased deposit in the amount of . . . .$ _____
      within _____ **Days** After Acceptance, or ☐ _____
   C. **FIRST LOAN IN THE AMOUNT OF** . . . .$ _____
      (1) NEW First Deed of Trust in favor of lender, encumbering the Property, securing a note payable at
         maximum interest of _____% fixed rate, or _____% initial adjustable rate with a maximum
         interest rate of _____%, balance due in _____ years, amortized over _____ years. Buyer
         shall pay loan fees/points not to exceed _____. (These terms apply whether the designated loan
         is conventional, FHA or VA.)
      (2) ☐ FHA ☐ VA: (The following terms only apply to the FHA or VA loan that is checked.)
         Seller shall pay _____% discount points. Seller shall pay other fees not allowed to be paid by
         Buyer, ☐ not to exceed $_____. Seller shall pay the cost of lender required Repairs
         (including those for wood destroying pest) not otherwise provided for in this Agreement, ☐ not to
         exceed $_____. (Actual loan amount may increase if mortgage insurance premiums,
         funding fees or closing costs are financed.)
   D. **ADDITIONAL FINANCING TERMS:** ☐ Seller financing, (C.A.R. Form SFA); ☐ secondary financing, ...$ _____
      (C.A.R. Form PAA, paragraph 4A); ☐ assumed financing (C.A.R. Form PAA, paragraph 4B)
      _____
      _____
   E. **BALANCE OF PURCHASE PRICE** (not including costs of obtaining loans and other closing costs) in the amount of . . .$ _____
      to be deposited with Escrow Holder within sufficient time to close escrow.
   F. **PURCHASE PRICE (TOTAL):** . . . .$ _____
   G. **LOAN APPLICATIONS:** Within **7 (or ☐ _____) Days** After Acceptance, Buyer shall provide Seller a letter from lender or mortgage loan broker stating that, based on a review of Buyer's written application and credit report, Buyer is prequalified or preapproved for the NEW loan specified in 2C above.
   H. **VERIFICATION OF DOWN PAYMENT AND CLOSING COSTS:** Buyer (or Buyer's lender or loan broker pursuant to 2G) shall, within **7 (or ☐ _____) Days** After Acceptance, provide Seller written verification of Buyer's down payment and closing costs.
   I. **LOAN CONTINGENCY REMOVAL: (i)** Within **17 (or ☐ _____) Days** After Acceptance, Buyer shall, as specified in paragraph 14, remove the loan contingency or cancel this Agreement; **OR (ii)** (if checked) ☐ the loan contingency shall remain in effect until the designated loans are funded.
   J. **APPRAISAL CONTINGENCY AND REMOVAL:** This Agreement is (**OR**, if checked, ☐ is NOT) contingent upon the Property appraising at no less than the specified purchase price. If there is a loan contingency, at the time the loan contingency is removed (or, if checked, ☐ within **17 (or _____) Days** After Acceptance), Buyer shall, as specified in paragraph 14B(3), remove the appraisal contingency or cancel this Agreement. If there is no loan contingency, Buyer shall, as specified in paragraph 14B(3), remove the appraisal contingency within **17 (or _____) Days** After Acceptance.
   K. ☐ **NO LOAN CONTINGENCY** (If checked): Obtaining any loan in paragraphs 2C, 2D or elsewhere in this Agreement is NOT a contingency of this Agreement. If Buyer does not obtain the loan and as a result Buyer does not purchase the Property, Seller may be entitled to Buyer's deposit or other legal remedies.
   L. ☐ **ALL CASH OFFER** (If checked): No loan is needed to purchase the Property. Buyer shall, within **7 (or ☐ _____) Days** After Acceptance, provide Seller written verification of sufficient funds to close this transaction.
3. **CLOSING AND OCCUPANCY:**
   A. Buyer intends (or ☐ does not intend) to occupy the Property as Buyer's primary residence.
   B. **Seller-occupied or vacant property:** Occupancy shall be delivered to Buyer at _____ AM/PM, ☐ on the date of Close Of Escrow; ☐ on _____; or ☐ no later than _____ **Days** After Close Of Escrow. (C.A.R. Form PAA, paragraph 2.) If transfer of title and occupancy do not occur at the same time, Buyer and Seller are advised to: **(i)** enter into a written occupancy agreement; and **(ii)** consult with their insurance and legal advisors.

RPA-CA REVISED 10/02 (PAGE 1 OF 8) Print Date

Buyer's Initials (_____)(_____)
Seller's Initials (_____)(_____)

Reviewed by _____ Date _____

EQUAL HOUSING
OPPORTUNITY

CALIFORNIA RESIDENTIAL PURCHASE AGREEMENT (RPA-CA PAGE 1 OF 8)

Property Address: _____ Date: _____

   C. Tenant-occupied property: (i) Property shall be vacant at least 5 (or ☐ _____) Days Prior to Close Of Escrow, unless otherwise agreed in writing. **Note to Seller: If you are unable to deliver Property vacant in accordance with rent control and other applicable Law, you may be in breach of this Agreement.**

   OR (ii) (if checked) ☐ **Tenant to remain in possession.** The attached addendum is incorporated into this Agreement (C.A.R. Form PAA, paragraph 3.);

   OR (iii) (if checked) ☐ **This Agreement is contingent** upon Buyer and Seller entering into a written agreement regarding occupancy of the Property within the time specified in paragraph 14B(1). If no written agreement is reached within this time, either Buyer or Seller may cancel this Agreement in writing.

   D. At Close Of Escrow, Seller assigns to Buyer any assignable warranty rights for items included in the sale and shall provide any available Copies of such warranties. Brokers cannot and will not determine the assignability of any warranties.

   E. At Close Of Escrow, unless otherwise agreed in writing, Seller shall provide keys and/or means to operate all locks, mailboxes, security systems, alarms and garage door openers. If Property is a condominium or located in a common interest subdivision, Buyer may be required to pay a deposit to the Homeowners' Association ("HOA") to obtain keys to accessible HOA facilities.

4. ALLOCATION OF COSTS (If checked): Unless otherwise specified here, this paragraph only determines who is to pay for the report, inspection, test or service mentioned. If not specified here or elsewhere in this Agreement, the determination of who is to pay for any work recommended or identified by any such report, inspection, test or service shall be by the method specified in paragraph 14B(2).

   A. WOOD DESTROYING PEST INSPECTION:

     (1) ☐ Buyer ☐ Seller shall pay for an inspection and report for wood destroying pests and organisms ("Report") which shall be prepared by _____, a registered structural pest control company. The Report shall cover the accessible areas of the main building and attached structures and, if checked: ☐ detached garages and carports, ☐ detached decks, ☐ the following other structures or areas _____ _____. The Report shall not include roof coverings. If Property is a condominium or located in a common interest subdivision, the Report shall include only the separate interest and any exclusive-use areas being transferred and shall not include common areas, unless otherwise agreed. Water tests of shower pans on upper level units may not be performed without consent of property below the shower.

     OR (2) ☐ **(If checked)** The attached addendum (C.A.R. Form WPA) regarding wood destroying pest inspection and allocation of cost is incorporated into this Agreement.

   B. OTHER INSPECTIONS AND REPORTS:

     (1) ☐ Buyer ☐ Seller shall pay to have septic or private sewage disposal systems inspected _____.

     (2) ☐ Buyer ☐ Seller shall pay to have domestic wells tested for water potability and productivity _____.

     (3) ☐ Buyer ☐ Seller shall pay for a natural hazard zone disclosure report prepared by _____.

     (4) ☐ Buyer ☐ Seller shall pay for the following inspection or report _____.

     (5) ☐ Buyer ☐ Seller shall pay for the following inspection or report _____.

   C. GOVERNMENT REQUIREMENTS AND RETROFIT:

     (1) ☐ Buyer ☐ Seller shall pay for smoke detector installation and/or water heater bracing, if required by Law. Prior to Close Of Escrow, Seller shall provide Buyer a written statement of compliance in accordance with state and local Law, unless exempt.

     (2) ☐ Buyer ☐ Seller shall pay the cost of compliance with any other minimum mandatory government retrofit standards, inspections and reports if required as a condition of closing escrow under any Law. _____.

   D. ESCROW AND TITLE:

     (1) ☐ Buyer ☐ Seller shall pay escrow fee _____. Escrow Holder shall be _____.

     (2) ☐ Buyer ☐ Seller shall pay for **owner's** title insurance policy specified in paragraph 12E _____. Owner's title policy to be issued by _____. (Buyer shall pay for any title insurance policy insuring Buyer's **lender**, unless otherwise agreed in writing.)

   E. OTHER COSTS:

     (1) ☐ Buyer ☐ Seller shall pay County transfer tax or transfer fee _____.

     (2) ☐ Buyer ☐ Seller shall pay City transfer tax or transfer fee _____.

     (3) ☐ Buyer ☐ Seller shall pay HOA transfer fee _____.

     (4) ☐ Buyer ☐ Seller shall pay HOA document preparation fees _____.

     (5) ☐ Buyer ☐ Seller shall pay the cost, not to exceed $ _____, of a one-year home warranty plan, issued by _____ with the following optional coverage: _____.

     (6) ☐ Buyer ☐ Seller shall pay for_____.

     (7) ☐ Buyer ☐ Seller shall pay for_____.

5. STATUTORY DISCLOSURES (INCLUDING LEAD-BASED PAINT HAZARD DISCLOSURES) AND CANCELLATION RIGHTS:

   A. (1) Seller shall, within the time specified in paragraph 14A, deliver to Buyer, if required by Law: **(i)** Federal Lead-Based Paint Disclosures and pamphlet ("Lead Disclosures"); and **(ii)** disclosures or notices required by sections 1102 et. seq. and 1103 et. seq. of the California Civil Code ("Statutory Disclosures"). Statutory Disclosures include, but are not limited to, a Real Estate Transfer Disclosure Statement ("TDS"), Natural Hazard Disclosure Statement ("NHD"), notice or actual knowledge of release of illegal controlled substance, notice of special tax and/or assessments (or, if allowed, substantially equivalent notice regarding the Mello-Roos Community Facilities Act and Improvement Bond Act of 1915) and, if Seller has actual knowledge, an industrial use and military ordnance location disclosure (C.A.R. Form SSD).

     (2) Buyer shall, within the time specified in paragraph 14B(1), return Signed Copies of the Statutory and Lead Disclosures to Seller.

     (3) In the event Seller, prior to Close Of Escrow, becomes aware of adverse conditions materially affecting the Property, or any material inaccuracy in disclosures, information or representations previously provided to Buyer of which Buyer is otherwise unaware, Seller shall promptly provide a subsequent or amended disclosure or notice, in writing, covering those items. **However, a subsequent or amended disclosure shall not be required for conditions and material inaccuracies disclosed in reports ordered and paid for by Buyer.**

Buyer's Initials (_____)(_____)
Seller's Initials (_____)(_____)

A-CA REVISED 10/02 (PAGE 2 OF 8)

Reviewed by _____ Date _____

CALIFORNIA RESIDENTIAL PURCHASE AGREEMENT (RPA-CA PAGE 2 OF 8)

Property Address: _____ Date: _____

(4) If any disclosure or notice specified in 5A(1), or subsequent or amended disclosure or notice is delivered to Buyer after the offer is Signed, Buyer shall have the right to cancel this Agreement within **3 Days** After delivery in person, or **5 Days** After delivery by deposit in the mail, by giving written notice of cancellation to Seller or Seller's agent. (Lead Disclosures sent by mail must be sent certified mail or better.)

(5) Note to Buyer and Seller: Waiver of Statutory and Lead Disclosures is prohibited by Law.

B. **NATURAL AND ENVIRONMENTAL HAZARDS:** Within the time specified in paragraph 14A, Seller shall, if required by Law: **(i)** deliver to Buyer earthquake guides (and questionnaire) and environmental hazards booklet; **(ii)** even if exempt from the obligation to provide a NHD, disclose if the Property is located in a Special Flood Hazard Area; Potential Flooding (Inundation) Area; Very High Fire Hazard Zone; State Fire Responsibility Area; Earthquake Fault Zone; Seismic Hazard Zone; and **(iii)** disclose any other zone as required by Law and provide any other information required for those zones.

C. **DATA BASE DISCLOSURE:** NOTICE: The California Department of Justice, sheriff's departments, police departments serving jurisdictions of 200,000 or more and many other local law enforcement authorities maintain for public access a data base of the locations of persons required to register pursuant to paragraph (1) of subdivision (a) of Section 290.4 of the Penal Code. The data base is updated on a quarterly basis and a source of information about the presence of these individuals in any neighborhood. The Department of Justice also maintains a Sex Offender Identification Line through which inquiries about individuals may be made. This is a "900" telephone service. Callers must have specific information about individuals they are checking. Information regarding neighborhoods is not available through the "900" telephone service.

6. **CONDOMINIUM/PLANNED UNIT DEVELOPMENT DISCLOSURES:**

A. **SELLER HAS: 7 (or ☐ _____) Days** After Acceptance to disclose to Buyer whether the Property is a condominium, or is located in a planned unit development or other common interest subdivision (C.A.R. Form SSD).

B. If the Property is a condominium or is located in a planned unit development or other common interest subdivision, Seller has **3 (or ☐ _____) Days** After Acceptance to request from the HOA (C.A.R. Form HOA): **(i)** Copies of any documents required by Law; **(ii)** disclosure of any pending or anticipated claim or litigation by or against the HOA; **(iii)** a statement containing the location and number of designated parking and storage spaces; **(iv)** Copies of the most recent 12 months of HOA minutes for regular and special meetings; and **(v)** the names and contact information of all HOAs governing the Property (collectively, "CI Disclosures"). Seller shall itemize and deliver to Buyer all CI Disclosures received from the HOA and any CI Disclosures in Seller's possession. Buyer's approval of CI Disclosures is a contingency of this Agreement as specified in paragraph 14B(3).

7. **CONDITIONS AFFECTING PROPERTY:**

A. Unless otherwise agreed: **(i) the Property is sold (a) in its PRESENT physical condition as of the date of Acceptance and (b) subject to Buyer's Investigation rights; (ii)** the Property, including pool, spa, landscaping and grounds, is to be maintained in substantially the same condition as on the date of Acceptance; and **(iii)** all debris and personal property not included in the sale shall be removed by Close Of Escrow.

B. **SELLER SHALL, within the time specified in paragraph 14A, DISCLOSE KNOWN MATERIAL FACTS AND DEFECTS affecting the Property, including known insurance claims within the past five years, AND MAKE OTHER DISCLOSURES REQUIRED BY LAW (C.A.R. Form SSD).**

C. **NOTE TO BUYER:** You are strongly advised to conduct investigations of the entire Property in order to determine its present condition since Seller may not be aware of all defects affecting the Property or other factors that you consider important. Property improvements may not be built according to code, in compliance with current Law, or have had permits issued.

D. **NOTE TO SELLER:** Buyer has the right to inspect the Property and, as specified in paragraph 14B, based upon information discovered in those inspections: **(i)** cancel this Agreement; or **(ii)** request that you make Repairs or take other action.

8. **ITEMS INCLUDED AND EXCLUDED:**

A. **NOTE TO BUYER AND SELLER:** Items listed as included or excluded in the MLS, flyers or marketing materials are **not** included in the purchase price or excluded from the sale unless specified in 8B or C.

B. **ITEMS INCLUDED IN SALE:**

(1) All EXISTING fixtures and fittings that are attached to the Property;

(2) Existing electrical, mechanical, lighting, plumbing and heating fixtures, ceiling fans, fireplace inserts, gas logs and grates, solar systems, built-in appliances, window and door screens, awnings, shutters, window coverings, attached floor coverings, television antennas, satellite dishes, private integrated telephone systems, air coolers/conditioners, pool/spa equipment, garage door openers/remote controls, mailbox, in-ground landscaping, trees/shrubs, water softeners, water purifiers, security systems/alarms; and

(3) The following items: _____
_____.

(4) Seller represents that all items included in the purchase price, unless otherwise specified, are owned by Seller.

(5) All items included shall be transferred free of liens and without Seller warranty.

C. **ITEMS EXCLUDED FROM SALE:** _____

9. **BUYER'S INVESTIGATION OF PROPERTY AND MATTERS AFFECTING PROPERTY:**

A. Buyer's acceptance of the condition of, and any other matter affecting the Property, is a contingency of this Agreement as specified in this paragraph and paragraph 14B. Within the time specified in paragraph 14B(1), Buyer shall have the right, at Buyer's expense unless otherwise agreed, to conduct inspections, investigations, tests, surveys and other studies ("Buyer Investigations"), including, but not limited to, the right to: **(i)** inspect for lead-based paint and other lead-based paint hazards; **(ii)** inspect for wood destroying pests and organisms; **(iii)** review the registered sex offender database; **(iv)** confirm the insurability of Buyer and the Property; and **(v)** satisfy Buyer as to any matter specified in the attached Buyer's Inspection Advisory (C.A.R. Form BIA). Without Seller's prior written consent, Buyer shall neither make nor cause to be made: **(i)** invasive or destructive Buyer Investigations; or **(ii)** inspections by any governmental building or zoning inspector or government employee, unless required by Law.

B. Buyer shall complete Buyer Investigations and, as specified in paragraph 14B, remove the contingency or cancel this Agreement. Buyer shall give Seller, at no cost, complete Copies of all Buyer Investigation reports obtained by Buyer. Seller shall make the Property available for all Buyer Investigations. Seller shall have water, gas, electricity and all operable pilot lights on for Buyer's Investigations and through the date possession is made available to Buyer.

Buyer's Initials (_____)(_____)
Seller's Initials (_____)(_____)

| Reviewed by _____ Date _____ |

CALIFORNIA RESIDENTIAL PURCHASE AGREEMENT (RPA-CA PAGE 3 OF 8)

Property Address: _____ Date: _____

10. **REPAIRS:** Repairs shall be completed prior to final verification of condition unless otherwise agreed in writing. Repairs to be performed at Seller's expense may be performed by Seller or through others, provided that the work complies with applicable Law, including governmental permit, inspection and approval requirements. Repairs shall be performed in a good, skillful manner with materials of quality and appearance comparable to existing materials. It is understood that exact restoration of appearance or cosmetic items following all Repairs may not be possible. Seller shall: **(i)** obtain receipts for Repairs performed by others; **(ii)** prepare a written statement indicating the Repairs performed by Seller and the date of such Repairs; and **(iii)** provide Copies of receipts and statements to Buyer prior to final verification of condition.

11. **BUYER INDEMNITY AND SELLER PROTECTION FOR ENTRY UPON PROPERTY:** Buyer shall: **(i)** keep the Property free and clear of liens; **(ii)** Repair all damage arising from Buyer Investigations; and **(iii)** indemnify and hold Seller harmless from all resulting liability, claims, demands, damages and costs. Buyer shall carry, or Buyer shall require anyone acting on Buyer's behalf to carry, policies of liability, workers' compensation and other applicable insurance, defending and protecting Seller from liability for any injuries to persons or property occurring during any Buyer Investigations or work done on the Property at Buyer's direction prior to Close Of Escrow. Seller is advised that certain protections may be afforded Seller by recording a "Notice of Non-responsibility" (C.A.R. Form NNR) for Buyer Investigations and work done on the Property at Buyer's direction. Buyer's obligations under this paragraph shall survive the termination of this Agreement.

12. **TITLE AND VESTING:**
    A. Within the time specified in paragraph 14, Buyer shall be provided a current preliminary (title) report, which is only an offer by the title insurer to issue a policy of title insurance and may not contain every item affecting title. Buyer's review of the preliminary report and any other matters which may affect title are a contingency of this Agreement as specified in paragraph 14B.
    B. Title is taken in its present condition subject to all encumbrances, easements, covenants, conditions, restrictions, rights and other matters, whether of record or not, as of the date of Acceptance except: **(i)** monetary liens of record unless Buyer is assuming those obligations or taking the Property subject to those obligations; and **(ii)** those matters which Seller has agreed to remove in writing.
    C. Within the time specified in paragraph 14A, Seller has a duty to disclose to Buyer all matters known to Seller affecting title, whether of record or not.
    D. At Close Of Escrow, Buyer shall receive a grant deed conveying title (or, for stock cooperative or long-term lease, an assignment of stock certificate or of Seller's leasehold interest), including oil, mineral and water rights if currently owned by Seller. Title shall vest as designated in Buyer's supplemental escrow instructions. THE MANNER OF TAKING TITLE MAY HAVE SIGNIFICANT LEGAL AND TAX CONSEQUENCES. CONSULT AN APPROPRIATE PROFESSIONAL.
    E. Buyer shall receive a CLTA/ALTA Homeowner's Policy of Title Insurance. A title company, at Buyer's request, can provide information about the availability, desirability, coverage, and cost of various title insurance coverages and endorsements. If Buyer desires title coverage other than that required by this paragraph, Buyer shall instruct Escrow Holder in writing and pay any increase in cost.

13. **SALE OF BUYER'S PROPERTY:**
    A. This Agreement is NOT contingent upon the sale of any property owned by Buyer.
    OR B. ☐ (If checked): The attached addendum (C.A.R. Form COP) regarding the contingency for the sale of property owned by Buyer is incorporated into this Agreement.

14. **TIME PERIODS; REMOVAL OF CONTINGENCIES; CANCELLATION RIGHTS: The following time periods may only be extended, altered, modified or changed by mutual written agreement. Any removal of contingencies or cancellation under this paragraph must be in writing (C.A.R. Form CR).**
    A. **SELLER HAS: 7 (or ☐ _____) Days** After Acceptance to deliver to Buyer all reports, disclosures and information for which Seller is responsible under paragraphs 4, 5A and B, 6A, 7B and 12.
    B. **(1) BUYER HAS: 17 (or ☐ _____) Days** After Acceptance, unless otherwise agreed in writing, to:
       (i) complete all Buyer Investigations; approve all disclosures, reports and other applicable information, which Buyer receives from Seller; and approve all matters affecting the Property (including lead-based paint and lead-based paint hazards as well as other information specified in paragraph 5 and insurability of Buyer and the Property); and
       (ii) return to Seller Signed Copies of Statutory and Lead Disclosures delivered by Seller in accordance with paragraph 5A.
       (2) Within the time specified in 14B(1), Buyer may request that Seller make repairs or take any other action regarding the Property (C.A.R. Form RR). Seller has no obligation to agree to or respond to Buyer's requests.
       (3) By the end of the time specified in 14B(1) (or 2I for loan contingency or 2J for appraisal contingency), Buyer shall, in writing, remove the applicable contingency (C.A.R. Form CR) or cancel this Agreement. However, if **(i)** government-mandated inspections/ reports required as a condition of closing; or **(ii)** Common Interest Disclosures pursuant to paragraph 6B are not made within the time specified in 14A, then Buyer has **5 (or ☐ _____) Days** After receipt of any such items, or the time specified in 14B(1), whichever is later, to remove the applicable contingency or cancel this Agreement in writing.
    C. **CONTINUATION OF CONTINGENCY OR CONTRACTUAL OBLIGATION; SELLER RIGHT TO CANCEL:**
       (1) Seller right to Cancel; Buyer Contingencies: Seller, after first giving Buyer a Notice to Buyer to Perform (as specified below), may cancel this Agreement in writing and authorize return of Buyer's deposit if, by the time specified in this Agreement, Buyer does not remove in writing the applicable contingency or cancel this Agreement. Once all contingencies have been removed, failure of either Buyer or Seller to close escrow on time may be a breach of this Agreement.
       (2) Continuation of Contingency: Even after the expiration of the time specified in 14B, Buyer retains the right to make requests to Seller, remove in writing the applicable contingency or cancel this Agreement until Seller cancels pursuant to 14C(1). Once Seller receives Buyer's written removal of all contingencies, Seller may not cancel this Agreement pursuant to 14C(1).
       (3) Seller right to Cancel; Buyer Contract Obligations: Seller, after first giving Buyer a Notice to Buyer to Perform (as specified below), may cancel this Agreement in writing and authorize return of Buyer's deposit for any of the following reasons: **(i)** if Buyer fails to deposit funds as required by 2A or 2B; **(ii)** if the funds deposited pursuant to 2A or 2B are not good when deposited; **(iii)** if Buyer fails to provide a letter as required by 2G; **(iv)** if Buyer fails to provide verification as required by 2H or 2L; **(v)** if Seller reasonably disapproves of the verification provided by 2H or 2L; **(vi)** if Buyer fails to return Statutory and Lead Disclosures as required by paragraph 5A(2); or **(vii)** if Buyer fails to sign or initial a separate liquidated damage form for an increased deposit as required by paragraph 16. **Seller is not required to give Buyer a Notice to Perform regarding Close of Escrow.**
       (4) Notice To Buyer To Perform: The Notice to Buyer to Perform (C.A.R. Form NBP) shall: **(i)** be in writing; **(ii)** be signed by Seller; and **(iii)** give Buyer at least **24 (or ☐ _____)** hours (or until the time specified in the applicable paragraph, whichever occurs last) to take the applicable action. A Notice to Buyer to Perform may not be given any earlier than **2 Days** Prior to the expiration of the applicable time for Buyer to remove a contingency or cancel this Agreement or meet a 14C(3) obligation.

Buyer's Initials (_____)(_____)
Seller's Initials (_____)(_____)

RPA-CA REVISED 10/02 (PAGE 4 OF 8)

| Reviewed by _____ Date _____ |

EQUAL HOUSING OPPORTUNITY

CALIFORNIA RESIDENTIAL PURCHASE AGREEMENT (RPA-CA PAGE 4 OF 8)

Property Address: _____   Date: _____

D. EFFECT OF BUYER'S REMOVAL OF CONTINGENCIES : If Buyer removes, in writing, any contingency or cancellation rights, unless otherwise specified in a separate written agreement between Buyer and Seller, Buyer shall conclusively be deemed to have: **(i)** completed all Buyer Investigations, and review of reports and other applicable information and disclosures pertaining to that contingency or cancellation right; **(ii)** elected to proceed with the transaction; and **(iii)** assumed all liability, responsibility and expense for Repairs or corrections pertaining to that contingency or cancellation right, or for inability to obtain financing.

E. EFFECT OF CANCELLATION ON DEPOSITS: If Buyer or Seller gives written notice of cancellation pursuant to rights duly exercised under the terms of this Agreement, Buyer and Seller agree to Sign mutual instructions to cancel the sale and escrow and release deposits to the party entitled to the funds, less fees and costs incurred by that party. Fees and costs may be payable to service providers and vendors for services and products provided during escrow. **Release of funds will require mutual Signed release instructions from Buyer and Seller, judicial decision or arbitration award. A party may be subject to a civil penalty of up to $1,000 for refusal to sign such instructions if no good faith dispute exists as to who is entitled to the deposited funds (Civil Code §1057.3).**

15. FINAL VERIFICATION OF CONDITION: Buyer shall have the right to make a final inspection of the Property within **5 (or _____) Days** Prior to Close Of Escrow, NOT AS A CONTINGENCY OF THE SALE, but solely to confirm: **(i)** the Property is maintained pursuant to paragraph 7A; **(ii)** Repairs have been completed as agreed; and **(iii)** Seller has complied with Seller's other obligations under this Agreement.

16. LIQUIDATED DAMAGES: If Buyer fails to complete this purchase because of Buyer's default, Seller shall retain, as liquidated damages, the deposit actually paid. If the Property is a dwelling with no more than four units, one of which Buyer intends to occupy, then the amount retained shall be no more than 3% of the purchase price. Any excess shall be returned to Buyer. Release of funds will require mutual, Signed release instructions from both Buyer and Seller, judicial decision or arbitration award.
BUYER AND SELLER SHALL SIGN A SEPARATE LIQUIDATED DAMAGES PROVISION FOR ANY INCREASED DEPOSIT. (C.A.R. FORM RID)

Buyer's Initials _____ / _____	Seller's Initials _____ / _____

17. DISPUTE RESOLUTION:

A. MEDIATION: Buyer and Seller agree to mediate any dispute or claim arising between them out of this Agreement, or any resulting transaction, before resorting to arbitration or court action. Paragraphs 17B(2) and (3) below apply whether or not the Arbitration provision is initialed. Mediation fees, if any, shall be divided equally among the parties involved. If, for any dispute or claim to which this paragraph applies, any party commences an action without first attempting to resolve the matter through mediation, or refuses to mediate after a request has been made, then that party shall not be entitled to recover attorney fees, even if they would otherwise be available to that party in any such action. THIS MEDIATION PROVISION APPLIES WHETHER OR NOT THE ARBITRATION PROVISION IS INITIALED.

B. ARBITRATION OF DISPUTES: (1) Buyer and Seller agree that any dispute or claim in Law or equity arising between them out of this Agreement or any resulting transaction, which is not settled through mediation, shall be decided by neutral, binding arbitration, including and subject to paragraphs 17B(2) and (3) below. The arbitrator shall be a retired judge or justice, or an attorney with at least 5 years of residential real estate Law experience, unless the parties mutually agree to a different arbitrator, who shall render an award in accordance with substantive California Law. The parties shall have the right to discovery in accordance with California Code of Civil Procedure §1283.05. In all other respects, the arbitration shall be conducted in accordance with Title 9 of Part III of the California Code of Civil Procedure. Judgment upon the award of the arbitrator(s) may be entered into any court having jurisdiction. Interpretation of this agreement to arbitrate shall be governed by the Federal Arbitration Act.
(2) EXCLUSIONS FROM MEDIATION AND ARBITRATION: The following matters are excluded from mediation and arbitration: **(i)** a judicial or non-judicial foreclosure or other action or proceeding to enforce a deed of trust, mortgage or installment land sale contract as defined in California Civil Code §2985; **(ii)** an unlawful detainer action; **(iii)** the filing or enforcement of a mechanic's lien; and **(iv)** any matter that is within the jurisdiction of a probate, small claims or bankruptcy court. The filing of a court action to enable the recording of a notice of pending action, for order of attachment, receivership, injunction, or other provisional remedies, shall not constitute a waiver of the mediation and arbitration provisions.
(3) BROKERS: Buyer and Seller agree to mediate and arbitrate disputes or claims involving either or both Brokers, consistent with 17A and B, provided either or both Brokers shall have agreed to such mediation or arbitration prior to, or within a reasonable time after, the dispute or claim is presented to Brokers. Any election by either or both Brokers to participate in mediation or arbitration shall not result in Brokers being deemed parties to the Agreement.
"**NOTICE: BY INITIALING IN THE SPACE BELOW YOU ARE AGREEING TO HAVE ANY DISPUTE ARISING OUT OF THE MATTERS INCLUDED IN THE 'ARBITRATION OF DISPUTES' PROVISION DECIDED BY NEUTRAL ARBITRATION AS PROVIDED BY CALIFORNIA LAW AND YOU ARE GIVING UP ANY RIGHTS YOU MIGHT POSSESS TO HAVE THE DISPUTE LITIGATED IN A COURT OR JURY TRIAL. BY INITIALING IN THE SPACE BELOW YOU ARE GIVING UP YOUR JUDICIAL RIGHTS TO DISCOVERY AND APPEAL, UNLESS THOSE RIGHTS ARE SPECIFICALLY INCLUDED IN THE 'ARBITRATION OF DISPUTES' PROVISION. IF YOU REFUSE TO SUBMIT TO ARBITRATION AFTER AGREEING TO THIS PROVISION, YOU MAY BE COMPELLED TO ARBITRATE UNDER THE AUTHORITY OF THE CALIFORNIA CODE OF CIVIL PROCEDURE. YOUR AGREEMENT TO THIS ARBITRATION PROVISION IS VOLUNTARY.**"
"**WE HAVE READ AND UNDERSTAND THE FOREGOING AND AGREE TO SUBMIT DISPUTES ARISING OUT OF THE MATTERS INCLUDED IN THE 'ARBITRATION OF DISPUTES' PROVISION TO NEUTRAL ARBITRATION.**"

Buyer's Initials _____ / _____	Seller's Initials _____ / _____

Buyer's Initials (_____)(_____)
Seller's Initials (_____)(_____)

Reviewed by _____ Date _____   EQUAL HOUSING OPPORTUNITY

CALIFORNIA RESIDENTIAL PURCHASE AGREEMENT (RPA-CA PAGE 5 OF 8)

Property Address: _____ Date: _____

18. **PRORATIONS OF PROPERTY TAXES AND OTHER ITEMS:** Unless otherwise agreed in writing, the following items shall be PAID CURRENT and prorated between Buyer and Seller as of Close Of Escrow: real property taxes and assessments, interest, rents, HOA regular, special, and emergency dues and assessments imposed prior to Close Of Escrow, premiums on insurance assumed by Buyer, payments on bonds and assessments assumed by Buyer, and payments on Mello-Roos and other Special Assessment District bonds and assessments that are now a lien. The following items shall be assumed by Buyer WITHOUT CREDIT toward the purchase price: prorated payments on Mello-Roos and other Special Assessment District bonds and assessments and HOA special assessments that are now a lien but not yet due. Property will be reassessed upon change of ownership. Any supplemental tax bills shall be paid as follows: **(i)** for periods after Close Of Escrow, by Buyer; and **(ii)** for periods prior to Close Of Escrow, by Seller. TAX BILLS ISSUED AFTER CLOSE OF ESCROW SHALL BE HANDLED DIRECTLY BETWEEN BUYER AND SELLER. Prorations shall be made based on a 30-day month.

19. **WITHHOLDING TAXES:** Seller and Buyer agree to execute any instrument, affidavit, statement or instruction reasonably necessary to comply with federal (FIRPTA) and California withholding Law, if required (C.A.R. Forms AS and AB).

20. **MULTIPLE LISTING SERVICE ("MLS"):** Brokers are authorized to report to the MLS a pending sale and, upon Close Of Escrow, the terms of this transaction to be published and disseminated to persons and entities authorized to use the information on terms approved by the MLS.

21. **EQUAL HOUSING OPPORTUNITY:** The Property is sold in compliance with federal, state and local anti-discrimination Laws.

22. **ATTORNEY FEES:** In any action, proceeding, or arbitration between Buyer and Seller arising out of this Agreement, the prevailing Buyer or Seller shall be entitled to reasonable attorney fees and costs from the non-prevailing Buyer or Seller, except as provided in paragraph 17A.

23. **SELECTION OF SERVICE PROVIDERS:** If Brokers refer Buyer or Seller to persons, vendors, or service or product providers ("Providers"), Brokers do not guarantee the performance of any Providers. Buyer and Seller may select ANY Providers of their own choosing.

24. **TIME OF ESSENCE; ENTIRE CONTRACT; CHANGES:** Time is of the essence. All understandings between the parties are incorporated in this Agreement. Its terms are intended by the parties as a final, complete and exclusive expression of their Agreement with respect to its subject matter, and may not be contradicted by evidence of any prior agreement or contemporaneous oral agreement. If any provision of this Agreement is held to be ineffective or invalid, the remaining provisions will nevertheless be given full force and effect. **Neither this Agreement nor any provision in it may be extended, amended, modified, altered or changed, except in writing Signed by Buyer and Seller.**

25. **OTHER TERMS AND CONDITIONS,** including attached supplements:
    A. ☑ Buyer's Inspection Advisory (C.A.R. Form BIA)
    B. ☐ Purchase Agreement Addendum (C.A.R. Form PAA paragraph numbers: _____)
    C. ☐ Statewide Buyer and Seller Advisory (C.A.R. Form SBSA)
    D. _____

26. **DEFINITIONS:** As used in this Agreement:
    A. **"Acceptance"** means the time the offer or final counter offer is accepted in writing by a party and is delivered to and personally received by the other party or that party's authorized agent in accordance with the terms of this offer or a final counter offer.
    B. **"Agreement"** means the terms and conditions of this accepted California Residential Purchase Agreement and any accepted counter offers and addenda.
    C. **"C.A.R. Form"** means the specific form referenced or another comparable form agreed to by the parties.
    D. **"Close Of Escrow"** means the date the grant deed, or other evidence of transfer of title, is recorded. If the scheduled close of escrow falls on a Saturday, Sunday or legal holiday, then close of escrow shall be the next business day after the scheduled close of escrow date.
    E. **"Copy"** means copy by any means including photocopy, NCR, facsimile and electronic.
    F. **"Days"** means calendar days, unless otherwise required by Law.
    G. **"Days After"** means the specified number of calendar days after the occurrence of the event specified, not counting the calendar date on which the specified event occurs, and ending at 11:59PM on the final day.
    H. **"Days Prior"** means the specified number of calendar days before the occurrence of the event specified, not counting the calendar date on which the specified event is scheduled to occur.
    I. **"Electronic Copy" or "Electronic Signature"** means, as applicable, an electronic copy or signature complying with California Law. Buyer and Seller agree that electronic means will not be used by either party to modify or alter the content or integrity of this Agreement without the knowledge and consent of the other.
    J. **"Law"** means any law, code, statute, ordinance, regulation, rule or order, which is adopted by a controlling city, county, state or federal legislative, judicial or executive body or agency.
    K. **"Notice to Buyer to Perform"** means a document (C.A.R. Form NBP), which shall be in writing and Signed by Seller and shall give Buyer at least 24 hours **(or as otherwise specified in paragraph 14C(4))** to remove a contingency or perform as applicable.
    L. **"Repairs"** means any repairs (including pest control), alterations, replacements, modifications or retrofitting of the Property provided for under this Agreement.
    M. **"Signed"** means either a handwritten or electronic signature on an original document, Copy or any counterpart.
    N. **Singular and Plural** terms each include the other, when appropriate.

Buyer's Initials (_____)(_____)
Seller's Initials (_____)(_____)

RPA-CA REVISED 10/02 (PAGE 6 OF 8)

Reviewed by _____ Date _____

CALIFORNIA RESIDENTIAL PURCHASE AGREEMENT (RPA-CA PAGE 6 OF 8)

Property Address: _____ Date: _____

27. AGENCY:

    A. DISCLOSURE: Buyer and Seller each acknowledge prior receipt of C.A.R. Form AD "Disclosure Regarding Real Estate Agency Relationships."

    B. POTENTIALLY COMPETING BUYERS AND SELLERS: Buyer and Seller each acknowledge receipt of a disclosure of the possibility of multiple representation by the Broker representing that principal. This disclosure may be part of a listing agreement, buyer-broker agreement or separate document (C.A.R. Form DA). Buyer understands that Broker representing Buyer may also represent other potential buyers, who may consider, make offers on or ultimately acquire the Property. Seller understands that Broker representing Seller may also represent other sellers with competing properties of interest to this Buyer.

    C. CONFIRMATION: The following agency relationships are hereby confirmed for this transaction:
Listing Agent _____ (Print Firm Name) is the agent of (check one): ☐ the Seller exclusively; or ☐ both the Buyer and Seller.
Selling Agent _____ (Print Firm Name) (if not same as Listing Agent) is the agent of (check one): ☐ the Buyer exclusively; or ☐ the Seller exclusively; or ☐ both the Buyer and Seller. Real Estate Brokers are not parties to the Agreement between Buyer and Seller.

28. JOINT ESCROW INSTRUCTIONS TO ESCROW HOLDER:

    A. The following paragraphs, or applicable portions thereof, of this Agreement constitute the joint escrow instructions of Buyer and Seller to Escrow Holder, which Escrow Holder is to use along with any related counter offers and addenda, and any additional mutual instructions to close the escrow: 1, 2, 4, 12, 13B, 14E, 18, 19, 24, 25B and 25D, 26, 28, 29, 32A, 33 and paragraph D of the section titled Real Estate Brokers on page 8. If a Copy of the separate compensation agreement(s) provided for in paragraph 29 or 32A, or paragraph D of the section titled Real Estate Brokers on page 8 is deposited with Escrow Holder by Broker, Escrow Holder shall accept such agreement(s) and pay out from Buyer's or Seller's funds, or both, as applicable, the Broker's compensation provided for in such agreement(s). The terms and conditions of this Agreement not set forth in the specified paragraphs are additional matters for the information of Escrow Holder, but about which Escrow Holder need not be concerned. Buyer and Seller will receive Escrow Holder's general provisions directly from Escrow Holder and will execute such provisions upon Escrow Holder's request. To the extent the general provisions are inconsistent or conflict with this Agreement, the general provisions will control as to the duties and obligations of Escrow Holder only. Buyer and Seller will execute additional instructions, documents and forms provided by Escrow Holder that are reasonably necessary to close the escrow.

    B. A Copy of this Agreement shall be delivered to Escrow Holder within **3** business days after Acceptance (or ☐ _____). Buyer and Seller authorize Escrow Holder to accept and rely on Copies and Signatures as defined in this Agreement as originals, to open escrow and for other purposes of escrow. The validity of this Agreement as between Buyer and Seller is not affected by whether or when Escrow Holder Signs this Agreement.

    C. Brokers are a party to the escrow for the sole purpose of compensation pursuant to paragraphs 29, 32A and paragraph D of the section titled Real Estate Brokers on page 8. Buyer and Seller irrevocably assign to Brokers compensation specified in paragraphs 29 and 32A, respectively, and irrevocably instruct Escrow Holder to disburse those funds to Brokers at Close Of Escrow or pursuant to any other mutually executed cancellation agreement. Compensation instructions can be amended or revoked only with the written consent of Brokers. Escrow Holder shall immediately notify Brokers: **(i)** if Buyer's initial or any additional deposit is not made pursuant to this Agreement, or is not good at time of deposit with Escrow Holder; or **(ii)** if Buyer and Seller instruct Escrow Holder to cancel escrow.

    D. A Copy of any amendment that affects any paragraph of this Agreement for which Escrow Holder is responsible shall be delivered to Escrow Holder within **2** business days after mutual execution of the amendment.

29. BROKER COMPENSATION FROM BUYER: If applicable, upon Close Of Escrow, **Buyer** agrees to pay compensation to Broker as specified in a separate written agreement between Buyer and Broker.

30. TERMS AND CONDITIONS OF OFFER:

This is an offer to purchase the Property on the above terms and conditions. All paragraphs with spaces for initials by Buyer and Seller are incorporated in this Agreement only if initialed by all parties. If at least one but not all parties initial, a counter offer is required until agreement is reached. Seller has the right to continue to offer the Property for sale and to accept any other offer at any time prior to notification of Acceptance. Buyer has read and acknowledges receipt of a Copy of the offer and agrees to the above confirmation of agency relationships. If this offer is accepted and Buyer subsequently defaults, Buyer may be responsible for payment of Brokers' compensation. This Agreement and any supplement, addendum or modification, including any Copy, may be Signed in two or more counterparts, all of which shall constitute one and the same writing.

Buyer's Initials (_____)(_____)
Seller's Initials (_____)(_____)

Reviewed by _____ Date _____

CALIFORNIA RESIDENTIAL PURCHASE AGREEMENT (RPA-CA PAGE 7 OF 8)

Displayed/Reprinted with permission, CALIFORNIA ASSOCIATION OF REALTORS®. Endorsement not implied.

Property Address: _____ Date: _____

31. EXPIRATION OF OFFER: This offer shall be deemed revoked and the deposit shall be returned unless the offer is Signed by Seller and a Copy of the Signed offer is personally received by Buyer, or by _____, who is authorized to receive it by 5:00 PM on the third Day after this offer is signed by Buyer (or, if checked, ☐ by _____ (date), at _____ AM/PM).

Date _____ Date _____

BUYER _____ BUYER _____

_____
(Print name)   **(Print name)**

_____
(Address)

32. BROKER COMPENSATION FROM SELLER:
    A. Upon Close Of Escrow, **Seller** agrees to pay compensation to Broker as specified in a separate written agreement between Seller and Broker.
    B. If escrow does not close, compensation is payable as specified in that separate written agreement.

33. ACCEPTANCE OF OFFER: Seller warrants that Seller is the owner of the Property, or has the authority to execute this Agreement. Seller accepts the above offer, agrees to sell the Property on the above terms and conditions, and agrees to the above confirmation of agency relationships. Seller has read and acknowledges receipt of a Copy of this Agreement, and authorizes Broker to deliver a Signed Copy to Buyer.
    ☐ (If checked) **SUBJECT TO ATTACHED COUNTER OFFER, DATED** _____.

Date _____ Date _____

SELLER _____ SELLER _____

_____
(Print name)   **(Print name)**

_____
(Address)

(___/___) **CONFIRMATION OF ACCEPTANCE:** A Copy of Signed Acceptance was personally received by Buyer or Buyer's authorized
(Initials) agent on (date) _____ at _____ AM/PM. **A binding Agreement is created when a Copy of Signed Acceptance is personally received by Buyer or Buyer's authorized agent whether or not confirmed in this document. Completion of this confirmation is not legally required in order to create a binding Agreement; it is solely intended to evidence the date that Confirmation of Acceptance has occurred.**

REAL ESTATE BROKERS:
A. Real Estate Brokers are not parties to the Agreement between Buyer and Seller.
B. Agency relationships are confirmed as stated in paragraph 27.
C. If specified in paragraph 2A, Agent who submitted the offer for Buyer acknowledges receipt of deposit.
D. **COOPERATING BROKER COMPENSATION:** Listing Broker agrees to pay Cooperating Broker **(Selling Firm)** and Cooperating Broker agrees to accept, out of Listing Broker's proceeds in escrow: **(i)** the amount specified in the MLS, provided Cooperating Broker is a Participant of the MLS in which the Property is offered for sale or a reciprocal MLS; or **(ii)** ☐ (if checked) the amount specified in a separate written agreement (C.A.R. Form CBC) between Listing Broker and Cooperating Broker.

Real Estate Broker (Selling Firm) _____
By _____ Date _____
Address _____ City _____ State _____ Zip _____
Telephone _____ Fax _____ E-mail _____

Real Estate Broker (Listing Firm) _____
By _____ Date _____
Address _____ City _____ State _____ Zip _____
Telephone _____ Fax _____ E-mail _____

ESCROW HOLDER ACKNOWLEDGMENT:
Escrow Holder acknowledges receipt of a Copy of this Agreement, (if checked, ☐ a deposit in the amount of $ _____), counter offer numbers _____ and _____, and agrees to act as Escrow Holder subject to paragraph 28 of this Agreement, any supplemental escrow instructions and the terms of Escrow Holder's general provisions.

Escrow Holder is advised that the date of Confirmation of Acceptance of the Agreement as between Buyer and Seller is _____

Escrow Holder _____ Escrow # _____
By _____ Date _____
Address _____
Phone/Fax/E-mail _____
Escrow Holder is licensed by the California Department of ☐ Corporations, ☐ Insurance, ☐ Real Estate. License # _____

(___/___) **REJECTION OF OFFER:** No counter offer is being made. This offer was reviewed and rejected by Seller on
(Seller's Initials) _____ (Date)

THIS FORM HAS BEEN APPROVED BY THE CALIFORNIA ASSOCIATION OF REALTORS® (C.A.R.). NO REPRESENTATION IS MADE AS TO THE LEGAL VALIDITY OR ADEQUACY OF ANY PROVISION IN ANY SPECIFIC TRANSACTION. A REAL ESTATE BROKER IS THE PERSON QUALIFIED TO ADVISE ON REAL ESTATE TRANSACTIONS. IF YOU DESIRE LEGAL OR TAX ADVICE, CONSULT AN APPROPRIATE PROFESSIONAL.

This form is available for use by the entire real estate industry. It is not intended to identify the user as a REALTOR®. REALTOR® is a registered collective membership mark which may be used only by members of the NATIONAL ASSOCIATION OF REALTORS® who subscribe to its Code of Ethics.

Published and Distributed by:
REAL ESTATE BUSINESS SERVICES, INC.
a subsidiary of the California Association of REALTORS
525 South Virginia Avenue, Los Angeles, California 90020

RPA-CA REVISED 10/02 (PAGE 8 OF 8)

Reviewed by _____ Date _____

CALIFORNIA RESIDENTIAL PURCHASE AGREEMENT (RPA-CA PAGE 8 OF 8)

Displayed/Reprinted with permission, CALIFORNIA ASSOCIATION OF REALTORS®. Endorsement not implied.

Appendix B

Example of a Good Inspection Report

• •

*I*n Chapter 13, we show you an example of a lousy inspection report. This appendix gives an example of what you should expect to see in a good inspection report.

Like our sample, your report should paint a vivid word picture of the home you may purchase. The inspection report should be brimming with in-depth explanations — not merely a list of checkmarks, generic boilerplate, and hastily scribbled notes.

Get the most out of your inspection dollar. Find a professional inspection company that will thoroughly inspect the property's mechanical and structural systems inside and out, from foundation to roof, and present you a solid report on which you can make an informed home-buying decision. (See Chapter 13 for advice on finding a great home inspector.)

Warren Camp Inspection Services

P.O. Box 986, Arnold, CA   95223

(209) 795-7661

- **Inspection Date:** _____ __, 2006
- **Date of Report:** _____ __, 2006
- **Report Number:** 06 - _____
- **Inspector:**   Warren Camp, ASHI® Certified Member, #732
- **Report:**   Prepurchase inspection at ___ _____ Street, San Francisco
- **Dwelling Description:** Single-family dwelling
- **Present During Inspection:**
  - **Weather:** No rain within past 10 days
  - **Buyer:** Red E. Toobuy
  - **Buyer's Agent:** Ken B. Elpful / *Manny Elpful and Associates*
  - **Seller's Agent:** A. Frank Lister / *Frank & Company, LLC*
  - **Others:** Bugzie O. Bliterate / *Nuke 'em, Treat 'em, Treat 'em Pest-Control Company*
- **The inspected unit was furnished at inspection.**
- **A structural/pest-control inspection report was not provided.**
- **The seller's disclosure form was not provided.**

As requested by the buyer or buyer's agent, this report is being prepared for the exclusive use of the buyer to accompany the on-site verbal presentation. In no way is it to be used by, nor are we obligated to review it with, any third parties. Because Warren Camp has not personally described the extent and nature of his findings to anyone but those present for the entire inspection, he strongly discourages third parties from using any part of this report. Interested parties should arrange with Warren Camp for an inspection that meets their more individualized needs.

This report provides a professional opinion of general nature and major deficiencies of the building and its systems at inspection. It does not necessarily analyze or report on adjacent properties, nor does it cover environmental / neighborhood concerns. It summarizes observations on components inspected in accordance with customary property-inspection standards. The scope of this inspection is limited only to items discussed. It is not technically exhaustive. Because certain findings are variable (separations and cracking lengths that increase in time, levelness and plumbness readings that may change over time, erosion and corrosion levels that do not remain static, and so on), no one should rely on any reported findings for more than 60 days.

This is not a code compliance report, home, product, or system guarantee of any kind; nor is it an evaluation of the property's saleability. It includes only items accessible to visual inspection; no furniture relocation, dismantling, demolition, or other manual handling, etc., would have occurred in its preparation. It does not fulfill the requirements set forth in California Civil Code Section 1102 as to the required disclosures of a transferor of real property.

Inspector Warren Camp explained to the client the two types of reports available. Rather than selecting the in-depth, narrative report with extensive recommendations, the client selected the present standard report. Findings and recommendations that would normally have been included in the extensive narrative report would be excluded from this report.

Please call with your questions.

TABLE OF CONTENTS

CERTIFIED MEMBER

• Prepurchase Inspection Report
___ _____ Street, San Francisco, California   _____ __, 2006

INTRODUCTION

The inspected property was a single-family dwelling. Most interior spaces were unfurnished. Low-voltage wiring, heat exchangers, gardens, fences, retaining walls, underground piping and storage tanks, and sprinklers are not included in the scope of this inspection report.

Warren Camp Inspection Service (WCIS) inspections are designed to meet or exceed recent "Standards of Practice" established by the American Society of Home Inspectors® (ASHI®) of which Warren Camp is a certified member. A copy of the Standards is available upon request.

For the most part, the building is a single-level, framed structure built over a crawl space. Built around 1955, the original structural work of this wood-framed building appeared customarily constructed. No unusual or extensive damage was apparent, however, several items need attention.

Portions of this single-family dwelling have been recently remodeled. Alteration of the plumbing and electrical systems, as well as several structural installations at the rear addition was made in a nonprofessional manner. These concerns are brought up in other sections of this report. Because many of the walls and ceilings were closed, it was not possible to ascertain the full extent of renovation. If more information about these altered areas is needed, (a) consult with a licensed structural engineer, (b) review copies of permits and remodeling contracts that may be made available, and (c) examine the seller's disclosure form.

The building interior and exterior were, for the most part, adequately maintained. But of course, *all* buildings have flaws. We'll discuss a number of these flaws, but we cannot discover and report on every one. This inspection and report is not technically exhaustive, and WCIS does not provide a thorough or fully detailed analysis of problem areas. With only a few hours to inspect the entire property, WCIS provides, at best, a professional opinion based upon experience. Inspector Warren Camp is not a licensed engineer or expert in every trade or craft. Only representative sample-checks of various exposed-to-view segments of this property were made. If additional items or conditions are found when repairs or improvements begin, call WCIS immediately before further work resumes.

All the main points of this report were fully discussed with Red E. Toobuy and his agent, Ken B. Elpful, at inspection. The following sections describe the findings discussed.

Repairs, corrections, and other follow-up items to consider (Note: Check-marked concerns are merely highlights of the inspector's findings. Read the entire *report to fully appreciate this effort. Where you have interest, follow these and the following recommendations and have specialists address those discussed items that may not have been included in this inspection and report.)*

> ✔ Check with the building inspection department about permits and inspections for any building construction, alterations, and additions.

EXTERIOR
Building Exterior
This building, with board-and-batten siding on the facade, and stucco on the balance, needs maintenance on the rear addition. Surfaces should be weathersealed in the not-too-distant future to prevent moisture entry. When references are made to the front, rear, left, and right, they are made facing the building from _____ Street.

Additional items not yet painted or waterproofed were found. They include five louvered wall vents, the garage door, one new entry door, and various windrow trim pieces.

At the garage rear, soil or pavement was close to or even with the foundation top. This condition can cause wood decay and deterioration. Because Warren Camp is not qualified as a structural/pest-control inspector, refer to a current report for findings and recommendations.

Wood-to-earth contacts were found at stairway posts and doorsills. Contacts encourage wood decay, entry of pests, and moisture retention. All contacts should be properly separated and appropriate grade levels maintained.

Rust deterioration was found on several exposed nails on the rear addition's roof eave trim. Prior to painting, these surfaces should either be fully prepared for paint or removed.

A few minor cracks in the stucco were evident at inspection. The cracking is likely due to material shrinkage or expansion, drought, seismic forces, or ordinary building movement. Cracks should be caulked and weathersealed. Contact a painting and waterproofing contractor to replenish and seal exterior surfaces to prevent water entry.

Stucco siding on the rear and side yard walls extended downward over the foundation and made contact with grade (ground covering). This is conducive to entry of wood-destroying pests or organisms from behind the stucco. As an upgrade, raise the base of stucco siding a few inches to expose the foundation or lower the grade level.

Windows and Doors

Aluminum windows on the rear addition appeared sound. WCIS suggests that exposed wooden frames, sills, and trim adjacent to the metal window frames be routinely maintained to prevent possible water entry. A sampling of these windows was operated at inspection and a number were openable to an acceptable degree.

Many of the original building's painted, wood-sash windows were unable to be opened when tested, causing some rooms to be without adequate ventilation. Further, with respect to fire egress and other emergency situations, it could be extremely difficult and dangerous to attempt exit through such inoperable closed windows. *This should be corrected immediately.* In addition, routine maintenance is recommended for exposed wooden sashes, adjacent window trim, and glazing putty to eliminate potential water seepage and extend lifespan.

The garage entry door was a tilt-up type without open-vent screens.

Its spring balances were not equipped with a safety device that prevents catapulting that might occur if the springs were to actually break under pressure. Contact a professional garage door installer for appropriate replacement/correction.

Pavement and Drainage

Excess changes in the height of pavement at the front walkway could be a trip hazard. Exercise caution in this area.

This building sits on a steep hillside. Erosive soil grooves were visible in a number of locations. Not being engineers of any kind, WCIS is unable to represent or evaluate this condition. Red E. Toobuy can contact qualified engineers regarding the stability of the building and hillside, as well as any past, present, or future soil embankment or ground or building movement.

Adequate soil drainage for Bay Area homes is imperative because soil types in this area swell when saturated and may damage a building's foundation. Grade at the front was noticeably sloped, likely providing adequate drainage away from the foundation during rainstorms.

A drainage pattern at the rear and side yards was not as easy to predict. Water entry is probable into the building subarea possibly because the soil and pavement was not significantly sloped away from the building but should be. Because calcification and/or staining were found on the inside of a few foundation walls, grading and drainage should be monitored regularly and should be improved.

Moisture and drainage conditions vary with specific soil types, landscape/hardscape designs, and weather changes. Consequently, reporting on seepage and ponding conditions or making representations regarding soil stability cannot be made by this inspection company. Refer to a seller's disclosure and/or a soil engineer's report to learn of the possible presence of a subterranean French-drain system and to fully appreciate the potential for water entry — whether caused by light rains, natural springs, prolonged heavy rains, or other causes. Routinely keep all drains, patios, and walkways clean and well maintained.

Underground Piping
Understandably, inspection of inaccessible, underground perimeter drainage systems could not be inspected. Neither could WCIS inspect other underground devices such as conduits, gas and water piping, waste and vent lines, and so on, as well as under-slab components. Absolutely no testing of sewer lines is done by WCIS.

WCIS detected no outward signs of presently existing or previously placed underground fuel storage tanks (USTs) within the inspected areas (e.g., a fill spout, vent pipe, supply tubing and return line, or a fuse box labeled "oil burner" — typical indicators of USTs). Interested parties may wish to explore further since such exploration is not within the scope of ASHI® standard inspection practices.

    ✔ Free and maintain windows, trim, and hardware.
    ✔ Refer to a current structural/pest-control inspection report for findings and corrective
       recommendations.
    ✔ Paint or waterproof all raw materials.
    ✔ Repair needed items.
    ✔ Regrade/refinish landscape and hardscape surfaces in needed areas.
    ✔ Contact a soil engineer regarding erosion and hillside stability.

FOUNDATION

The foundation was only partially accessible because of low headroom throughout the subarea. No ratproofing membrane was yet placed beneath the family room, which might be a thoughtful consideration.

Visible foundation stem walls, as viewed from the subarea doorway and building exterior have been installed according to customary practiced standards.

Garage and crawl space legs were made of continuous concrete, which is often reinforced with internally placed steel bars that could not be examined or verified.

There was hairline or minor cracking on foundation sections of the family room addition. Such cracking in a building of this type and age is not uncommon and should be routinely monitored. If the cracking increases, or new cracks develop, contact a qualified engineer for an evaluation. Looking for any direct and current transference of foundation movement to adjacent finished walls, ceilings, and floors, no outward sign was detectable. It was not possible to determine if this cracking was a current condition. Determining whether foundations shift, settle, or rotate, or cracks will appear, or if existing cracks will extend further, is not within the scope of ASHI® inspections. Neither can WCIS predict the likelihood of future foundation failures, shifting, or settlement. If more information is needed, a qualified structural engineer, experienced in similar structures, should be contacted to fully inspect and evaluate findings on these and any other structural concerns, such as earthquake-preparedness measures.

✔ Routinely monitor the foundation.

STRUCTURAL FRAMING

Substructure

New and original framing was seen at the rear addition. The lower areas of partially accessible, exposed framing, were limited to portions of the crawl space. Framing, for the most part, was customary, with no visible sign of critical sags, cracks, deterioration, or movement.

Wood posts in the crawl space below the family room were in unsatisfactory condition. The bottoms of support posts beneath the center girder were not connected to embedded concrete piers. No fastening devices (screws, nails, or bolts) could be found. Corrective work is needed and would be easy to accomplish at the direction of a structural engineer.

The header supporting the garage access opening was some cause for concern because of the nonconforming size of fasteners used at each end. The header has also begun to rotate (shift) causing the fastening connections to weaken. Structurally, connections made between one structural member and another are essential. Post base-and-top connections, and beam connections to each other and to joists, were also minimal but could easily be supplemented.

Cripple-wall studs in the garage and subarea were tied together customarily, however, they were not yet benefited with supplemental fasteners or plywood shearwall panels known today to strengthen wooden structures located in earthquake country.

Many structural posts, beams, and studs had also not yet been retrofitted for earthquake preparedness. As a standard recommendation, these measures should be taken. All upgrade recommendations should come from a qualified, licensed, structural engineer.

Moisture staining was found on garage interior walls. These stains looked and felt dry, and, when tested with the biprobe electric moisture meter, accessible stains were dry. Because the cause of water staining, and the determination of its currentness, is difficult to determine, refer to a seller's disclosure statement to learn what efforts were made in each of these areas.

Rodent dropping was found throughout the subarea. Contact a pest-control company for an evaluation.

Portions of the subarea's ceiling were installed with thermal insulation, however, a calculated "energy inspection" is not within this industry's standards of practice. Several sections were loose or had fallen onto subarea soil. Corrective work is needed.

Main Structure

No evidence of *current* structural movement was noted during inspection of samplings of doors, windows, floors, walls, and ceilings. The tops of some doors were taper-cut to allow for wall shifting over the years. Any separations on walls, molding, or ceilings, or sagging or sloping of floors appeared to be the result of ordinary shifting and/or expansion within framing and supporting soils. In WCIS's opinion, the findings do not represent significant, current movement.

Attic Area

An attic had its access door in the hallway ceiling. No floor boards were yet sitting on attic joists making this area risky to traverse. In addition, thermal insulation covered many of the ceiling joists. Consequently, only a limited visual inspection of the adjacent attic space was made from the access doorway.

Attic floor joists had runs of electrical wiring laid through and over their tops. Care must be taken whenever attic access is required.

Ceiling insulation was installed throughout much of the attic floor. Reporting on adequacy of building insulation is not within inspection-industry standards. Neither would we be able to examine or suspect any failures or hazards beneath or amid insulation. An electrical contractor could inspect the embedded wiring fully as a safety evaluation and provide a safety certificate.

Insulation baffles, required around most heat-producing elements, such as lighting fixtures and flues, were not readily visible and should be provided as needed.

Visually accessible roofing supports on the main building were customarily framed. A representative number of purlins (supporting members) and/or collar ties (members connecting two roof sections) were found. Unfortunately, the family room addition's attic was completely inaccessible so no inspection whatsoever was made.

There were beneficial vent openings at overhanging roof eaves. Ventilation was customarily provided and maintained.

✔ Hire a structural engineer to evaluate family room framing.
✔ Seismically retrofit structural posts, beams, plates, and studs for wind load and earthquake preparedness.
✔ Correct the rotated header and refasten it appropriately.
✔ Refer to a current structural/pest-control inspection report for findings and corrective recommendations.
✔ Provide insulation baffles where needed and refasten fallen crawl space insulation.

FIRE SAFETY and SECURITY

Fire Safety

WCIS has some fire-safety concerns with this property. Garage wall surfaces, adjacent to habitable rooms, were not completely fire-resistant. Currently, there is risk of potential flame spread, as well as radon infiltration, into habitable spaces. Fully separate mechanical rooms from habitable rooms (e.g., by installing or patching all openings and separations with fire-resistant drywall, plaster, sheet metal, etc., or undertaking fire-resistant construction where appropriate). WCIS was unable to locate any smoke detectors or sprinklers in this area. A monitored alarm system with adequate smoke and heat detectors could be installed.

A few smoke detectors were installed in this building: on walls in three bedrooms and the ceiling of the common hallway. Because state and local codes change frequently, consult the building department for direction on optimal number, type, and location of units. Be certain to replace batteries every year with fresh batteries. Providing appropriately specified and located fire extinguishers also improves fire safety.

Security

The building's front door was equipped with a lock, deadbolt, and large glass pane. Glazing did not have a label certifying specification (e.g., tempered or safety). Door and window panes without safety glazing can be hazardous when broken, so current building codes require safety-labeled glass to minimize possible injury. Replacement is not customarily required; however, exercise caution and common sense in this area to prevent accidental breakage and possible bodily injury.

The front entry door lock requires minor adjustment for security as well as quick and easy operation.

It was a solid-core door, which is more resistant to breaking and entering, as well as to flame spread than a hollow-core door. (Not all solid-core doors are fire-resistant unless label-certified.)

The glass-and-flat-panel door from the garage to the side entry was a weak door offering little in the way of security.

Front and rear pedestrian garage doors were without at least a 1-inch-throw lock or dead-bolt. At all exterior doors, deadbolts are the recommended auxiliary locking devices.

The side entrance (kitchen) deadbolt was a "double-keyed" type—a key for the inside as well as outside lock cylinder is required. If these keys are not easily accessible, emergency egress could be impossible, and bear serious safety consequences. Conversion to single-keyed bolts is easy, affordable, and should be considered. Contact a locksmith.

Glazing and Egress

Family room addition windows were installed close to the floor. Unfortunately, each glass pane lacked glazing labels certifying specification (e.g., tempered or safety). Replacement glazing, plastic film, or barrier installation may not now be required, but exercise caution and common sense in these areas until improvements are made.

Means of egress was a concern. When attempting to freely operate the fire-exit windows leading outside from each bedroom, the windows were painted shut and unable to open.

Interior and exterior lighting should be supplemented for overall security and safety.

And, as a reminder before taking possession of your new home, rekey all existing door-lock cylinders to improve overall security and provide peace of mind.

> ✔ Provide and install needed fire protection, separations, devices, and safety systems or components.
> ✔ Improve security and door-lock safety.
> ✔ Make fire egress windows freely and fully openable.

PLUMBING

Water Supply

The main water-service shutoff valve was on the building's front wall. It was operable; no leakage was detected. A 3/4-inch copper waterline joined the building from the street. Visible domestic hot- and cold-water-supply lines were mostly made of copper.

WCIS found a combination of galvanized iron and copper waterlines at the front of the building. The seller might be able to provide information about the extent of copper piping replacement. Galvanized iron water piping is subject over time to corrosion from mineral build-up that can restrict water flow to fixtures. Corrosion may or may not be extensive and WCIS cannot predict at what rate this will occur.

Measured at the main valve, static pressure on the waterline was 89 pounds per square inch (PSI), which is a moderate-to-high level. Prescribed water-pressure-ratings are set at 55 to 65 PSI to prevent leakage from excessive pressures. A water-pressure regulator, pressure gauge on the incoming waterline, and routine water-pressure monitoring are always recommended.

Part of the hot-water piping in the subarea had no thermal insulation. Full insulation would reduce energy consumption and improve the hot-response time for each water fixture.

This area's copper water piping was also without proper or sufficient wall and ceiling fasteners. This omission might contribute to leakage or hammering noises in these lines, such as those WCIS detected in both bathrooms.

Vents, Drains, and Traps

Throughout this structure, visible waste and vent piping was made of cast iron. A 2-inch cast iron waste or vent line beneath the crawl space access door was cracked and deteriorated, requiring replacement of this piping in the not-too-distant future.

A waste/vent line in the garage was incomplete, lacking a cap or clean-out plug. Located to the right of the furnace, a plumber should simply install a proper cap or plug.

A number of drains were inspected and maintaining an effective water trap-seal.

Traps for both bathroom washbasins were a concern for WCIS because they were not fastened to a tailpiece and *each leaked*. Competent plumbing connections are essential. Trap replacement would be inexpensive and easy.

Gas Supply

The main gas-shutoff valve, located on the building's front exterior wall, was tight. If a shutoff valve is not now, or in cases of emergency, accessible or operable, PG&E could be contacted for correction.

✔ Install a water-pressure regulator and gauge on the incoming water line.
✔ Strap water and waste lines securely to the structure.
✔ Replace cracked/deteriorated cast iron piping.
✔ Cap or plug the open waste/vent pipe.
✔ Replace defective traps on both bathroom washbasins.

WATER HEATER

The hot-water heater in the garage was a gas-fueled type that was operating during inspection. It had no fiberglass thermal jacket. A new thermal insulation blanket, equipped with a razor-cut, insulated access door placed directly over the heater's ID plate, should be installed.

The water heater also lacked adequate cross-strapping and restraining blocks designed to resist movement during an intense earthquake.

It was apparently a recently installed model. With a fiberglass tank, an identification plate indicated that this A. O. Smith appliance had a 40-gallon capacity, a setting of 38,000 BTUs, and a 40.4-gallon-per-hour recovery rating.

The tank bottom was free of rust. No leaks were evident.

A safety valve on water heater tops, referred to as a "temperature and pressure relief valve," is necessary for the safe operation of these appliances. The T&PR valve was properly located and a water overflow tube was connected to the valve according to accepted trade practices.

The shutoff valve on the cold-water supply piping was operational. No leakage was evident.

Hot-water piping immediately adjacent to the water heater had some thermal wrapping, however, an "energy inspection" is not within the scope of our inspections.

The drain valve at the base of the tank, when opened, showed minimal sludge deposits.

The gas-shutoff valve was difficult to operate and should be adjusted.

Fresh air needed for complete combustion was minimal in this area. Additional, continuous ventilation is suggested. Open air vents and windows provide such ventilation.

Gas-fueled heaters must always be vented safely. Visible portions of the exhaust vent flue were installed in a questionable and possibly unsafe condition (inaccessible portions of piping were not inspected). Flue connections were inappropriately "taped over" with asbestos-like materials. The mere presence of asbestos in a building material does not necessarily represent a health hazard. Many factors must be considered before making such determination (e.g., the percentage of asbestos make-up, exact type of asbestos, and current physical condition). Considering the age of this building, other asbestos-containing materials that may not be visibly detectable or identified in this report may be present. Contact specialty contractors to conduct lab-tests for asbestos presence and analysis, and if found to be positive, provide estimates for removal or encapsulation of these materials following the U.S. Environmental Protection Agency's standards of practice.

The flue was also stained, suggesting either leakage at the roofline or condensation from a lack of fresh air in this area. However, no moisture was evident in this area at inspection.

As a standard earthquake-preparedness consideration, some or all of the following installations should always be undertaken if not already present:
   a. Flexible water-supply piping to water heaters
   b. Fully functional seismic cross-strapping (see enclosed WCIS brochure)
   c. Flexible gas-supply piping to heaters and all gas-fueled appliances

   ✔ Provide continuous fresh-air circulation.

LAUNDRY

A garage-area laundry area was no longer operational. No appliances were on location.

Air chambers on the water lines above the laundry sink had not yet been installed. Because they benefit the circulation of hot and cold water within these lines, air chambers should be installed by a qualified plumbing contractor before the sink is made operational.

The concrete-and-iron sink was adequately secured to the garage rear wall. Neither a sewer vent line above nor trap seal beneath this laundry tray had been installed. Contact a licensed plumbing contractor for such installation.

The gas-shutoff valve was tight and will require adjustment when connecting gas piping.

"Fresh air exchange" was minimal in this laundry area. Regularly opened windows aid such ventilation.

There was concern with the looseness of the 120-volt electric outlet next to the sink. This is a small repair job, and because looseness could compromise grounding protection, *a licensed electrician should promptly examine and fasten this outlet to its box.*

   ✔ Make the various recommended plumbing improvements when making the laundry
        area operational.
   ✔ Install a vent and trap for the sink and secure the loose electrical receptacle.

ELECTRICAL
Service and Main Disconnect
Electrical wiring for this building was fed from overhead and provided approximately 240 volts to the meter.

The contents of this report have been prepared for the exclusive use of Red E. Toobuy.
Reliance by others is prohibited.

• Page 8

The main disconnect switch and panel on the right exterior wall had a 60-amp overcurrent protection device for the building. Gauge markings on the conductors were taped over but their size suggested #8 wire gauge. Ampacity (the service entrance capacity) was marginal, based on the building's current load-demands. To *ensure* adequate electrical size, or to increase it, contact a licensed electrician for a load calculation and evaluation.

The main electrical panel was fastened to the building exterior but was unprotected from the weather. Corrosion was found inside the panel and gutter chamber. Because it has been known to cause shorting, deteriorated parts should be replaced.

This panel was also extremely dirty, inside and out. Caution must be exercised in this location because foreign matter can allow arcing that can lead to shorting.

Subpanel Distribution
The building's main disconnect device was combined in a panel with other circuits. No other subpanels were easily located or inspected.

Protected by circuit breakers, the combined main-disconnect-and-distribution panel had the following circuitry distribution:

1 @ 120-volt circuit at 15 amps
4 @ 120-volt circuits at 20 amps

This subpanel was not fully circuit-labeled but should be. It was, however, benefited by a closed-front protection cover.

"Double-tapping" (connecting two conductors to one circuit breaker) occurred within this panel. *Such wiring should be corrected immediately* because double tapping increases the possibility and frequency of tripping the overcurrent protection device.

As a part of regular property maintenance, all circuit breakers should be trip-tested, then re-set yearly, to insure that they are, and will remain, fully operational.

Grounding and Polarity
Of course, all electrical systems should be safely and properly grounded. An appropriately driven grounding rod was not easily located beneath the main panel. When sample testing outlets requiring adequate grounding, some had *little or no grounding protection*.

There was an "open ground" (ungrounded) condition in the living room, three bedrooms, and family room, which can be hazardous. *This should be corrected immediately for maximum personal safety.*

In a random sampling of receptacles, "reverse polarity" was present in a few locations (in both bathrooms and at each side of the kitchen sink). This condition, hazardous in certain instances, can be easily corrected and should be. What's more, the receptacle in the master bathroom was not protected with a ground-fault circuit interrupter (GFCI) device as expected.

Wiring
Electrical wiring for this building was comprised of original as well as supplemental wiring. Much of the exposed wiring was the Romex® type.

The following is only a sampling of wiring concerns and is not intended to take the place of an electrical contractor's findings:

a. A defective light switch for the kitchen's above-sink lighting fixture needs replacement.

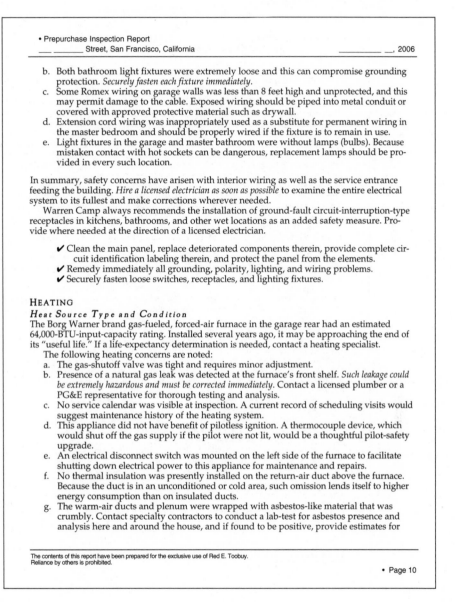

b. Both bathroom light fixtures were extremely loose and this can compromise grounding protection. *Securely fasten each fixture immediately.*

c. Some Romex wiring on garage walls was less than 8 feet high and unprotected, and this may permit damage to the cable. Exposed wiring should be piped into metal conduit or covered with approved protective material such as drywall.

d. Extension cord wiring was inappropriately used as a substitute for permanent wiring in the master bedroom and should be properly wired if the fixture is to remain in use.

e. Light fixtures in the garage and master bathroom were without lamps (bulbs). Because mistaken contact with hot sockets can be dangerous, replacement lamps should be provided in every such location.

In summary, safety concerns have arisen with interior wiring as well as the service entrance feeding the building. *Hire a licensed electrician as soon as possible* to examine the entire electrical system to its fullest and make corrections wherever needed.

Warren Camp always recommends the installation of ground-fault circuit-interruption-type receptacles in kitchens, bathrooms, and other wet locations as an added safety measure. Provide where needed at the direction of a licensed electrician.

✔ Clean the main panel, replace deteriorated components therein, provide complete circuit identification labeling therein, and protect the panel from the elements.
✔ Remedy immediately all grounding, polarity, lighting, and wiring problems.
✔ Securely fasten loose switches, receptacles, and lighting fixtures.

HEATING
Heat Source Type and Condition

The Borg Warner brand gas-fueled, forced-air furnace in the garage rear had an estimated 64,000-BTU-input-capacity rating. Installed several years ago, it may be approaching the end of its "useful life." If a life-expectancy determination is needed, contact a heating specialist.

The following heating concerns are noted:

a. The gas-shutoff valve was tight and requires minor adjustment.

b. Presence of a natural gas leak was detected at the furnace's front shelf. *Such leakage could be extremely hazardous and must be corrected immediately.* Contact a licensed plumber or a PG&E representative for thorough testing and analysis.

c. No service calendar was visible at inspection. A current record of scheduling visits would suggest maintenance history of the heating system.

d. This appliance did not have benefit of pilotless ignition. A thermocouple device, which would shut off the gas supply if the pilot were not lit, would be a thoughtful pilot-safety upgrade.

e. An electrical disconnect switch was mounted on the left side of the furnace to facilitate shutting down electrical power to this appliance for maintenance and repairs.

f. No thermal insulation was presently installed on the return-air duct above the furnace. Because the duct is in an unconditioned or cold area, such omission lends itself to higher energy consumption than on insulated ducts.

g. The warm-air ducts and plenum were wrapped with asbestos-like material that was crumbly. Contact specialty contractors to conduct a lab-test for asbestos presence and analysis here and around the house, and if found to be positive, provide estimates for removal or encapsulation of these materials following the U.S. Environmental Protection Agency's standards of practice.

Circulation and Ventilation

The return-air duct, flame ports, shelf, and furnace bottom were dirty. On the hall floor, the warm-air supply register and its interior were extremely dirty. These areas should be vacuumed promptly and regularly.

The filter box allows for a 14 x 25 x 1-inch filter. The filter was clean and properly installed. Furnace filters need to be changed every two to four months. Dirty filters actually block airflow to the heat exchanger causing it to overheat. Improper filter maintenance is a primary cause of premature cracking of a furnace's heat exchange components.

Oxygen sources necessary for complete combustion were minimal in the furnace chamber. Fresh-air entry was obstructed by boxes of personal belongings blocking the wall's ventilation screens. Remove obstructions and continually enable sufficient fresh-air exchange in this area.

Vent and Flue Piping

A cement-asbestos flue pipe (Transite®) was found. (See the discussion of asbestos elsewhere in this report.)

The flue was in a nonconforming location and may be dangerous to the building and occupants. Flues that do not pass the roofline should be properly extended upward or reinstalled.

Heat Exchanger

This heater's gas burners appeared to be out of balance with unusual flame characteristics known as "dancing flames." Unevenness is difficult for anyone but a heating contractor or utility company technician to analyze. Such a check-up should be made as soon as possible.

There was minor corrosion and pitting around the frontal entry of the heat exchanger area.

The firebox (heat exchanger) of this furnace separates and redirects hot air from ambient air, which it also warms and circulates. A full inspection of a heat exchanger is not possible without dismantling a furnace, which was not done by WCIS. There was also no access for an inspection mirror. Ask PG&E or a heating contractor to conduct a standard safety check of this and all gas appliances, supply lines, and flues, now and at every change of occupancy.

✔ Correct the gas leak at once.
✔ Loosen the shutoff valve.
✔ Address the nature and risk of asbestos-like material.
✔ Clean the ventilation and circulation components.
✔ Provide adequate fresh-air ventilation.
✔ Extend the flue top so it is sufficiently above the roofline.
✔ Ask PG&E or a heating contractor to activate the heater and conduct a standard test and safety check of *all* gas-fueled appliances, supply lines, and flues.

INTERIOR

General Condition

Generally, walls, ceilings, and floors were adequately maintained. The inspection industry does not report on cosmetic details.

• Prepurchase Inspection Report
___ _____ Street, San Francisco, California _____ __, 2006

Windows, Doors, and Stairs
Because the operability of most windows has been affected by painting, fresh air availability has been diminished and should be increased by routinely opened. Repair as needed.

Windows in a number of rooms need additional attention. Some window locks and hardware need adjustment. In addition, at least three double-hung sashes in the master bedroom had broken wires. And one garage window had a cracked glass pane that should be replaced. Generally, any broken, deteriorated, and/or missing doors and windows, locks, and components, even though not specifically called out in this report, should be replaced or repaired.

Floors and Walls
Much of the family room flooring was carpeted. Uncovered hardwood flooring in the living room was in good condition and adequately maintained.

A hole was noticed on the hall wall. Apparently a missing door stop is responsible for this wall damage, which needs repair before repainting.

✔ Repair or adjust windows, doors, and hardware as needed.
✔ Install a missing doorstop device and repair the hole in the hall wall.

FIREPLACE
The living room fireplace had a sound firebox. Little cracking of bricks or mortar joints was detected. The firebox was empty.

Needing attention was the matter of cleanliness of the firebox, damper throat, and full extent of the chimney. The National Fire Prevention Association recommends that an in-depth inspection of the entire fireplace system be performed whenever there's a change of ownership of a home having a solid-fuel-burning fireplace. Thereafter, contact a professional chimney-sweep contractor to fully examine, repair, and clean all needed areas, as well as those that were not readily accessible for today's inspection, on a regular basis. This will insure continued safe and efficient fireplace operation.

The chimney flue had a cap on its top and it was the spark-arresting type. This protective ember screen was in satisfactory condition.

The fireplace damper door was operational and well fitted. However, neither a protective ember screen nor a glass-door assembly was presently in place at the firebox's outer hearth. Provide either type of protective barrier before lighting the next fire.

The wood mantle and breastplate, as well as the tiled outer hearth, were in good condition and well maintained.

✔ Provide a protective ember screen or glass-door assembly at the firebox's outer hearth.
✔ Hire a professional, full-service chimney-sweep inspector/contractor before activating the fireplace.

KITCHEN
The kitchen was well maintained. The sink, faucet, trap and drain, and shutoff valves were working when tested. Water pressure was adequate.

Leakage at the faucet ball needs *immediate correction*.

The electric garbage disposer was operational and functioned as expected. There was no unusual or excessive noise or vibration.

Inner surfaces of the dishwasher were empty and clean. It did not have an anti-siphoning device but was well secured to the underside of the counter. An anti-siphoning device, installed above the sink rim, prevents backflow of waste products into the clean dishwasher appliance if the sewer system were to become blocked. A licensed plumber should be contacted for this installation.

Stained hardwood cabinetry was in satisfactory condition; however, only a sampling of this kitchen's cabinet doors, drawers, and connections was made.

Plastic-laminated counters were in satisfactory condition, however, the backsplash to the right of the range was loose and needs securing and caulking. Joints in all counter, backsplash, and sink areas should be continuously sealed with a good quality, flexible caulk to help prevent moisture penetration.

A ducted exhaust fan in the overhead microwave appliance was operational. The exhaust fan filter was greasy, and the fan motor drew air weakly and may be grease-bound. For an efficient exchange of air, clean, repair, or replace components as needed.

Resilient vinyl flooring was recently installed and well maintained.

> ✔ Install an anti-siphoning device for the dishwasher.
> ✔ Secure the loose backsplash piece and apply caulking where needed.
> ✔ Clean, repair, or replace exhaust fan components.

BATHROOM

This building had two bathrooms that were recently remodeled. The sinks and faucets, traps and drains, and angle stops worked well when tested.

Water pressure was adequate; however, measurement is only a relative comparison rating. New owners should personally test each fixture to become familiar with each and make desired modifications.

Testing "dynamic water flow" (the running of two or more cold water fixtures concurrently) showed a noticeable drop in volume. Red E. Toobuy and his real-estate agent were told how to perform a "homeowner's dynamic water flow and temperature test" on each fixture to ascertain the risk of accidental scalding when cold faucets are activated while someone is taking a shower.

No evidence of significant or unusual deterioration was evident on visible drain lines and trap piping. Tested drains ran freely, however, water leakage was found at the guest bathroom sink drain. This leak needs *immediate repair and/or correction.*

Both toilets were secured and caulk-sealed to the floor. The guest bathroom's toilet seat was extremely loose and needs to be tightened.

Shower glass in the master bathroom did have a glazing label certifying composition (e.g., tempered or safety). Both tub and shower areas had well-fastened grab bars.

The guest bathroom ceiling fan drew air weakly and seemed to need cleaning, servicing, or replacement.

The guest bathroom's resilient floor covering had an open seam that needs adhesive and caulk.

> ✔ Correct the leaking guest bathroom sink drain.
> ✔ Fasten the loose toilet seat of the guest bathroom.
> ✔ Clean, service, or replace the exhaust fan.
> ✔ Secure the guest bathroom floor seam and apply caulk.

• Prepurchase Inspection Report
___ _____ Street, San Francisco, California _____ __, 2006

ROOFING

Accessibility

The roof was accessible by ladder. Inspector Warren Camp physically performed a full roof inspection. Only the general condition of visible roofing surfaces was observed. Watertesting of roof surfaces, membranes, chimneys, gutters, flashing, and so on, is not typically performed by home inspectors.

Membrane Type and Condition

Multiple layers of composition shingles appear to have been laid over this structure. The actual number or combined weight placed on structural members could not be determined. Multiple layers concern roofers and inspectors for different reasons: they create an uneven surface; retain moisture and/or gas vapors between membranes; may transfer decay to structural members in their contact; and may add excessive weight to the structure. Whenever multi-layered roofs receive their next membrane, all existing roofing materials should be torn off and discarded. Consider installing appropriately specified plywood sheathing at that time.

Although not fresh, and showing routine wear and tear due to exposure, the composition shingles on each roof slope appeared sound. There was little or no evidence of unusual or significant roof deterioration however moss growth was evident on the lower portion of the north-facing slope. Contact a roofing contractor to determine ways to eliminate this growth.

Debris was found on the front roof slope where the tall tree has been dropping leaves and branches over time. Roofing must be promptly and regularly cleaned and maintained.

Chimneys, Gutters, and Flashing

Step-shingle flashing is a quality feature. It was visible at the base of the fireplace chimney. Rust was observed on a portion of this flashing, suggesting further exploration and analysis by a sheet metal contractor.

Pipe vent and perimeter flashing were in satisfactory condition.

Sections of valley flashing were exposed. Overall, the condition was satisfactory.

Three gutter seams were noticeably rusted, especially on the unpainted interior face. In addition, two separated or missing gutter ends were found that need correction. Hire a sheet metal contractor to make needed repairs or replacements.

Gutters had collected organic debris from overhead trees. Keep gutters, downspouts, and all other drain openings free of debris for proper drainage throughout the year.

The downspout system was, for the most part, customarily installed. Unfortunately, a number of downspouts likely dump water directly onto foundation areas below, which can cause erosion and building settlement over time. Splash blocks or extenders can be placed at the base of such downspouts to divert collected water. As an option, see if a licensed plumbing contractor can connect downspout piping to an existing drain line.

Additional Concerns

Roofs are seldom, if ever, regularly inspected. Regardless of whether a Warren Camp Inspection Services roof inspection was made, roofing problems are often subtle and difficult to evaluate. Because property inspectors don't often have the hands-on training and accessibility roofers have, whenever questions of roofing adequacy arise, a licensed roofing contractor should be asked to provide a thorough inspection and evaluation.

• Prepurchase Inspection Report
___ _____ Street, San Francisco, California   _____ __, 2006

Biennially, before the rainy season, roofs should be examined by a qualified roofing contractor, and routinely maintained.

✔ Clean the roof system of moss growth and tree dropping.
✔ Have the rusted step shingle flashing analyzed by a sheet metal contractor.
✔ Repair or replace rusted gutters and separated/missing gutter end pieces.
✔ Extend or redirect downspout bottoms to divert rainwater away from the building foundation.

Seismic Map Evaluation Notations (an optional evaluation that was ordered by Red E. Toobuy)

Map #1 — Intensity of Ground Shaking During a Major Earthquake (having a Richter rating of 8.0 or higher). . . From "A" to "E," this property's location is rated "E" (the *least* intense shaking rating in the city)

Map #2 — Potential Landslide Location . . . This building is *within* such location. It's approximately three blocks from an active slide area.

Map #3 — Estimated Building Damage from a Major Quake . . . Anticipate *minimal* damage to this building and from adjacent structures.

Map #4 — Potential Reservoir Failure . . . This building is *outside* such location.

Map #5 — Geologic Makeup Beneath This Building . . . This building sits on unsheared Franciscan rock (designated KJU), which has the *highest stability* rating in the city.

Map #6 — Liquefaction Potential . . . This building is *outside* such location.

Map #7 — Subsidence Potential . . . This building is *outside* such location.

Map #8 — Tsunami Potential . . . This building is *outside* such location.

— • —

Thank you for calling Warren Camp, your ASHI-certified-member property inspector.

Additional articles/pamphlets provided:

All-Points Bulletin — a home remodeling and repair newsletter; a PG&E utilities pamphlet; published articles by Warren Camp about smoke detectors, asbestos, water intrusion, and GFCI electrical receptacles; and his year-round home-maintenance checklist.

Copies to:	delivery	mail	pick-up	fax	email
Buyer:	[ ]	[X]	[ ]	[ ]	[ ]
Buyer's Agent:	[ ]	[ ]	[X]	[ ]	[ ]
Seller's Agent:	[ ]	[ ]	[ ]	[ ]	[ ]

— • —

• Page 15

Appendix C

Glossary

• •

*T*he terms that appear in italic type within the definitions are defined in this glossary.

acceleration clause: Watch out for an *acceleration clause* in your mortgage contract. This provision gives the lender the right to demand payment of the entire outstanding balance if you miss a monthly payment, sell the property, or otherwise fail to perform as promised under the terms of your mortgage. (See also *due-on-sale clause.*) Ouch!

adjustable-rate mortgage (ARM): An *adjustable-rate mortgage* is a mortgage whose interest rate and monthly payments vary throughout its life. ARMs typically start with an unusually low interest rate (see *teaser rate*) that gradually rises over time. If the overall level of interest rates drops, as measured by a variety of indexes (see *index*), the interest rate of your ARM generally follows suit. Similarly, if interest rates rise, so does your mortgage's interest rate and monthly payment. Caps (see also *periodic cap* and *life cap*) limit the amount that the interest rate can fluctuate. Before you agree to an adjustable-rate mortgage, be sure that you can afford the highest payments that would result if the interest rate on your mortgage increased to the maximum allowed.

adjusted cost basis: For tax purposes, the *adjusted cost basis* is important when you sell your property, because it allows you to determine what your profit or loss is. You can arrive at the adjusted cost basis by adding the cost of the capital improvements that you've made to the home to the price that you paid for the home. Capital improvements increase your property's value and its life expectancy.

adjustment period or **adjustment frequency:** This term has nothing to do with the first few weeks after you've broken up with your sweetheart; it refers to how often the *interest rate* for an *adjustable-rate mortgage* changes. Some adjustable-rate mortgages change every month, but it is more typical to have one or two adjustments per year. The less frequently your loan rate shifts, the less financial uncertainty you may have. But less frequent adjustments in your mortgage rate mean that you will probably have a higher teaser, or initial interest rate. (The initial interest rate is also called the "start rate.")

annual percentage rate (APR): This figure states the total yearly cost of a mortgage as expressed by the actual rate of interest paid. The *APR* includes the base *interest rate, points,* and any other add-on loan fees and costs. Thus, the APR is invariably higher than the rate of interest that the lender quotes for the mortgage.

appraisal: You must pay for the mortgage lender to hire an appraiser to give an "opinion of value" (that is, the appraiser gives a measure of the market value) of the house you want to buy. This professional opinion helps protect the lender from lending you money on a home that is worth less than what you've agreed to pay for it. For typical homes, the *appraisal* fee is usually several hundred dollars.

appreciation/depreciation: *Appreciation* refers to the increase of a property's value. *Depreciation* (the reverse of appreciation) is when a property's value decreases.

arbitration of disputes: A method of solving contract disputes that is generally less costly and faster than going to a court of law. In *arbitration,* buyers and sellers present their differences to a neutral arbitrator who, after hearing the evidence, makes a decision that resolves the disagreement. The arbitrator's decision is final and may be enforced as though it were a court judgment. Consult a real estate lawyer if you are ever a party in an arbitration. (Also see *mediation of disputes.*)

assessed value: The *assessed value* is the value of a property (according to your local county tax assessor) for the purpose of determining your *property tax.*

assumable mortgage: Some mortgages allow future buyers of your home to take over the remaining loan balance of your mortgage. If you need to sell your house, but the *interest rate* is high, having an *assumable mortgage* may be handy. You may be able to offer the buyer your assumable loan at a lower interest rate than the current going interest rate. Most assumables are *adjustable-rate mortgages — fixed-rate, assumable mortgages* are nearly extinct these days because lenders realize that they lose a great deal of money on these types of mortgages when interest rates skyrocket.

balloon loans: These loans require level payments just as a 15- or 30-year *fixed-rate mortgage* does. But well before their maturity date (the date when you pay them off) — typically, three to ten years after the start date — the full remaining balance of the loan becomes due and payable. Although *balloon loans* can save you money because they charge a lower rate of interest relative to fixed-rate loans, balloon loans are dangerous. Being able to *refinance* a loan is never a sure thing. Beware of balloon loans!

bridge loan: If you find yourself in the inadvisable situation where you have closed on a new home before you have sold your old one, you may need a short-term *bridge loan.* Such loans enable you to borrow against the *equity* that is tied up in your old house until it sells. We say "bridge" because such a loan is the only thing keeping you above water financially during this period when you own two houses. Bridge loans are expensive compared with other alternatives, such as using a *cash reserve,* borrowing from family or friends, or using the proceeds from the sale of your current home. In most cases, you need the bridge loan for only a few months in order to tide you over until you sell your house. Thus, the loan fees can represent a high cost (about 10 percent of the loan amount) for such a short-term loan.

broker: A real estate *broker* is one level higher on the real estate professional totem pole than a *real estate agent* (or salesperson). Real estate agents can't legally work on their own — a broker must supervise them. To become a broker in most states, a real estate salesperson must have a number of years of full-time real estate experience, meet special educational requirements, and pass a state licensing exam. See also *real estate agent* and *Realtor.*

buydown: A *buydown* is a *VA loan* plan that is available only in some new housing developments and targets veterans with low or modest incomes. Buydown simply means that a builder agrees to pay part of the home buyer's mortgage for the first few years. Sellers also sometimes do interest-rate buydowns to create attractive financing for buyers of their houses by paying lenders a predetermined amount of money so lenders will reduce their mortgage interest rates.

buyer's brokers: Historically, *real estate agents* and *brokers* worked only for sellers. The *buyer's broker* owes allegiance only to the buyer and does not have an agent relationship with the seller. Although this may seem to be an improvement for all the buyers in the world, don't be too ecstatic. Buyer's brokers are still paid on *commission* when you buy, so don't expect them to be supportive of you if you habitually lollygag. Also keep in mind that the higher the purchase price of the house, the more money the buyer's broker makes.

capital gain: For tax purposes, a *capital gain* is the profit that you make when you sell a home. If you buy a home for $175,000 and then (a number of years later) sell the house for $325,000, your capital gain is $150,000. A sizable amount of capital gain on a house sale is excluded from federal tax: up to $250,000 for qualifying single taxpayers and $500,000 for married couples filing jointly.

caps: Real estate *caps* have nothing to do with dental work. Two different types of caps for *adjustable-rate mortgages* exist. The *life cap* limits the highest or lowest *interest rate* that is allowed over the entire life of your mortgage. The *periodic cap* limits the amount that your interest rate can change in one *adjustment period.* A one-year *ARM,* for example, may have a start rate of 7.5 percent with a plus or minus 2 percent periodic adjustment cap and a 6 percent life cap. On a worst-case basis, the loan's interest rate would be 9.5 percent in the second year, 11.5 percent in the third year, and 13.5 percent (7.5 percent start rate plus the 6 percent life cap) forevermore, starting with the fourth year.

cash reserve: Most mortgage lenders require that home buyers have sufficient cash left over after closing on their home purchase in order to make the first two mortgage payments or to cover a financial emergency.

closing costs: After you've passed every home-buying obstacle and reached the safe clearing in order to buy your home, one final potential land mine appears in the form of *closing costs*. These costs generally total 2 percent to 5 percent of the home's purchase price and are completely independent of (and in addition to) the *down payment*. Closing costs include such things as *points* (that is, the loan *origination fee* to cover the lender's administrative costs), an *appraisal* fee, a *credit report* fee, mortgage interest for the period between the closing date and the first mortgage payment, the *homeowners insurance* premium, *title insurance,* prorated *property tax*es, and recording and transferring charges. So when you are finally ready to buy, you need to have enough cash to pay all these costs in order to buy your dream home.

commission: The *commission* is the percentage of the selling price of a house that is paid to the *real estate agent* and *broker*. Because most agents and brokers are paid by commission, understanding how the commission can influence the way that agents and brokers work is important for home buyers. Agents and brokers make money only when you make a purchase, and they make more money when you make a bigger purchase. Choose an agent carefully, and take your agent's advice with a grain of salt, because this inherent conflict of interest can often set an agent's visions and goals at odds with your visions and goals.

community property: Along with *joint tenancy* and *tenancy-in-common, community property* is a way that married couples may take title to real property. Community property offers two major advantages over joint tenancy and tenancy-in-common. First, community property ownership allows spouses to transfer interests, by a will or otherwise, to whomever they wish. The second advantage of holding title to a home in community property is that the surviving spouse gets favorable tax treatment. The market value of the entire house as of the spouse's date of death (such market value is also called the house's "stepped-up basis") is used rather than the house's original cost, which reduces the taxable profit (assuming that the home has appreciated in value) when the house is sold.

comparable market analysis (CMA): Buying a Ford Taurus from the first dealer that you visit would be impulsive and foolish. You need to shop around to find out where the best deal on that type of car is. The same is true with home buying. If you're interested in buying a home, you need to find out how much money houses in the area have been selling for. You must identify "comparable" homes that have sold within the past six months; are in the immediate vicinity of the home that you desire to purchase; and are as similar as possible to the one that you're interested in buying in terms of size, age, and condition. You must do the same thing for comparable houses currently on the market to see if prices are rising, flat, or falling. A written analysis of comparable houses currently being offered for sale and comparable houses sold in the past six months is called a *comparable market analysis (CMA)*.

conditions: See *contingencies*.

condominiums: *Condominiums* are housing units that are contained within a development area in which you own your actual unit and a share of everything else in the development (lobby, parking areas, land, and the like, which are known as common areas). Condominiums are a less-expensive form of housing than single-family homes. For this reason, some people mistakenly view them as good starter houses. Unfortunately, condominiums generally don't increase in value as rapidly as single-family houses do because the demand for condos is lower than the demand for houses. And because condominiums are far easier for builders to develop than single-family homes, the supply of condominiums often exceeds the demand for them.

contingencies: *Contingencies* are conditions contained in almost all home purchase offers. The seller or buyer must meet or waive all contingencies before the deal can close. These conditions relate to such things as the buyer's review and approval of property inspections or the buyer's ability to get the mortgage financing that is specified in the contract.

convertible adjustable-rate mortgage: Unlike a conventional *adjustable-rate mortgage,* a *convertible adjustable-rate mortgage* gives you the opportunity to convert to a *fixed-rate mortgage,* usually between the 13th and 60th month of the loan. For this privilege, convertible adjustable-rate mortgage loans have a higher rate of interest than conventional adjustable-rate mortgages, and a conversion fee (which can range from a few hundred dollars to 1 percent or so of the remaining balance) is charged. Additionally, if you choose to convert to a fixed-rate mortgage, you will pay a slightly higher rate than what you can get by shopping around for the best rates available at the time you convert.

cooperatives (co-ops): *Cooperatives* are apartment buildings where you own a share of a corporation whose main asset is the building that you live in. In high-cost areas, cooperatives (like their cousins, *condominiums* and *townhouses*) are cheaper alternatives to buying single-family houses. Unfortunately, cooperatives also resemble their cousins in that they generally lag behind single-family homes in terms of *appreciation.* Co-ops are also, as a rule, harder to sell and obtain loans for than condominiums.

cosigner: If you have a checkered past in the credit world, you may need help securing a mortgage, even though you're financially stable. A friend or relative can come to your rescue by cosigning (which literally means being indebted for) a mortgage. A *cosigner* can't improve your *credit report* but can improve your chances of getting a mortgage. Cosigners should be aware, however, that cosigning for your loan will adversely affect their future creditworthiness, because your loan becomes what is known as a contingent liability against their borrowing power.

cost basis: See *adjusted cost basis.*

covenants, conditions, and restrictions (CC&Rs): *CC&Rs* establish a condominium by creating a homeowners association, by stipulating how the *condominium*'s maintenance and repairs will be handled, and by regulating what can and can't be done to individual units and the condominium's common areas. These restrictions may apply to lawn maintenance, window curtain colors, and the like. Some CC&Rs put community decision-making rights into the hands of a homeowners association.

credit report: A *credit report* is the main report that a lender uses to determine your creditworthiness. You must pay for the lender to obtain this report, which the lender uses to determine your ability to handle all forms of credit and to pay off loans in a timely fashion.

debt-to-income ratio: Before you go out home buying, you should determine what your price range is. Lenders generally figure that you shouldn't spend more than about 33 to 40 percent of your monthly income for your housing costs. The *debt-to-income ratio* measures your future monthly housing expenses, which include your proposed mortgage payment (debt), property tax, and insurance, in relation to your monthly income.

deed: A *deed* is the document that conveys title to real property. Before you receive the deed, the *title insurance* company must receive the mortgage company's payment and your payments for the *down payment* and *closing costs*. The title-insurance company must also show that the seller holds clear and legal title to the property for which title is being conveyed.

default: *Default* is the failure to make your monthly mortgage payments on time. You're officially in default when you have missed two or more monthly payments. Default also refers to other violations of the mortgage terms. Default can lead to *foreclosure* on your house.

delinquency: At first you are in *delinquency;* then you are in *default.* Delinquency occurs when a monthly mortgage payment isn't received by the due date.

down payment: The *down payment* is the part of the purchase price that the buyer pays in cash, upfront, and doesn't finance with a mortgage. Generally, the larger the down payment, the better the deal you can get on a mortgage. You can usually get access to the best mortgage programs with a down payment of 20 percent of the home's purchase price.

due-on-sale clause: A *due-on-sale clause* contained in the mortgage entitles the lender to demand full payment of all money due on your loan when you sell or transfer title to the property.

earthquake insurance: Although the West Coast is often associated with earthquakes, other areas are also prone to earthquakes. An *earthquake insurance* rider on a homeowners policy pays to repair or rebuild your home if it is damaged in an earthquake. If you live in an area with earthquake risk, get earthquake insurance coverage!

equity: In the real estate world, *equity* refers to the difference between the market value of your home and what you owe on it. For example, if your home is worth $250,000, and you have an outstanding mortgage of $170,000, your equity is $80,000.

escrow: *Escrow* isn't an exotic dish; it's the holding of important documents and money (related to the purchase/sale of a property) by a neutral third party (the escrow officer) prior to the close of the transaction. After the seller accepts the buyer's offer, the buyer doesn't immediately move into the house. A period during which *contingencies* have to be met or waived exists. During this period, the escrow service holds the buyer's *down payment* and the buyer's and seller's documents related to the sale. "Closing escrow" means that the deal is completed. Among other duties, the escrow officer makes sure that the previous mortgage is paid off, your loan is funded, and the *real estate agent*s are paid.

Fannie Mae: See *Federal National Mortgage Association.*

Federal Home Loan Mortgage Corporation (FHLMC): The *FHLMC* (or *Freddie Mac*) is one of the best-known institutions in the secondary mortgage market. Freddie Mac buys mortgages from banks and other mortgage-lending institutions and, in turn, sells these mortgages to investors. These loan investments are considered safe because Freddie Mac buys mortgages only from companies that conform to its stringent mortgage regulations, and Freddie Mac guarantees the repayment of *principal* and interest on the mortgages that it sells.

Federal Housing Administration mortgages (FHA): *Federal Housing Administration mortgages* are marketed to people with modest means. The main advantage of these mortgages is that they require a small *down payment* (usually between 3 percent and 5 percent). FHA mortgages also offer a competitive *interest rate* — typically, 0.5 to 1 percent below the interest rates on other mortgages. The downside is that with an FHA mortgage, the buyer must purchase mortgage *default* insurance (see *private mortgage insurance*).

Federal National Mortgage Association (FNMA): The *FNMA* (or *Fannie Mae*) is one of the best-known institutions in the secondary mortgage market. Fannie Mae buys mortgages from banks and other mortgage-lending institutions and, in turn, sells them to investors. These loan investments are considered safe because Fannie Mae buys mortgages only from companies that conform to its stringent mortgage regulations, and Fannie Mae guarantees the repayment of *principal* and interest on the loans that it sells.

fixed-rate mortgage: The *fixed-rate mortgage* is the granddaddy of all mortgages. You lock into an *interest rate* (for example, 7.5 percent), and it never changes during the life (term) of your 15- or 30-year mortgage. Your mortgage payment will be the same amount each and every month. Compare fixed-rate mortgages with *adjustable-rate mortgage*s.

flood insurance: "When the flood waters recede, the poor folk start from scratch" (Richard Wright, author). They start from scratch unless they have *flood insurance.* In federally designated flood areas, flood insurance is required. If there's even a remote chance that your area may flood, having flood insurance is prudent.

foreclosure: *Foreclosure* is the legal process in which the mortgage lender takes possession of and sells the property to attempt to satisfy indebtedness. When you *default* on a mortgage, and the lender deems that you're incapable of making payments, you may lose your house to foreclosure. Being in default, however, does not necessarily lead to foreclosure. Some lenders are lenient and help you work out a solution if they see that your problems are temporary. Foreclosure is traumatic for the homeowner and expensive for the lender.

formula: We're not talking about baby food here. In real estate lingo, the formula is how you calculate the *interest rate* for an *adjustable-rate mortgage*s. Add the *margin* to the *index* to get the interest rate (margin + index = interest rate).

Freddie Mac: See *Federal Home Loan Mortgage Corporation.*

graduated-payment mortgage: A rare bird these days, the *graduated-payment mortgage* gives you the opportunity to cut your total interest costs. With a graduated-payment mortgage, your monthly payments are increased by a predetermined formula (for example, a 3 percent increase each year for seven years, after which time payments no longer fluctuate). If you expect to land a job that may allow you to make these higher payments, you may want to consider this option.

home-equity loan: *Home-equity loan* is technical jargon for what used to be called a *second mortgage.* With this type of loan, you borrow against the *equity* in your house. If used wisely, a home-equity loan can help people pay off high-interest consumer debt, which is usually at a higher *interest rate* than a home-equity loan and is not tax deductible; or a home-equity loan can be used for other short-term needs, such as for payments on a remodeling project.

homeowners insurance: Required and necessary. No ifs, ands, or buts about it — you need "dwelling coverage" that can cover the cost to rebuild your house. The liability-insurance portion of this policy protects you against accidents that occur on your property. Another essential piece is the personal property coverage that pays to replace your lost worldly possessions and usually totals 50 to 75 percent of the dwelling coverage. Finally, get *flood insurance* or *earthquake insurance* if you're in an area susceptible to these natural disasters. As with other types of insurance, get the highest deductibles with which you are comfortable.

home warranty plan: A *home warranty plan* is a type of insurance that covers repairs to specific parts of the home for a predetermined time period. Because home warranty plans typically cover small-potato items, such plans aren't worth buying. Instead, spend your money on a good *house inspection* before you buy the home in order to identify any major problems (electrical, plumbing, or structural).

house inspection: Like *homeowners insurance,* we think that a *house inspection* is a necessity. The following should be inspected: overall condition of the property, inside and out; electrical, heating, and plumbing systems; foundation; roof; pest control and dry rot; and seismic/slide risk. A good house inspection can save you money by locating problems. With the inspection report in hand, you can ask the seller to either do repairs or reduce the purchase price. Hire your own inspector. Never be satisfied with a seller's inspection reports.

hybrid loans: Combining the features of *fixed-rate* and *adjustable-rate mortgages* is the objective of *hybrid loans.* The initial *interest rate* for a hybrid loan may hold at the same rate for the first three to ten years of the loan (as opposed to only 6 to 12 months for a standard adjustable-rate mortgage); then the interest rate adjusts biannually or annually. Remember that the longer the interest holds at the same initial rate, the higher the interest rate will be. These hybrid loans are best for people who plan to own their house for a short time (fewer than ten years) and who don't like the volatility of a typical adjustable-rate mortgage.

index: The *index* is the measure of the overall level of *interest rates* that the lender uses as a reference to calculate the specific interest rate on an adjustable-rate loan. The index plus the *margin* is the *formula* for determining the interest rate on an *adjustable-rate mortgage.* One index used on some mortgages is the six-month Treasury bill. If the going rate for these Treasury bills is 5.5 percent, and the margin is 2.5 percent, your interest rate would be 8 percent. Other common indexes used are certificates of deposit index, 11th District Cost of Funds index, and LIBOR index.

interest-only mortgage: A mortgage that in its early years has the borrower making only interest payments. Typically a number of years after it starts, the payment jumps significantly as the borrower begins to make principal and interest payments.

interest rate: Interest is what lenders charge you to use their money. Lenders generally charge higher rates of interest on higher-risk loans. For *fixed-rate mortgages,* remember that the *interest rate* has a seesaw relationship with the *points.* A high number of points is usually associated with a lower interest rate, and vice versa. For an *adjustable-rate mortgage,* make sure that you understand the *formula* (the *index* plus the *margin*) that determines how the interest rate is calculated after the *teaser rate* expires.

investment property: Real estate is a good long-term investment — it has produced returns similar to those from diversified stock portfolios over the years. In practice, investment in real estate is different from investment in stocks. You can also *leverage* your real estate investment — that is, you can make a profit on your investment as well as on borrowed money. Investing in real estate is time intensive (although investing in stocks can be, too, if you don't use a professional money manager). You also need to be adept at managing people and money if you are to bear fruit with real estate investments.

One drawback of *investment property* is that you can't shelter your investment-property profits in a retirement account the way you can shelter profits earned through stock investments.

joint tenancy: *Joint tenancy* is a form of co-ownership that gives each tenant equal interest and rights in the property, including the right of survivorship. At the death of one joint tenant, ownership automatically transfers to the surviving joint tenant. This form of ownership is most appropriate for unmarried people in a long-term relationship. Some of the limitations of joint tenancy are, first, that each person must own an equal share of the house and, second, the right of survivorship terminates if one person transfers his *deed* from joint tenancy to *tenancy-in-common.*

late charge: A *late charge* is a fee that is charged if a mortgage payment is received late. A late charge can be steep — as much as 5 percent of the amount of your mortgage payment. Ouch! Get those payments in on time!

lease-option: A *lease-option* is something of which syndicated real estate columnist Robert J. Bruss is a big fan. A property that you can lease with an option to purchase at a later date has a lease-option contract. These contracts usually require an upfront payment (called "option consideration") to secure the purchase option. The consideration is usually credited toward your *down payment* when you exercise your option to buy the home. An important factor in a lease-option agreement is what portion of the monthly rent payments (typically, one-third) is applied toward the purchase price if you buy. You'll usually pay a slightly higher rent because of the lease-option privilege.

leverage: *Leverage* refers to exerting great influence with little effort. Buying a house allows you to leverage your cash in two ways. Suppose that you make a 20 percent *down payment* on a $100,000 house — thus investing $20,000. The first leverage is that you control a $100,000 property with $20,000. If your house appreciates to a value of $120,000, you've made a $20,000 profit on a $20,000 investment — a 100 percent return thanks to leveraging. However, leverage works both ways, so if your house depreciates. . . .

lien: A *lien* is a legal claim against a property for the purpose of securing payment for work performed and money owed on account of loans, judgments, or claims. Liens are encumbrances, and they need to be paid off before a property can be sold or title can be transferred to a subsequent buyer. The liens that exist on a property for sale appear in a property's preliminary title report.

life cap: The *life cap* determines the total amount that your *adjustable-rate mortgage interest rate* and monthly payment can fluctuate up or down during the duration of the loan. The life cap is different from the *periodic cap*, which limits the extent to which your interest rate can change up or down in any one *adjustment period.*

liquidated damages: In most real estate contracts, buyers and sellers may agree at the beginning of the transaction regarding how much money one party would receive if the other party violates the terms of the contract without good cause. *Liquidated damages* confine and define how much money the injured party may recover. Buyers, for example, generally limit their losses to the amount of their deposit. Discuss the advisability of using the liquidated damages provision with a lawyer or *real estate agent.*

lock-in: A *lock-in* is a mortgage lender's commitment and written agreement to guarantee a specified *interest rate* to the home buyer, provided that the loan closes within a set period of time. The lock-in also usually specifies the number of *points* to be paid at closing. Most lenders won't lock in your mortgage *interest rate* unless you have made an offer on the property and the property has been appraised. For the privilege of locking in the rate in advance of the closing of a loan, you may pay a slight interest-rate premium.

margin: The *margin* is the amount that is added to the *index* to calculate your *interest rate* for an *adjustable-rate mortgage.* Most loans have margins around 2.5 percent. Unlike the index (which constantly moves up and down), the margin never changes over the life of the loan.

mediation of disputes: *Mediation of disputes* is a fast, inexpensive way to resolve simple contract disputes. In mediation, buyers and sellers present their differences to a neutral mediator who does not have the power to impose a settlement on either party. Instead, the mediator helps buyers and sellers work together to reach a mutually acceptable solution of their differences. It is probably in your best interest to mediate your problem before going to an arbitrator or suing in a court of law. (Also see *arbitration of disputes.*)

mortgage broker: A *mortgage broker* is a person who can help you find a mortgage. Mortgage brokers buy mortgages wholesale from lenders and then mark the mortgages up (typically, from 0.5 to 1 percent) and sell them to buyers. A good mortgage broker is most helpful for people who won't shop around on their own for a mortgage or for people who have blemishes on their *credit report.*

mortgage life insurance: *Mortgage life insurance* guarantees that the lender will receive its money in the event that you meet an untimely demise. Many people may try to convince you that you need this insurance to protect your dependents and loved ones. We recommend that you don't waste your time or money with this insurance! Mortgage life insurance is expensive. If you need life insurance, buy low-cost, high-quality term life insurance rather than mortgage life insurance.

Multiple Listing Service: A *Multiple Listing Service* (or *MLS*) is a *real estate agents*' cooperative service that contains descriptions of most of the houses that are for sale. Real estate agents use this computer-based service to keep up with properties listed for sale by members of the Multiple Listing Service in their area.

negative amortization: Although it may sound like science-fiction jargon, *negative amortization* occurs when your outstanding mortgage balance increases despite the fact that you're making the required monthly payments. Negative amortization occurs with *adjustable-rate mortgage*s that cap the increase in your monthly payment but don't cap the *interest rate*. Therefore, your monthly payments don't cover all the interest that you actually owe. If you have ever watched your credit card balance snowball as you made only the minimum monthly payment, you already have experience with this phenomenon. Avoid loans with this feature!

origination fee: See *points.*

partnership: A *partnership* is a way for unmarried people to take title of a property. Partnerships most often occur among people who have a business relationship and who buy the property as either a business asset or for investment purposes. If you intend to buy property with partners, have a real estate lawyer prepare a written partnership agreement for all the partners to sign before making an offer to purchase.

periodic cap: This cap limits the amount that the *interest rate* of an *adjustable-rate mortgage* can change up or down in one *adjustment period.* See also *caps.*

points: Also known as a loan's *origination fee,* points are interest charges paid upfront when you close on your loan. Points are actually a percentage of your total loan amount (one point is equal to 1 percent of the loan amount). For a $100,000 loan, one point costs you $1,000. Generally speaking, the more points that a loan has, the lower its *interest rate* should be. All the points that you pay on a purchase mortgage are deductible in the year that you pay them. If you *refinance* your mortgage, however, the points that you pay at the time that you refinance must be amortized over the life of the loan. If you get a 30-year mortgage when you refinance, for example, you can deduct only one-thirtieth of the points on your taxes each year.

prepayment penalty: One advantage of most mortgages is that you can make additional payments to pay the loan off faster if you have the inclination and the money to do so. A *prepayment penalty* discourages you from doing this by penalizing you for early payments. Some states prohibit lenders from penalizing people who prepay their loans. Avoid mortgages that penalize prepayment!

principal: The *principal* is the amount that you borrow for a loan. If you borrow $100,000, your principal is $100,000. Each monthly mortgage payment consists of a portion of principal that must be repaid plus the interest that the lender is charging you for the use of the money. During the early years of your mortgage, your loan payment is primarily interest.

private mortgage insurance (PMI): If your *down payment* is less than 20 percent of your home's purchase price, you will likely need to purchase *private mortgage insurance* (also known as "mortgage default insurance"). The smaller the down payment, the more likely a home buyer is to *default* on a loan. Private mortgage insurance can add hundreds of dollars per year to your loan costs. After the *equity* in your property increases to 20 percent, you no longer need the insurance. Don't confuse this insurance with *mortgage life insurance.*

probate sale: A *probate sale* is the sale of a home that occurs when a home-owner dies and the property is to be divided among inheritors or sold to pay debts. The executor of the estate organizes the probate sale, and a probate-court judge oversees the process. The highest bidder receives the property.

property tax: You have to pay *property tax* on the home you own. Annually, property tax averages 1 to 2 percent of a home's value, but property tax rates vary widely throughout this great land.

prorations: Certain items such as *property tax*es and homeowners-association dues are continuing expenses that must be prorated (distributed) between the buyers and sellers at close of *escrow.* If the buyers, for example, owe the sellers money for property taxes that the sellers paid in advance, the pro-rated amount of money due the sellers at close of escrow appears as a debit (charge) to the buyers and a credit to the sellers.

real estate agent: A *real estate agent* is the worker bee of real estate sales. Also called "salespeople," agents are supervised by a real estate broker. The state licenses agents; their pay is typically based totally on *commission*s generated by selling property.

real estate investment trust (REIT): A *real estate investment trust* is like a mutual fund of real estate investments. Such trusts invest in a collection of properties (from shopping centers to apartment buildings). REITs trade on the major stock exchanges. If you want to invest in real estate while avoiding the hassles inherent in owning property, real estate investment trusts may be the right choice for you.

Realtor: A *Realtor* is a *real estate agent,* or *broker,* who belongs to the National Association of Realtors, a trade association whose members agree to its ways of doing business and code of ethics. The National Association of Realtors offers its members seminars and courses that deal with real estate topics.

refinance: *Refinance,* or "re-fi," is a fancy word for taking out a new mortgage loan (usually at a lower *interest rate*) to pay off an existing mortgage (generally at a higher interest rate). Refinancing is not automatic; neither is refinancing guaranteed. Refinancing can also be a hassle and expensive. Carefully weigh the costs and benefits of refinancing.

return on investment: The *return on investment* is the percentage of profit that you make on an investment. If you put $1,000 into an investment, and one year later your account is worth $1,100, you have made a profit of $100. Your return is the profit ($100) divided by the initial investment ($1,000) — 10 percent. See also *leverage.*

reverse mortgage: A *reverse mortgage* enables elderly homeowners, typically those who are low on cash, to tap into their home's *equity* without selling their home or moving from it. Specifically, a lending institution makes a check out to you each month, and you can use the check as you want. This money is really a loan against the value of your home; because the money that you receive is a loan, the money is tax free when you receive it. The downside of these loans is that they deplete your equity in your estate, the fees and *interest rates* tend to be on the high side, and some require repayment within a certain number of years.

second mortgage: A *second mortgage* is a mortgage that ranks after a first mortgage in priority of recording. In the event of a *foreclosure,* the proceeds from the sale of the home go toward paying off the loans in the order in which they were recorded. You can have a third (or even a fourth) mortgage, but the farther down the line the mortgage is, the higher the risk of *default* on the mortgage — hence, the higher *interest rate* that you'll pay on the mortgage. See also *home-equity loan.*

72-hour clause: The *72-hour clause,* also called a release clause, is commonly inserted into real estate purchase offers when the purchase of a home is contingent upon the sale of the buyer's current house. The seller accepts the buyer's offer but reserves the right to accept a better offer if one should happen to come along. However, the seller can't do this arbitrarily. If the seller receives an offer that he wants to accept, he must notify the buyer of that fact in writing. Then the buyer usually has 72 hours (though the allotted amount of time can vary) from the seller's notification to remove the contingency-of-sale clause and move on with the purchase; otherwise, the buyer's offer is wiped out.

shared-equity transaction: In a *shared-equity transaction,* a private investor contributes money toward the purchase of a house and subsequently shares *equity* as a co-owner. When the house is sold, the investor takes a share of the profit or loss. These shared-equity transactions can become fairly complicated because the investor co-owner and the resident co-owner may have conflicts of interest. For example, the investor co-owner may want to sell the property to make a profit, but the resident co-owner may want to stay put. If you intend to participate in an equity-sharing transaction, have a lawyer who works with residential real estate *partnerships* prepare a written partnership agreement for all parties to sign prior to purchasing the property.

tax deductible: *Tax deductible* refers to payments that you may deduct against your federal and state taxable income. The interest portion of your mortgage payments, loan *points,* and *property tax*es are tax deductible; your employment income is not!

teaser rate: Otherwise known as the initial *interest rate,* the *teaser rate* is the attractively low interest rate that most *adjustable-rate mortgage*s start with.

Don't be sucked into a mortgage because it has a low teaser rate. Look at the mortgage's *formula (index + margin* = interest rate) for a more reliable method of estimating the loan's future interest rate — the interest rate that will apply after the loan is "fully indexed."

tenancy-in-common: *Tenancy-in-common* is probably the best way for unmarried co-owners to take title to a home (except for those unmarried co-owners who are involved in close, long-term relationships — see *joint tenancy*). Co-owners don't need to own equal shares of the property they hold as a tenancy-in-common. A tenancy-in-common also does not provide for the right of survivorship that automatically passes the deceased partner's ownership to the survivor without *probate sale.* The deceased's share of the property involved in a tenancy-in-common passes to the person named to receive that share of the property in the deceased's will or living trust.

title insurance: *Title insurance* covers the legal fees and expenses necessary to defend your title against claims that may be made against your ownership of the property. The extent of your coverage depends upon whether you have an owner's standard coverage or extended-coverage title-insurance policy. To get a mortgage, you also have to buy a lender's title-insurance policy to protect your lender against title risks.

top producers: People remark that 20 percent of all *real estate agent*s account for 80 percent of all real estate sales. Be cautious. Why are those agents *top producers?* Some agents get to the top by being pushy and selling a great deal of property without patiently educating buyers — not the kind of agent that you want! If, however, the agent is a top producer because she works hard to meet the needs of her clients, being a top producer is a good thing.

townhouses: *Townhouse* is the decorative name for a row (or attached) home. Townhouses are cheaper than single-family homes because they use common walls and roofs, thus saving land. In terms of investment appreciation potential, townhouses lie somewhere between single-family homes and *condominiums.*

VA (Department of Veterans Affairs) loan: Congress passed the Serviceman's Readjustment Act, commonly known as the GI Bill of Rights, in 1944. One of its provisions enables the VA to help eligible people on active duty and veterans obtain mortgages on favorable terms (generally, 0.5 to 1 percent below the *interest rate* currently being charged on conventional loans) to buy primary residences. Like the *FHA,* the VA has no money of its own. It guarantees loans granted by conventional lending institutions that participate in VA mortgage programs.

Index

USINESS, CAREERS & PERSONAL FINANCE

0-7645-5307-0

0-7645-5331-3 *†

Also available:

- Accounting For Dummies †
  0-7645-5314-3
- Business Plans Kit For Dummies †
  0-7645-5365-8
- Cover Letters For Dummies
  0-7645-5224-4
- Frugal Living For Dummies
  0-7645-5403-4
- Leadership For Dummies
  0-7645-5176-0
- Managing For Dummies
  0-7645-1771-6

- Marketing For Dummies
  0-7645-5600-2
- Personal Finance For Dummies *
  0-7645-2590-5
- Project Management For Dummies
  0-7645-5283-X
- Resumes For Dummies †
  0-7645-5471-9
- Selling For Dummies
  0-7645-5363-1
- Small Business Kit For Dummies *†
  0-7645-5093-4

OME & BUSINESS COMPUTER BASICS

0-7645-4074-2

0-7645-3758-X

Also available:

- ACT! 6 For Dummies
  0-7645-2645-6
- iLife '04 All-in-One Desk Reference
  For Dummies
  0-7645-7347-0
- iPAQ For Dummies
  0-7645-6769-1
- Mac OS X Panther Timesaving
  Techniques For Dummies
  0-7645-5812-9
- Macs For Dummies
  0-7645-5656-8

- Microsoft Money 2004 For Dummies
  0-7645-4195-1
- Office 2003 All-in-One Desk Reference
  For Dummies
  0-7645-3883-7
- Outlook 2003 For Dummies
  0-7645-3759-8
- PCs For Dummies
  0-7645-4074-2
- TiVo For Dummies
  0-7645-6923-6
- Upgrading and Fixing PCs For Dummies
  0-7645-1665-5
- Windows XP Timesaving Techniques
  For Dummies
  0-7645-3748-2

OD, HOME, GARDEN, HOBBIES, MUSIC & PETS

0-7645-5295-3

0-7645-5232-5

Also available:

- Bass Guitar For Dummies
  0-7645-2487-9
- Diabetes Cookbook For Dummies
  0-7645-5230-9
- Gardening For Dummies *
  0-7645-5130-2
- Guitar For Dummies
  0-7645-5106-X
- Holiday Decorating For Dummies
  0-7645-2570-0
- Home Improvement All-in-One
  For Dummies
  0-7645-5680-0

- Knitting For Dummies
  0-7645-5395-X
- Piano For Dummies
  0-7645-5105-1
- Puppies For Dummies
  0-7645-5255-4
- Scrapbooking For Dummies
  0-7645-7208-3
- Senior Dogs For Dummies
  0-7645-5818-8
- Singing For Dummies
  0-7645-2475-5
- 30-Minute Meals For Dummies
  0-7645-2589-1

NTERNET & DIGITAL MEDIA

0-7645-1664-7

0-7645-6924-4

Also available:

- 2005 Online Shopping Directory
  For Dummies
  0-7645-7495-7
- CD & DVD Recording For Dummies
  0-7645-5956-7
- eBay For Dummies
  0-7645-5654-1
- Fighting Spam For Dummies
  0-7645-5965-6
- Genealogy Online For Dummies
  0-7645-5964-8
- Google For Dummies
  0-7645-4420-9

- Home Recording For Musicians
  For Dummies
  0-7645-1634-5
- The Internet For Dummies
  0-7645-4173-0
- iPod & iTunes For Dummies
  0-7645-7772-7
- Preventing Identity Theft For Dummies
  0-7645-7336-5
- Pro Tools All-in-One Desk Reference
  For Dummies
  0-7645-5714-9
- Roxio Easy Media Creator For Dummies
  0-7645-7131-1

eparate Canadian edition also available
eparate U.K. edition also available

ailable wherever books are sold. For more information or to order direct: U.S. customers visit www.dummies.com or call 1-877-762-2974.
. customers visit www.wileyeurope.com or call 0800 243407. Canadian customers visit www.wiley.ca or call 1-800-567-4797.

WILEY

SPORTS, FITNESS, PARENTING, RELIGION & SPIRITUALITY

0-7645-5146-9

0-7645-5418-2

Also available:
- Adoption For Dummies
  0-7645-5488-3
- Basketball For Dummies
  0-7645-5248-1
- The Bible For Dummies
  0-7645-5296-1
- Buddhism For Dummies
  0-7645-5359-3
- Catholicism For Dummies
  0-7645-5391-7
- Hockey For Dummies
  0-7645-5228-7

- Judaism For Dummies
  0-7645-5299-6
- Martial Arts For Dummies
  0-7645-5358-5
- Pilates For Dummies
  0-7645-5397-6
- Religion For Dummies
  0-7645-5264-3
- Teaching Kids to Read For Dummies
  0-7645-4043-2
- Weight Training For Dummies
  0-7645-5168-X
- Yoga For Dummies
  0-7645-5117-5

TRAVEL

0-7645-5438-7

0-7645-5453-0

Also available:
- Alaska For Dummies
  0-7645-1761-9
- Arizona For Dummies
  0-7645-6938-4
- Cancún and the Yucatán For Dummies
  0-7645-2437-2
- Cruise Vacations For Dummies
  0-7645-6941-4
- Europe For Dummies
  0-7645-5456-5
- Ireland For Dummies
  0-7645-5455-7

- Las Vegas For Dummies
  0-7645-5448-4
- London For Dummies
  0-7645-4277-X
- New York City For Dummies
  0-7645-6945-7
- Paris For Dummies
  0-7645-5494-8
- RV Vacations For Dummies
  0-7645-5443-3
- Walt Disney World & Orlando For Dummies
  0-7645-6943-0

GRAPHICS, DESIGN & WEB DEVELOPMENT

0-7645-4345-8

0-7645-5589-8

Also available:
- Adobe Acrobat 6 PDF For Dummies
  0-7645-3760-1
- Building a Web Site For Dummies
  0-7645-7144-3
- Dreamweaver MX 2004 For Dummies
  0-7645-4342-3
- FrontPage 2003 For Dummies
  0-7645-3882-9
- HTML 4 For Dummies
  0-7645-1995-6
- Illustrator cs For Dummies
  0-7645-4084-X

- Macromedia Flash MX 2004 For Dummies
  0-7645-4358-X
- Photoshop 7 All-in-One Desk Reference For Dummies
  0-7645-1667-1
- Photoshop cs Timesaving Techniques For Dummies
  0-7645-6782-9
- PHP 5 For Dummies
  0-7645-4166-8
- PowerPoint 2003 For Dummies
  0-7645-3908-6
- QuarkXPress 6 For Dummies
  0-7645-2593-X

NETWORKING, SECURITY, PROGRAMMING & DATABASES

0-7645-6852-3

0-7645-5784-X

Also available:
- A+ Certification For Dummies
  0-7645-4187-0
- Access 2003 All-in-One Desk Reference For Dummies
  0-7645-3988-4
- Beginning Programming For Dummies
  0-7645-4997-9
- C For Dummies
  0-7645-7068-4
- Firewalls For Dummies
  0-7645-4048-3
- Home Networking For Dummies
  0-7645-42796

- Network Security For Dummies
  0-7645-1679-5
- Networking For Dummies
  0-7645-1677-9
- TCP/IP For Dummies
  0-7645-1760-0
- VBA For Dummies
  0-7645-3989-2
- Wireless All In-One Desk Reference For Dummies
  0-7645-7496-5
- Wireless Home Networking For Dummies
  0-7645-3910-8